CONTENTS

D0185566

THE WALKS

MAPS & PLANS

PRACTICAL INFORMATION

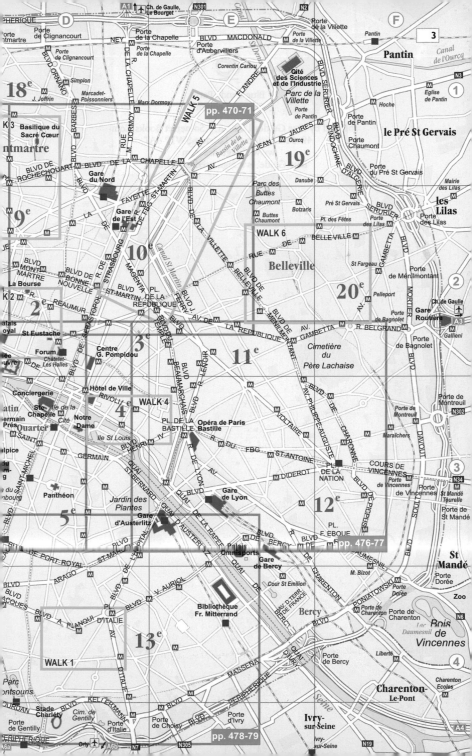

Pu   pany

Text © Delia Gray-Durant 2007
Maps, plans and diagrams © Blue Guides Limited
The right of Delia Gray-Durant to be identified as author of this work has been asserted by her in accordance with the Copyright Designs and Patents Act, 1988.

ISBN 978–1–905131–19–8

A CIP catalogue record of this book is available from the British Library.

Published in the United States of America by
WW Norton and Company, Inc.
500 Fifth Avenue, New York, NY 10110
USA ISBN 978-0-393-33009-0

The author and the publisher have made reasonable efforts to ensure the accuracy of all the information in Blue Guide Paris; however, they can accept no responsibility for any loss, injury or inconvenience sustained by any traveller as a result of information or advice contained in the guide.

Cover photographs: Top: Eiffel Tower (photo: Phil Robinson).
Bottom: *Diana's Return from the Hunt* by François Boucher
(© Musée Cognac-Jay / photo Lifermann).
Spine: Rose window, west front of Notre Dame.
Title page: *Georges Sand* (1838) by Auguste Charpentier in the Musée de la Vie Romantique.

All other acknowledgements, photo credits and copyright information are given on p. 480, which forms part of this copyright page.

Statement of editorial independence: Blue Guides, their authors and editors, are prohibited from accepting any payment from any restaurant, hotel, gallery or other establishment for its inclusion in this guide, or for a more favourable mention than would otherwise have been made.

Every effort has been made to contact the copyright owners of material reproduced in this guide. We would be pleased to hear from any copyright owners we have been unable to reach.

About the author
Delia Gray-Durant's association with France began more than 30 years ago when she went to live and work in Paris. Subsequently she read French and History of Art at university and had a home in the Midi-Pyrénées. Now she writes books, leads art history tours and spends a large part of the year in France. She has been writing for *Blue Guides* since 1993 and is also the author of *Blue Guide Southwest France*.

INTRODUCTION

Paris is a magnetic and compelling city. Seen once or 20 times, it often challenges but rarely disappoints. A radiant city, bathed in the reflective light of the Ile de France, crossed by a great river, it has consciously created itself: not by chance does it boast some of the greatest cityscapes and vistas in the world. The Champs-Elysées, like the gardens of Versailles, were carefully planned, as was the drama of the Opéra Garnier at the end of the Avenue de l'Opéra, the sweep of gardens from the Palais de Chaillot to the Champs de Mars, the statement of the Montparnasse Tower at the end of Rue de Rennes, the continuum westwards from the Louvre to La Défense. This represents an extraordinary vision. Despite tight control on high-rise buildings in the centre of Paris, the opportunities to look upon this remarkable city from above are legion: from the natural heights of Montmartre, Belleville and Père Lachaise Cemetery; from the more distant terraces of St-Germain-en-Laye and the Parc de St-Cloud; from old buildings such as the Panthéon, the Basilica of Sacré Coeur, and cathedral of Notre-Dame; from modern buildings such as the Pompidou Centre and La Grande Arche de la Défense; and of course, most famously, from the Eiffel Tower.

Paris reveres its culture. It contains over 1,800 classified monuments, and around 170 museums. The great museums are in a constant flux of renewal, improvement and renovation. But the city does not remain focused solely on the past. In 2006 the Musée du Quai Branly, the latest presidential *grand projet*, opened its doors, revealing an architectural revolution, a museum on stilts above a garden, with a wall of vegetation; inside are mystery, magic, and free-flowing spaces. Revamps and rethinks have transformed museum settings, a common factor being the return to natural light. One such recent metamorphosis is the Musée des Arts Décoratifs, reopened in 2006. Further transformations have occurred at two large museums belonging to the city, the Petit Palais and the Musée d'Art Moderne de la Ville de Paris. The Orangerie has gone part underground. The two major Asian arts museums—the National collections at the Guimet, and the city collection at the Musée Cernuschi—are resplendent. The reorganised 4th and 5th floors at the Pompidou Centre have now both reopened. At the Louvre, the Arts of Islam has become the 8th department. The Musée Rodin has a new entrance and exhibition space. A new centre for Architecture and Heritage at the Palais de Chaillot is on the way. At Bercy there is the new Musée du Cinéma, as well as the new Simone de Beauvoir footbridge linking two reawakened districts.

Paris now has a *plage* in the summer months and in October stays awake for a whole night during the *Nuit Blanche*. The hotels and restaurants of Paris become ever more innovative: every type of décor, comfort or gimmick is to be found. The cuisine blends unlikely flavours or marries the traditional with the exotic, while with diligent searching the traditional Parisian bistrot or brasserie can still be found. This 11th edition of Blue Guide Paris includes a variety of walks exploring different parts of the city, old and new, on routes comfortably accomplished of a morning or afternoon.

HISTORICAL SKETCH

by Matthew Kidd

The Paris of the popular imagination is a sensuous place, as captured by phrases such as 'belle époque' and 'ville lumière'. And it is easy to approach the city in this way: the phrases do reflect elements of Parisian history. But it is not the full story. For Paris has also known hard times: disease, famine, economic hardship, absentee rulers, political strife. It has undergone repeated siege and occupation. These aspects too have left their traces on the Paris we see now, and can help us to understand how it came to be as it is, and what deeper currents underlie the gaiety.

The beginnings

The Seine was a navigable river and a commercial highway as far back as historical evidence can take us. At what is now Paris, the river intersected with a main north–south route; and the islands in the river offered natural defensive advantages. The first people to establish a permanent base here, probably in the 4th century BC, were a Celtic tribe later called (by the Romans) *Parisii*. They established themselves on what is now the Ile de la Cité, the biggest of what were then a dozen islands, in a river probably twice as wide then as now. They were semi-nomadic, trading up and down the river, leaving no trace of grand buildings or paved streets, and with no bridges to connect their settlement to the banks. They worshipped the water: a fact worth recalling when one sees modern Paris' coat of arms (of a ship afloat) and motto (*fluctuat nec mergitur*: she is tossed on the waves but not engulfed). And Paris remains a working port, France's fifth largest, with a freight canal running directly beneath the Place de la Bastille.

The Romans arrived in 54 BC. Julius Caesar identified the settlement (apparently known to the Celts as *Louk-tier*, place of marshes) as a good base for his campaign to subjugate the tribes of northern Gaul. The Romans Latinised the name as *Lutetia*. The Romans built the first bridges, connecting the Ile de la Cité to both banks. The settlement slowly expanded, particularly on the southern side. By the 2nd century AD, they had built a forum (on the hill where the Sorbonne now stands), an arena (remains still visible near the Rue Monge; *see p. 60*) and baths. The size of the arena suggests a population of 20–30,000. There was a temple to Jupiter on the island where Notre-Dame now stands.

Christianity came to Lutetia probably in the 3rd century. The first bishop, Dionysius (or Denis), was martyred on the hill north of Lutetia which later became known as Montmartre (*Mons Martyrum*). The legend had it that, after his head had been cut off, he picked it up and carried it to where the cathedral of St-Denis was later built in his memory (providing the mausoleum in which a thousand years of French kings were buried; *see p. 407*).

By the end of the 3rd century, Roman Gaul was under attack from Goths and Huns. The emperor Constantius Chlorus made Lutetia for the first time the provincial capital, closer than Lyon (the previous capital) to the front line at the Rhine. In the mid-4th century, the emperor Julian (nephew of Constantine the Great and known as the Apostate) spent three years in Lutetia, writing affectionately of its charms, and in effect making it the capital of the Western Empire. He was formally acclaimed Augustus there in 360 AD, an event not to be repeated until Napoleon's imperial coronation in 1804. Julian changed the city's name from Lutetia to *Civitas Parisiorum*, combining Roman status with Celtic history.

The barbarian pressure on Roman Gaul grew over the following century. In 451 Attila the Hun led a fierce army against Paris, but the inhabitants kept their nerve, urged on by a young girl, later St Geneviève, who had had a vision that he would turn away. Indeed he did. In 497, however, Paris was occupied by the equally fierce Franks under Clovis. Geneviève this time advised the Parisians to open their gates to him as long as he converted to Christianity. Clovis did so, defeated the Romans, and made Paris the capital of a Christian Frankish kingdom in 508. His name—the modern Louis—has proved the most popular of all French royal names, reflecting his status as the founding father of France. His dynasty (the Merovingians, after his grandfather Merovius) remained based in Paris for two and a half centuries. The Roman buildings were plundered for their stone, including the city walls, thus leaving Paris vulnerable. But the first monasteries were founded (including the abbey of St Geneviève, where Clovis was buried, and where the Lycée-Henri IV now stands; *see p. 51*). The first proto-French texts were written.

The later, weaker Merovingian kings allowed power in the city to pass into the hands of indigenous *maires*: already in the 8th century sowing the seeds of conflict between local powerbrokers and an alien monarchy. The best known *maire*, Charles Martel, succeeded in checking the Moslem advance into France, at Poitiers in 732, and used the authority he had won by so doing to depose the last Merovingian king in 754 and impose his own son instead, establishing the Carolingian dynasty. Charlemagne (r. 768–814), his grandson, crowned Holy Roman Emperor in 800, had no use for Paris, and moved his capital to Aachen (Aix-la-Chapelle). By the 9th century Paris had shrunk back to its original dimensions on the Ile de la Cité; and, like the rest of what had once been Gaul was weakened by the squabbling of Frankish nobles. It lay wide open to the attacks of the Norse invaders.

Six times they came between 825 and 925, mostly by ship, the fiercest assault being in 885–886 (*see p. 56*), when Paris withstood a year-long siege under Eudes (or Odo), Count of Paris and eldest son of Robert the Strong. It was the first time that any Frankish settlement had dared to resist the Norsemen so robustly; three years later Eudes was crowned king. By the early 10th century, the Norsemen were established permanently in Normandy (hence the name), and challenged the Franks for territorial supremacy. In 987 the Franks picked Hugues Capet (r. 987–996), Parisian and great-nephew of Eudes, as their leader, replacing the enfeebled Carolingians. He was crowned in Paris, establishing his dynasty, the Capetians.

The Capetians

Hugues Capet's kingdom was modest—just Paris and the hinterland of the Ile de France—and its inhabitants lacked even a common language. But during the three centuries of Capetian rule, Paris started to grow, both physically and intellectually. Hugues Capet's son, Robert le Pieux, was perhaps the first ruler since the Romans to take an interest in the city's fabric. He restored the Palais de la Cité and started rebuilding the monasteries outside the walls. A century later, Suger, Abbot of St-Denis, became the first in a series of ecclesiastical administrators and patrons who over the centuries, in the name of the kings they served, both provided government to France and changed the face of Paris. Suger ordered the rebuilding of St-Denis (1136–47), stimulating the development of the Gothic style in cathedrals across northern France. He encouraged also the building of Notre-Dame, though it was started only after his death. Under the authority of Louis VI (r. 1108–37), he had marshlands on the Left Bank drained, and had the fort (or *châtelet*) governing the northern end of the bridge linking the Ile de la Cité to the Right Bank rebuilt of stone, creating thereby a new focal point for the expanding city.

In the same generation, Peter Abelard transformed the status of Paris as a seat of learning. He brought a new questioning spirit to the theological seminaries already present, and started the process of consolidating them into a single university. Maurice de Sully, who oversaw the construction of Notre-Dame from 1163 onwards, also led the building of Paris' first hospital, the Hôtel-Dieu, next door. It was a period of enlightenment, of intellectual and artistic experiment. The decision to knock down buildings around Notre-Dame, in order to permit straight roads over which the stone for the cathedral could be more easily hauled to the site, must have seemed a radical change of priorities.

Philippe-Auguste (r. 1180–1223), Louis VI's grandson, was one of the kings of France who had most impact on the development of Paris, despite many conflicting calls on his attention: Crusades, tangling with the pope and fighting the English. He ordered the construction of the first complete stone wall around the city, up to six metres high (with traces still visible today; *see p. 306*). He built aqueducts to bring fresh water, and sought (without much success) to alleviate the problems of refuse and sewerage (*see p. 325*). He gave the University of Paris its first charter, and its students ecclesiastical privileges (which led to town versus gown frictions over the centuries to come). He promoted trade by establishing the first permanent market at Les Halles. He built the first fortress on the site of the Louvre, then outside his city walls. He strengthened the city's mechanisms for running its own affairs, including allowing it to levy taxes on river traffic. Much of the funding for his projects came from money confiscated from the Jews; Philippe-Auguste's persecution of them in the 1180s stained his record, and his partial relenting in the following decade was prompted less by conscience than by a realisation that without them his funds were running dry. But Paris as a whole profited from his reign. He promoted the city's sense of itself as capital of France, for example by holding there the triumphal procession following the Battle of Bouvines, the victory over King John of England and his allies which resulted in French gains of English lands in France, and established France as a military power. By the time Philippe died, Paris' population had grown to 200,000.

The 13th century saw a growth in the influence of the Parisian bourgeoisie, supported by the city's growing trading wealth. Philippe-Auguste's grandson, Louis IX (r. 1226–70; later St Louis after being canonised by Pope Boniface VIII for his personal holiness and his contribution to the Crusades), set up administrative structures for France (courts, treasury, and a *parlement*, though without legislative powers) which remained in place until 1789. He turned the old Palais de la Cité into an administrative centre. He also incorporated into it the Sainte-Chapelle, one of the only elements to survive today, to house the Crown of Thorns, which he had acquired from the Frankish emperor of Constantinople (*see p. 32*). The university was further developed, and acquired its name (from Robert de Sorbon, Louis IX's personal confessor). But Louis turned his back on the free thinking of the previous century, even allowing the Inquisition, which St Dominic in his preaching against the Albigensians had introduced to southern France some years before, to establish itself in Paris.

Few of the later Capetians left much trace on the city. The exception was Philippe IV (Philip the Fair; r. 1285–1314), who continued his grandfather Louis' work on France's administration. When he died, France was more populous than at any point over the next four centuries, and Paris had 300,000 inhabitants. But Philippe was a spendthrift, always in need of new sources of revenue. Having harassed the Jews and the Lombards, he turned his attention to the Knights Templar, long and prosperously established in the area still known as the Quartier du Temple (*see p. 277*). With the connivance of Pope Clement V, their headquarters were raided, the knights tortured and burnt by the Inquisition, their property seized by the state. As their Grand Master was burnt at the stake, roughly where the statue of Henri IV at the eastern end of the Ile de la Cité now stands (*see p. 37*), he cursed both pope and king; within the year, both were dead. Within fifteen more years Philippe's three sons, kings in succession, had died too, all childless.

The end of the Middle Ages and the Renaissance

For France and for Paris, the 14th century was marked by the long attrition of the Hundred Years War against England. In addition, the Black Death hit Paris in 1348, following several years of famine. Public disenchantment with the kings' insistence on pursuing the war burst out into rioting led by the merchant class. Unlike other French cities, Paris had no charter to protect it from the monarch's caprices. In 1355 Etienne Marcel, merchants' provost, sought to establish a new constitution limiting the king's powers over the city. But his revolt was put down, and he lost public support by seeking alliance with the English.

The English occupied Paris in 1420 with their Burgundian allies; the Duke of Bedford (brother of the English king, Henry V) ran the city from the Palais des Tournelles, on the site of what is now the Place des Vosges (*see p. 283*). In 1429 came an attempt—in which Joan of Arc participated—to storm the Porte St-Honoré. It was unsuccessful, and the English remained in occupation until 1436, having the young Henry VI (Henry V's son) crowned King of France in Notre-Dame in 1431.

After the end of the Hundred Years War, in 1453, when England was expelled from all her holdings in France except Calais, France recovered quickly—though successive French kings involved themselves in fighting for territory on the Italian peninsula, with a series of expeditionary campaigns culminating in humiliating defeat at Novara in 1513. But these campaigns also provided a conduit for the ideas of the Italian Renaissance. Cultivated Frenchmen decorated their speech with Italianisms. This was also the period when Paris acquired its first printing press, in 1470. The kings of the late 15th century spent little time there, however; and the first evidence of new architectural styles reaching France was rather to be seen in the Loire châteaux.

François I (r. 1515–47) had to contend with a new strategic threat: the Holy Roman Empire under the Habsburg Charles V, who ruled both Austria and Spain. The contest culminated in François' defeat and temporary imprisonment after the Battle of Pavia in 1525. He nevertheless gave Paris plenty of his attention. He had the Marais cleared and opened for development by private entrepreneurs. He built the first stone *quais* along the Seine. He demolished the old fortress of the Louvre and started its reconstruction in the new style as a residential palace. He founded the Collège de Paris, not only to teach the new humanism emanating from Italy, but to do so in French (this was the period when Rabelais was giving the language a new vigour). He brought to Paris the paintings which were to form the nucleus of the Louvre's collections, including the *Mona Lisa*. Indeed, François was Leonardo da Vinci's last and most generous patron, inviting him to France, and giving him a country house near Amboise. Leonardo died there in 1519.

François also brought from Italy, as a bride for his second son (later Henri II), Catherine de Médicis, of the Florentine ruling house. Henri II (r. 1547–59) died in a jousting accident in the courtyard of the Palais des Tournelles. Catherine was mother of the next three kings, all of whom inherited the throne young and died young, leaving her influential as regent. This period saw bitter conflict between Catholics and Protestants. In Paris, the populace were mostly Catholic, as were the feudal nobility. But many in the merchant classes had embraced Protestantism, partly out of disenchantment with the monarch's claim of divine right as well as with the corruption and degeneracy of the court.

In 1572, Catherine's second son, the young Charles IX (r. 1560–74), was brought to issue an order for the massacre of Protestants (or Huguenots, from the German *Eidgenossen*, confederates) on St Bartholomew's Eve (23rd August). Six days before, at Catherine's instigation, his sister Marguerite de Valois (later La Reine Margot) had been married to the Protestant Henri of Navarre, an event which brought many Protestants into the city. Some estimates suggest that up to 15,000 were killed, as the massacre spread from Paris to other cities. Paris' international reputation (and consequently its trade) suffered. Over the following decade, it fell further, as the city came under the influence of the vigilantes of the Catholic League, led by the Duc de Guise. The League operated in open rivalry to the king, the unpopular and irresolute Henri III (r. 1574–89), the youngest of Catherine de Médicis' sons. In 1588 Henri ordered the assassination of the Duc de Guise. In revenge he himself was stabbed to death by a Dominican friar at St-Cloud.

The Bourbons to the Revolution

There was no direct heir. The Catholic League hoped to manoeuvre their way to the succession. But Henri III proposed on his deathbed that the throne should pass to his brother-in-law (by Marguerite de Valois) and distant cousin, Henri of Navarre, even though he was a Protestant. Henri had to fight for this inheritance. After failing to defeat the League in open battle, and concluding that the walls of Paris, built by Philippe-Auguste nearly four hundred years earlier, were too strong for him to storm the city, he laid siege to it. Famine ensued; 30–40,000 died, and still the Catholic hard-liners urged no surrender. The hard-pressed populace became increasingly impatient for a solution. Eventually, after three years of siege, a deal was reached: Henri submitted to Catholicism in a formal mass at St-Denis in July 1593, and the following spring the city opened its gates to him. He ascended the throne as Henri IV (r. 1589–1610), the first of the Bourbon monarchs of France. His dynasty, destined to occupy the thrones of France, Spain and Naples, was to struggle for the next century and a half for hegemony in Europe.

One of Henri IV's first moves was to announce a general amnesty, and the same year he issued the Edict of Nantes, establishing freedom of religion. He then turned his attention to transforming Paris, which after the siege, and two outbreaks of plague in the 1580s and 1590s, was in a sorry state. He had the Pont Neuf completed, and other bridges modernised. He started a programme of replacing medieval wooden buildings by new squares of brick and stone, of which the Place des Vosges is the best completed example (compare with the nearby Rue des Prévôts to understand how novel it must have seemed). The transformation he set in hand led to a 50 per cent increase in population over the first half of the following century. It all cost money (the Pont Neuf was funded by a tax on wine), but Henri IV preferred to invest in his own capital rather than follow the fashion of seeking territories in the New World (French colonisation of Canada had begun under François I). Despite all his efforts to rule equitably, the Catholic League remained active. There were frequent assassination attempts on him. In May 1610 a fanatical would-be monk named Ravaillac stabbed him fatally as he sat in his carriage in the Rue de la Ferronnerie (still there, near Les Halles), trapped in a traffic jam caused by an overturned cart of straw.

The next three Bourbon rulers, Louis XIII, XIV and XV, between them, reigned for 164 years. Each inherited the throne as a child, the first two under the regency of their mothers. None of the three felt particularly at home in Paris. Louis XIII (r. 1610–43) preferred to be out hunting, and built himself a hunting-box at Versailles. Louis XIV (r. 1643–1715) hugely enlarged it, and it remained the residence of his successors until the Revolution. Louis XIV returned to his capital only 25 times in the last forty years of his reign.

Paris certainly changed during this long period. But others were primarily responsible. Louis XIII's mother had the Palais du Luxembourg built (later a prison under the Revolution, now the home of the Sénat). Cardinal Richelieu, Louis XIII's chief minister, created the Ile St-Louis, joining two existing smaller islands, embellished the Sorbonne and built himself the Palais Cardinal, which later became the Palais Royal (see p. 248). This helped to stimulate growth of the city westwards and northwards from the Marais.

Richelieu's tyrannical ways created predictable public resentment, intensified by the cost of the Thirty Years War against Spain and Austria. Richelieu died in 1642, Louis XIII the following year. Louis XIV's mother, as regent, called on Richelieu's secretary, Mazarin, to succeed him as First Minister. In 1648, Mazarin sought to re-impose an unpopular tax, and provoked riots which forced the boy king and his mother to flee Paris. The rioters used the catapult, or *fronde*, as their weapon; the rebellions against the crown during these years came to be named after it. Several years of confusion followed, with rebellious nobles joining the urban rioters in seeking to bring the king down. But in 1652 Mazarin forced the *parlement* to renounce any claims to a political role. The king had won. But the experiences of the Fronde had brought him to the conclusion that to rule effectively, he must rule absolutely. Three years later, still only seventeen, he was told while out hunting that the *parlement* had met without seeking his approval. He appeared at their session and laid down the law: 'l'Etat, c'est moi'.

Louis conducted a series of wars, in Spain and the Netherlands, to extend the territory of France, and Paris saw the effects in projects designed to commemorate his victories: the adjacent triumphal arches at the Porte St-Denis and the Porte St-Martin, and the Place des Victoires. The Hôtel des Invalides was founded, to accommodate up to 7,000 war veterans. It was an era with a taste for grandeur and spectacle. Parts of the earlier fortifications were demolished to make room for grand boulevards (named after the bulwarks they replaced). Pageants were popular, including the one in 1662 in which Louis XIV wore for the first time the symbol of the sun, which became identified with him. This was also the great age of the Paris theatre, with Corneille and later Racine writing tragedies, Molière comedies, and Lully incidental music. Wealthy nobles vied to build elegant châteaux around Paris. But the king did not care to be outshone: when his finance minister Fouquet invited him to a splendid pageant at his new château at Vaux-le-Vicomte, Louis had him arrested for embezzlement.

While Louis was conquering on land, his able new finance minister, Colbert, was seeking to make France mistress of the seas. France now administrated colonies in Africa and the Americas, and exotic commodities were pouring into the capital, along with considerable wealth. During this period Paris saw its first cafés, its first streetlights and fire service, the first carriages for public hire (known as *fiacres*, because they waited to be hired by the church of St-Fiacre, now remembered only in a tiny alley near the Beaubourg). It had by now a population of half a million, the rich increasingly in the west, the poorer in the east. But taxes to pay for the wars were heavy, and the court was not popular. In 1682, Louis XIV decreed that he would rule henceforth from Versailles. Work on his projects in the capital, including completing the Cour Carrée of the Louvre, was suspended (and the scaffolding remained up for the next seventy years). But the withdrawal of the court did little to dent Paris' prosperity. If anything, it had less impact than the Revocation of the Edict of Nantes in 1685, which led to another exodus of Protestants, who took with them their wealth and skills. Persecution of Protestants was followed by action in 1709 to break up the convent at Port-Royal, home of the Jansenists, an austere Catholic sect (though marked by Calvinist ideas), unsympathetic to the luxury of the court, but attractive to influential figures such as Pascal and Racine.

The Duc de Saint-Simon's memoirs give a picture of the stultifying life of the Versailles court in Louis XIV's last years. The king's insistence that his nobles remain in attendance on him there made it hard for them to engage in political activity, or to administer their own estates effectively. Gloom was heightened by a famine following a failed harvest in 1693; by military reverses, which saw French armies defeated by the Duke of Marlborough at Blenheim, Ramillies, Oudenarde and Malplaquet, and which in 1707 brought Dutch cavalry Scouts almost to the gates of Versailles; and by the coldest winter ever in Paris, in 1709. In 1712 Louis recognised the Protestant succession in England and gave up his ideas of uniting the French and Spanish crowns. The War of the Spanish Succession ended with the accession of his grandson Philip to the throne of Spain. In 1715, Louis XIV died, having outlived his son, two out of his three grandsons and his oldest great-grandson.

Louis XV (r. 1715–74), another great grandson, was five when he came to the throne. Philippe, Duc d'Orléans, son of Louis XIV's younger brother, was appointed regent. In his forties, free-thinking and licentious, he moved the court back to Paris. He was initially popular, especially for negotiating settlements of France's wars. But the public never forgave him for the collapse of his attempt to introduce a paper-based bank, which then speculated heavily in developing Louisiana (New Orleans was named after him).

When Philippe died in 1723, Louis XV moved back to Versailles. Without Louis XIV's early experience of hardship, he had grown up feckless, extravagant, accustomed to flattery. He engaged France once again in dynastic wars: those of the Polish and Austrian successions, and the Seven Years War against Prussia. Under the influence of Madame de Pompadour, his mistress for twenty years, there were some further grand projects in Paris: the Ecole Militaire, and the Place Louis XV (now Place de la Concorde), which moved the city's centre of gravity a further step westward. The decorative arts flourished, as seen in the works of Boucher, Boulle and Gouthière. But the contrast between the light comedies of Marivaux, popular at Versailles, and the intellectual ferment stimulating Diderot and the *encyclopédistes* in Paris (and Voltaire from his exile near Geneva) is telling. Louis lived for the pleasures of the day, and neglected his people; as Madame de Pompadour expressed it, 'après nous le déluge'. His popularity in Paris declined so far that he preferred to travel from Versailles to Fontainebleau without passing through the city. It took three successive subscriptions to raise the funds for his pet project, the Panthéon. When he died, in 1774, his burial at St-Denis had to be conducted in secret.

His successor, Louis XVI (r. 1774–93), inherited a dire economic situation. But he was not strong-minded enough to endorse, over the resistance of his court, reform proposals which would have abolished some of their tax privileges. Instead, France's public purse remained over-burdened by accumulated debt and continuing military expenditure, even while private wealth funded the building of elegant *hôtels particuliers* in the areas beyond the Place Louis XV. The population continued to grow, now reaching 600,000; and the economic screws continued to tighten. In 1784 an unpopular new wall was built around Paris, to enable customs dues to be collected more efficiently on goods entering and leaving the city (*see p. 318*). The harvest failed across France in 1787 and 1788. In May 1789, the king convoked (for the first time since 1614) a full meeting of the Etats-Généraux to consider further reform proposals prepared by his finance minister Necker. The Etats-Généraux had three constituent parts: the First Estate (the clergy), the Second Estate (the nobility), and the Third Estate (the commoners). The Third Estate, always outvoted by the other two, then proceeded to meet independently, and proclaimed itself an assembly in its own right. Louis responded by sacking Necker. But he had misjudged the popular mood, especially in Paris. The mob attacked Les Invalides, capturing 30,000 muskets, and the next day, 14th July, they stormed and occupied the Bastille prison, symbol of royal autocracy. The French Revolution had begun.

The French Revolution

The next decade and a half saw France ruled in a bewildering succession of political formats. Paris was at the centre of the turmoil and bloodshed, losing a tenth of its population. The fabric of the city suffered too: royal buildings were damaged and statues toppled, Church property was sequestrated and churches themselves either given new functions or pulled down (with the atmospheric paintings of Hubert Robert recording their decay). But bringing down the monarchy was not the rebels' immediate objective. A new constitution sworn into operation on the following 14th July, including by the king himself, still provided for a constitutional monarchy, although it severely diminished the powers of the Church.

This new constitution then came under increasing attack from both sides. Radicals, especially those known as the Jacobins (because they met in what had been the Jacobin convent in the Rue St-Honoré), felt that it did not go far enough. Conservative Catholics, swayed by the pope's condemnation of it, felt that it went too far, and sought to recover the ground it had ceded. Caught in the middle were the moderate Girondins (so called because many of their leaders came from the Gironde region around Bordeaux). In June 1791 the king and his queen Marie-Antoinette tried to flee, and were captured at Varenne in eastern France; but, though the Assembly took this as a reason to suspend Louis from his functions, he was later reinstated. Emigrés, and the wealth they had taken with them, and those priests refusing to accept the constitution, were more urgent targets of popular wrath.

Over the winter of 1791–92 a third focus for resentment developed: the foreign powers thought to be scheming to reverse reforms. In April 1792 the king, reflecting the will of the Assembly, declared war on Austria and Prussia. But the weak French army's disastrous performance encouraged public suspicions that the king and his Girondin government had sought to bring about French defeat. The mob stormed the

Tuileries; the Assembly established a Convention to draw up a new, more radical, republican constitution; and the royal family was imprisoned in the Temple Tower. Radical and popular frustration boiled over: prisons were stormed and emptied, and aristocrats executed. The king himself was guillotined in January 1793 after a show trial. Marie-Antoinette met the same fate in October. The Convention established a Revolutionary Tribunal and a Committee of Public Security which gradually assumed power and pursued anyone suspected of royalist or clerical sympathies. Twenty thousand died in the Terror, including Madame du Barry, the once-beautiful courtesan and former mistress of Louis XV, who went to her death pleading with the executioner for 'encore un moment... encore un petit moment...'.

Only by the second half of 1794, by which time many of the Committee's own original leaders (including Danton and Robespierre) had been executed, did the pendulum swing back. In 1795 a five-member Directoire took power. Though feeble, increasingly corrupt, and dependent on the Army, it was committed to trying to restore stability. The following years saw military success too, especially under the young Corsican general Napoleon Bonaparte; and at home, after the Terror, people began to develop a taste for self-indulgence. The first restaurants were established, mainly run by former chefs to aristocrats: it was thought democratic to eat well in public. Clockmakers and other craftsmen easily incorporated republican motifs into their luxury products.

Napoleon and the French Empire

Bonaparte's military successes continued apace. In 1797 he extinguished the Venetian Republic; in 1798 he occupied Rome, declared a Roman republic, and took the pope into custody to France; in 1799 he usurped the Directoire and established a Consulat, with himself as First Consul; fortified by his crushing of the Austrians at the Battle of Marengo in 1800, he became consul for life. Then he declared himself Emperor, and staged a coronation in Notre-Dame in 1804, in the presence of the pope, in evocation of the papal coronation of Charlemagne (in this case, however, it was Napoleon himself, and not the pontiff, who placed the crown on the imperial head). In 1805 Napoleon crowned himself with the iron crown of Lombardy in Milan. In 1806 he abolished the Holy Roman Empire and married Marie-Louise, daughter of the last Holy Roman Emperor Francis II, as a way at last of brokering peace between France and Austria. Napoleon had created a new European empire, and Paris was its capital.

Though often absent from Paris, Napoleon nevertheless took a close interest both in France's civil administration and in the amenities of the city. He had four new bridges started. He remodelled the Madeleine, began the Rue de Rivoli, and had medieval houses around Notre-Dame removed to make more space for his coronation parade. He planned his Arc de Triomphe, but in open country to the west of the city rather than in the Place de la Bastille as first intended, because of popular disillusionment with his policies. He inaugurated the Louvre as a museum, in particular to display his spoils from Italy and Germany.

By 1810, Napoleon's luck seemed to change. The long campaign in Spain ended in defeat; so did the disastrous march on Moscow. At home, there was a financial crash in 1811. In March 1814, the combined forces of France's enemies, led by Austria, Prussia and Russia, occupied Paris, the first time it had been occupied by foreign troops for four centuries. Napoleon abdicated, and in May Louis XVI's younger brother returned to reoccupy the royal throne. (He took the title Louis XVIII, remembering Louis XVI's eight-year-old son, the Louis XVII that might have been, thought to have been murdered in the Temple after his father's death.)

The occupying forces behaved magnanimously, though the Cossacks' impatience in restaurants (*bistro*—quickly) gave rise to a new form of eating establishment. But the new king did little to endear himself. When Napoleon, the following year, escaped from Elba and sought to re-establish his empire, Paris received him phlegmatically back. After the Battle of Waterloo finally settled his prospects, the Allies occupied Paris once again, while Napoleon was exiled to St Helena.

Further cycles of revolution

Louis XVIII (r. 1815–24) returned, this time supported by 300,000 soldiers, half the population of the city. He surrounded himself with ministers of reactionary tendencies, tendencies which were only encouraged by the assassination of his nephew, the Duc de Berry, outside the opera in 1820.

Economically, France and Paris recovered well under Louis XVIII and his brother Charles X (r. 1824–30). Albeit later than London, Paris started to see the effects of the Industrial Revolution. But Charles was even more resistant to the pull of democracy than his brother; and his attempt in 1830 to dissolve the Chamber of Deputies and suspend freedom of the press led to riots. The rioters took over the whole city in three days in July, using urban guerrilla tactics which the narrowness of the streets made it hard to counter.

Rather than re-establish the Republic, however, the rebels invited Louis-Philippe (r. 1830–48), Duc d'Orléans, to become 'citizen-king', establishing the 'July Monarchy'. Although he was a direct descendant of Louis XIII, he carefully distinguished his style from that of the Bourbons. He had been a prosperous banker, and he continued to promote bourgeois interests. Most of the changes to Paris during his reign were new residential developments in areas such as Batignolles. His reign saw the first omnibuses and the first department stores. The railway arrived. The city's population increased by a third in only a generation, to over a million for the first time. Balzac's novels chart this rapidly changing city. But the king's popularity declined, not helped by the authoritarian ways of his police force, nor by the cholera epidemic in the city in 1832 and food shortages in 1847. When a small demonstration in February 1848 was violently suppressed, with several hundred deaths, the National Guard took the insurgents' side; and France's last king fled. The rioters sacked the Tuileries, and burnt the royal throne in front of the Place de la Bastille monument to those who had died in the 1830 riots.

During 1848, that year of upheaval across Europe, France saw four forms of government. After the monarchy came the Second Republic, unprepared and ineffectual. When, within months, it proved unable to meet public expectations, and unemployment in Paris rose alarmingly, there was more rioting, this time savagely put down by Cavaignac, Minister for War. Several thousand were killed, many more imprisoned or deported; for a while Paris was under effective military dictatorship. Finally, at the end of the year, elections—the first with mass male suffrage—brought Napoleon's nephew-by-marriage, Louis-Napoléon to power as President, his 75 per cent of the vote reflecting how strong Bonapartist feeling still was in the provinces, compared to radical, republican Paris. Three years later, he mounted a coup against his own presidency and was appointed Emperor in a plebiscite.

As Napoléon III (in acknowledgement of the two-week reign of Napoleon's four-year-old son in 1815), the new emperor had ambitious ideas for Paris. He and Baron Haussmann, appointed as Préfet de Paris, wanted wide modern streets and were ruthless in demolishing the crowded and insalubrious old quarters that stood in their way. Planning regulations required housing to follow uniform proportions, emphasised by long horizontal lines of balconies overlooking the new boulevards. The emperor's great pride in his city, and in its railway stations and other public buildings exploiting the developing possibilities of iron and glass, was reflected also in Great Exhibitions in 1855 and 1867.

Napoléon III's foreign policy was less successful. Militarily he was an adventurer, and involved France in a number of wars, including the battle to drive Austria from Italy in return for Savoy and Nice. Disaster struck when he was manoeuvred by Bismarck into declaring war on Prussia in 1870. Within six weeks, the French army had to surrender at Sedan. The emperor was captured, deposed, and a (Third) Republic was declared, under Favre and Gambetta. The Germans occupied Versailles and besieged Paris. The city, unprepared, quickly ran out of food and was reduced to communicating with the outside world by sending out hot air balloons, made of cotton, varnished and filled with coal gas. Finally, it had to capitulate. The Germans imposed harsh terms: France was to cede Alsace and part of Lorraine, pay a hefty indemnity, and recognise Germany as an empire under Kaiser Wilhelm I. The government saw no alternative to accepting. The poorer classes in Paris, however, were in no mood to sit quiet. Napoléon III's modernisation had created an outwardly grandiose city, but his town planning was socially divisive: the poor could not afford the new rents and had retreated to the eastern districts, where gentrification emphatically did not reach. Now, still bitter at the killings of 1010, and fearing that their interests were once again being sacrificed to those of the bourgeoisie, they seized an armoury of weapons and succeeded in occupying the whole of Paris and declaring a Commune.

The *communards*, however, had no strategy for holding on to what they had gained, and a government counter-strike forced them to retreat gradually back across Paris. The traditional barricades were less effective at holding the new broad streets than they had been in the cramped medieval alleys of the pre-Haussmann era. As they retreated eastwards, the *communards* set fire to the *quartiers* they were leaving. Within two months, it was all over, after a last stand in the Père-Lachaise cemetery (in the corner where later French Communist Party leaders liked to be buried). Three to four thousand *communards* had died in the fighting; another 20,000 were executed in retribution. The chasm between bourgeois and working class deepened further.

Economic and cultural recovery was nevertheless rapid, and the reparations imposed by the Prussians were quickly paid off. Already by 1878 the city was confident enough to put on another Great Exhibition; and another in 1889, for which Eiffel built his Tower. The Impressionists held their first exhibition in 1874. Ironically, too, the 'scorched earth' policy of the Commune made it all the easier to complete Haussmann's plans. In 1898 the first Métro lines opened, with stations designed in the Art Nouveau style by Guimard (who also designed the little synagogue in the Rue Pavée in the Marais). By 1914 Paris' population stood at 2.5 million: it had quintupled within a century.

Politically, France remained riven: between Church and State, between conservative provinces and a radical capital. Against popular resentment, the government started building the Sacré-Coeur on Montmartre, in expiation of the Commune (it was not finally consecrated until 1919). The Dreyfus affair (in which a Jewish officer was accused, falsely as it was eventually proven, of passing military secrets to Germany) polarised society for a decade.

Paris in the two world wars

When the First World War came in August 1914, France—although united by resentment of the Germans—was neither politically nor militarily prepared. Within a month, German forces came within 50 miles of Paris, and the city faced siege again. The government fled for Bordeaux. But lucky capture of a German campaign map enabled veteran general Gallieni to counter-attack. The city's taxis made an odd but essential logistic contribution by bringing troops to the front line (*see p. 113*). The Germans retreated to northern France, where fighting focused on trench warfare for the rest of the war, though Paris experienced bombardment again in the spring of 1918 during the Germans' last, unsuccessful offensive.

After the War, the Peace Treaties were negotiated in Paris. The French Prime Minister, Clémenceau, insisted that they be signed in the Hall of Mirrors (Galerie des Glaces; *see p. 380*) in Versailles, where Bismarck had had the German Empire proclaimed in 1870. The treaties were displeasing to France. Exhausted and resentful, having sustained huge loss of life and a ravaged land, she felt angered that Germany was being allowed to survive. On the day the Peace Treaty was signed in Versailles, the Paris bus-drivers went on strike. Recovery was slow. Though the fortifications built around Paris after the Franco-Prussian War (where the Boulevard Périphérique now runs) were dismantled, there were no ambitious ideas, and no funds, for using the space created. Immigration into Paris, from abroad and from the provinces, combined with economic depression, led to social tensions and anti-Semitism. There were serious riots in 1934; and in the seven years up to 1939 no fewer than 19 governments. One of them, in 1936, brought together Socialists and Communists in a pioneering Popular Front under Léon Blum. Mutual suspicions between the two soon undermined it, as did a wave of celebratory strikes and factory occupations which put economic revival at risk. But some of its innovations (such as paid holiday entitlements) have kept its memory fresh.

On the outbreak of the Second World War, France was in no state to resist the Germans when they sidestepped the defensive Maginot Line in May 1940 and marched once again on Paris. The Germans occupied the northern half of France, including Paris, while a collaborationist government was established at Vichy. French officials connived at the deportation of around half of Paris' Jewish population. But many French began to resist the German occupation, especially once Germany had attacked the Soviet Union. Over the four years to 1944, around 11,000 partisans of various political leanings were killed. In 1944, the Allied forces landed in Normandy, prompting insurgents of both Left and Right to try to take control of Paris. General de Gaulle persuaded the Allied commanders to help his Free French forces take the city, to prevent it falling into Communist control. General Leclerc arranged to enter the city by the Porte d'Orléans, as Napoleon had in 1815. Meanwhile, the departing German *Kommandant* ignored Hitler's orders to destroy the city behind him. Two days later, to make clear that Paris was once again under French authority, de Gaulle marched from the Arc de Triomphe to the Place de la Concorde, courageously ignoring the danger from Communist snipers still active.

The Fourth and Fifth Republics

De Gaulle remained in control of France until the end of the war, and claimed for France a place among the victorious Allied Powers. But the shattered economy needed external support, from the US Marshall Plan. Savage reprisals were taken against alleged collaborators with the Germans: the underlying moral dilemma helped stimulate the development, by Sartre and others, of Existentialism. In 1946 de Gaulle stepped back from power, and the (Fourth) Republic was established. It struggled to achieve economic recovery due to endemic strikes; joined the first efforts to build a new peaceful community between the states of Europe; and grappled with colonial problems, first in Indo-China, then in Algeria. It successfully disentangled France from the former; but lacked the strength to deal with the latter's demands for independence, especially once the violence spread to France itself.

In 1958 the Republic collapsed, and was replaced by a new Constitution (the Fifth Republic) designed by de Gaulle around a powerful President: himself. It came as a shock to many of his supporters when in 1962 he decided to grant Algerian independence. There was fierce resistance within France to this decision (including attempts to assassinate him), led by disaffected generals.

During the 1960s he was able to turn his attention to cleaning up Paris. For the first time, some official support was provided for preserving the city's existing character, starting in the Marais, rather than just imposing new development. This was, nevertheless, also the era of the Tour Montparnasse, still one of only two skyscrapers inside the Périphérique, and of the decision to demolish the old Halles market. In 1968 there were, once again, serious riots in Paris, started this time by students. Though de Gaulle re-established control, he stepped down the following year.

All of de Gaulle's successors as President have sought to leave their mark on Paris, though none have been Parisians by birth. François Mitterrand, the longest serving (1981–95), initiated the most ambitious projects: a new opera house at the Bastille; a new arch at La Défense, to continue westwards the perspective of triumphal arches from the Arc du Carrousel to the Arc de Triomphe; the glass pyramids at the Louvre. The election as Mayor of Paris in 1977 (the first time for over a century that it had been an elective rather than bureaucratic office) of Jacques Chirac, from the political Right, seemed to hint that centuries-old social divisions within Paris, and between Paris and France, were finally healed. The racial rioting that spread from the *banlieues* in 2005 suggests that it would still be wrong to judge Paris as a city at peace with itself; nevertheless, it remains—as it has always been—a magnet for all the cultural and artistic vitality of France.

THE ISLANDS IN THE SEINE

At the heart of Paris, where the River Seine widens to encompass them, are two islands, the Ile de la Cité and the Ile St-Louis. Closely connected but different in character, their history and position on the Seine makes them exceedingly attractive to visitors. The freighted vessel on a sea argent has figured in the arms of Paris since the *sceau des marchands de l'eau* (the seal of the water merchants) became the seal of the first municipal administration at the time of St Louis in the 13th century, with its device *fluctuat nec mergitur* (tossed but not engulfed). In its stylised form as the logo of the Mairie de Paris, the coat of arms can be found right across the city.

The Ile de la Cité is of major historical and administrative importance and has outstanding monuments including the cathedral of Notre-Dame de Paris, the Sainte-Chapelle and the Conciergerie.

HISTORY OF THE ILE DE LA CITE

The Ile de la Cité was the earliest inhabited part of Paris. According to Caesar, it was the site of the *oppidum* of the Celtic tribe known as the Parisii. The island was settled c. 52 BC by the Romans and became known as *Lutèce* or *Lutetia Parisiorum*. There was a temple towards the east, on the site of the present cathedral, and traces of the Roman settlement can be explored (*see p. 30*). *Lutetia* gradually spread to the Left Bank (*see p. 41*) and c. 300 the settlement became known as Paris, chosen as the capital of the Franks in 508, under Clovis I (r. 481–511). The island, protected by the river, but also a convenient crossing point, centre for river traffic, and close to ancient overland routes, became a strategic focal point. From the 10th century, the Capetian kings were responsible for the great buildings of the Cité, including the palace. For many centuries the island continued to be the royal, legal and religious centre, with 14 parishes in the Middle Ages. It remained barely altered from 1300 until the mid-19th century, when the medieval quarters were run through by Baron Haussmann's city improvement projects (*see p. 223*) creating pretty much what can be seen today. The island continues to be an ecclesiastical, judicial and legal centre.

NOTRE-DAME DE PARIS
Map p. 475, E2

Open Mon–Sat 8–6.45, Sun 8–7.45; T: 01 42 34 56 10.
The oldest of the great emblems of Paris, Notre-Dame cathedral has been described as the ribcage of the the city, with all its associations, from pre-Christian times to Quasimodo (*see p. 28*) via royal marriages and presidential funerals. The building of Notre-Dame played an important role in the history of medieval architecture. Begun in 1163, it expanded on the new style initiated at St-Denis (*see p. 408*), which became known as Gothic. The west front, with its magnificent rose window, was completed in the 13th century. Notre-Dame in its turn influenced ecclesiastical architecture in the Ile-de-France and all over Europe. Despite successive alterations, this building represents a textbook example of the evolution of the Gothic style from the 12th to 14th centuries.

NOTRE-DAME: THE WEST FRONT

Bishop Maurice de Sully (d. 1196), was the inspiration behind the move to replace two earlier churches, St-Etienne and Notre-Dame, by a single building on a much larger scale. St-Etienne, founded by Childebert in 528, had itself replaced a Roman temple dedicated to Jupiter. Tradition holds that the foundation stone of the new cathedral was laid by Pope Alexander III in 1163. Between that date and the consecration of the main altar on 19th May 1182, the choir and double ambulatory were finished except for the high vault. The second phase of work, which completed the transepts and most of the nave, extended from c. 1178–1200. From 1190–1220 the west front was built up to the rose window and during this period the second nave aisle was being erected. The rose itself dates from 1220–25 and the towers from 1225–50. Modifications were already being made around this time to the earlier sections, notably the enlargement of the clerestory windows all around the church. In 1235–50 a series of chapels was built between the nave buttresses. Around 1250 the north transept was extended and the porch built by Jean de Chelles who began c. 1258 the extension of the south transept which was completed by Pierre de Montreuil. Pierre de Chelles built the *jubé* at the beginning of the 14th century and he, followed by Jean Ravy, was responsible for the chapels around the apse (1296–1330). The latter *maître d'oeuvre* began the flying buttresses, which took the strain of the high vaults and whose dramatic proportions encourage comparisons with the rigging of a ship. Jean Ravy's successors, Jean le Bouteiller and Raymond du Temple, completed work on the great vessel by the second half of the 14th century.

Adam and Eve and the Serpent: sculpted decoration (1166–75; restored) on the west front of Notre-Dame.

For some three centuries the fabric of the cathedral remained relatively untouched and provided the setting for many important events. The School of Music at Notre-Dame was influential during the late 12th and 13th centuries. In 1186 Geoffrey Plantagenet (son of Henry II) was buried here after his sudden death in Paris, and Henry VI of England in 1431 at the age of 10 was crowned King of France in the cathedral. Many royal marriages were celebrated within its walls, including those of James V of Scotland to Madeleine of France in 1537, François II to Mary Stuart (1558), Henri of Navarre, the future Henri IV, to Marguerite de Valois (1572), and Charles I of England (by proxy) to Henrietta Maria (1625).

Changes in taste and emphasis during the reigns of Louis XIV and Louis XV brought about major alterations. Tombs and stained-glass were destroyed, the *jubé* and the stalls were condemned, and in 1771 Soufflot desecrated the trumeau and part of the tympanum of the central portal to allow a processional dais to pass through. Much of what survived this destruction was lost during the Revolution. But the cathedral was still used for great ceremonies: in 1804, Napoleon was crowned Emperor here by Pius VII and in 1853 Napoléon III and Eugénie de Montijo were married in the church. By 1844, due in great part to Victor Hugo's Romantic novel *Notre-Dame de Paris* (1831; *see p. 28*), which helped to engender an interest in Gothic architecture, the cathedral was considered worth a thorough restoration. This was begun under the direction of Lassus and Viollet-le-Duc. A century later, on 26th August 1944, the thanksgiving service following General de Gaulle's entry into liberated Paris took place at Notre-Dame. The cathedral has continued to be the scene of occasional ceremonial functions, including the state funeral of François Mitterand in January 1996. The first stage of a long renovation of the building was completed to coincide with the start of the 21st century.

The exterior

The west front, composed of three distinct levels, is a model of clarity and harmony. A masterful design of verticals and horizontals divides the elevation into regular and complementary sections, its construction continued through the first half of the 13th century. The central Porte du Jugement, c. 1220, is medieval only in essence. The figure of Christ on the trumeau dates from 1885, the *Last Judgement* was restored by Viollet-le-Duc, and most of the other sculptures are also 19th century. The Porte de la Vierge on the left is slightly earlier. The Virgin on the central pier has been restored, and the statues of saints remade by Viollet-le-Duc. However, the scenes relating to the *Life of the Virgin* in the tympanum are 13th-century: in the lower register, the *Ancestors of the Virgin*; in the middle, the *Resurrection of the Virgin*; and in the upper register, her *Coronation*. The sculptures of the Porte de Ste Anne (on the right) are mostly of 1165–75, designed for a narrower portal, with additions of c. 1240. On the pier is St Marcellus (19th century); above are scenes from the lives of St Anne and the Virgin, and the *Virgin in Majesty*, with Louis VII (right) and Maurice de Sully (left). The two side doors retain their medieval wrought-iron hinges. In the buttress niches flanking the doors are modern statues of St Stephen, the Church, the Synagogue and St Denis. Above, across the full width of the façade, is the *Gallery of the Kings of Judah*, reconstructed by Viollet-le-Duc. Its 28 statues were destroyed in 1793 because the Parisians assumed that they represented the kings of France and fragments discovered in 1977 are in the Musée du Moyen Age (*see p. 43*). The magnificent rose window, 9.6m in diameter, is flanked by double windows within arches. Higher still is an open arcade on slender columns.

Like the west front, the side façades and apse also consist of three distinct and receding storeys; the bold and elegant flying buttresses of the latter were an innovation by Jean Ravy. The south porch, according to a Latin inscription at the base, was begun in 1257 under the direction of Jean de Chelles. The *Story of St Stephen* (a reference to the earlier church dedicated to him) in the tympanum and the medallions depicting student life, are original. The north porch, slightly earlier, has an original statue of the Virgin and, in the tympanum, the *Story of Theophilus*. Just to the east of this porch is the graceful Porte Rouge, probably by Pierre de Montreuil. To the left, below the windows of the choir chapels, are seven 14th-century bas-reliefs. The *flèche* (90m above the ground), a lead-covered oak structure, was rebuilt by Viollet-le-Duc in 1860.

The Towers of Notre-Dame
Open daily July–Aug 9–7.30, Sat and Sun to 11pm; Apr–June, Sept 9.30–7.30; Oct–Mar 10–5.30; last entry 45mins before closing; free for under 18s on 1st Sun of month and Oct–Mar; T: 01 53 10 07 00; enter by the north tower. www.monum.fr
There are 387 steps inside the massive towers, which never received the spires that were originally intended. The climb is worthwhile for the view of Viollet-le-Duc's *flèche* and the rooftops. It includes an exhibition about the building, and a close-up from the gallery between the towers of the suitably chimerical creatures redesigned by Viollet-le-Duc. The great bell, *Emmanuel*, recast in 1686 and weighing 13 tonnes, was made famous by Victor Hugo's novel *Notre-Dame de Paris* and his hunch-backed bell-ringer Quasimodo. Named after the first Sunday following Easter, when he was found on the cathedral steps by Archdeacon Frollo, Quasimodo (literally 'as if in the manner of' from the introit for that day: *Quasi modo geniti infantes* 'new born babes') and the story of his devotion to the gypsy girl Esmeralda have been the subject of at least five film adaptations, although the central character of the novel remains the cathedral itself.

The interior
The interior is fairly regular in its layout with only slight discrepancies. The shift in axis between the nave and choir and the increased width of the latter (48m) over the former are hardly discernible. Despite the large clerestory windows with modern glass (1964), the interior tends to be rather sombre, and is usually very busy. On the left when entering is a book-stall; visitors are encouraged not to enter the ambulatory except for devotional purposes. The height of the ten-bay nave, 33m—very daring for the time—confirmed the prestige of the principal ecclesiastical building in Paris. The sheer elevations of the nave and shallow mouldings of the upper storey emphasise the thinness of the walls relative to their height. In contrast, short cylindrical piers, a throwback to St-Denis (*see p. 408*), surround the nave and the apse. Triple shafts of equal size rise uninterrupted from the capitals to the springing of the sexpartite vaults. The nave is flanked by double aisles and a double ambulatory surrounds the choir (five bays) and 37 chapels surround the whole. The total length of the cathedral is 130m. A vaulted triforium overlooks the nave whereas the gallery around the choir has double openings. The change in master of works c. 1178 resulted in the contrast between the piers with shafts on the east and the piers with pilasters to the west. The upper part of the transept bays and west bay of the choir were remodelled in the 19th century to approximately their original 12th-century disposition.

The shallow transepts contain two of the three rose windows that have retained some original 13th-century glass. The north is the finest and best preserved and represents kings, judges, priests and prophets around the Virgin. The south was much restored in 1737 and, with Christ at the centre, it depicts saints, apostles and angels, with the *Wise and Foolish Virgins*. The rose in the west contains scenes of the *Labours of the Months*, the *Signs of the Zodiac*, Vices, Virtues and prophets with the Virgin, but was almost entirely remade in the 19th century.

In the side-chapels of the nave hang seven 17th-century paintings from an original 76 (by Charles le Brun, Sébastian Bourdon and others), presented by the Goldsmiths' Guild of Paris between 1630 and 1707. Against the southeast pillar at the crossing stands a 14th-century image of the Virgin, as Notre-Dame de Paris, and against the northeast pillar is St Denis by Nicolas Coustou (18th century).

The choir was completely altered in 1708–25 by Louis XIV in fulfilment of his father's vow of 1638 to place France under the protection of the Virgin should he father a son; this vow was realised after 23 years of marriage when the future Louis XIV was born (*see p. 98*). The work was carried out under the direction of Robert de Cotte, but was not spared by Viollet-le-Duc. Behind Viollet-le-Duc's altar is a *Pietà* (1723) by Nicolas Coustou, the base by Girardon, part of the *Voeu de Louis XIII*. The statue of Louis XIII (south) is also by Coustou; that of Louis XIV (north) by Coysevox (both 1715). Of the original 114 stalls, 78 remain, adorned with bas-reliefs from the designs of Jules Degoulon, with canopied archiepiscopal stalls at either end. The bronze angels (1713) against the apse-pillars are rare survivors of the Revolutionary melting-pot. In the first four bays of the choir are the remains of the mid-14th-century choir screen which, until the 18th century extended round the whole apse; the expressive reliefs on the exterior were unhappily restored and repainted by Viollet-le-Duc. In the blind arches below are listed some of the eminent people buried in the church.

The ambulatory contains the tombs of 18th–19th-century prelates. Behind the high altar is the tomb-statue of Bishop Matiffas de Bucy (d. 1304). In the second chapel south of the central chapel is the theatrical tomb, by Jean-Baptiste Pigalle, of the Comte d'Harcourt (d. 1769); here also are the restored tomb-statues of Jean Jouvenel des Ursins and his wife (d. 1431, 1451).

On the south side of the ambulatory is the entrance to the **Treasury** (*open daily 9–6*), a collection of ecclesiastical plate, reliquaries and cult objects. including relics purporting to be from the Crown of Thorns and the True Cross (see p. 33). In the west is the main organ, 1733, by Cliquot rebuilt in 1868 by the Cavaillé-Coll workshops. The Cavaillé-Coll dynasty originated in the south of France, and the best known, Aristide (1811–99), was one of the originators of the symphonic organ.

Parvis Notre-Dame

The cathedral rises to the east of the vast forecourt, Parvis Notre-Dame, which was increased sixfold in the 19th century. Road distances are calculated from a symbolic centre in the Parvis (which means 'paradise') marked by a bronze flagstone engraved with the arms of the town and the four points of the compass. Traced on its paving is the outline of part of the earlier cathedral of St-Etienne (Stephen). To the left of the cathedral is the Hôtel Dieu, the hospital for central Paris, rebuilt in 1868–78, north of the first hospital, founded c. 660 by St Landry, Bishop of Paris. The old Hôtel Dieu, built in the 12th century at the same time as Notre-Dame, was razed by Haussmann (*see p. 223*). In the past, ecclesiastical authorities brought condemned heretics to trial on the Parvis where they begged for absolution before execution. The Pont au Double (1882) replaced a mid-17th century bridge where the toll was a diminutive coin known as a *double*. Rue d'Arcole leads north to Pont d'Arcole (1855), named after a youth killed in 1830 leading insurgents against the Hôtel de Ville.

Crypte Archéologique
Open 10–6, closed Mon; T: 01 43 29 83 51.
Near the west end of the Pl. du Parvis Notre-Dame is the entrance to the Crypte Archéologique. Superimposed layers of architectural remains of all periods of the Cité's past were uncovered here in 1965 during excavation work for the adjacent underground car-park. The site is well presented with dioramas and models explaining the growth of the district prior to the ravaging fire of 1772. Sections are illuminated by press-button lighting and explanatory notes in French and English. The path runs above the foundations of the late 3rd-century Gallo-Roman rampart, more of which is seen later. Further to the east, beyond the excavated area, lie the foundations of the west end of the Merovingian cathedral of St-Etienne (6th century). There are display cases containing artefacts from the dig, and the route then follows the foundations of the demolished Hospice des Enfants-Trouvés and other medieval buildings which flanked Rue Neuve Notre-Dame—some on the right close to the exit dating from as early as the 2nd century. On the left are vestiges of hypocausts.

Rue de la Cité which crosses the island at the level of Pl. du Parvis Notre-Dame, is an ancient route which crossed Roman bridges, replaced to the north by Pont Notre-Dame, rebuilt in 1913, and to the south by the Petit Pont (1853).

Musée Notre-Dame
Open Wed, Sat and Sun 2.30–6; T: 01 43 25 42 92; enter at 10 Rue du Cloître Notre-Dame.
The museum has collections illustrating the history of the cathedral and alterations made to it and to the surroundings. There is information on ancient ceremonies, the music and people connected with the building, and two gilded bronze bees from the coronation of Napoleon. A great admirer of industry, the Emperor adopted bees as his symbol instead of the royal *fleur-de-lys*.

East of the cathedral
East of the cathedral is Sq. Jean XXIII, a pleasant garden on the site of the 17th-century archbishop's palace, demolished in 1831. On the eastern tip of the island, in Sq. de l'Ile-de-France, is the stark but deeply moving Mémorial des Martyrs et de la Déportation (*open summer 10–12 & 2–7; winter 2–7; T: 01 49 74 34 00*) of 1962 by Henri Pingusson. The names of some 200,000 French men, women and children deported to German concentration camps during the 1939–45 war are recorded here.

THE PALAIS DE JUSTICE
Map p. 475, E2

Visits to the interior or hearings, access via the entrance to the Sainte-Chapelle (see p. 32).
The Palais de Justice, standing on Blvd du Palais, is a huge block occupying the whole width of the island, the great but inglorious result of 19th-century rebuilding under Louis Duc and P.-J.-H. Daumet.

HISTORY OF THE PALAIS DE JUSTICE

The site was occupied in the Roman period by the palace where Julian the Apostate was proclaimed emperor in 360; the Merovingian kings, when in town, divided their time between the *thermae* (*see p. 44*) and their palace within the city walls. Louis VI died here in 1137 and Louis VII in 1180. St Louis (Louis IX) altered the building and built the Sainte-Chapelle. From 1431 it was occupied entirely by the *Parlement*, which had previously shared it with the king, but it was at the Revolution that it acquired its present function. Here, in the 16th Chambre Correctionelle, the trials of Flaubert's *Madame Bovary* and Baudelaire's *Les Fleurs du Mal* took place (29th January and 20th August 1857 respectively). The 18th-century buildings were greatly enlarged in 1857–68 and again in 1911–14. In the mid-19th century, the 14th-century tower at the northeastern corner, Tour de l'Horloge, with a clock copied from the original dial designed c. 1585 by Germain Pilon (1528–90), was virtually rebuilt. This handsome timepiece replaced the first public clock in Paris. The upper part of the north façade was rebuilt in the 19th century in an attempt to reproduce the original 14th-century work. The domed Galerie Marchande, dominating the Cour du Mai, is embellished with Neoclassical 18th-century sculptures by Augustin Pajou. Unlikely as it may now seem, the Cour du Mai was named after the maypole set up here annually by the society of law clerks.

Visiting the law courts

The most interesting part of these law courts is accessed up steps from the Cour du Mai. The Salle de Pas-Perdus is a magnificent hall, which replaced the great hall of the medieval palace where in 1431 the coronation banquet of Henry VI of England was celebrated. It was rebuilt in 1622 by Salomon de Brosse and restored in 1878 after being burned by the Communards. The room is divided in two by a row of arches, and at the far end is the entrance to the Première Chambre Civile, formerly the Chambre Dorée (restored in the style of Louis XII), a vestige of the old palace and perhaps originally the bedroom of Louis IX. Later it was used by the *Parlement*, in contempt of which Louis XIV here coined his famous epigram *L'Etat, c'est moi*. The Conciergerie and the extraordinary Sainte-Chapelle are the oldest surviving parts and are both now embraced within the precincts of the Palais de Justice.

THE SAINTE-CHAPELLE

Open daily March–Oct 9.30–6; Nov–Feb 9–5; T: 01 53 40 60 80. Enter from Blvd du Palais. Binoculars useful to study the stained glass. Narrow stairs link the lower and upper chapels. The Sainte-Chapelle was built by the saintly Louis IX (*see p. 11*) and dedicated in 1248. It is best known for the remarkable concentration of medieval stained glass in a building of exceptional lightness and delicacy. It was once part of the royal palace.

HISTORY OF THE SAINTE-CHAPELLE

The Sainte-Chapelle was planned both as the royal chapel of the palace, and as a resting place for the precious and costly relics acquired from Badouin II, the new Emperor of Constantinople, among them the Crown of Thorns and fragments of the True Cross, in 1239. An acquisition of both religious and political significance, the importance attributed to these relics is reflected in the sumptuousness of the building, whose design has been ascribed (in an oral tradition dating back to the 16th century) to Pierre de Montreuil, who also worked at St-Denis, Notre-Dame and St-Germain-en-Laye. The west window was replaced in 1485 by a Flamboyant rose. Damaged by fire in 1630, the chapel was slowly rebuilt only to be put under risk of demolition at the end of the 18th century as the Revolution left it in a perilous state. Thankfully the chapel, including many of the statues, was saved by the archaeologist Alexandre Lenoir (1762–1839). A full-scale restoration was undertaken between 1837 and 1857 by Duban, Lassus (who reconstructed a leaden *flèche* in the 15th-century style, the fifth on this site), Viollet-le-Duc and his successor Boeswillwald.

The exterior

From the outside, the impression of great height, actually 42.5m, in proportion to its length (36m) and breadth (17m) is accentuated by the buildings that crowd in around it. The chapel consists of two superimposed levels: the smaller lower one, the Chapelle Basse, dedicated to the Virgin Mary, was for the use of royal servants and retainers during solemn mass. The upper chapel, the part that is richly endowed with lofty windows and medieval stained glass, originally connected directly with the palace and was reserved for the royal family and court. The entrance consists of superimposed porches; the statues are 19th-century restorations. The balustrade is decorated with a motif of *fleurs de lys* and carved on the pinnacle above the south tower is a Crown of Thorns.

Chapelle Basse

The interior of the Chapelle Basse, with carved oak bosses and 40 columns supporting the upper chapel, is darkened by the decoration of Emile Boeswillwald, who attempted to reproduce its medieval décor painted with the *fleurs de lys* of France and the towers of Castille (emblem of Blanche de Castille, mother of Louis IX). The glass is 19th-century and three-lobed arcades and medallions enhance the walls. There are several 14th–15th-century tombstones in the pavement.

Chapelle Haute

A narrow staircase leads to the Chapelle Haute (20.5m high), though not the route taken by royalty, who entered directly at the upper level from buildings now demolished to the west. In contrast to the gloominess of the lower chapel, the upper chapel is a revelation, appropriate to the shrine of the holy relics. In one of the greatest virtuoso achievements of medieval architecture, the structure is reduced to an essential skeleton of tracery, supporting walls of richly coloured glass totalling almost 600 square metres. The chapel's bold design (1243–48) has been attributed on stylistic grounds to the architect Pierre de Montreuil. The Royal Chapel was designed to house the supremely important relic of the Crown of Thorns, which Louis IX had acquired from Constantinople in the aftermath of the Fourth Crusade of 1204. The design of the chapel, likened to the filigree work of a goldsmith, and the decorative scheme, originally inlaid with gilt and glass to give the effect of enamels, emphasised the relationship to a shrine or reliquary. The effect, with the stained glass, was a powerful and splendid setting designed to echo the physical reality and the mystical significance of the relics. Linking the blind traceried arcades of the lower part and the soaring windows are statues of Apostles under baldaquins—the 4th and 5th on the left and the 4th and 5th to the right are 13th-century. The uplifting translucence of the stained glass can only be fully appreciated on a day of clear sunlight. The two deep recesses under the windows of the 3rd bay were the seats reserved for the royal family. On the south side is a small chapel built at the time of Louis XI to enable the monarch to participate in mass without being seen. In the centre of the restored arcade across the apse is a wooden canopy beneath which the relics used to be exhibited on Good Friday; those few that survived the Revolution can now be seen in the treasury of Notre-Dame (*see p. 29*).

The stained glass was skillfully restored in 1845 and, although some has been lost, a large proportion dates from the 13th century. The glass reads from left to right and from bottom to top. Of the three east windows, on the left are scenes from the Life of St John the Evangelist and the *Childhood of Christ*; the central one, considered the most outstanding, dwells on the *Passion*; and on the right are the stories of John the Baptist and of Daniel. All the other windows, except one, deal with the Old Testament, reading from northwest: Genesis, Exodus, Numbers, Deuteronomy and Joshua, Judges, Isaiah and the Rod of Jesse. Then the three apse windows are followed by Ezekiel—92 of the 121 scenes are original—Jeremiah and Tobit, Judith and Job, Esther, and the Book of Kings. The southwest window depicts the Legend of the True Cross with illustrations of the *Translation of the Relics to Paris by St Louis*. However, this is one of the least well preserved and contains only 26 of the original 67 scenes. The 86 panels from the *Apocalypse* in the large rose-window, which are the easiest to read, were a gift of Charles VIII, some 250 years later.

THE CONCIERGERIE

Opening times and details as for the Sainte-Chapelle.

The Conciergerie occupies part of the lower floor of the Palais de Justice. It was a stately royal palace before it became one of the world's most infamous prisons during the Revolution. The medieval rooms constitute a very fine and rare example of medieval architecture in Paris.

HISTORY OF THE CONCIERGERIE

Roman governors and the French kings had palaces on this site until the second half of the 14th century. The three distinctive round towers facing the river are vestiges of the royal residence built by Philippe IV le Bel (1285–1314). After the old palace was abandoned in favour of the Louvre and Vincennes, it was used only for major receptions and celebrations. It became the seat of power for the *Parlement*, a judicial body, and residence of the *Concièrge*, a high-ranking officer of the Crown with powers of justice. Over time the name became associated with the place of imprisonment of those judged and its former role of royal palace was forgotten. Its infamy grew during the Revolution when a succession of the condemned, some 2,780 people both Royalist and Jacobin, passed their last hours here. Among them were Queen Marie-Antoinette, Mme du Barry, Camille Desmoulins, Charlotte Corday, Danton, André Chénier, the poet, and Robespierre. From 1793, the Revolutionary Tribunal was installed in the Great Chamber marking the reign of the Terror.

Visiting the Conciergerie

The present entrance is 19th-century; the original palace entrance was from the eastern side of the Cour du Mai. The three handsomely proportioned rooms of the medieval palace, albeit heavily restored, contrast with the macabre second part of the visit, to the prison cells. The vast four-aisled Gothic Salle des Gens-d'Armes (63.3m long), constructed 1302–13 by Enguerrand de Marigny, bears witness to the past splendour. The great hall served as a refectory for some 2,000 members of the royal household and contains a portion of the black marble table (against the south wall) once used here. In the east (near the entrance), are the lower part of the vaulted kitchens, with four huge fireplaces built during the reign of Jean II le Bon (1350–64); the upper kitchen (not always open), was originally on two levels, and is now devoid of decoration. The decoration to the west of the hall is more elaborate. The neo-Gothic spiral staircase is 19th-century. Great banquets took place here: Philip IV le Bel sponsored eight days of celebration, when the whole island was illuminated, to welcome his son-in-law Edward II of England; Charles V held a reception for the Emperor Charles IV in 1378; wedding celebrations included François I's marriage to

Eleanor of Habsburg in 1530, and Mary Queen of Scots to François II (1558). The Grand'Salle Haute, which was above, has been replaced by the Salle des Pas-Perdus (*see p. 31*). Temporary exhibitions are held in the Salle des Gens-d'Armes. The Salle des Gardes, (c. 1310), on a smaller scale, is divided down the middle by three pillars.

The four western bays of the great hall are known as the Rue de Paris, after the executioner during the Revolution who was known as Monsieur de Paris. The overflow prisoners, or *pailleux* (prisoners who slept on straw, being too poor to pay for their term in jail), slept here. The Revolutionary Prison of 1780 was rebuilt following a fire, and was altered again in the 19th century, so that visitors only see a small portion of the original. Off the Couloir des Prisonniers are small spaces reserved for the Clerk, who took the prisoners' names, the Concierge's office, and the room where prisoners were prepared for execution. The chapel where the Girondins were incarcerated was a small royal chapel modified in 1776. Marie-Antoinette's Chapel was built at the Restoration on the exact place where the Queen's cell had been. A poignant reminder of the tragic past of the Conciergerie is the re-creation of her cell in the last room on this level. Outside, the Cour des Femmes, where the female prisoners took exercise, has a fountain and stone tables. Above are prison memorabilia, the blade of a guillotine, lists of names, and reconstructions of cells. A bizarre memento is the wooden ladder from 396 Rue St-Honoré, where Robespierre (1758–94) lived from 1791 until his death.

ENVIRONS OF THE PALAIS DE JUSTICE

In front of the Palais de Justice, Blvd du Palais leads north to Place du Châtelet across the river over the Pont au Change (1860), thus named in the 12th century when gold-smiths and moneylenders set up shop on the bridge. The present one replaces a 17th-century stone bridge lined with buildings; to the south, Pont St-Michel, rebuilt several times since the late 14th century (most recently in 1857), leads to Blvd St-Michel and the Latin Quarter (*see p. 41*). Opposite the Palais de Justice, Rue de Lutèce leads between (right) the Préfecture de Police and (left) the domed Tribunal de Commerce (by Bailly; 1860–65), to the Marché aux Fleurs on Quai de la Corse. This provides a colourful and sweetly scented contrast to the sombre judicial buildings. It is supplied with drinking water from a Wallace Fountain (*see box overleaf*), and a bird market is held here on Sundays.

The Quai des Orfèvres on the south side of the island owes its name to goldsmiths established here between 1580 and 1643. Much later, as the site of the headquarters of the detective branch of the French police, the *quartier* became famous through Chief Inspector Jules Maigret of the Homicide Squad (*Brigade spéciale*), Georges Simenon's detective hero of 103 novels and short stories written between 1930 and 1972. Maigret entered his office in the Palais de Justice from the Quai des Orfèvres.

Behind the Palais de Justice are Place Dauphine, named in honour of the future Louis XIII (1610–43), as was the road on the Left Bank, and flanked by some attractive old houses. Tucked away here is the long-established restaurant Chez Paul, at No. 15.

WALLACE FOUNTAINS

Known in Paris simply as 'wallaces', these fountains were donated to the city by Sir Richard Wallace (*see p.357*) in 1872. Two years previously, upon inheriting his father's estate, Sir Richard had been caught up in the Siege of Paris and the painful birth of the Third Republic. Staying on in the city, he paid for an ambulance and a hospital, but the city's violent suppression of the Paris Commune in the following year persuaded Wallace to move his art collection to London for safe-keeping. He offered 50 fountains as a farewell gift. Conceived by Wallace himself in two different models (free-standing and also wall-mounted, the last remaining example now on Rue Cuvier) and designed by the sculptor Charles Auguste Lebourg, the fountains provided a free supply of clean drinking water and were enthusiastically received by pedestrian Parisians. The ornamental dome of the fountain is supported by four caryatids representing the gowned goddesses of Simplicity, Temperance, Charity and Kindness, distinguishable by their knees—whether left or right is covered or bare, held forward or back. The locations of the first batch of installations were decided by Eugène Belgrand (*see p. 223*). Eighty-two Wallace Fountains can now be found in different parts of Paris, none in the 1st and 2nd arrondissements but an average of five in each of the rest, with at least six in other French cities and towns. Others exist in more than 20 cities worldwide, with one most recently installed in Macao (the second in Asia after Tokyo).

The Wallace Fountain in the Marché aux Fleurs on Quai de la Corse.

PONT NEUF
Map p. 475, D2

The picturesque Pont Neuf is in fact two bridges which meet on the western point of the island between the Quai du Louvre and (south) the Quai des Augustins. The two parts are unified by the same cornice supported by corbels decorated with expressive and varied heads. Despite its name (New Bridge), it is the oldest existing bridge in Paris, begun by Baptiste du Cerceau. It was conceived so that the king could travel between the Louvre and the Abbey of St-Germain-des-Prés (*see p. 68*) and was the first bridge to be lined with side-walks instead of houses. Henri III (1574–89) laid the foundation stone in 1578; it was completed in 1607 and has required little maintenance until major renovations in 2006. Much admired from the start, paintings of it in former times can be found in the Musée Carnavalet (*see p. 284*). The Pointe de la Cité is occupied by the Square du Vert-Galant, a shaded area with fine panoramas of the banks of the Seine. Its name alludes to the amorous adventurer Henri IV (*see p. 13*). The equestrian statue of the king, by Jean de Bologne (1529–1608), given to Paris in 1604 by Marie de Medicis (1573–1642), was the first royal statue to be erected in a public place. Destroyed at the Revolution, the four slaves of the pedestal are at the Louvre. In 1818 the new statue by Lemot was inaugurated. Sightseeing boats, Vedettes du Pont Neuf (*T: 01 46 33 98 38, www.pontneuf.net*), depart from here.

ILE SAINT-LOUIS

Just a footbridge away from the Ile de la Cité, across the Pont St-Louis (1969), is the Ile St-Louis, a tranquil and elegant backwater and sought-after residential area. The island boasts no major monuments nor a Metro station, but does shelter some pleasant hotels and restaurants. Formerly two islets, these were linked in the 17th century when, as annex to the Marais, it became the site of a number of imposing mansions, several of which were designed by Louis Le Vau (*see box below*), the leading French Baroque architect. These jostle for place in the few narrow streets, the best presenting a dignified and subtly hued cordon facing out to the river. Four bridges link the island to the 'mainland': Pont Marie (1635), in the middle, was named after the original developer of the island, Christophe Marie.

Louis Le Vau (1612–70)
The leading Baroque architect at the time of Louis XIV, Le Vau was a highly successful master of the grand manner and overall effect, if not of fine detail. He married ingenuity and drama and knew how to adapt to his clients' tastes. He also had a talent for designing showy interiors on which he always worked with a dedicated team of decorative craftsmen. Born in Paris, he learned his trade from his father, a master mason, and in the late 1630s built himself a house on the Ile St-Louis. There followed several private commissions for mansions on the island which at that time was in full expansion, the most outstanding of which was the Hôtel de Lambert (1641–44). In 1643 Le Vau was engaged by the king's *Surintendent*, Nicolas Fouquet, for the Château de Vaux-le-Vicomte, and after Fouquet's fall managed to keep in good grace with Colbert, subsequently succeeding Lemercier as *Premier architecte du Roi*. From 1661 he worked at the Louvre, on the rebuilding of the Galerie d'Apollon and with Perrault on the great east façade. He produced the first designs for the Institut de France begun in 1662, and at Versailles in 1669 he remodelled the garden façade, altered later by Hardouin-Mansart.

Rue St-Louis en l'Ile

The main street, Rue St-Louis en l'Ile, has no river frontage, but has retained an aura of times past. It is endowed with one or two good buildings, including at no. 51 the Hôtel Chenizot, with a fine decorated doorway and balcony of 1726. The church of St-Louis en l'Ile could be passed by unnoticed if it were not for the curious openwork spire and the clock of 1741. Begun in 1664 to replace the then-outgrown original chapel, it was based on designs by the great architect Louis Le Vau and completed in 1726 by Jacques Doucet. The bright Baroque interior has ornamental stone-carving executed under the direction of the painter Philippe de Champaigne's nephew, Jean-Baptiste de Champaigne, who is buried here (d. 1681). As well as several 18th-century paintings and furnishings of some interest, the church contains a 16th-century Flemish polychromed wood relief of the *Dormition of the Virgin*, and six Nottingham alabaster reliefs.

Camille Claudel (1864–1943)

An exceptionally gifted artist and Rodin's pupil and lover, Camille Claudel lived and worked for a very productive but difficult period of her life at no. 19 Quai de Bourbon on the Ile St-Louis (*see below*). Well represented in the Musée Rodin (*see p. 116*), she first met Rodin in 1883 when at the Academie Colarossi studying under Alfred Bouchier. Strong, passionate, beautiful, independent and serious about her artistic future, she had rebelled against her parents and by the age of 20 was established in her own studio on the Left Bank. Rodin was bowled over by Claudel. She joined Rodin's studio in 1884, as model and assistant, which resulted in an intense love affair and a deeply rewarding artistic partnership. During their association Rodin derived the inspiration for a more intense expression in his works. Their tempestuous affair lasted for 11 years in the shadow of Rose Beuret, Rodin's lifelong companion. This situation provoked Claudel to make vicious drawings aimed at the couple, as she came to realise that Rodin would never marry her. As the affair waned, Claudel's strength as a sculptress emerged: despite similar characteristics, her work tends to be more lyrical and imaginative than Rodin's, notably in *Waltz* (1893). The relationship was intermittent between 1889 and 1894, and by 1898 they no longer had any contact. Claudel made her first maquette of *Maturity* in 1894, an allegory of the breakup; one figure, *The Implorer*, was produced as a separate edition. Her work was well received in the 1903 Salon d'Automne and *The Wave* (1897) shows a conscious advance on the Rodin years. From 1905 her mental health deteriorated and she destroyed many works. After her supportive brother, poet and diplomat Paul Claudel (1868–1955), married and moved abroad, she took refuge from the world in her studio, accusing Rodin of plagiarism. She was not informed of her father's death in 1913, and was committed to a psychiatric hospital by her mother. Despite pleas from medical staff that her daughter should return to her family, her mother refused. Camille Claudel died on 19th October, 1943, after 30 years in an asylum. About 90 of her sculptures, sketches and drawings survive. A biographical film, *Camille Claudel*, was made in 1988 with Isabelle Adjani as Claudel and Gérard Depardieu as Rodin.

The north bank of the island

Typical of the grander *hôtels particuliers* (*see p. 43*) built on the eastern part of the island is the Hôtel de Lambert (privately owned) at no. 2 Quai d'Anjou, begun in 1641 by Le Vau, the interior decorated by Eustache Le Sueur and Charles Le Brun, among others. Over three centuries, Quai d'Anjou has seen a variety of illustrious residents. Le Vau himself lived at no. 3.

No. 9 was the home from 1846 of the artist Honoré Daumier (1808–79), whose paintings, inspired by the quays, include *Laveuse au Quai d'Anjou* (c. 1860, Buffalo, New York). Born in Marseille, Daumier was apprenticed to a bookseller but soon discovered that his passion lay in drawing and politics. He studied the former under Alexandre Lenoir, and the latter contributed to his remarkably incisive caricatures of contemporary political figures. In 1832, his caricature of King Louis Philippe as Gargantua earned him six months in prison. Baudelaire considered Daumier one of the greatest artists of his day.

No. 17, the Hôtel de Lauzun (1657; *occasional visits with Centre des Monuments Nationaux, 7 Blvd Morland, T: 01 44 54 19 30*) attributed to Le Vau, was the residence from 1682–84 of the Duc de Lauzun, commander of the French forces at the Battle of the Boyne in Ireland in 1690, when he was defeated by King William of Orange. From 1842, as the Hôtel de Pimodan, this grand old address hosted the Club des Hachichins, a popular meeting place for artists and writers to experiment with cannabis, an exotic import that had arrived in the wake of Napoleon's North African campaigns. Charles Baudelaire (1821–67) rented three rooms on the top floor and squandered his inheritance here from 1843–45, although according to Théophile Gautier (1811–72), who became a regular visitor, the great Romantic poet did not indulge. The artists responsible for the splendid decoration of the *hôtel* were Le Brun, Le Sueur, Patel and Sébastien Bourdon.

The English writer Ford Madox Ford (1873–1939) published the literary periodical *Transatlantic Review* (*see p. 55*) from no. 29 around 1919; Hemingway was its deputy editor. Ford Madox Ford was the grandson of the pre-Raphaelite painter Ford Madox Brown. In 1908 he had founded the *English Review*, publishing authors such as Wyndham Lewis, D.H. Lawrence and Norman Douglas for the first time. His own tetralogy *Parade's End* (1924–25) is a vivid portrayal of the life of a junior officer in the trenches of the First World War.

The sculptress, Camille Claudel (*see box on previous page*) lived at no. 19 Quai de Bourbon from 1899–1913. No. 1, with wrought iron decorated with palms and grapes, was the cabaret or wine-bar Franc-Pinot, patronised by sailors.

To the south, at no. 6 Quai d'Orléans is the Polish Library and Museum (*see p. 422*). The island became a refuge for a number of Polish immigrants after the Polish uprising against Russian occupation in 1831, including the Romantic poet, Adam Mickiewicz, who was a friend of Chopin and Victor Hugo.

THE LEFT BANK

The Seine arrives from the south and describes a large arc dividing Paris in two, then leaves the centre by the southwest. The smaller section of the capital within the arc, relative to the flow of the river, is the Left Bank or Rive Gauche. Gallo-Roman *Lutetia* spread onto the mainland here opposite the islands, the area which later became the academic quarter, or Latin Quarter, around the medieval university reaching as far as the Mont Ste-Geneviève. The abbey of St-Germain was established in the fields (*prés*) west of the medieval fortified walls. By the 17th century this area was expanding with the construction of major buildings such as the Luxembourg Palace, the Institut de France, Les Invalides, the Jardin des Plantes and the Salpetrière hospital. Each introduced a certain distinction and character, particularly around St-Germain, which then became an increasingly fashionable residential area. By the 18th century the Ecole Militaire and the Champs de Mars were created. These districts correspond today to the 5th, 6th and 7th arrondissements. It was not until the 19th century, when the *faubourgs* and outlying villages became part of Paris that new districts, such as Montparnasse, Vaugirard, Grenelle and Tolbiac, the 13th, 14th and 15th arrondissements today, came into existence. The National Assembly and the Senate are both on this side of the Seine, as is the Eiffel Tower, and the new Musée du Quai Branly of non-European ethnology and ethnography.

THE LATIN QUARTER

Although associated with the young, the Latin Quarter is one of the oldest parts of Paris. It contains the majority of the educational and scientific institutions of the University of Paris (*see p. 53*). There are still many signs of student life, though probably little Latin spoken. During the student revolution of 1968, the old *pavés* (paving stones) were used as missiles, to be replaced by dull slabs. The district holds a vague yet irresistible attraction to many visitors, and cafés and bookshops abound, but the crass commercialism, fast-food restaurants and constant frenetic bustle of the main artery, the *Boul Mich* (Blvd St-Michel, part of Haussmann's scheme, *see p. 223*), can be a disincentive to linger. The more picturesque character of the area can be found in the side streets, where there are many reminders of the past, despite being bisected by Blvd St-Germain in the mid-19th century. The two major Gallo-Roman remains of Paris—the Arènes de Lutèce (*see p. 60*) and the Thermes de Cluny (*see p. 44*)—are here, along with interesting lesser known medieval churches, and the great necropolis on the hill, the Panthéon.

HISTORY OF THE LATIN QUARTER

By the 1st century AD, Roman *Lutetia* began to spread from the Ile de la Cité to the left bank of the Seine. A military camp was established on Montagne Ste-Geneviève, and the forum, arena (*see p. 60*), theatre, and three *thermae* (*see p. 44*) were constructed, while an aqueduct carried water from the Bièvre valley (*see p. 372*). The main Roman roads south from the the the Ile de la Cité were the *Via Inferior*, roughly the route of Blvd St-Michel, and the parallel *Via Superior*, the present Rue St-Jacques. Overrun by the Huns in the 5th century, the salvation of Paris c. 451 is traditionally attributed to the courageous example and prayers of a young Christian woman, Geneviève (*Genovefa*), born c. 420 at Nanterre, coming under the protection of St Germanus of Auxerre. Although romantically described as a shepherdess, she was from a prosperous Gallo-Roman background. Her faith and generosity of spirit raised her to sainthood and she became patron saint of Paris. Latin was the language spoken by scholars who gathered around the brilliant and outspoken theological scholar, Pierre Abélard (d. 1142) on the Montagne Ste-Geneviève. He settled on the Left Bank following his removal, c. 1100, from the school attached to Notre-Dame where he had confounded his master, Guillaume of Campeaux, in disputation. Abélard continued to challenge the Church and later proved to be a writer of genius, but his place in history was established by the scandal of his seduction and marriage of Heloïse, his pupil and niece of Canon Fulbert of Notre-Dame. After the couple failed to keep their vow of celibacy, Fulbert ordered Abélard's castration. They are commemorated at Père Lachaise (*see p. 327*).

MUSEE NATIONAL DU MOYEN AGE
Map p. 475, E3

*Open 9.15–5.45, closed Tues; T: 01 53 73 78 16; www.musee-moyenage.fr. Entrance at 6
Place Paul-Painlevé. Free on the 1st Sunday of the month and for under-18s. Frequent
guided tours, cultural activities and concerts. Audio guides, and sound and touch equipment
for the non- or partially sighted are available.*

The 15th-century Hôtel de Cluny is not only one of the finest surviving examples of
medieval French domestic architecture in Paris but also incorporates the best conserved
vestige of antique Paris, the Gallo-Roman *thermae*. Gathered here in the National
Museum of the Middle Ages are precious collections of religious and domestic artefacts
dating from Gallo-Roman times to the 15th century. The greatest single attraction is the
series of 15th-century tapestries, *The Lady with the Unicorn*. The collections are exhibited in 22 rooms of the medieval *hôtel particulier*, thematically, and to a certain extent
chronologically. In 2000 a 'Medieval Garden' was created to complement the building.

History of the Hôtel de Cluny
From around 1280, young monks from the great Benedictine monastery of Cluny in
Burgundy had lived in the Collège de Cluny attending the University of Paris. In 1340,
Pierre de Chalus, Abbot of Cluny, Chancellor to Philippe VI, purchased land in the area
to establish a residence in the capital. The 14th-century building was replaced by the
present U-shaped *hotel particulier* built by Jacques d'Amboise, Abbot of Cluny
(1485–1510), in 1485–98. His emblems are on the stair-tower in the courtyard. The
Hôtel de Cluny is an early example of a house standing between courtyard and garden,
an arrangement developed further in later centuries. Although rarely used by the abbots,
it was important enough to be mentioned by Rabelais in *Pantagruel*; Louis XII's widow,
Mary Tudor (1496–1533), younger sister of Henry VIII of England, lived here for a time,
as did James V of Scotland before his marriage to Madeleine, daughter of François I. By
the 17th century the building was neglected. In the 19th century, isolated by the new
Blvd St-Michel, it became national property. Alexandre du Sommerard moved in his
family and the treasures that he had spent his life collecting. After his death, the
collection was purchased by the State and thoroughly supplemented during the long
curatorship of his son, Edmond du Sommerard (d. 1009). Objects from the Renaissance
period, and part of the collections of this museum, are at Ecouen (*see p. 415*).

Ground floor

Room 2: The Grande Salle of the 15th-
century building has religious carvings
and secular tapestries, including a 16th-
century altarpiece with scenes of the
Passion, typical of northern France or
the Low Countries and a touchingly
detailed French *Annunciation* group
with a lively and elegant Virgin and
Gabriel, which is contemporary with
the building. Six tapestry scenes of *La
Vie Seigneuriale* (c. 1500–25) illustrate
domestic life in a noble household.

Room 3: Fragile 4th–6th-century textiles and embroideries are shown in rotation, including Coptic or Byzantine, French, Italian and Spanish pieces. A high-quality early 14th-century English piece in gold on velvet is the *Embroidery with Leopards*.

Rooms 5 and 6: Alabasters, mainly from Nottingham in England, can be seen in room 5. In room 6 are small panels of stained glass (12th–14th centuries), displayed at eye level, including a section of a circular medallion from St-Denis (before 1144) and fragments from the Sainte-Chapelle (*see p. 32*).

Rooms 7 and 8: Room 7 is the corridor linking the medieval and antique buildings, containing 13th–14th-century tombstones and Pierre de Montreuil's doorway for St-Germain-des-Prés (*see p. 68*). The spacious Room 8, where concerts are held, displays fragments of sculpture from Notre-Dame de Paris removed during the Revolution including the original 13th-century heads from the gallery of the Kings of Judah, discovered in 1977, and a heavily restored nude *Adam*, c. 1260, originally from a *Last Judgement* in the transept.

Rooms 9–11: These three rooms are dedicated to Carolingian and Romanesque carvings. Ivories (4th–12th centuries) include the sensual *Ariadne* (Constantinople; 6th century), and an 8th-century English diptych, which was re-used in the 9th century during the Carolingian Renaissance. Mid-to-late 12th-century architectural elements from Paris include a group of 12 capitals from St-Germain-des-Prés and some richly carved examples from Ste-Geneviève. The Gothic period in Paris is represented by statues of the Apostles from the Sainte-Chapelle and a stone retable showing the *Baptism of Christ*, from St-Denis. Two painted wood *Crucifixions* (12th century) were carved in provincial France.

The Thermae

Room 12: The *frigidarium* of the Gallo-Roman baths below this room is unique in France in that the 2nd-century vault is still intact. This large space (14m high) plus the *piscina* on the northern side, is all that remains of the baths, probably built during the 1st century and modified c. 212–17 AD. Partial ruins remain of the *tepidarium*, the *caldarium* and the *palestra* (gymnasium) and underground chambers still exist. The rest of the *thermae* were demolished in the 16th and 19th centuries. Exhibited here are the *Pilier des Nautes* (c. 14–37 AD), with elements of a monument dedicated to Jupiter by Parisian boatmen, and the votive *Pilier de St-Landry* (2nd century), both discovered on the Ile de la Cité.

First floor

Room 13: This circular room contains the series of six exquisite *millefleurs* tapestries known as *La Dame à la Licorne* (*see box on facing page*). The gallery is equipped with fibre optic lighting, deliberately kept dim for conservation reasons.

Room 14: Here are late medieval religious works from Europe, including

LA DAME A LA LICORNE TAPESTRIES

These tapestries, probably designed by a Parisian artist but woven, in silk and wool, in Northern Europe between 1484 and 1500, were commissioned by Jean le Viste, a Lyonnais lawyer whose family arms—gules, a band azure with three crescents argent—are frequently repeated in the designs. The tapestries hung for a long time in the Château of Boussac in the Creuse until brought to public notice by Prosper Mérimée, Inspector of Historic Monuments, and the writer George Sand. They were acquired by the museum in 1882 and have undergone a number of restorations. With rich red backgrounds, blue islands of colour, and different types of trees, the six panels are scattered with thousands of delicate flower, animal and bird motifs. In each, the lady appears differently attired, sometimes accompanied by her maid, and always flanked by the mythical symbol of purity, the elusive Unicorn, as well as a Lion. In several of the panels a monkey and a pet dog are also included. Five of the tapestries present the theme of the senses: in *Taste* the lady feeds the monkey and a parakeet from a bowl of sweetmeats; in *Hearing* she plays a portable organ; in *Sight* the Unicorn gazes into the mirror held before him by the lady; in *Smell* the monkey sniffs a flower while the lady weaves a garland; and in *Touch* the lady gently grasps the horn of the Unicorn. The sixth tapestry in the series (*pictured above*), known by the enigmatic motto *A mon seul désir* embroidered above the pavilion before which the lady stands, shows her returning jewels to a casket held by her maid. The iconography remains a mystery.

a collection of altarpieces, and representations of the Virgin and female saints. The *Altarpiece of the Blessed Sacrament* from Averbode in Brabant (1513) by Jan de Molder, has carved images of the *Mass of St Gregory* and the *Last Supper*. An early 16th-century *Virgin reading to the Child* comes from the Lower Rhine and there is an elegantly carved funeral effigy of Jeanne of Toulouse (c. 1280). A rare example of a medieval English painting in a French museum depicts *Scenes of the Life of the Virgin* (c. 1325).

Rooms 15 and 16: In the corridor Room 15 are medieval domestic objects and examples of the locksmith's craft. Room 16 contains a glittering array of the goldsmiths' and enamellers' arts. The centrepieces—part of the magnificent *Treasure of Gurrazar*, near Toledo, capital of the Visigoth kings—are three Visigothic votive crowns with their pendant crosses (late 7th century) which demonstrate the complexity of the craftsmanship of this civilisation. The fragile *Golden Rose* (1330), made in Siena in gold and coloured glass, was given by the Avignon Pope John XXII to a count of Neuchâtel in recognition of his support in a struggle against Emperor Louis of Bavaria. Among Gallo-Roman and Merovingian jewellery are gold torques, bracelets, buckles, ornamented belts and fibulas as well as late Roman and Byzantine cloisonné enamelwork. Representative of medieval reliquaries and the high-quality 12th–14th-century Limoges enamels are two reliquaries of St Thomas Becket (1190–1200), illustrating his murder; and the 13th-century *Reliquary of La Sainte-Chapelle*, commissioned by Louis IX, resembling a miniature chapel. The central plaque of the finely engraved portable triptych of the *Dormition of the Virgin* (Nuremberg, 15th century) was found in London in 1994.

Rooms 17 and 18: Room 17 displays 14th- and 15th-century stained glass, as well as enamels, ivories, and a fine collection of Hispano-Moresque ware and other lustreware from Manises (Valencia). Room 18 contains choir stalls, with irreverently carved misericords from the abbey of St-Lucien at Beauvais (1492–1500). Among the illuminated manuscripts which can be leafed through is the text of law written for Louis IX.

Rooms 19 and 20: The original late Gothic chapel and adjacent room contain some choice silver and gold pieces: the early 11th-century gold antipendium was possibly intended as a donation for Monte Cassino from Emperor Henry II and Empress Cunegonde, who are portrayed as minuscule figures at the feet of Christ (it in fact ended up in Basle Cathedral); the 12th-century *Stavelot* (Meuse) retable, with a Pentecostal scene; and a gospel binding of the 12th century in nielloed and gilded silver. The chapel itself is a masterpiece of Flamboyant vaulting from a central pillar, with a filigree of delicate moulding between the main ribs and sophisticated undercutting of the architectural canopies. The niches originally contained figures representing the powerful Amboise family, including Cardinal d'Amboise, destroyed in 1793. The tapestries depict the *Life and Martyrdom of St Stephen* and the *Legend of the Relics*. They were woven c. 1500 for Jean Baillet, Bishop of Auxerre.

Acquired in 1880, they have never been restored although the colours are still strong and every painstaking detail is clearly revealed. Like a strip cartoon with captions, the scenes are arranged in alternate interior and exterior settings.

Rooms 21–23: Late medieval objects, both religious and domestic, are shown here. A charming wooden *Christ astride a donkey* (late 15th century), which stands on a platform with wheels, is typical of religious processional objects produced in southwestern Germany from the 12th century to the Reformation. Among domestic artefacts are games pieces in ivory and bone, dating from the 11th and 12th centuries to 1500, wooden combs with intricate decoration, embroidered alms purses and bakery moulds. The mid-15th-century painting of the Jouvenel des Ursins family kneeling in line was commissioned for their chapel in Notre-Dame de Paris.

Square Paul Painlevé and the Jardin Médiéval

The small Square Paul Painlevé, opposite the entrance to the museum, contains statues of Michel de Montaigne (1533–92) by Landowski and of Puvis de Chavannes (*see p. 48 below*) by Desbois; also a replica of the Roman She-Wolf which suckled Romulus and Remus in the 8th century, given by Rome to Paris in 1962. On the north side of the museum, the Jardin Médiéval was created in 2000 as a contemporary interpretation of themes and symbolism found in the museum's famous tapestries (*see box on p. 45*). Composed of distinct enclosed areas, it makes no claim to reproduce an actual 15th-century garden. The enclosed terrace behind the museum represents a domestic medieval garden and other sections attempt to evoke the *hortus conclusus*, rivers of paradise, the Montagne Sainte-Geneviève, and medieval woodland glades.

THE PANTHEON
Map p. 475, E3

Open April–Sept 10–6.30; Oct–March 10–6; April–Oct with access to the colonnade; last admission 45 minutes before closing; T: 01 44 32 18 00.

Across Pl. Ste-Geneviève is the unmistakable and grandiose bulk of the Panthéon. This is the site of Mont Ste-Geneviève, the highest point on the Left Bank (60m), and legendary burial place of Geneviève, patron saint of Paris, in the 6th century (*see p.42*). The building was inspired by the Pantheon in Rome, with dome and peristyled portico; but Gallo-Roman excavations of the site nearly put paid to the structure.

History of the Panthéon

In 1744, lying ill at Metz, Louis XV vowed that if he recovered he would replace the abbey church of Ste-Geneviève, then ruinous, with a new church to house the saint's shrine. Work began in 1755, in the old abbey gardens, but the foundations disappeared into the labyrinth of Roman clay pits dug 16 centuries earlier. Louis finally laid the first stone above ground in 1764. The building was only completed in 1790 and its architect,

Jacques-Germain Soufflot, is said to have died of anxiety. By the Revolution there were three churches on the hill, the old abbey church, the new church, and St-Etienne (*see p. 49*). In 1791, the Constituent Assembly decided that the building should be used as a *panthéon* or burial place for distinguished citizens, 72 of whom are buried here, and the pediment was inscribed with the words *Aux Grands Hommes la Patrie reconnaissante*. From the Restoration to 1831 and from 1851–85 it was reconsecrated, but on the occasion of Victor Hugo's internment in 1885 it was definitively secularised.

The building

In the shape of a Greek cross, it is 110m long, 82m wide and 83m high to the top of its majestic dome. It was radically altered after 1791, with the demolition of twin belfries and the recarving by David d'Angers of the pediment above the portico of Corinthian columns, with a masterful relief representing France between Liberty and History, distributing laurels to famous men. Inside, the effect is coldly Classical, using the giant Corinthian Order. The space below the cupola was intended for Saint Geneviève's tomb. The vast interior is enlivened with a series of huge murals (everything is on a colossal scale here), made possible when 42 windows were walled up during the Revolution. The most notable is the series of the *Life of Ste Geneviève* by the Symbolist painter Puvis de Chavannes, recognisable by their calm dignity and quiet colours. The only true exponent of the technique of fresco painting to work in the Panthéon, and admirer of the Italian Quattrocento painters, Puvis began the series in 1874 in this ideal setting and it brought him general acclaim. Note in particular the panel showing the saint watching over Paris and bringing supplies to the city after the siege by the Huns. In the east end is a work representing the Convention, by Sicard and against the central pillars are monuments, right, to Jean-Jacques Rousseau by Bartholomé, and left, to Diderot and the Encyclopédistes by Terroir. The dome, supported by four piers united by arches, is made up of three distinct shells, of which the first is open in the centre to reveal the second. It carries a fresco by Antoine Gros. Within the dome, in 1852, the physicist Léon Foucault gave the first public demonstration of his pendulum experiment proving the rotation of the Earth, which is dramatically reconstructed in audio-visual displays in the aisles. It is possible to climb up to the Colonnade encircling the dome for an unusual and thrilling view of historic Paris.

The crypt contains the tombs of Jean-Jacques Rousseau (1712–78) and Voltaire (1684–1778) and of the architect, Soufflot. Of the famous men whose remains have been re-interred in the vaults, the most eminent are the writers Victor Hugo (1802–85) and Emile Zola (1840–1902); Marcelin Berthelot (1827–1907), the chemist; Jean Jaurès, the socialist politician (1859, assassinated 1914); Louis Braille (1809–52), benefactor of the blind; the explorer Bougainville (1729–1811); and the Resistance hero Jean Moulin (1899–1944). The heart of Léon Gambetta (1838–82), a proclaimer of the Republic in 1870, is enshrined here. Jean Monnet (1888–1979), the 'Father of Europe', was buried here on the centenary of his birth. More recently, the remains of Pierre and Marie Curie (in 1995; the first woman thus honoured), André Malraux (in 1996) former Minister of Culture, and novelist Alexandre Dumas (in 2002) were re-interred here.

Bibliothèque Ste-Geneviève

Open on request in writing or with one-day pass; T: 01 44 41 97 97; www-bsg.univ-paris1.fr
In the northwest corner of the Place du Panthéon, on Rue Soufflot, is the Law Faculty building, begun by Soufflot in 1771, and subsequently enlarged. The Bibliothèque Ste-Geneviève, on the north at no. 10, began as the library of the Abbaye Ste-Geneviève. The Collège de Montaigu, founded in 1314, where Erasmus (c. 1469–1536) the Dutch humanist, and Ignatius Loyola (c. 1491–1556) Spanish founder of the Jesuit Order, and John Calvin (1509–64) the French Protestant reformer, all studied, stood on this site until the 19th century. The present building (1844–50), designed by Henri Labrouste, is an important early example of a metal framed building, using both wrought and cast iron, the exterior resembling a cross between a 16th-century Florentine palace and a 19th-century railway station. Students work under the splendid iron and glass roof of the reading room. The library contains a large collection of manuscripts, incunabula, and some 120,000 volumes from the 16th to 19th centuries, as well as MSS of Rimbaud, Verlaine, Baudelaire, Gide and Valéry.

SAINT-ETIENNE DU MONT
Map p. 475, E3

Open Tues–Sun 8–7.30, Mon 12–7.30; Sat, Sun and holidays closed 12–2; T: 01 43 54 11 79.
St-Etienne du Mont is an unusually pretty church with some original features. Essentially a late-Gothic structure with Renaissance decoration, it was almost continuously under construction from 1492 to 1586. It has sheltered the shrine of Ste-Geneviève, patron saint of Paris (*see p. 42*), since the destruction of the old abbey church. The church is on the hill where the saint was buried, c. 502, in the basilica built by Clovis, king of the Franks, also buried there in 511, as well as his queen, Clothilde. The most unusual feature of St-Etienne du Mont is the Renaissance *jubé*, or rood screen (*pictured overleaf*), rarely found intact in French churches.

The exterior

Originally St-Etienne was joined to the abbey church, which may account for the choir, nave and façade being on slightly different axes. In 1610, Marguerite de Valois (1553–1615), daughter of Catherine de Médicis and, as first wife of Henri IV, known as *La Reine Margot*, laid the foundation stone of the façade. This has three pedimented tiers with a small rose window in each of the upper ones in a curious combination characteristic of the transitional style of architecture from late Gothic to Renaissance. The tower, begun in 1492, was completed in 1628. On the north flank is a picturesque porch of 1632.

The interior

The luminous interior gives an impression of height because of the tall aisles. Its originality lies in the elegant gallery that links the supporting pillars of the nave and

The fretted stone rood screen or *jubé* (1525–35) in the church of St-Etienne du Mont.

choir. Several of the large windows contain Renaissance stained glass. The ambulatory is wide with ribbed vaulting and heavy pendant bosses, the longest above the crossing. The celebrated fretted stone *jubé*, built 1525–35, is a virtuoso piece of stone carving with magnificent sweeping spirals at either side of the central pierced balustrade. The design is attributed to the great French Renaissance humanist architect Philibert de l'Orme (1510–70; *see p. 71*), and the work was probably carried out by Antoine Beaucorps. The date 1605 on the side refers only to the door to the spiral.

The organ, over the west door, has a richly carved case by Jean Buron dating from 1631–32, with *Christ of the Resurrection* at the summit; the instrument dates from the 17th century, renovated in the 19th. The pulpit is the work of Germain Pilon, with later sculptures designed by Laurent de la Hyre and at the crossing is a pendant boss with the *Lamb of God*. There is stained glass dating from c. 1550–c. 1600; the high nave windows by N. Pinaigrier, date from 1587–88, and include scenes of the *Resurrection*, *Ascension* and *Coronation of the Virgin*. The transept glass (1585–87), also by Pinaigrier with J. Bernard, includes various saints and *The Crucifixion*. The high windows in the choir contain glass of the 1540s onwards, and in the ambulatory are fragments of 16th-century glass mixed with 19th-century work.

In the chapel south of the choir is the copper-gilt shrine of Ste-Geneviève (1853), containing a fragment of her tomb; her remains were burned by the mob in the Pl. de Grève—now the Pl. de l'Hôtel de Ville (*see p. 282*) in 1801. Various important monuments include an *ex-voto* to Ste-Geneviève, with the provost and merchants of Paris, by François de Troy (1726) and higher, to the right, a similar subject painted by Largillière of 1696. In the adjacent chapel are epitaphs of philosopher Pascal (1623–62) and tragedian playwright Racine (1639–99), whose graves are at the entrance to the Lady Chapel. In the southwest chapel is a 16th-century *Pietà*.

On the site of the *charnier*, or gallery of the graveyard, are 12 superb windows of 1605–09; the joy of these is that the glass panels are at eye level. The most notable are no. 1 *The Miracle of Rue des Billettes (see p. 280)*, no. 2 *Noah's Ark*, no. 9 *Manna from Heaven*, and no. 10 *The Mystic Wine-press*.

Lycée Henri-IV

South of St-Etienne du Mont at 23 Rue Clovis is the Lycée Henri-IV (*no visits*), one of Paris' great schools, which took over the site of the old Abbaye Ste-Geneviève in 1796. It was on this site in 510 that Clovis founded his church and where he was buried. By the 6th century it was a rich abbey. Little remains of the abbey demolished in 1802, except the tower with Romanesque base and Gothic upper storeys and the cloister (1746). Many sons of great men studied here, such as those of Haussmann and Viollet-le-Duc. Part of Philippe-Auguste's 13th-century perimeter wall is visible in Rue Clovis.

THREE SMALLER CHURCHES

SAINT-SEVERIN
Map p. 475, E2

The church of St-Séverin, between Rue St-Jacques and Rue de la Harpe, is an interesting 13th–16th-century church, combining early and late Gothic styles overlaid by various later modifications. The first simple church was built here on the site of an oratory of the time of Childebert I in which Foulque of Neuilly-sur-Marne had preached the Fourth Crusade (c. 1199). It was enlarged at the end of the 13th and beginning of the 14th centuries, but only the first three bays of the nave escaped a fire in 1448. Rebuilding began in 1452 and went on until 1498. In the 17th century the church was drastically altered, like many other churches at the time, and the *jubé* was demolished and the choir partially classicised at the request of Mlle de Montpensier, *La Grande Mademoiselle*, niece of Louis XIII.

The exterior

The early 13th-century west door, with foliate carvings between the colonettes, was brought piecemeal from St-Pierre-aux-Boeufs in the *Cité* in 1837 (*Virgin and Child*, 19th century). The upper two storeys date from the 15th century. On the left is a 13th-century tower completed in 1487, with a door that was once the main entrance; the tympanum dates from 1853, but in the frame is a 15th-century inscription *Bonnes gens qui par cy passés, Priez Dieu pour les trespassés* ('Good people who pass through here, pray to God for your sins'). On the south are the galleries of the 15th-century charnel house, the only one to survive in Paris.

The interior

The church is impressively broad compared to its length, with a double ambulatory but no transept. The difference in style between the first three bays, built in the 13th century, and the remainder, which are 15th-century, is quite obvious. The earlier bays contain late 14th-century glass from St-Germain-des-Prés (*see p. 68*), but much restored; from the fourth bay on, the glass is mid-15th-century. One of the subjects on the south side of the nave is the *Murder of Thomas Becket*. The west rose window contains a *Tree of Jesse* (c. 1500) masked by the organ of 1745, once played by the composers Gabriel Fauré (1845–1924) and Camille Saint-Saëns (1835–1921). The double ambulatory is a tour de force of Flamboyant architecture with a dynamic central column around which shafts spiral to burst into leaf in the vaults like a palm tree. The stained glass of the apse chapels is by Jean Bazaine (1966). Off the southeast chapel is the Holy Communion Chapel designed by Jules Hardouin-Mansart (*see p. 110*) in 1673. The liturgical furnishings (1985–89) are by Georges Schneider and the chapel contains a series of engravings, *Miserere* (1922–27), by Georges Rouault, displayed here since 1993.

SAINT-JULIEN LE PAUVRE & ENVIRONS
Map p. 475, E2

The church of St-Julien le Pauvre, rebuilt c. 1170–1230 by monks of Longpont, an abbey attached to Cluny in Burgundy, stands on the site of a succession of chapels dedicated to St-Julien. Despite many restorations it retains the air of a solid late-Romanesque country church. There are two original carved capitals in the chancel. It was used from the 13th–16th centuries as a university church and from 1655–1877 for various secular purposes. Since 1889 it has been occupied by Melchites (Greek Catholics) and an iconostasis obscures the east end. The present west front was built in 1651. Unfortunately the church is usually closed.

Rue Galande, close to the church of St-Julien, is one of the oldest streets in Paris (14th century). At no. 42 is a carved relief, mentioned in 1380, of St Julian the Hospitaller (or the Poor Man) and his wife ferrying Christ across a river.

The small garden adjacent to the church, Sq. René Viviani, contains some architectural elements, possibly from Notre-Dame, and claims the oldest tree in Paris, a *Robinia* (False Acacia) planted in 1601. From here is a classic view of Notre-Dame.

From the northeast side of this square runs Rue de la Bûcherie where at no. 37 is the shabby little secondhand bookshop, Shakespeare & Co., which was the rendezvous of interwar American writers. Its first home was in Rue de l'Odéon, and its fame rests on publishing James Joyce's *Ulysses* in 1922 (*see p. 55*). Now owned and run by George Whitman 'as a socialist utopia' for penniless writers, the shop has been described by one such, Canadian journalist Jeremy Mercer, in two recent books: *Time was soft there* and *Books, Baguettes and Bedbugs*. No. 13 Rue de la Bûcherie was occupied by the Ecole de Médecine for more than two centuries from 1483–1775, and has a rotunda of 1745.

The area on the other side of Rue St-Jacques, west towards Place St-Michel, is also worth exploring. The Pl. St-Michel is linked to the Ile de la Cité by Pont St-Michel. The *Fontaine St-Michel* (1860) incorporates a memorial to the Resistance of 1944. Immediately to the east of Pl. St-Michel is a still decrepit but picturesque corner of Old Paris penetrated by ancient streets or alleys such as Rue de la Huchette, Rue Xavier-Privas and Rue du Chat-qui-Pêche (named after an old shop-sign of a cat fishing).

SAINT-NICOLAS-DU-CHARDONNET
Map p. 475, E3

On Rue Monge stands St-Nicolas-du-Chardonnet, a reminder that an earlier church was built here in a field of thistles (*chardons*). The major part of the present church was built 1656–1709; only the tower (1625) remains from the previous building. Le Brun designed the finely carved door on Rue des Bernardins. In the 19th century, Blvd St Germain shaved the east of the church necessitating a rearrangement of the apsidal chapel, and the main façade on Rue Monge was not completed until the last century. The interior contains some good paintings and sculptures while the ornamental glass chandeliers add a decadent touch. In the first bay is Le Brun's painting the *Martyrdom of St John the Evangelist*, and in the first chapel on the right is Corot's study for the *Baptism of Christ*; the transept contains two paintings by Nicolas Coypel. Outstanding are a monument by Girardon of Bignon, the jurist, d. 1656 (2nd chapel south of the choir), and the splendidly theatrical tomb of Le Brun's mother, designed by Le Brun (in the apse); in the same chapel is a monument to Le Brun (d. 1690) and his widow, by the sculptor Antoine Coysevox.

THE UNIVERSITY OF PARIS & ITS INSTITUTIONS
Map p. 475, F3

The University of Paris, which disputes with Bologna the title of the oldest university in Europe, arose in the first decade of the 12th century out of the schools of dialectic attached to Notre-Dame. It later transferred to the Montagne Ste-Geneviève, and received its first statutes in 1215, which served as the model for Oxford and Cambridge and other universities of northern Europe. By the 16th century it comprised no fewer than 40 separate colleges.

THE SORBONNE

Occasional visits with Centre des Monuments Nationaux (CMN) T: 01 44 54 19 30.
The Sorbonne was founded as a theological college in 1253 by Robert de Sorbon (1201–74), chaplain to Louis IX. Before the end of the 13th century it had become synonymous with the faculty of theology, overshadowing the rest of the university and possessing the power of conferring degrees. It was noted for its religious rancour, supporting the condemnation of Joan of Arc, justifying the St Bartholomew's Day

massacre of Protestants and refusing to recognise King Henry IV, a former Protestant. In 1470 it was responsible for the introduction of printing into France. Other colleges (from *colligere*, to assemble) followed, with charters defining their principles: mainly to provide secure shelter for poor students; study was in the schools, the ancestors of faculties. From the 15th century the university experienced a period of crisis and criticism, and by the end of the next century, the buildings were in a poor condition.

Cardinal Richelieu (1585–1642) undertook the rebuilding of the Sorbonne in 1629, employing the architect Jacques Lemercier. The huge project continued until Richelieu's death in 1642. In the 18th century the university was still traditional in its teaching and had not assimilated progress in ideas and the sciences. At the Revolution the corporation that was the university gradually disappeared, and in 1792 the Sorbonne was suppressed, to become a Musée des Arts in 1801.

Napoleon refounded the university 1806–10, and the Sorbonne became the seat of the University of Paris in 1821. During the last third of the 19th century the institutions were reorganised. The college buildings, apart from the chapel, which had fallen into disrepair, were replaced by the present sombre collection (1885–1901). Around a large courtyard with galleries are the great staircase and Grand Amphithéâtre or main lecture hall, decorated with a mural by Puvis de Chavannes (*see p. 48*).

The modern university

Student unrest was simmering in 1968, provoked by poor academic standards and overcrowding. In early May unrest turned to riot at the University of Nanterre on the outskirts of Paris, and spread to the Sorbonne which was occupied. The leader who emerged was Daniel Cohn-Bendit. The university buildings were closed for only the third time in its history (the first during riots in 1229, the second during the invasion in 1940). The student revolt escalated to a nationwide general strike lasting until 30th May when President de Gaulle's appeal finally restored calm. The action brought about overdue reforms in the university system and in 1970 the University of Paris was replaced by 13 autonomous universities, *Universités de Paris I-XIII*. The 5th arrondissement (the Latin Quarter) is still the historical campus. Four of the universities have a presence in the Sorbonne and about half are outside the city in areas such as Nanterre, Vincennes and Val-de-Marne. The universities come under a common chancellor, who is Rector of the Académie Française (*see p. 73*).

Chapelle de la Sorbonne

Open during temporary exhibitions or concerts.

The Chapelle de la Sorbonne, facing Pl. de la Sorbonne, was founded in the 13th century. It was rebuilt by Jacques Lemercier in 1635–42 and paid for by Richelieu. The west elevation makes a direct reference to Italian Baroque with superimposed orders linked by volutes, innovative in Paris at the time. The unusual plan places the dome centrally, between nave and choir of equal length, and shallow transepts. Richelieu's dramatic tomb (1694), sculpted by Girardon is designed to give maximum effect either from the west or from the alternative north entrance.

THE 'LOST GENERATION'

After the First World War, young American and foreign writers, such as F. Scott Fitzgerald, James Joyce and Ernest Hemingway, came to Paris in search of political freedom and intellectual stimulation. They first settled in the Latin Quarter, particularly around Rue St-Jacques, to live, work and drink. Gertrude Stein (1874–1946), the Jewish American writer and friend of Matisse and Picasso, dubbed these disillusioned expatriates the 'Lost Generation'. Stein's apartment at 27 Rue des Fleurs became a place of pilgrimage, although in Hemingway's case their friendship did not last. The expatriate community's base shifted from the Latin Quarter to the cafés of Montparnasse. Following the stock market crash of 1929, the economic Depression forced many Americans to return home. George Orwell meanwhile arrived in 1928, as did Samuel Beckett, and Evelyn Waugh a year later. The second wave descended on Paris in the aftermath of the Second World War, Hemingway notably entering the city with the American troops to 'liberate the cellars of the Ritz'. Many expatriates were attracted to the French capital by nostalgia for the achievements of the 'Lost Generation'. Café culture at this time favoured the watering holes of the St-Germain-des-Prés and Luxembourg districts—Café de Flore, Les Deux Magots, the Mabillon, and the Pergola.

During both periods the visitors brought a new energy to the cultural life of Paris and also supported and relied upon English-language presses, periodicals and bookstores. Small presses included the Contact Press (American poet, Robert McAlmon), the Three Mountains Press (William Bird), the Hours Press (Nancy Cunard), the Black Sun Press (Harry and Caresse Crosby), the Obelisk Press (Jack Kahane), and the Olympia Press (Maurice Girodias, son of Kahane). They published the works of many writers in Paris, often before they were well known elsewhere, as in the case of Ernest Hemingway and Henry Miller. Most of these early presses disappeared with the Depression, as did many expatriate periodicals, among the more important of which were *The Transatlantic Review*, edited by Ford Madox Ford (and one issue by Ernest Hemingway; see p. 40), and *This Quarter*, featuring poetry, short stories and prose. Possibly the best known contribution which Joyce usually called *A Work in Progress*, was later incorporated into *Finnegans Wake* in 1939. Only *transition* survived the onset of the Depression, lasting until 1938. Of the English-language bookstores, the most important was undoubtedly Sylvia Beach's (1887–1962) famous Shakespeare & Co., opened in 1919 on Rue Dupuytren and then removed to Rue de l'Odéon. As well as running the bookstore and library, Beach published Joyce's *Ulysses* in 1922, but business declined during the war and she finally closed her shop in late 1941. Le Mistral, founded by Walt Whitman's great grandson, George Whitman, in 1951, later took the name Shakespeare & Co. in memory of Sylvia Beach's bookshop.

RUE SAINT-JACQUES & THE COLLEGES

Behind the Sorbonne runs Rue St-Jacques, an ancient thoroughfare which existed even before it became the *Via Superior* or *cardo*, the north-south artery in Gallo-Roman times linking *Lutetia* to northern France and to *Cenabum* (Orléans). It crossed the Seine via the Petit Pont which, until 1782 was defended at the southern end by the Petit Châtelet, the successor of the Tour de Bois that in 885–6 held Viking or Norman marauders at bay (*see p. 9*). It was adopted in the Middle Ages as the pilgrimage route to Santiago de Compostela, taking its name from a pilgrim hospice dedicated to St-Jacques which was occupied in 1218 by the future St Dominic and Dominican friars from Toulouse. Rue St-Jacques links the Latin Quarter with Montparnasse to the south, and continues northwards on the Right Bank as Rue St-Martin.

Collège de France

The Collège de France has its entrance in the Pl. Marcelin-Berthelot, Rue des Ecoles. In the graceful porticoed courtyard is a statue of the scholar Guillaume Budé (Budaeus; 1468–1540) under whose influence it was founded by François I in 1530 with the intention of spreading Renaissance humanism, counteracting the narrow scholasticism of the Sorbonne. Independent of the University, its teaching was free and public. The present building was begun in 1610, completed c. 1778 by Jean-François Chalgrin.

Sq. A.-Mariette-Pacha, next to the Collège de France, contains statues of Dante (1882), the Renaissance poet Ronsard (1928) and C. Bernard (1946), Professor of Medicine 1947–78. In Impasse Chartière nearby is a monument to the *Pléiade*, a group of Renaissance poets that originated in the vanished Collège Coqueret, founded on this site 1418–1643.

Lycée Louis-le-Grand and Collège Ste-Barbe

On Rue St-Jaques is the Lycée Louis-le-Grand, formerly the Jesuit Collège de Clermont, founded in 1560 and rebuilt 1887–96. Among those who studied here were the playwright Molière (1622–73; *see p. 246*), philosopher Voltaire (1694–1778), politician Robespierre (1758–94), supporter of the Reign of Terror at the Revolution, and another revolutionary, Camille Desmoulins (1760–94), as well as the painter Delacroix (*see p. 70*) and the writer Victor Hugo (*see p. 283*).

The Collège Ste-Barbe, Rue Cujas, is the oldest existing public educational establishment in France founded in 1460.

Around the Panthéon

The Jardin Carré is a modern public garden with a bronze, *La Spirale* (1986) by Meret Oppenheim. It was created in the courtyard of the former Ecole Polytechnique (at 5 Rue Descartes) which was founded in 1794 for the training of artillery and engineer officers. This was the most prestigious of the Grandes Ecoles, institutions created by the Convention to provide the technical experts needed by the Empire. From 1805 it occupied old college buildings, and relocated to the outskirts of Paris in 1977. Steps lead down to Sq. Paul Langevin (on Rue Monge) with an 18th-century fountain and headless statues from the old Hôtel de Ville (*see p. 282*), as well as a statue of the poet François Villon.

The private dwellings in the courtyard at no. 34 Rue Montagne-Ste-Geneviève once belonged to the Collège des Trente-Trois, after its 33 scholarships, one for each year of Christ's life, established here in 1657. The Musée de la Préfecture de Police occupies the first floor of no. 5 (*see p. 422*).

On Rue d'Ulm is the Maronite church of Notre-Dame du Liban, for Christians of Syrian origin living in Lebanon. The Ecole Normale Supérieure, established in 1794 to train teachers, has been at no. 45 since 1843.

The Collège des Irlandais, founded in 1578 by John Lee and re-founded in 1687 by English Catholics as a seminary, at 5 Rue des Irlandais, is now the Centre Culturel Irlandais (*open Tues–Sat, 2–6, Wed to 8; Sun, 12.30–2.30; closed Mon and public holidays; T: 01 58 52 10 30*), showing a wide range of different art forms.

Pasteur from 1864–88, and Pierre and Marie Curie in 1883–1905, worked in the laboratories of the Ecole de Physique et de Chimie industrielles in Rue Pierre-Brossolette. The aquariums of the Centre de la Mer et des Eaux are in the Institut Océanographique, 195 Rue St-Jacques (*see p. 421*).

The unadorned Classical church of St-Jacques-du-Haut-Pas (1630–88) was originally the site of a hospice for pilgrims on the road to Santiago de Compostela and its 17th-century severity reflects its Jansenist connections. It was completed in 1712 with the help of the Duchesse de Longueville (1619–79) who is buried here, together with Jean Duvergier de Hauranne (1581–1643), prominent Jansenist (*see p. 99*), and Jean-Dominique Cassini (1625–1712), the astronomer. It has a fine organ, with a case dating mainly from 1609, transferred here from the church of St-Benoît-le-Bétourné and entirely rebuilt in 1971.

At the corner of Rue de l'Abbé-de-l'Epée, is the Institut National des Sourds-Muets, a hospital for the deaf and dumb, founded by the Abbé de l'Epée (1712–89) about 1760. It was taken over by the State in 1790 and reconstructed in 1823. In the courtyard is a statue of the Abbé by Félix Martin, a deaf and dumb sculptor (1789).

RUE DE L'ECOLE-DE-MEDECINE
Map. 175, D3

West of Blvd St-Michel, on the corner of Rue de l'Ecole de Médecine and Rue de Hautefeuille (no. 32), Gustave Courbet had his studio in the former chapel of the Collège des Prémontrés. Most of the block on Rue de l'Ecole de Médecine is occupied by the Faculty of Medicine, Université René Descartes Paris V. Jacques Gondouin was responsible in 1769–76 for the courtyard, colonnaded façade and pedimented entrance, a grandiose Classical structure; the building was enlarged 1878–1900. It contains a library of around 600,000 volumes, the Medical Faculty archives since 1395, and the Musée d'Histoire de la Médecine (*see p. 420*). In the courtyard is a statue of the anatomist Xavier Bichat (1771–1802) by David d'Angers (1788–1856).

Opposite the Faculty of Medicine is the entrance to the beautiful Gothic refectory of the **Couvent des Cordeliers** (*open 10.30–6.30; 10–7 during exhibitions; closed Mon; T: 01 40 46 05 47*), used as a municipal exhibition gallery. The 15th-century Franciscan house was rebuilt c. 1500 around a 13th-century church, on land lent by the Abbey of St-Germain-des-Prés for theology lessons. Space was later rented out, and the urbanist, Edmé Verniquet, worked here from 1785 on the masterly plan requested by Louis XVI for the restructuring of Paris. In 1790 the chapel became the meeting place of the Cordeliers' Club, the most vocal and violent of the pre-Revolutionary groups. Led by Georges-Jacques Danton (1759–94) and Jean-Paul Marat (1743–93), who lived nearby, as did Danton's friend, the rabble-rousing journalist Camille Desmoulins (1760–94), it was even more left-wing than the Jacobins Club. Marat was buried in the convent garden after his assassination by Charlotte Corday. The club was closed in 1795. After the Revolution, Citizen Verniquet's designs became the basis for the proposal to subdivide nationalised land.

At the western end of Rue de l'Ecole-de-Médecine a flight of steps ascends to Rue Monsieur-le-Prince (de Condé) where it meets Rue de Vaugirard with the Lycée St-Louis, built by Bailly on the site of the Collège d'Harcourt (1280), where the writers Racine and Boileau studied. Its entrance faces Pl. de la Sorbonne. Adjacent to the south end of Rue Monsieur-le-Prince is Pl. Edmond-Rostand, looking across to the Panthéon (*see p. 47*). To the south, on the right of Blvd St-Michel, the Ecole Supérieure des Mines occupies the Hôtel de Vendôme, an 18th–century building enlarged after 1840, its principal façade facing towards the Luxembourg Gardens. It contains a Museum of Mineralogy (*see p. 421*).

QUARTIER DE LA MOUFFE
Map p. 475, E4

Rue Mouffetard or Quartier de la Mouffe is a narrow and ancient thoroughfare with a laid-back atmosphere. Extremely popular, packed with cafés, and also with some interesting old houses, it continues to the north the story of the Bièvre River as it relates to the Manufacture des Gobelins and La Butte aux Cailles (*see p. 101*). In the lower part of La Mouffe is a lively street market every morning.

History of La Mouffe

Rue Mouffetard follows a section of the old Roman road leading from the Ile de la Cité out of Paris towards Italy alongside the Bièvre River. In the Middle Ages it linked the University quarter and the outskirts of Paris, as far as the present Place d'Italie, crossing the semi-rural *bourgs* of St-Médard and St-Marcel. Once a desirable rural area outside Charles V's ramparts (*see p. 244*), over the centuries it evolved into a thoroughly urban working-class quarter with cabarets and dance halls mainly dependent on leather-related industries, especially tanning which polluted the river water and filled the air with putrid odours. These smells, described as *moffettes*, may be the origin of

Decorative detail above a shopfront at the southern end of Rue Mouffetard.

its present name. The Bourg St-Médard gradually spread as far as the walls of Paris and was annexed to the city in 1724. By the 18th century the district was considered dangerous, dirty and generally to be avoided, and its inhabitants participated in Revolutionary uprisings and insurrections. A section of La Mouffe disappeared with Haussmann's urban reorganisation in the 19th century and around 1910 the unhealthy and stinking Bièvre was channelled underground. Before the Second World War the area was still insalubrious and many buildings were not linked to main drains. Yet it attracted writers such as Georges Duhamel, Ernest Hemingway and George Orwell who could live inexpensively here, and its colourful market became famous. Close to the University of Paris it also felt the effects, for better or for worse of the 1968 student riots.

SAINT-MEDARD

Open 10–12 & 4–7.30; Sun 10–12.30 & 5–8; closed Mon.
The church of St-Médard, the French equivalent of St Swithin, is the major monument of the quarter. An earlier church came under the protection of the Abbey of St-Germain-des-Prés until the Revolution. The nave and west front of the existing church are late 15th-century. The choir was constructed 1560–86, and the aisles from 1665. A classical touch was added when the Doric columns of the choir were fluted in 1784

when the Lady Chapel was also added. The church was sacked by the Huguenots in 1561. There is a fine organ case by Germain Pilon of 1644, and the pulpit dates from 1718. The church was the centre of a scandal in the 17th century around the grave of a notable Jansenist, François Pâris (d. 1727, aged 37) becoming a focus for persecuted Jansenists (*see p. 99*) and a cult of cures and visions leading to collective hysteria and violence; female *convulsionnaires*, so it was said, rent their clothes. The cemetery was closed in 1732 and an anonymous message was pinned to the gate that read: *De par le Roi, défense à Dieu de faire miracle en ce lieu* ('On the part of the King, God is forbidden to carry out miracles in this place').

ARENES DE LUTECE
Map p. 475, F4

Between Rue Monge and Rue Linné is Rue des Arènes leading to the remains of the 1st-century amphitheatre of *Lutetia*, the Arènes de Lutèce. The second most important Gallo-Roman site in Paris after the *thermae* (*see p. 44*), and one of the largest arenas in France, it now gives little idea of its former glory days when around 17,000 spectators would have watched fights as well as theatre performances. The structure fell into ruin in the 3rd century, was used as a necropolis in the 4th, and the stone was removed. It was mentioned in the 12th century, but was filled in during the building of Philippe-Auguste's wall (*see p. 10*) and disappeared from view. In 1869, during the Haussmann era, construction works uncovered underlying remains, but despite opposition, it was turned into an omnibus depot. Funds were raised as a result of a public outcry instigated by Victor Hugo that led to more excavations 1883–85, and its consequent conservation. Dr Joseph-Louis Capitan (1854–1929) restored the ruins to their present state in 1917–18. Sq. Capitan on two sides of the arena is a green, redeeming feature on the site of an old reservoir. Instead of blood-thirsty spectacles, it is now a popular place for *le foot*, *les boules* or eating *les sandwiches*.

INSTITUT DU MONDE ARABE
Map p. 475, F3

Open 10–6, closed Mon; library closed Sun; T: 01 40 51 38 38; www.imarabe.org
Located at 1 Rue des Fossés-Saint-Bernard, the Institute contains a museum, temporary exhibition spaces, a cinema, book and gift shop, library and documentation centre. Annually, Oct–Feb, is a major exhibition on different aspects of the Arab world; also intermittent smaller exhibitions. On level 0 is the Café Littéraire; on the roof terrace (level 9) are the Restaurant Ziryab, open midday and evenings (T: 01 53 10 10 16), and a self-service Cafeteria Le Moucharabieh (both open Tues–Sun); also a bird's eye view onto the Seine and Notre-Dame.
The Institut du Monde Arabe (IMA), beside the Seine, is well known to Parisians but sometimes overlooked by overseas visitors. The Institute's excellent temporary

exhibitions are an important part of the Parisian cultural scene. Inaugurated in 1987, it was founded to further cultural and scientific relations between France and some 21 Arab countries. The sleek and complex building, designed by Jean Nouvel (*see p. 124*), has nine levels above ground and two below. The 20th-century design echoes certain aspects of Arabic architecture such as the unique window shutters, or *moucharabiehs*, of the south façade which function like a camera lens, expanding and contracting in reaction to the sun's intensity through the medium of photo-electric cells; they can also be operated mechanically. The building is arranged around an interior court or *ryad* (with glass lifts), and a book tower or *ziggourat*.

The museum

The permanent collection is exhibited on three levels (starting on level 7 and working down), dedicated to the art and civilisation of the Arab world from pre-Islamic time to the present day. Small and elegantly laid out, the museum is mainly concerned with the development of the religion of Islam and the part played by the Arab world in the history of science. Examples of the arts and crafts of Islam on display include ceramics, manuscripts, metalwork, ivories, fabrics and glass objects; also textiles, rugs, costumes and jewellery from throughout the Arab world.

ENVIRONS OF THE INSTITUT

Behind the Institute, on Rue Jussieu, is the unlovely 1960s block and tower which houses the Science Faculties of *Université Marie Curie, Paris VI et Paris VII*, where the Collection of Minerals can be visited (*see p. 64*). Here, until their transfer to Bercy, stood the huge bonded warehouses of the Halles aux Vins, itself on the site of the Abbaye de St-Victor. Dispersed in 1790, Thomas Becket and Abélard had resided in the abbey and Rabelais studied in its library.

At the top of 15–17 Quai de la Tournelle, is the old-established restaurant, La Tour d'Argent (*T: 01 43 54 23 31*), with views of Notre-Dame; below is the Musée de la Table. At 32 Rue du Cardinal Lemoine, stood the Collège des Bons-Enfants, where Vincent de Paul (1581–1660) founded his congregation of mission-priests in 1625. No. 49 is the Hôtel le Brun, built by Germain Boffrand, occupied at times by the painter Watteau and by the naturalist, the Comte de Buffon (*see p. 62*)

At the Seine end of Rue de Poissy, at no. 57 Quai de la Tournelle, stands the restored 17th-century Hôtel de Nesmond, now occupied by La Demeure Historique (*T: 01 55 42 60 00*), the organisation founded in 1924 by Dr Joachim Carvallo, owner of the Château de Villandry, to support and preserve historically important private properties across France. The building at no. 24 Rue de Poissy was the 14th-century refectory of the ancient Collège des Bernardines, founded in 1244 by the English Abbot of Clairvaux, Etienne de Lexington. The Musée de l' Assistance Publique of the history of Paris hospitals, is at 47 Quai de la Tournelle (*see p. 419*). Rue de Bièvre marks the line of the canal built by the Abbey St-Victor in the 12th century that re-routed the Bièvre River into the Seine.

JARDIN DES PLANTES

The Jardin des Plantes, officially the Muséum National d'Histoire Naturelle, is an oasis of 28 hectares encompassing botanic gardens, a group of museums, and other attractions such as the *ménagerie* (zoo), and the maze. As well as unrivalled collections of wild and herbaceous plants, it includes a sunken alpine garden, rose and ecological gardens, tropical greenhouses and, in May and June, magnificent displays of peonies and iris. In the 13th arrondissement to the southeast, beyond Gare d'Austerlitz, are L'Hôpital de la Salpêtrière and the Bibliothèque National Mitterand.

MUSEUM NATIONAL D'HISTOIRE NATURELLE
Map p. 475, F4

Gardens open summer 8–8, winter 8–5.30; Greenhouses open 10–5, closed Tues; Sat, Sun and holidays April–Sept 1–6; T: 01 40 79 56 01; www.mnhn.fr
Founded in 1626 under Louis XIII for the cultivation of medicinal herbs by the royal physician Guy de la Brosse, the garden was first opened to the public in 1640. Its present importance is mainly due to the eminent naturalist, biologist and mathematician, the Comte de Buffon (1707–88), who was superintendent from 1739 and greatly enlarged the grounds. Known until 1793 as the Jardin du Roi, it was then reorganised by the Convention under its present official title and provided at that time with 12 professorships. The National Museum of Natural History is a public institute with the triple role of research, conservation and dissemination of knowledge. The library owns a remarkable collection of botanical manuscripts, including the *Vélins du Roi*, illustrated by Nicolas Robert (1614–85) and others; also works by P.-J. Redouté (1758–1840), watercolourist and botanical painter. Several of the distinguished French naturalists who taught and studied here are commemorated by monuments in or near the garden. An early 20th-century statue by Léon Fagel of the naturalist associated with early theories of evolution, J.-B. Lamarck (1744–1829), faces the Place Valhubert entrance, and another by the same artist of the chemist Eugène Chevreul (1786–1889) stands in the northern part of the gardens. Chevreul's research on the principles of harmony and colour contrasts had an important influence on the Impressionist and Post-Impressionist painters' colour theories (*see p. 352*). For a time he was director of the dyeing department at the Gobelins tapestry factory (*see p. 100*). The Administrative Department is housed in the Hôtel de Magny, built in 1690, and behind it is the Grand Amphitheatre, begun by Verniquet, and where Chevreul worked. The Maison de Cuvier was the home of Georges Cuvier (1769–1832), zoologist, paleontologist and educator, founder of the study of comparative anatomy and Secretary of the Academy of Science from 1803. The house was later occupied by Henri Becquerel (1852–1908) who discovered radioactivity here in 1896.

Exploring the gardens

From the Esplanade Milne-Edwards (an eminent 19th-century zoologist) in front of the Central Library, formal gardens bordered by curtains of planes planted in 1882 create an orderly floral vista with a backdrop of modern Paris. Behind the northern avenue is a host of less regimented gardens. The Butte is a fanciful hillock encased in a maze. At its foot is the first Cedar of Lebanon (from Kew Gardens) to be planted in France, in 1734, and at its summit an *Acer Orientale* (Turkish maple) planted in 1702 close to the Gloriette, the oldest metal structure in Paris, dating from 1786, designed by Edmé Verniquet (1727–1804; *see p. 58*). A sundial bears the inscription *Horas non numero nisi serenas*: 'I only count the hours of happiness'.

The sunken Alpine Garden protects some 2,000 worldwide species of mountain plants and can be viewed from Allée Cuvier. A recent addition is vines which are accompanied by the plants typical of Ile de France. Roses and irises are on the southern side and greenhouses (1830–33)—described as Australian and Mexican—are to the west.

Animals from the royal collection at Versailles and of street showmen formed the nucleus of a *ménagerie* in 1792, which now occupies most of the northern side of the gardens (*open summer Mon–Sat 9–6, Sun and holidays 9–6.30; winter 9–5*) and contains more than a thousand animals .

GRANDE GALERIE DE L'EVOLUTION

Open Wed–Mon 10–6; closed Tues; T: 01 40 79 56 01/01 40 79 54 79.
Part of the Museum of Natural History, the Grande Galerie de l'Evolution was one of President Mitterrand's *grands projets*, opened in 1994 at 36 Rue Geoffroy-St-Hilaire after a closure of nearly 30 years. It combines an exciting visual experience with its rich natural history content. The exhibition space uses the central nave, balconies and side galleries of the old building of the Zoological gallery of 1889. The theme of the museum revolves around the History of Evolution, whose drama unfolds through the different levels of the museum. The innovations of modern museology manage to convey a powerful scientific message in quite a magical way. Outside is the colourful *Dragon* (1998) by Niki de Saint-Phalle (*see p. 264*).

The exhibition

The permanent exhibition combines carefully selected and restored specimens—the smaller ones suspended in transparent display cases to great effect—with audio visual presentations, models and etched glass. Level 0, excavated to reveal stone arcades, evokes the watery underworld and takes you across various marine zones, from the deep to the shallows and on to the coast and dry land. Arctic regions have to be crossed on the way to Level 1 and a change in climate. Here, among other displays, is a cavalcade of animals across the African savannah and the tropical forests of South America. Lifts fly you past exotic birds to Level 3 where the balconies, devoted to the evolution of living organisms, provide a spectacular view down onto the nave of Level 1. The exhibition continues on Level 2 with the science of selectivity and mankind's role in evolution, including some of our most disturbing effects on the environment. Behind the balcony on the east side is a gallery devoted to extinct and endangered species. This chapel-like room, with its original wooden display cabinets, is classified as an historic monument and contains a clock made for Marie-Antoinette.

Other departments of the Muséum

Open Wed–Mon 10–5; April–Sept Sat, Sun and holidays 10–6; closed Tues; T: 01 40 79 54 79/01 40 79 56 01.

The Mineralogy and Geology Gallery (also at 36 Rue Geoffroy St-Hilaire) in its original building of 1837, has a huge collection of rocks and minerals, as well as precious stones. The collection includes a group of giant crystals from Brazil, originally destined for industrial use, which amount to three-quarters of the world's known stock.

The Palaeontology and Compared Anatomy Galleries (at 2 Rue Buffon), have preserved the spirit of the period (1898) where bones, skeletons and fossils are presented in the manner of the 17th century. The oldest specimen in the museum is the rhinoceros that belonged to Louis XV. The staircase sweeping up to the upper floor has a splendid metal ramp with a chrysanthemum and fern motif.

MOSQUEE DE PARIS
Map p. 475, F4

Guided visits Sat–Thur 9–10 & 2–6; 2bis Place du Puits-de-l'Ermite; T: 01 45 35 97 33. Tea-room and shop entrance on the corner of Rue Daubenton and Rue G. St-Hilaire.

To the west of Rue Geoffroy-St-Hilaire is the green-tiled Mosquée de Paris. Easily identified by its minaret, the mosque was inaugurated in 1926, inspired by those in Fez. It commemorates the 100,000 Moslems who died for France in 1914–18. The religious buildings are grouped around a courtyard and in the prayer room are some magnificent carpets. The decorative materials were made in North Africa and much of the décor is Hispano-Moresque in style. The 1960s' utilitarian architecture nearby on Rue Censier belongs to the University of Paris III, Faculty of Letters, Languages and Sociology.

HOPITAL DE LA PITIE-SALPETRIERE
Map p. 479, D1

Entrance on Square Marie-Curie, 47 Bvld de l'Hôpital. The chapel is usually open to visitors.

The 17th-century buildings of the hospital still exist, albeit surrounded by modern departments making it one of the largest hospitals in Paris. As a whole, it is a notable example of the austere magnificence of the architecture of the reign of Louis XIV. The Chapelle de St-Louis can be visited. It returned to the Church in 1802, and was then abandoned. Following restoration work it reopened in 1974 as a religious and cultural centre. Diana, Princess of Wales died in the hospital on 31st August, 1997.

HISTORY OF LA SALPETRIERE

In the 17th century the State took over from the Church the responsibility for the sick and needy. By an edict of 1656 it created the Hôpital Général to contain all undesirables: the destitute, poor, old, women of ill repute and so on. At the same time the huge Hôpital de la Salpêtrière was founded to shelter desolate women. The hospital was built on the site of the old Arsenal (saltpeter is a component of gunpowder), then on the outskirts of Paris, by Le Vau (*see p. 38*), and by Pierre Le Muet (*see p. 278*). The domed chapel of St-Louis, built in 1670–78 by Libéral Bruant, who worked on Les Invalides (*see p. 111*) can hold 4,000 people. The criminal wing, *La Maison de la Force*, was added in 1680. Mental patients were admitted from 1796. Dr Jean-Martin Charcot (1825–93), who used hypnosis as a diagnostic tool to study hysteria, and was an influence on Freud, is commemorated by a monument to the left of the gateway. In 1964 the hospital was combined with the Hôpital de la Pitié, founded by Marie de Médicis in 1612.

Chapelle de St-Louis de la Salpetrière

The Chapelle de St-Louis de la Salpêtrière is grandiose yet simple and, with Les Invalides and the Val-de-Grace (*see p. 98*), is among the most important examples of Baroque in Paris. In designing the chapel Bruant, *Premier Architect du Roi*, needed to be ingenious in creating separate areas which would accommodate the large numbers drawn from different sectors of the hospital, and who had to be kept apart. His solution was a central domed octagon with four identical rectangular naves separated by small octagonal chapels. Each compartment is linked to the central space by a small arched bay. The articulation of the vast, empty space is unusual in French architecture of the period, and the integral decoration is minimal. Statues by Antoine Etex were added after 1832. Outside are formal gardens and a sundial on the south wall.

GARE D'AUSTERLITZ & TOLBIAC

North of the Pitié-Salpêtrière Hospital is **Gare d'Austerlitz**, the railway terminus for southwest France. Between 1870 and 1871 (during the Siege of Paris), the station, then known as the Gare d'Orléans, was turned into a hot-air balloon factory. On the riverbank, between Quai St-Bernard and the Seine, in the Tino-Rossi gardens, extends the **Musée de Sculpture en Plein Air**. Created in 1980 with examples of large 20th-century sculpture, there are works by some 29 artists, including Ipoustéguy (b. 1920), Augustin Cardenas (b. 1927), Bernard Pagès (b. 1940), Luiba (b. 1923), and Guy de Rougemont (b. 1935). The **Tolbiac** district to the southeast of the station has undergone major urban renewal in the last 20 years, now linked by the new Simone de Beauvoir footbridge with Bercy (*see p. 311*).

BIBLIOTHEQUE NATIONALE MITTERRAND
Map p. 479, F2

Open Mon 2–8; Tues–Sat 10–8; Sun 12–7; T: 01 53 79 59 59 (reservations/visits) and 01 53 79 49 49 (information); www.bnf.fr. The area immediately surrounding the library, and parts of the interior, are open to the public. Frequent temporary exhibitions on Upper Garden Level. Bookshop, cafeteria. Free guided visits by appointment.
Beside the Seine half way between the Pont de Bercy and the Pont de Tolbiac, is the Bibliothèque Nationale de France François Mitterrand, a veritable fortress for books to which the major part of the national collection was transferred 1996–98 from the Bibliothèque Nationale, Cardinal de Richelieu. The Richelieu site has retained certain collections (*see p. 241*).

The exterior
The last of Mitterrand's *grands projets*, the mammoth and controversial construction was designed by Dominique Perrault and was begun in 1990. It consists of four L-shaped 80m-high towers, each of 20 storeys, simulating books opened at right angles, standing at the corners of a hollow rectangular podium. The whole Tolbiac site covers 7.5 hectares. The stark and open esplanade (60,000 square metres) is approached by wide steps of silvery-grey hard-wood, and decorated with evergreen bushes trapped in metal cases. Only on reaching the top of the steps do the sunken gardens (12,000 square metres), planted with tall pines and silver birches, come into view.

The interior
The 11 upper floors of each glazed tower block, designed to contain offices and the book stacks, had to be lined with wooden shutters for protection. Altogether, there is a storage capacity for over 15 million volumes. The reading rooms themselves, arranged around the gardens designed to resemble a vast, glassed-in cloister, cover a total area of 58,000 square metres. The library is equipped with all the latest technological services and facilities. The vast interior spaces are panelled in woven metal, wood and concrete and softened with hectares of rust-colour carpet. The furnishings are also Perrault's designs.

There are escalators (east and west) from the esplanade down to the two main entrances and entrance halls at each end of the *haut-de-jardin* (upper garden level). Anyone may visit this area. The 1,650-seat library on this level is open to anyone over 16 with a daily or annual reader's ticket (on sale in the entrance halls) and provides open access to some 300,000 specifically acquired volumes, not part of the patrimonial collection. The *rez-de-jardin* (garden level) is open only to readers and has 2,000 places for researchers who have access to the closed stack collections as well as a collection on open access of some 400,000 volumes. The reading rooms and collections on both levels are organised into five departments, four of them thematic and one devoted to audio-visual material.

FAUBOURG SAINT-GERMAIN

As emblematic of Paris as the Latin Quarter or Montparnasse, timelessly elegant and fashionable, the Faubourg (suburb) St-Germain fascinates every visitor to the city. It stretches south from the Seine between the Institut de France to the east and the Pont de la Concorde to the west. Named after the oldest of the major churches of Paris, the *quartier* evokes famous literary cafés, smart but discreet hotels and restaurants, antiquarians selling books and bibelots alongside modern galleries, the best in fashion boutiques as well as colourful street markets in Rue de Buci and meandering urban lanes. In the eastern part, between Blvd St-Michel, Rue des Saints-Pères and Blvd Raspail (6th and 7th arrondissements), are the churches of St-Germain-des-Prés and St-Sulpice and the Musée Delacroix. The grander western part of Faubourg St-Germain accommodates several embassies and ambassadorial residences in elegant 17th–18th-century *hôtels particuliers* while the Palais Bourbon is home to the Assemblée Nationale, and the former Gare d'Orsay has become the magnificent Musée d'Orsay.

HISTORY OF THE FAUBOURG SAINT-GERMAIN

In the Middle Ages much of this area, the property of the Abbaye St-Germain-des-Prés (*see p. 68*), was open country with a *bourg* which developed outside Philippe-Auguste's walls (*see p. 10*) bounded in the 13th century by Rues du Vieux-Colombier and des Saints-Pères. Early in the 14th century more houses were built, and in the 17th century the abbey enclosure was gradually dismantled. With the 16th–17th-century religious revival, several convents were established and, in 1670, the Hôtel des Invalides (*see p. 111*) was constructed on the western outskirts. By 1685 the new Pont Royal provided easy access to the Palais des Tuileries (*see p. 193*), the home of the court during the Regency (1715–23). This, together with the creation of the Ecole Militaire (*see p. 134*), was the main reason for building the new 18th-century aristocratic quarter which gradually supplanted the Marais (*see p. 282*).

About half of the houses were built 1690–1725, a quarter of them 1725–50, and most of the remainder 1750–90. In style they are nonetheless very similar; often the more handsome façades face the interior garden, and the gateway or *porte-cochère* from the street leads to the *cour d'honneur*. Haussmann (*see box on p. 223*) created the new main axes of Blvd St-Germain, Rue de Rennes, and Blvd Raspail in the mid-19th century, cutting across many small streets and destroying a number of grand houses. Blvd Raspail is the link between Blvd St-Germain and Montparnasse (*see p. 105*).

SAINT-GERMAIN-DES-PRES

Map p. 475, D2

*Open 8–7; visits to Chapel St-Symphorian (guided tour in French), Tues and Thur at 1.30;
T: 01 55 42 81 18. 1 Place St-Germain-des-Prés.*
The revered and reassuring tower of the church of St-Germain-des-Prés dominates its
surroundings. Although heavily rebuilt and restored, this is the oldest church in Paris
and the only one retaining any considerable remains of Romanesque work.

History of St-Germain-des-Prés

The church was a part of the great Benedictine abbey founded in 558 by Clovis I's son
Childebert I (r. c. 511–558) who was buried here, and who endowed the abbey with
relics of St Vincent of Saragossa. St Germanus, Bishop of Paris (d. 576), was also interred
on this site. It became the burial place of the Merovingians. The church was rebuilt at
the beginning of the 11th century, and the nave completed up to the vaults by 1050.
The base of the west tower dates from this time. Pope Alexander III consecrated the
enlargement of the chancel in 1163 and in the 13th century the master mason, possibly
Pierre de Montreuil (*see p. 32*), came up with a solution to the long-standing problem of
how to vault the curved section of an ambulatory. The ensemble was embellished at this
time with a Gothic Lady Chapel and cloisters. A small section of the cloisters stands in
the gardens. In the 17th century, when it was the chief house of the reformed
Congregation of St-Maur, the wooden roof of the nave was replaced by a neo-Gothic
vault, the transepts were remodelled (c. 1644), and the bell-chamber of the tower was
added. Badly desecrated at the Revolution, drastic alterations in the 19th century included the rebuilding of the Lady Chapel in 1819, the truncation in 1822 of the two towers
flanking the choir and the restoration of the upper part of the west belfry.

The exterior

The massive flying buttresses of the choir are among the earliest in France. And while
the west porch dates from 1607, it retains the jambs of a 12th-century door and a
battered lintel depicting the *Last Supper*. A fragment of the 11th-century tympanum
was found during excavations in 1971–73. The beautiful Chapel St-Symphorian,
begun in the 6th century and once the Merovingian necropolis, with 11th–12th-
century frescoes, is on the right (south) of the entrance.

The interior

The interior (65m by 21m, and 19m high), an important architectural document of
the transition from Romanesque in the nave to the earliest Gothic in the choir, was
painted all over with murals from 1842–64, by Hippolyte Flandrin and friends. The
neo-Gothic vaults of the nave and the aisles date from 1644–46. The sculpted capitals
are copies (1848–53) of the originals now in the Musée du Moyen Age (*see p. 44*),
with the exception of one in the northwest corner. To the right in the south aisle is a
marble image of *Notre Dame de Consolation*, presented to the Abbey of St-Denis by

Queen Jeanne d'Evreux in 1340. In the south transept is the tomb, by Girardon, of Olivier and Louis de Castellan, killed in the king's service in 1644 and 1669.

The small marble columns in the triforium of the choir are re-used material from the 6th-century abbey of St-Vincent, and their bases and capitals are 12th-century. Renovations in the ambulatory in the 1950s revealed the 12th-century structure and capitals of some of the eastern chapels. In the first ambulatory chapel is the tomb of Lord James Douglas (1617–45), commander of Louis XIII's Scots regiment, killed near Arras. In the second chapel is Descartes' (1596–1650) tombstone, moved from Ste-Geneviève in 1819. The fourth chapel has fragments of mid-13th-century stained glass. The Lady Chapel was rebuilt in the 19th century. In the north aisle is the tombstone of the poet and critic Nicolas Boileau (1636–1711) transfered from the Sainte-Chapelle, and the tomb of William Douglas, 10th Earl of Angus (1554–1611), who died in the service of Henri IV. In the north transept are a statue of the Jesuit missionary St Francisco Xavier (1506–52), by G. Coustou, and the theatrical tomb, by G. and B. Marsy, of the Jesuit John Casimir II, King of Poland, Abbot of St-Germain in 1669 (d. 1672).

ENVIRONS OF THE CHURCH

In the little gardens of Square L.-Prache to the north are fragments of sculptures from the Lady Chapel (1212–55) and Picasso's *Head of a Woman* given in 1959 in homage to Guillaume Apollinaire. In Square F.-Desruelles on the Blvd St-Germain side of the church is a statue of the potter, Bernard Palissy (*see p. 185*), and a monumental portico in ceramic and stone made at the Sèvres works by Risler for the Great Exhibition of 1900.

Opposite the church, around the lively intersection Place Jean-Paul Sartre et Simone de Beauvoir (formerly Place St-Germain-des-Prés) is a trio of brasseries made famous by the elite of the artistic and literary world—Romantics, Surrealists and Existentialists—until the 1950s. No longer the haunt of impoverished cutting-edge intellectuals they are still packed with visitors (and the odd local) seeking something of the old atmosphere or simply a good rendezvous. Each retains a certain individuality: **Café des Deux Magots** (*T: 01 45 48 55 25*), opposite the church, was named after the wooden Chinese statues inside and has a corner terrace; next door on Blvd St-Germain, **Café de Flore** (*T: 01 45 48 55 26*), has an Art Deco interior and is marginally less hectic; and across the boulevard is the once ultra-fashionable **Brasserie Lipp** (*T: 01 45 48 53 91*), specialising in Alsatian food, where it is still difficult to get seated in the downstairs area.

RUE BONAPARTE

Rue Bonaparte runs south from the Seine, linking the two main churches of the district, St-Germain-des-Prés and St-Sulpice as well as the Institut de France (*see p. 71*) with the Palais du Luxembourg (*see p. 93*). A commercial street, narrower and more interesting north of Blvd St-Germain, it is a great place to linger among numerous antique shops and art galleries. The Hôtel du Marquis de Persan (nos. 7–9) was the birthplace of the painter Edouard Manet in 1832.

MUSEE DELACROIX
Map p. 475, D2

Open 9.30–5, closed Tues; T: 01 44 41 86 50.
In 1857, six years before he died, Delacroix moved from Rue Notre-Dame de la Lorette (*see p. 253*) to the first floor apartment at 6 Rue de Furstenberg (or Fürstemberg). Seriously ill, he needed to be close to St-Sulpice, for which he was preparing three large paintings and was delighted to discover this abode, with its little square of garden (now returned to its 1850s' layout). The studio was later shared by Monet and Bazille. The Musée Delacroix is an intimate space that gives a fascinating insight into the artist's life through memorabilia such as his palette and paint table, objects which he brought back from Morocco in 1832, as well as letters written by, and photos of, the painter. There is also a collection of small paintings by Delacroix, including *Madeleine au désert* (1845), portraits, and works on paper, and also works by other artists.

Place de Fürstemberg, which is no more than a bulge in the Rue de Fürstemberg, picturesquely shaded by four Paulownias and lit by a five-globed street lamp, has been the subject of many paintings. It was opened in 1699 by Cardinal Egon de Fürstemberg, Abbot of St-Germain-des-Prés, to serve the abbey palace and was in fact built as an outer courtyard surrounded by stabling and accommodation, including No. 6.

ECOLE DES BEAUX-ARTS
Map p. 475, D2

Main entrance at 14 Rue Bonaparte; the courtyard may be visited with permission from the porter; certain buildings can be visited on Mon (except during academic holidays); T: 01 47 03 50 14. Occasional visits with CMN, T: 01 44 54 19 30. Entrance for temporary exhibitions at 13 Quai Malaquais, open 1–7, closed Mon.
The origins of the Ecole des Beaux-Arts (School of Fine Arts) go back to the L'Académie Royale de Peinture et de Sculpture which Mazarin created in 1648, and which was partly closed in 1793. The Ecole Académique and the Académie d'Architecture, however, continued to function and later fused to create one single institution which became the Ecole Nationale Supérieure des Beaux-Arts. Its first home was the Louvre, then it moved to Rue Mazarine (*see p. 77*), and since 1829 it has occupied the site of the former convent of the Petits-Augustins, founded in 1608, across the river from the Louvre. The school inherited part of the varied collections of the Royal Academies.

The buildings
The large group of buildings making up the School occupies a vast space between Rue Bonaparte and Quai Malaquais. The transformation was begun in 1820 by Debret (1777–1850) and finished in 1862 by his pupil Félix Duban (1797–1872). Some parts of the old convent were incorporated into it, notably the 17th-century chapel. It was here that Alexandre Lenoir (1762–1839), archaeologist and fervent protector

of French monuments, collected together numerous pieces of sculpture, including the tombs of the kings from St-Denis, saving them from destruction during the Revolutionary period. At the Restoration many, but not all, were returned to their place of origin or dispersed among museums (*see p. 409*). The building was further enlarged in 1883 by the acquisition of the Hôtel de Chimay, built by François Mansart c. 1640, and altered in the 18th century (*see p. 90*). This was the first great architectural school. Most great names in art studied here at some point during the 19th and 20th centuries.

From the street it is possible to glimpse on the right, against the former convent church, the re-erected central part of the façade of the Château d'Anet (c. 1540), a rare extant work of Philibert de l'Orme, celebrated architect to François I. This façade is cited as the earliest example in France of the correct use of the three orders of architecture according to Vitruvius. Inside there are more souvenirs of Anet, the château built west of Paris for Diane de Poitiers. The hexagonal Chapel des Louanges, on the Rue Bonaparte side, was built by Marguerite de Valois (*see p. 49*). Its dome is the earliest built in the city (1608).

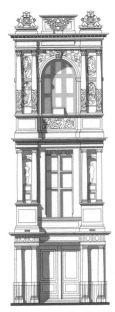

CENTRAL FAÇADE OF THE CHATEAU D'ANET

INSTITUT DE FRANCE
Map p. 475, D2

Guided tours Sat, Sun and public holidays at 3 pm; for individual visits, contact Mme Danielle Bigorgne, T: 01 44 41 44 42 (weekdays). Occasional visits with CMN, T: 01 44 54 19 30. Entrance at 23 Quai de Conti.

Place de l'Institut, on the south bank of the Seine, facing the Louvre, is flanked by the curved wings of the Institut de France. These prestigious premises, with their gilded dome, are the most beautiful on this reach of the river.

History of the Institut

This is an outstanding structure, without parallel in 17th-century France, the oval cupola and semi-circular façade embodying characteristics typical of Roman Baroque. Louis Le Vau (*see p. 38*) was responsible for the initial design, on the axis of the Cour Carrée of the Louvre, built between 1662–91, the architects Lambert and d'Orbay carrying on where Le Vau left off. The Institute, founded in 1795, acquired the building in 1806 and moved from the Louvre. The building was erected in accordance with the bequest of Cardinal Mazarin, powerful statesman and first Minister of France while Anne of Austria acted as regent (1643–61) during the minority of Louis XIV. He gave

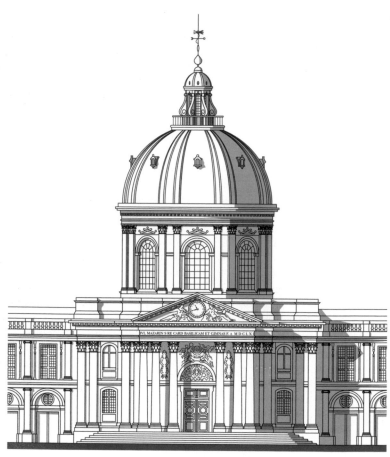

CENTRAL FRONT ELEVATION OF THE INSTITUT DE FRANCE

two million *livres* in silver and 45,000 *livres* a year for the establishment of a college for 60 gentlemen of the four provinces acquired by the Treaty of the Pyrénées: Artois, Alsace, Roussillon and Piedmont (Pinerolo), known from then as the Collège des Quatre-Nations rather than by its official title, Collège Mazarin. The east wing of the Institut and the adjacent Hôtel de la Monnaie (*see opposite*) cover the site of the Hôtel de Nesle (13th century), in which was incorporated the Tour Nesle or Hamelin, the river bastion of Philippe-Auguste's wall (which ran southeast parallel to Rue Mazarine). The western part, known as the Petit-Nesle, the workshop of the goldsmith Benvenuto Cellini in 1540–45 who was invited to France by François I, was demolished in 1663. The eastern part, or Grand-Nesle, rebuilt in 1648 by François Mansart, became the Hôtel de Conti, and in 1770, the Hôtel de la Monnaie.

The academies

The Institut de France comprises five academies: the exclusive Académie Française, founded by Cardinal Richelieu in 1635 and restricted to 40 members, with the particular task of editing the dictionary of the French language; the Académie des Beaux-Arts (1816), founded by Mazarin in 1648 as the Académie Royale de Peinture et de Sculpture; the Académie des Inscriptions et Belles-Lettres, founded by Colbert in 1663; the Académie des Sciences, also founded by Colbert, in 1666; and the Académie des Sciences Morales et Politiques, founded in 1795 and reorganised in 1832. The *institut* is also responsible for several collections, among them the Musée Marmottan Monet (*see p. 351*). An annual general meeting of all five academies is held on 25th October. The Académie Française holds special receptions for newly elected members who are known as *Les Immortels* (because their ranks are always refilled). Only in 1980 was the first woman member elected, the writer Marguerite Yourcenar (1903–87), author of the *Memoirs of Hadrian* (1951).

Visiting the Institut de France

From the first octagonal courtyard, beyond which are two others, one of them the Kitchen Courtyard of the old college, an elegant staircase (1824) by Vaudoyer leads to the Bibliothèque Mazarine. Little-changed since the 17th century, it contains some 450,000 volumes, 4,600 manuscripts and 2,100 incunabula. Originally the Cardinal's personal library, it opened to scholars in 1643, became the first public library in France and was considerably augmented by other collections during the Revolutionary period. The Institut library is also in this wing, together with several rooms decorated with academic statues and busts of eminent academicians. In the former chapel in the west wing is the Salle des Séances Solennelles. Restoration has undone the damage caused by Vaudoyer, and Mazarin's tomb, by Coysevox, has been returned from the Louvre. The room contains some 400 seats (green for members of the Académie Française; red for the others), and is used for receptions and general meetings.

MUSEE DE LA MONNAIE
Map p. 475, D2

Open 11–5.30, Sat–Sun 12–5.30, closed Mon and holidays; T: 01 40 46 55 35; audio guide. There are a number of guided visits available. The workshops can be visited by prior appointment on Wed and Fri afternoons (telephone two days in advance). On sale in the adjacent boutique are medals and replicas, as well as jewellery.

The Hôtel de la Monnaie, at 11 Quai de Conti, the former Mint, is a dignified building by Jacques-Denis Antoine, who made it his home. The doorway is ornamented with Louis XV's monogram and elegant bronze knockers; above is the *fleur-de-lys* escutcheon supported by Mercury and Ceres. From the 18th-century vestibule, a double staircase on the right ascends to Salle Guillaume Dupré, which is mainly Louis XVI style. This and the adjacent rooms are used for temporary exhibitions. Although in 1973 the minting of French coins was transferred to Pessac, near Bordeaux, some pieces are still minted here such as medals, prototypes and *coins d'essais* as well as collectables and jewellery.

Across the courtyard are the former *ateliers* or workshops of the mint. The visit starts on the ground floor to the right. This gallery is divided into nine sections and takes you through the evolution of French currency from the time of Roman Gaul to the Revolution with the aid of coins and medals displayed in transparent vertical mounts. The audio-guide presentation brings to life the history of money exchange through the ages with the aid of enacted scenes. The visit continues on an upper floor with three sections devoted to the period from the Revolution to the present day. As well as the historic background, the major stages used in minting coins are demonstrated. On a lower level, the last section is the Machine Room.

MUSEE DES LETTRES & MANUSCRITS
Map p. 475, D2

Open Wed 1–9, Tues–Sun 10–6, closed Mon; T: 01 43 25 25 41.
This unusual museum, dedicated entirely to old letters and rare manuscripts, opened in 2004 in a mansion at 8 Rue de Nesle built in 1608. The permanent display, over three floors, benefits from a totally up-to-date museum design and the collection is wide-ranging and fascinating. Among the precious documents it contains are a Mozart score, an original manuscript by George Sand (*see p. 259*), and a whole raft of letters written by Voltaire, Napoleon, the artists Géricault and Manet, and works by Paul Eluard, the surrealist poet. There is also a manuscript relating to Einstein's calculations for the Theory of Relativity.

SAINT-SULPICE
Map p. 475, D3

Open 7.30–7.30; guided visits Sun 3 pm; visits to organ loft Sun 12pm; T: 01 42 34 59 98.
The wealthiest church on the Left Bank, St-Sulpice is a fine Italianate building whose size imposes on the surrounding area. The sober west front, like a Roman theatre, features a two-storey colonnade of superimposed Doric and Ionic orders. The north tower, topped by a balustrade, is 73m high; the unfinished south tower is 5m lower. The scale of the project and the change in style of the elevations, notably the Jesuit or Baroque characteristics of the transept arm, are evident from Rue Palatine on the south flank. A succession of masons and a succession of designs mark the character of this church. Begun in 1646 to replace an older church, it was continued on a larger scale in 1670. After an interval from 1678 to 1719, work was resumed by Gilles-Marie Oppenordt, following Gittard's design, but the tower added above the crossing had to be demolished after 1731. The building of the west front was entrusted to

The organ (1781; re-modelled 1860–62) in the church of St-Sulpice.

Giovanni Servandoni, a Florentine, who was replaced in 1766 by Oudot de Maclaurin. His successor, Chalgrin, built the north tower in 1778–80, but the south tower was left incomplete. More recently, a crucial scene in Dan Brown's *Da Vinci Code* was set in St-Sulpice.

The interior

In the form of a Latin cross, the interior is spacious and regular in Counter-Reformation style, measuring 115m long, 57m wide and 33m high, with high arcades to the aisles. The organ, one of the largest in existence (6,588 pipes), was built in 1781 and remodelled in 1860–62; the case was designed by Chalgrin, with statues by Clodion and decoration by Duret. The church is noted for its music and organ recitals. Among the furnishings are two huge *Tridacna gigas* (Giant Clam) shells serving as holy-water stoups, presented to François I by the Venetian Republic, which are supported on 'rocks' carved from marble by Pigalle. The late 18th-century pulpit, designed by Wailly, bears gilded figures of Faith and Hope by Guesdon, and Charity by Dumont. The lateral chapels are decorated with frescoes. The most important are the late works (1855–61) by Delacroix in the first chapel on the right (*see p. 70*). These vigorous images of spiritual conflict represent, in the vault, *St Michael Vanquishing the Devil*, on the left, *Jacob Wrestling with the Angel*, and on the right *Heliodorus Chased from the Temple*. In the fifth chapel is the tomb of the curé Jean-Baptiste-Joseph Languet de Gergy (1675–1750) by Michel-Ange Slodtz (1705–64) who trained in Rome for 17 years. The sculpture represents the power of the Christian soul over death, with an

Luxembourg and provincial museums, as well as through donation and acquisition. The collections include all aspects of the visual arts, concentrating mainly on painting, pastels and drawings and sculpture, but the decorative arts and photography are also represented. On the forecourt of the museum are bronzes commissioned for the first Trocadero Palace built for the Paris *Universal Exposition* of 1878, and on Rue de Lille are works of 1925 by Bourdelle.

Some 4,000 works are permanently on display, arranged chronologically and thematically, illustrating the rapid changes in art from mid-19th century to the First World War, providing a dialogue between different styles. Separate sections are devoted to individual collections. The permanent exhibition space is divided into around 80 separate sections or galleries over three main floors. The recommended visit begins on the ground floor, Level 0, with the 19th-century works, followed by Level 5, Impressionism and Post-Impressionism, and then Level 2. Access via escalators directly to Level 5 is at the opposite end from the main entrance (undergoing maintenance at the time of writing). A new innovation is the introduction of an Artist in Residence, and the incorporation of occasional contemporary works on three-month loan by such artists as Boltanski or Pierre Soulages.

Ground floor (0)

In the central aisle, a large, lucid area flanked by severely geometric partitions watched over by the great station clock, are sculptures of the period 1850–70. Three contrasting 19th-century sculptures include an extreme example of Romanticism, albeit in a Classical guise, *Napoleon Awakening to Immortality* (1846) a plaster of the monument made for Fixin, Burgundy; *Sappho* (1852) is a typical work by the rigidly classical and successful sculptor Pradier; and the marble nude *Woman Bitten by a Snake* (1847) by Auguste Clésinger (1814–83) characteristic of the erotic sensuality of the period. The bronze *Ugolin* (1862) encapsulates the creative energies of Jean-Baptiste Carpeaux and led to important public commissions including the controversial *La Dance* for Opéra Garnier. The plaster design for the fountain the *Four Quarters of the World bearing the celestial sphere* (1867–72; see p. 96), was one of his last works. Thomas Couture's huge canvas, *Romans of the Decadence* (1847), facing the main aisle, is an eclectic piece combining classicism with subtle 18th-century colouring. Intended as a metaphor for the vices of contemporary society, it was equally appreciated for its dimensions, technical skill and orgiastic content. Manet studied under this gifted teacher for several years before rebelling against his rigid academicism.

Rooms 1–3: Academic tendencies of 1850–80 are compared here. Neoclassicists are grouped around Jean-Auguste-Dominique Ingres, whose classicism applies to his refined, linear style rather than to the subject matter which lacks the universal truths expressed in *La Source* (completed in 1856), by his master, Jacques-Louis David. The leading Romantic painter, Eugène Delacroix (*see p. 70*), drew inspiration from colourists such as Rubens and Veronese, and his close ally Géricault. The two poles are combined in *The Tepidarium* (1853) by Théodore Chassériau—student of Ingres, admirer of Delacroix, and later the teacher of Moreau. The subject was based on one of the *thermae* discovered at Pompeii. The stiff and formal Salon paintings on this side of the aisle set up a dialogue with contemporary works produced by artists reacting against the Academic stranglehold on the other side, never more clearly demonstrated than the comparison of the technically competent but vacuous *Birth of Venus* by Salon painter Alexandre Cabanel (Room 3) with Manet's *Olympia* (Room 14; *see below*), both painted in 1863. *Olympia*, derived from Titian's *Venus of Urbino*, presents a defiant woman who holds the viewer in her gaze. The black velvet bow, the slippers, the jewellery and flower in her hair contrast with her pale nudity and increase the provocation; the little black cat is equally challenging, while the bouquet is a mini-masterpiece of still life painting.

Rooms 8–10 and Lille Gallery:
Rotating exhibitions of photographs, the decorative arts of the period 1850–80, and works on paper are shown here.

Rooms 11–13:
Represented here are two of the most important Symbolist painters. Puvis de Chavannes (1824–98) whose *Poor Fisherman* (1881) had a profound influence on many later painters, including Seurat; and Gustave Moreau (*see p. 260*) whose *Orphée* (1865), is a deeply detailed and bejewelled mythological fantasy. Pre-1870 works by Edgar Degas, include *Semiramis Watching the Construction of Babylon* (1861) an experimental work influenced by medieval Italian painting, and the finely tuned family group, *The Bellelli Family* (1858/60), which shows a debt to 16th–17th-century northern painters.

Rooms 4–6 and Seine Gallery:
The realities of contemporary life in the mid-19th century are in sharp contrast to antique decadence. Important statements of developing social awareness include Honoré Daumier's *The Washerwoman* (c. 1863), a small painting handled in a monumental manner, the figures silhouetted against the quays of Paris—Daumier's studio was on the Ile St-Louis (*see p. 40*)—whereas his series of 36 painted clay busts of Parliamentarians, modelled from 1831, caricature the ruling classes. Ernest Meissonier, master of Napoleonic subjects, was more important in his day than his contemporary, Manet. The gentle silvery landscapes of Jean-Baptiste Corot and the bucolic nostalgia of Jules Breton (1827–1906) or Rosa Bonheur (1822–99) do not attain the quiet dignity of everyday toil found in Jean-François Millet's *The Gleaners* (1857) and *The Angelus* (1859), albeit overlaid with a touch of sentimentality. The Barbizon painters, Théodore Rousseau (1812–67), and Diaz de la Peña, paved the way for later open-air painters such as Charles Daubigny, in the Forest of Fontainebleau.

Room 7:
The large, and sometimes sombre, works of Gustave Courbet (and smaller works in Room 15) were both controversial and influential. The flamboyant, outspoken, anti-clerical Republican was criticised for the blatant realism of *Burial at Ornans* at the Salon

of 1850, when *The Romans of the Decadence* (*see p. 80*) was the received style. Shocking was the no-frills, straightforward presentation of a group of humble peasants treated in a monumental manner. The *Artist's Studio* (1855) shows recognisable men, all clothed, including (on the right), Baudelaire (1821–67), surrounding a nude female model, but being an artist's studio, did not cause undue comment. The two nude studies, the voluptuous *La Source* (1868) and erotic *The Origin of the World* (1866) demonstrate Courbet's skill and pleasure in painting luminous flesh.

Room 14: The stunning group of pre-1870 paintings by Edouard Manet here prove the versatility and elegance of this supremely confident painter. *Lola de Valence* (1862), and *The Balcony* (c. 1868–69), with Berthe Morisot in the foreground, show his admiration for Spanish painting and Goya. *Olympia* (*see above, p. 81*) appears in the background of the *Portrait of Zola* (1868), who spoke out in defence of Manet's work.

Room 17: Delicate pastels by Millet, Degas and Manet.

Rooms 18–21: Works from three collections, Moreau-Nélaton, Personnaz and Mollard. The *Studio in the Batignolles* (1870) records Henri Fantin-Latour's support for the Impressionists with his friend and colleague Manet at the easel, and grouped around him Renoir, Bazille, Monet and Emile Zola. Two important precursors of Impressionism are Eugène Boudin, whose *Beach at Trouville* (1864), is typical of many paintings of atmospheric seascapes and fashionable seaside outings in his native Normandy; and Jongkind (1819–91), who, like Boudin, places emphasis on weather and a vast expanse of sky in *The Seine at Notre-Dame*. Sisley, with *The Bridge at Moret-sur-Loing* (1893), and Camille Pissarro wholeheartedly embraced landscape painting in the Impressionist manner to record the effects of nature from frozen winters to lush green summers. The 14 landscapes (1870–1902) by Pissarro mark the evolution of his style. Early works by Claude Monet such as *Portrait of Mme Gaudibert*, and two sections of his huge unfinished *Le Déjeuner sur l'herbe* (1865/6), reveal early experiments leading to Impressionism. *Women in a Garden* (1867) was painted in the open air, and two years later his style evolved further in *The Magpie*. In 1873 he painted one of his most popular and emblematic works, *Coquelicots*, a halcyon moment recording his wife and child in a cascade of poppies, whereas *The Railway Bridge at Argenteuil* (c. 1875) admires 19th-century engineering. *Woman Sewing* (c. 1880/82) is the only painting in the Musée d'Orsay by the American, Mary Cassatt, who studied in Paris and was an admirer of Courbet, Manet and the Impressionists. Other works executed before 1870 include *Bazille Painting* (1867) by Auguste Renoir and *Portrait of Renoir* by Frédéric Bazille.

Opéra room: At the far end of the building, this room is devoted to architect Charles Garnier and the construction of the Paris Opéra (*see p. 235*), started in 1862. On the Seine side, Richard Peduzzi's *Architectural Tower* comprises successive elevations of architectural features from the period 1850–1900.

Upper level (5)

The main Impressionist collection is in Rooms 29–34, displayed in roughly chronological order. Post-Impressionism occupies Rooms 35, 36, 39, and 41–46. The Rooftop Café provides a curious vision of Paris through the hands of the huge clock, and panoramic views from the terrace.

Rooms 29 and 30: A close associate of Fantin-Latour (*Hommage à Delacroix*, 1864) and Courbet (Room 7), the American, James MacNeil Whistler, divided his time between London and Paris. A combination of Japanese influences and the simplification of shapes and spaces, led to the austere harmony of *Arrangement in Grey and Black, Whistler's Mother* (1871). Two tender interpretations by Berthe Morisot, *The Cradle* (1872) and *Young Woman in a Ballgown* (1879), contrast with the vigorous *Floor Planers* (1875) by Gustave Caillebotte. Degas' moving portrayal of café life, *The Absinthe Drinkers* (1876), a theme of addiction and despair addressed by Zola in his book *L'Assommoir* (1877), is an exercise in spatial harmony and colour; Degas' mastery of the oblique glance and textured use of colour is used to capture dancers and horses either in repose or in movement. Manet is at his most

Henri Fantin-Latour: *The Studio at Batignolles* (1870) showing (left to right): Scholderer, Manet at the easel, Renoir, Astruc, Zola, Maître, Bazille and Monet.

Edouard Manet: *Le Déjeuner sur L'Herbe* (1863).

impressionistic in *On the Beach* (1873), and in the portraits such as *Lady with the Fans* (1873–74).

Rooms 31, 33, and 39: Here are Renoir's joyful *Dance in the Country*, and the more restrained *Dance in the Town* of 1883, modelled by his future wife Aline. He uses dappled light to great effect in paintings of 1876 such as *Bal du Moulin de la Galette*, in Montmartre on a Sunday afternoon. *Large Bathers* (c. 1918–19) is considered the culmination of his art.

Rooms 32 and 34: Monet painted many scenes celebrating modern life, including seven versions of the *Gare St-Lazare* (1877) inspired by the steam and smoke.

Woman with the Sunshade (1886) was a sketch painted out of doors, and there are five versions of *Cathedral at Rouen* (1892–93), showing the effects of light at different times of day. Late works include *The Houses of Parliament, London, Sunlight in the Fog* (1904), *Lily Pond* (1899 and 1900), and *Blue Waterlilies* (c. 1916–18).

Room 35: The Post-Impressionist collections have rich pickings including a large number of canvases by Vincent van Gogh. From the dark and brooding early paintings, Van Gogh's work erupts into vigorous impasto and intense colour in *Portrait of Dr Paul Gachet* (1890), one of three portraits of the doctor who befriended the Impressionists and whose

MANET & LE DEJEUNER SUR L'HERBE

Two of the most exciting works painted by Manet are *Olympia* (Room 14) and *Le Déjeuner sur l'Herbe* (Room 19). Both painted in 1863, they both portray naked women, were considered scandalous and condemned as ugly at the time. They were Manet's last nudes. *Déjeuner* follows in the tradition of the Fête Champêtre as seen in Titian's *Concert Champêtre* (c. 1510) and Watteau's *Pilgrimage to Cythera* (1717) both in the Louvre (*see pp. 159 and 149*). Manet's version became one of the most notorious picnics of all time, heavily criticised not only for its subject matter but also for the non-conformist technique—freely applied paint, 'blocks' of colour, ambiguous perspective, lack of tonal modelling, and sketchy background. Manet was a bourgeois revolutionary rebelling against the idealism and impersonality of Couture's studio (*see p. 80*). He was also a true Parisian, loved art, and was seeking a formula to reconcile style and modern life, an ardent believer in spontaneously capturing real scenes. Daumier, Courbet and the Barbizon painters had gone some way towards this through landscape, which did not interest Manet in the way that figures did. In 1838 Louis-Philippe's Spanish Collection opened to the public, and here Manet discovered works by Velazquez and Goya, which influenced *Absinthe Drinker* (1858/59), modelled by a rag picker. Velazquez's abrupt handling of colour and dramatic contrasts strongly influenced Manet. *Concert in the Tuileries* (c. 1860–62), using numerous sketches of modern people at leisure, was Manet's first 'instant' record of modern life, but he still kept a foot in the past, a tension that emerges in *Le Déjeuner sur l'Herbe*. The idea was based on sketches of bathers in the Seine, but the composition was borrowed from a small group of naked divinities in an engraving by Marcantonio of a lost *Judgement of Paris* by Raphael as well as from Titian's *Concert Champêtre*. The huge canvas was painted in his studio using models. The result is a disconnected painting, implausible but fascinating. Predictably it was turned down at the official Salon, and at the alternative Salon des Refusés, crowds came along for a good laugh. Manet's painting proved a *succès de scandale*. Few who derided *Déjeuner* were unaware of the classical influences. The furore was caused above all by the depiction of an insolent looking floozy sitting stark naked in the company of men wearing mid-19th-century clothes, placing the subject fairly and squarely in the contemporary period. The nude has the face of the artist's favourite model Victorine Meurent and the body of his wife Suzanne. The loose paint handling in the naturalistic background; the almost cut-out figures; ambiguous perspective; the contrasts of tone; Manet's hallmark strong greens and blacks; the abandoned clothes in the foreground; the man's tasselled hat, not usually worn out of doors; the modernity of it all was incomprehensible to the public and disturbed their accustomed norms. Today, while still provocative and inscrutable, it is considered a masterpiece.

collection was donated to the museum by his children. Others include works from the two years that Van Gogh spent in Provence, *L'Hôpital à St-Paul de Mausole near St Remy, Provence* (1889), where he was treated for epilepsy and schizophrenia, a version of *The Bedroom at Arles* (1889), of which he wrote 'everything depends on the colour' and it 'ought to rest the mind'. Two *Self-portraits* (1887 and 1889) are electrifying in the use of colour and the tense energy of the brushstrokes; and equally intense is the *Church at Auvers-sur-Oise* (1890); *The Siesta, after Millet* (1889–90) is a rhapsody in blue and gold.

Rooms 36 and 41: A significant cross-section of Paul Cézanne's works includes *Portrait of Achille Emperaire* (1869/70), which was refused by the Salon in 1870. As a consquence Cézanne abandoned figure painting until 1880. Almost forgotten at dealer Julien Tanguy's gallery, it was a revelation to Emile Bernard and Vincent van Gogh. Monumental mature works include *The Card-players* and *Woman with a Coffee-pot* (both 1890–95). Landscapes of Provence are represented by the *Bay at Estaque*, and *Mont Ste-Victoire* of which there are over 40 versions in oil plus many watercolours. One of a series of six still lifes in the collection is *Apples and Oranges* (c. 1899) where Cézanne combines the textures of voluptuous fruit and heavy fabrics with his favourite pots and jars. *Bathers* (c. 1890) was Cézanne's last and largest canvas of male nudes.

Rooms 36 and 47: Toulouse-Lautrec, from one of the oldest aristocratic families in France, but more at home with the *demi-monde*, frequently painted popular entertainers, such as *Jane Avril Dancing* (c. 1891), and the female clown *Cha-U-Kao* (1895), as well as decorative panels for the dancer La Goulue's booth at the Foire du Trône.

Room 40: Pastels by Degas, and a water-colour by Piet Mondrian (1872–1944), *Départ pour la Pêche* (c. 1900). Examples of the mysterious and luminous work of Symbolist, Odilon Redon (also in Room 49), include *The Buddha* (1906/07), and *Portrait of Gauguin* (1903/05).

Room 41: The Gachet Collection here has works by Cézanne, Guillaumin, Monet, Pissarro, Sisley and Renoir.

Rooms 42–46: Works from the 1890s are a far cry from the Salon paintings and show a shift from Impressionism. The styles of this period are loosely termed Post-Impressionist, a name coined by the English writer and art critic, Roger Fry, for an exhibition of French paintings in London in 1910–11. Impressionism experienced a crisis in the 1880s and certain artists sought more spiritual or symbolic values. The flat colours and naïve style that characterise Henri (le Douanier) Rousseau's *Portrait of a Woman* (c. 1897) were an important influence on the new movement.

Rooms 43 and 44: These are devoted to Paul Gauguin and painters who

Henri (Le Douanier) Rousseau: *Portrait of a Woman* (c. 1897).

Paris region. At the time of the Liberation considerable fighting in the neighbourhood caused some damage to the building and the destruction of over 30,000 volumes in the library.

The building

The north façade (1804–07), a neo-Hellenistic piece of imperial bombast designed principally to balance the Madeleine (*see p.* 237) when seen from Pl. de la Concorde, is entirely decorative and consists of a portico of twelve Corinthian columns. The low reliefs on the wings are by Rude and Pradier. Inside, the semicircular *salle de séances* (1828–32) has statues by Pradier, Desprez and others, and a Gobelins tapestry after the School of Athens (Raphael). Other rooms contain historical paintings by Horace Vernet (1789–1863) and by Delacroix. The Galerie des Fêtes (1848) connects the building to the Hôtel de Lassay (1724), the official residence of the President of the Assembly.

Place du Palais Bourbon

Behind the building is Pl. du Palais Bourbon, an elegant ensemble of Louis XVI houses built to the same pattern after 1776. On the northeast corner, on Rue de l'Université (entrance at 121 Rue de Lille), in the former Hôtel Turgot (18th century), is the **Institut Néerlandais** (*T:* 01 53 59 12 43), which owns a collection of Dutch and German drawings and is open to the public during exhibitions.

BOULEVARD SAINT-GERMAIN & RUE DU BAC
Map p. 474, C2

A large section of the western end of Blvd St-Germain, including Hôtel de Roquelaure (no. 246; 1722), is occupied by Government offices. Guillaume Apollinaire (1880–1918), poet, writer and champion of avant-garde artists, lived and died (of Spanish flu) at no. 202, near the boulevard's junction with Rue du Bac which weaves south from the river and took its name from the ferry operating before the construction of the Pont Royal, carrying stone from the Vaugirard quarries across to the Louvre in 1550–64. The former Dominican church of **St-Thomas-d'Aquin**, begun in 1682 by Pierre Bullet in the Jesuit style, was completed in 1722 with the construction of the monks' choir in the east behind the altar; the façade dates from 1765–69. The light interior with pale stained glass is very effective. *The Transfiguration* on the vaults of the choir was painted by François Lemoyne shortly before his departure for Italy. Further east off Blvd St-Germain, at no. 27 Rue St-Guillaume, is the 16th-century Hôtel de Mesmes, enlarged in 1933, now the Institut National d'Etudes Politiques, and no. 16, the **Hôtel de Créqui**, built 1660–64, and extended in 1772, was for a time the home of poet, statesman and historian Alphonse Lamartine (1790–1866). An early French Romantic, Lamartine was unusual in combining his literary endeavours with a career in politics, though without much success, being involved in the birth of the Second Republic in 1848, advocating the abolition both of slavery and of the death penalty.

LUXEMBOURG & GOBELINS

THE PALAIS DU LUXEMBOURG
Map p. 475, D3

Group visits only, by appointment: Mon, Fri, Sat, T: 01 42 34 20 00; occasional visits with CMN, T: 01 44 54 19 30; frequent temporary exhibitions in the Orangery, open Mon–Thur 11–7, Fri 11–10, Sat–Sun 9–7; T: 01 42 34 25 95.

The Palais du Luxembourg was once a royal residence. The northern façade, where the main entrance is surmounted by an octagonal dome, is original; the south façade, facing the gardens, is a 19th-century copy. The two wings, terminating in double steep-roofed pavilions with three orders of columns superimposed, are connected by a single-storeyed gallery. It is an early example of a building visualised in terms of mass, thus preparing the way for classicism, rather than decoration of the surface. The main entrance of the Palais du Luxembourg is in Rue de Vaugirard, the longest street in Paris, stretching from Blvd St-Michel to the Porte de Versailles.

HISTORY OF THE PALAIS DU LUXEMBOURG

Marie de Médicis, queen mother, widow of Henri IV, commissioned the most distinguished architect of the time, Salomon de Brosse, to design the Luxembourg. Following the assassination of the king, the queen supposedly wished to quit the gloomy Louvre for a more rural setting reminiscent of Tuscany, and a place recalling the Pitti Palace, her birthplace in Florence. The Luxembourg, built 1615–27, stands on the site of the Petit-Luxembourg (1570–1612), the mansion she acquired from the Duc de Tingry-Luxembourg. After Louis XIII's death in 1643, the palace passed to Marie's second son Gaston, Duc d'Orléans (1608–60), and the Palais Médicis became known as the Palais d'Orléans. Subsequently, it belonged in succession to Mlle de Montpensier, daughter of Gaston d'Orléans, the Duchesse de Guise (1672), Louis XIV (1694) and the Orléans family. The building was altered in 1808 and enlarged in 1831–44 including a new façade facing the Jardin du Luxembourg. It was used as a prison during the Revolution and in 1794 the Directory transferred the seat of government from the Tuileries to the Luxembourg. In 1800 it became the Palais du Consulat, under the Empire it was the Palais du Sénat and later the Chambre des Pairs (House of Lords). Several important people were tried here, including Louis-Napoleon Bonaparte after his attempted coup in 1840. From 1852 to 1940, except for a short time, the Palais became the meeting place of the Senate, the upper chamber of the French Republic. In 1940–44 it was occupied as the Luftwaffe's headquarters and reverted in 1958 to the Senate.

The interior of the palace

The interior, drastically remodelled by Jean Chalgrin under Napoleon, is decorated in the sumptuous 19th-century manner, replete with an indifferent group of statues and paintings, historical and allegorical. The celebrated series of paintings devoted to the life of Marie de Médicis, by Rubens, painted for the palace, is in the Louvre (*see p. 154*). Of the rooms that can be visited, Marie de Médicis' audience chamber, the Cabinet Doré, is outstanding. Other rooms occasionally open to the public are the Salles des Conférences, the hemicycle of the Salle de Séances and the library with paintings by Delacroix including *Alexander Placing the Poems of Homer in Darius's Golden Coffer* and, in the cupola, the *Limbo* of Dante's *Inferno*.

The Petit-Luxembourg and St-Joseph-des-Carmes

The adjoining Petit-Luxembourg, now the residence of the President of the Senate, was presented to Richelieu by Marie de Médicis in 1626. It includes the cloisters and chapel of the Filles du Calvaire, for whom the queen built a convent; the chapel is a charming example of the Renaissance style; the cloister forms a winter-garden.

On Rue de Vaugirard is the domed St-Joseph-des-Carmes, once the chapel of a Carmelite convent, dating from 1613–20, containing several 17th-century canvases. In the crypt are the bones of some 120 priests massacred in the convent garden in September 1792. Josephine de Beauharnais (1763–1814), later Madame Bonaparte, was one of many imprisoned here during the Terror.

Adjacent are the buildings of the Institut Catholique, founded in 1875, one of the most prestigious Catholic teaching establishments in France where, in 1890, radio waves were discovered by Edouard Branly (1844–1940).

JARDIN DU LUXEMBOURG

Alongside Blvd St-Michel, and close to both St-Germain and Montparnasse, the atmosphere and setting of the Jardin du Luxembourg are less formal and more varied than the Champs de Mars or the Tuileries. Covering 23 hectares and embellished by more than 80 statues, two fountains and a pond, this is a pleasantly refreshing area in a quarter with few green spaces and consequently popular on sunny weekends. Planned in the 17th century, it was radically altered in 1782 and 1867, although the basic layout follows to some extent the one that was first created for Marie de Médicis. The Luxembourg Palace provides a handsome backdrop giving the ensemble the air of a country property rather than town mansion. In the garden are cafés, a bandstand, carousel, marionette theatre and children's play area, and frequently chess-players locked in combat.

Steps descend from the east terrace to lawns surrounding an octagonal pond with a fountain. Beyond the formal west terrace is the Jardin Anglais enclosing a small-scale

The Triumph of Silenus (1884) by Jules Dalou in the Jardin du Luxembourg.

replica of the *Statue of Liberty* by Bartholdi that was given to the United States in 1886. To the southwest is a fruit garden. Due south, beyond Pl. André-Honnorat, the impressive perspective between the two branches of Av. de l'Observatoire was achieved at the cost of the Carthusian monastery demolished at the Revolution. Landscaped during the First Empire (1804–15), these gardens are named Jardin Robert-Cavelier-de-la-Salle and Jardin Marco-Polo (*see below*).

North of the central octagonal pond, on the right, at the end of an oblong pool, is the *Fontaine Médicis*, attributed to Salomon de Brosse (c. 1627), in the style of an Italianate grotto. It was moved here in 1861. In the central niche is Polyphemus about to crush Acis and Galatea; on either side are Pan and Diana, by Augustin Ottin (1866). At the back is a low-relief, the *Fontaine de Léda*, brought from the Rue du Regard in 1855.

A selection of the many sculptures placed around the gardens includes *Stendhal* by Rodin, a *Monument to Watteau* by Henri Gauquié, a bust of Beethoven by Bourdelle, and the monument to Eugène Delacroix by Jules Dalou, the pupil of Jean-Baptiste Carpeaux. Also here, Dalou's *Triumph of Silenus* (1884; *pictured on previous page*) shows one of the most celebrated companions of Dionsyus in a typically inebriated state, just about maintaining his seat on a donkey thanks to supporting satyrs and nymphs. A tremendous piece of neo-Baroque, the sculpture provided inspiration for the *Bacchus* paintings of the 1970s by Elaine de Kooning (1920–89).

Jardin Marco Polo

To the south of the Luxembourg, in the Jardin Marco Polo at the end of Avenue de l'Observatoire, is the extravagant *Fontaine de l'Observatoire* (1875) by Gabriel Davioud, with Carpeaux's group of figures representing the *Four Quarters of the Globe* (*see p. 80*). The bronze horses and turtles are the work of Frémiet. On Carrefour de l'Observatoire stands François Rude's statue of Marshal Ney (1769–1815), who was shot nearby for supporting Napoleon on his return from Elba.

Closerie des Lilas

171 Blvd de Montparnasse; T: 01 43 26 70 50/43 54 21 68. See also p. 442.
The bar and restaurant, Closerie des Lilas, is now a rather smart affair. The original Closerie was a simple *guinguette* which was the first watering place on the road to Fontainebleau. At the end of the 19th century it became a favourite destination on the edge of Paris for poet Charles Baudelaire, and the painter Dominique Ingres brought his models here. Other writers and poets such as Verlaine, Theophile Gautier and the Goncourt brothers, as well as Emile Zola frequented the café. In 1901, the American poet, Stuart Merrill and Scandinavian writers, including Strindberg, became habitués, along with exiles from Café Guerbois such as Manet, Jongkind, Gauguin and the Impressionist painters. The American painter-dandy James McNeil Whistler who spoke French learned at St-Petersburg, also frequented it. The café was rebuilt in 1903 and every Tuesday evening was dedicated to *Vers et Prose*, where the likes of André Salmon, Guillaume Apollinaire or Max Jacob might declaim a verse, and heated discussions sometimes developed. In 1925, the Closerie modernised, a banquet in

honour of the poet Saint-Pol-Roux turned into a rumpus provoked by leading Surrealist André Breton. The list of patrons goes on. In the 21st century the terrace is populated at midday by business people, and it is a wonderfully nostalgic place to sip a *coup de champagne* of an evening.

MUSEE ZADKINE
Map p. 475, D4

Open Tues–Sun 10–6, closed Mon and public holidays; T: 01 55 42 77 20.
Tucked away on the south (left) side of Rue d'Assas, at no. 100, entered through a mini sculpture garden, is the Musée Zadkine. This museum is particularly attractive because it is installed in the former home and studio, from 1928, of the Russian-born sculptor Ossip Zadkine. Zadkine came to Paris in 1909 but only began to achieve public acclaim around 1920. The garden has changed little since the sculptor's time, although the studio was radically altered by his widow, the painter Valentine Prax, who bequeathed about 100 of the 300 works shown here. These demonstrate the range of Zadkine's sculptures and carving, from his early Cubist-inspired work through Expressionism and Abstraction. The earlier 'mannerist' works are reminiscent of Modigliani or Brancusi, but in the 1920s he adopted the geometric tendencies of Cubism. Towards the end of his life his work became more decorative and abstract. Among the pieces is a model for *La Ville Détruite* for Rotterdam and tributes to Van Gogh. Zadkine's main production was cast in bronze, but he continued all his life to carve, one beautifully simplified example being the ebony *Torse violoncello* (c. 1956).

THE OBSERVATOIRE
Map p. 475, D4

Application to attend a guided tour should be made in writing, enclosing a s.a.e., to the Secrétariat at 61 Av. de l'Observatoire, 75014 Paris, T: 01 40 51 22 21, www.obspm.fr. The Observatory is open during Journées Européennes du Patrimoine, la Fête de la Science and other special events such as the Nuits des Planètes.
The Observatoire, the oldest working observatory in the world, was founded by Louis XIV. On 21st June, 1667, the Meridian of Paris was established and determined the orientation of the building. It is indicated by a copper line embedded in the paving of the second floor (2° 20' 14" east of Greenwich). It was replaced by Greenwich in 1884. The four sides of the building face the cardinal points of the compass, and the latitude of the southern side is the recognised latitude of Paris (48° 50' 11" north) which, until 1912, was the basis for the calculation of longitude on French maps. The Observatoire is also the headquarters of the Bureau International de l'Heure. Set in gardens, the building was designed by Claude Perrault and completed in 1672. One of its directors was Jean-Dominique Cassini (1625–1712), the first of the family of

definitely not for veggies, such as *andouillette, pieds de cochons, boudin noir,* and *os à la moëlle*. Le Temps des Cerises (*T: 01 45 89 69 48*), at nos. 18–20, was a workers' canteen. Further on is the bright, modern Café Fusion (*T: 01 45 80 12 02*). The tea shop, L'Oisivethé (*T: 01 53 80 31 33, closed Mon*) at 1 Rue Jean-Marie Jégo offers good-looking desserts, cakes and salads.

At the top of the Butte, **Place Paul Verlaine** is a pretty open space cut in two by Rue Bobillot. On one half are trees and on the other a drinking-water fountain and swimming baths. Both fountain and baths are supplied by natural spring water. The search for a deep well was authorised by Haussmann (*see p. 223*) in 1863 to supplement the supply of river water to the Butte. Drilling went to a depth of 532m, but was abandoned in 1872, to be revived 20 years later with the discovery in 1903 of abundant springs—nearly 6,000 cubic metres per day 582m down—slightly sulphurous and warm (28°C). The exercise lost its utility because the Bièvre was gradually covered and homes were soon supplied with running water. In 1924, however, the hot water came into its own with the creation of a swimming pool and **public baths** (*open Mon 2–5.30; Tues, Wed, 7–6.30; Thur, Sat 7–6; Sun 8–5.30; closed Fri; T: 01 45 99 60 05.*) housed in a small red-brick building reminiscent of Arts and Crafts style with a wavy roofline. It was used by Dr Pierre

Macleuf in 1943–46 for research into remedial swimming. The original bore-hole worn out, a new one was drilled to a depth of 620m, to the benefit of locals who fill their water bottles with the pure water which flows from the fountain. Across from the swimming pool is a wine bar/restaurant, La Bouche à Oreilles (*T: 01 45 89 74 42*).

Rue Vandrezanne leads to a triangular area surrounded by white modern blocks. On the corner is the charming little restaurant Chez Nathalie (*T: 01 45 80 20 42*) at no. 45. Also on this street is a gallery/shop AGAAP (no. 43) and Le Timri Restaurant (*T: 01 45 65 23 87*) at no. 41, specialising in Berber cooking such as tagines and couscous.

Passage Vandrezanne is a narrow lane running downhill; to the left the refreshing little Jardin de la Montgolfière has shady pergolas. A reminder of the mills which once stood in the fields of the Butte is Rue des Moulins des Prés which crosses busy Rue de Tolbiac to Square des Peupliers, surrounded with pretty houses built in 1926, the name referring to the poplars which stood along the banks of the Bièvre. In the other direction, Rue des Moulins des Près runs uphill, behind the baths, back to Place Verlaine. From here Rue Simonet runs into Rue Gérard, where there are more attractive houses and gardens, a Spanish restaurant and the unusual black and white Service d'Electricité building. Rue P. Méry leads to the large and bustling Place d'Italie.

MONTPARNASSE

Montparnasse, best known for its former literary and bohemian associations, has inevitably changed since the 1920s, retaining only faded associations with the artists and intellectuals who once lived in the area. Now it is a busy shopping and residential district with a slightly seedy charm, watched over by the dark silhouette of the Tour Montparnasse. Blvd du Montparnasse is imbued with a modern vitality in the evenings, when the large brasseries, while altered in character, are all crammed to bursting.

HISTORY OF MONTPARNASSE

'Mount Parnassus' was named, so it is said, by students from the Latin Quarter who gathered on the rising ground outside Paris. In the 18th century, it became a centre of popular entertainment where cabarets and *guinguettes* could serve tax-free alcohol, and even when incorporated into Paris in the 19th century the tradition continued. With the construction of Blvd Montparnasse and the train station (1852) in the 19th century the ground was levelled off. At the turn of the 19th and 20th centuries, Montmartre (*see p. 256*), suffering from its bohemian fame and rising subculture, was supplanted by the Left Bank as the centre of artistic and literary activity. Montparnasse had new abundant housing and inexpensive studios readily available. Prior to the First World War, artists, musicians and poets began to move in. Famously, the social life of the intellectual community was centered on the café-brasseries at the junction of Blvd Montparnasse and Rue Vavin—Le Select, La Rotonde, and Le Dôme—and later La Coupole. During the *Années Folles*, after the First World War, the café society reached its zenith. Everyone and anyone gathered in Montparnasse. Blaise Cendrars, Jean Cocteau, Aragon and André Breton were among the literary newcomers, and musicians included Denis Milaud and Francis Poulenc. Jazz was in the air thanks to the likes of Sydney Bechet; anti-art movements such as Dada and Surrealism were taking off, Paul Poiret liberated women from the corset; and Maurice Chevalier, Mistinguette and Josephine Baker entertained Paris. Young, energetic writers and artists from the United States, escaping prohibition, (1919) also gathered in the *quartier*, and many Eastern European and Russian émigrés arrived to swell the crowd. Although most of the American colony (*see p. 55*) abandoned France during the Wall Street crash of 1929, the popularity of Montparnasse barely waned during the early '30s. After the Second World War, Americans returned and a new wave of enthusiasm hit the area which lasted until the '50s. Both Henry Miller and Ernest Hemingway described the café life, disreputable and otherwise, of the district in its heyday.

THE CAFES OF MONTPARNASSE
Map p. 474, B4

At no. 108 Blvd Montparnasse, from the 1870s **Le Dôme** (*T: 01 43 35 25 81*) was the original café and meeting place for Germans and East Europeans including the Bulgarian painter, Pascin. In 1907 Matisse, already well regarded, met other painters here as well as Gertrude Stein (*see p. 55*). It is suggested that Russian political refugees, including Lenin and Trotsky, were seen at Le Dôme.

La Rotonde (*T: 01 43 26 48 26*) at no. 105 started as a modest bistrot, but in 1911 its expansive owner, Victor Libion, extended into the butcher's next door. All were welcome, and he instructed his waiters not to wake the down-and-outs who came to sleep there. Picasso and the Cubist painters, apart from Braque, moved to Montparnasse and frequented La Rotonde. So did Amedeo Modigliani, a most striking character, ceaselessly sketching, who met other émigrés and members of the School of Paris such as Soutine and Kisling. La Rotonde was so famous that it was the first place Charlie Chaplin, accompanied by Douglas Fairbanks and Mary Pickford, visited on his arrival in Paris in 1921 to a tumultuous reception.

In 1924, **Le Select** (*T: 01 45 48 38 24*), at no. 99 Blvd Montparnasse, was the first café to open all night (now only until 2am), and among its specialities was welsh rarebit which attracted an American clientele. The café brought together Ernest Hemingway (also fond of Le Cluny and La Closerie des Lilas, *see p. 96*), Henry Miller, Scott Fitzgerald, Ezra Pound, William Faulkner, and the American engineer-sculptor, Alexander Calder, along with British writers such as James Joyce and T.S. Eliot.

La Coupole (*T: 01 43 20 14 20*), at no. 102, the largest of them all, with seating for 600, opened in 1927, a genuine Art Deco brasserie, supported by 24 pillars and decorated with 33 murals which were renovated in the 1990s. Its famous clients were legion, from Cocteau to Man Ray, and from Braque to Simone de Beauvoir and Jean-Paul Sartre. It still has an American bar.

TOUR MONTPARNASSE

Open April–Sept 9.30–11.30; Oct–March Sun–Thur 9.30–10.30; Fri, Sat, day prior to a Public Holiday, 9.30–11; (last lifts 30mins before closing); T: 01 45 38 52 56; entrance on Rue de l'Arrivée in front of the station.

The area is now dominated by the insolent Tour Montparnasse (200m high), a high-rise office block built in 1973, the first of its kind. The only way to beat it is to go to the top (196m) and revel in one of the most impressive views in the city from the 56th floor. The ride in the lift takes 38 seconds. There are audio visuals and interactive facilities providing information, an open-air terrace and a panoramic bar. The cost is 9 euros. Alternatively, take the lift up to the glamorous modern bar and restaurant Le Ciel de Paris (*open 8.30–11; T: 01 40 64 77 64*) and spend the money on some food or an aperitif—although you only get half the view.

GARE DE MONTPARNASSE

Adjacent to the tower is the mainline station, Gare de Montparnasse, serving Brittany and the Atlantic coast. An 18-storey glass and concrete structure surrounds the station platforms on three sides and above it is Le Jardin Atlantique, which can be entered from Place des Cinq-Martyrs-du-Lycée-Buffon or from the mainline station. This urban breathing space uses metal, wood, marble and granite structures, with an intermittent fountain evoking the sound of waves on a seashore, and coastal plants are used to harmonise with the theme. A raised walkway and a group of small thematic gardens are arranged around the pavilions of the Blue Waves and of the Pink Rocks, intended to evoke ocean and sky. At the tower end of the garden is the entrance to the **Museums of Marshal Leclerc and Jean Moulin** (*open 10–6; closed Mon; T: 01 40 64 39 44*), dedicated to the roles of these two heroes of the Second World War, Free French and Resistance. One room is dedicated to the Liberation of Paris.

Musée de la Poste
Open 10–6, closed Sun; T: 01 42 79 23 23.
The Musée de la Poste at 34 Blvd de Vaugirard presents some 500 years of the history of the French postal system in 15 rooms. The main sections, displayed chronologically and thematically, cover history, philately, art and society and the postal service today, illustrated using a range of exhibits. There are scale models,

View of the Eiffel Tower and the Champ de Mars from Tour Montparnasse, with the office blocks of La Défense in the distance beyond. The gilded Dôme des Invalides is on the right.

unusual objects and old letter-boxes, the earliest stamps and their printing, methods of communication and transport, through to postmen evoked by old costumes and prints. There is also a room devoted to the development of the airmail service, telecommunication and mechanisation.

Cartier Foundation for Contemporary Art
Open 12–8, closed Mon; T: 01 42 18 56 50.
At no. 261 Blvd Raspail the Cartier Foundation for Contemporary Art occupies a building by Jean Nouvel. Exhibitions of contemporary art by international artists are held here. The garden was landscaped by Lothar Baumgarten.

Just north of the junction of Blvd du Montparnasse and Blvd Raspail stands the statue of Balzac by Rodin (*see p. 117*). Further to the west on Rue du Docteur-Roux is the Musée Pasteur (*see p. 421*).

CIMETIERE MONTPARNASSE

The main entrance to the famous Cimetière Montparnasse is from Blvd Edgar-Quinet; there are others from Rue Froidevaux. (A plan is available at the office just inside the main gate.) The land originally belonged to the Hôtel Dieu (*see p. 29*) and was used by the monks as a burial ground for those who died in the hospital. In the southwest, near Porte Frodevaux, is the tower of a mill that existed here in the 15th century. The mill became a *guinguette* after the Revolution, and in 1824, when the City of Paris decided to open a new cemetery, it became the guardian's home. Although this cemetery is not quite as spectacular as Père Lachaise, the forest of monuments and gravestones is a tribute to all the marble cutters and engravers who found work here in the 19th century. On the impressive list of the late and great buried here are Maupassant, Baudelaire, J.-K. Huysmans, Jean-Paul Sartre, Ionesco and Beckett among the writers; composers and musicians including César Franck, Saint-Saëns and Gainsbourg; many artists such as Fantin-Latour, Gérard, Houdon, Rude, Soutine, Zadkine, Bourdelle, Bartholdi, and Brancusi, whose work *Le Baiser* (*The Kiss*) is tucked away in the northeast corner; Pierre-Joseph Proudhon, the social reformer; Arago, the scientist and politician; Alfred Dreyfus; Charles Garnier, the architect; and André Citroën, the car manufacturer.

MUSEE BOURDELLE
Map p. 474, B4

Open 10–5.40, closed Mon and holidays; T: 01 49 54 73 73.
The discreet Musée Bourdelle, at 16 Rue Antoine-Bourdelle, is devoted to the eponymous sculptor, who lived and worked here from 1885 until his death in 1929. Bourdelle's entire collection was donated to the Ville de Paris by his widow in 1949. This charming time-warp encompasses a small courtyard open to the street and the

studios and furnished living apartments. A gallery for plaster models was added in 1961 and in 1990–92 a two-level extension was built for permanent and temporary exhibitions as well as a gallery for graphic arts (*by appointment only*) and a library.

On display are studies, plaster casts and bronzes of his best known works. A pupil of Rodin (*see p. 116*), Bourdelle's earlier works, such as *Beethoven aux Grands Cheveux* (1891) show his master's influence. He made several studies of Beethoven to whom, when he was young, he felt he had a physical resemblance, and he likened the composer's artistic journey to his own artistic development. Bourdelle's later, Classical style, appears in the reliefs for the Théâtre des

Antoine Bourdelle photographed at the age of 28.

Champs-Elysées (1912–13; *see p. 219*) strongly influenced by the dances of Isadora Duncan (1878–1927). He tended to work on a monumental scale. Among powerful models and casts for larger works are the *Monument to General Alvear*, for Buenos Aires (1913–23); one of his most successful works is *Hercules the Archer*; and also *La France*, a bronze of which is outside the Palais de Tokyo (*see p. 338*). Among his pupils were Giacometti (1901–66) and Germaine Richier (1904–59).

THE CATACOMBES: DENFERT-ROCHEREAU
Map p. 478, A2

Open Tues–Fri 2–4; Sat, Sun 9–11 & 2–4; T: 01 43 22 47 63. Dress warmly.

Place Denfert-Rochereau was known as the Place d'Enfer until 1879, when it was named after the defender of Belfort during the Franco-Prussian War in 1870. In the square is a reduced version of the most famous lion in France, Bartholdi's *Lion of Belfort* (the original is in Belfort, Franche-Comté). In Square Ledoux on the west are the heavily rusticated remains of the twin pavilions of the Barrière d'Enfer for collecting tolls, designed by Claude Nicolas Ledoux (*see p. 318*), in the old wall of the Farmers' General. Surely one of the most dispiriting visits in Paris, yet remarkably popular with visitors of all ages, the Catacombes are entered via the eastern pavilion of the Barrière. The tour starts with the historic background, then a macabre series of galleries lined with bones and skulls leading to a huge ossuary containing the debris of over six million skeletons. The labyrinthine series of underground quarries, covering about 850 hectares and 20m down, first provided stone in Roman times, with 160km of tunnels extending from the Jardin des Plantes to the Porte de Versailles and as far as Montrouge and Montsouris. In the 1780s they became a charnel-house for bones removed from four overfull graveyards in the city, particularly the Cimetière des Innocents (*see p. 264*), and most of the victims of the Terror were transferred here. It took 15 months to transport these remains. In 1944 the Catacombes served as a headquarters of the Resistance Movement.

PARC DE MONTSOURIS

Some way south of Pl. Denfert-Rochereau is the 16-hectare Parc de Montsouris, laid out in 1875–78 as part of Haussmann's scheme to provide green spaces around the capital. The gardens imitate the informal English style with lawns, some 1,400 trees in groups, and a lake. As well as sculptures in stone and bronze, such as Etex's *Shipwrecked* (1882) and *Drama in the Desert* (1891), there is also a bandstand, and a puppet theatre.

Facing the south side of the park, spread over about a kilometre along Blvd Jourdan, is the **Cité Internationale Universitaire**, founded in 1922 on the site of the 19th-century Thiers fortifications to provide accommodation for about 6,000 students in a park-like setting. This area is worth exploring for examples of 20th-century architecture among the 39 national halls of residence (1922–2005), designed to evoke national characteristics in a wide spectrum of styles. The Maison Internationale (1936) was financed by John D. Rockefeller. The most innovative building of the time was Le Corbusier's sleek Swiss Hall (1930–32) introducing revolutionary new elements, including the pilotis or piers which support it above the ground. A later example of Le Corbusier's work, in conjunction with Lúcio Costa, is the partly painted, exposed-concrete, brutalist Brazilian Hall (1952). Other important buildings are the Japanese pavilion, designed by P. Sardou; the Dutch Hall, by M. Dudok (1927); and the Fondation Avicenne (1966–68), typical of French architecture of the late 1960s.

LES INVALIDES

The spacious avenues west of Faubourg St-Germain are dominated by the magnificent building of Les Invalides, unmistakable from its gilded dome which announces the burial place of Napoleon. On the south side of Les Invalides is the Jardin de l'Intendant, a fine formal garden based on plans by Robert de Cotte but carried out only in 1980. It is organised around a large pool and the borders are punctuated by cone-shaped yews; the architect Jules Hardouin-Mansart (1646–1708) is remembered in a 19th-century statue. The grandest approach to the sweeping panorama of Les Invalides at the end of its esplanade is from the ornate Pont Alexandre-III (*see p. 219*). As well as the Eglise St-Louis and Dôme des Invalides (with the tomb of Napoleon), the huge complex encompasses several important museums.

HOTEL DES INVALIDES
Map p. 474, A2

Open Apr–Sept 10–6; Oct–March 10–5; closed first Mon of month; T: 01 44 42 37 72.
The Hôtel des Invalides, covering 13 hectares, is the headquarters of the Military Governor of Paris. Founded by Louis XIV as a home for disabled and old soldiers, it was the first enduring institution of its kind, it encouraged recruitment to the king's army and at one time housed between 4,000 and 6,000 pensioners or *invalides*. Today, some 80 war veterans are accommodated here.

HISTORY OF THE HOTEL DES INVALIDES

The majestic ensemble is based on designs by Libéral Bruant, which included the church of St-Louis. Work began in 1671 and, after Bruant's death in 1697 was carried on by the great nephew of François Mansart and master of Parisian Baroque, J. Hardouin-Mansart, responsible for the Eglise du Dôme. So revolutionary was the idea of the *hôtel* that foreign monarchs came to visit. Peter the Great of Russia even chose to stay here. Restoration work was carried out under Napoleon, who was later buried beneath its dome. Between the Esplanade and Les Invalides are fortifications in the style of the king's engineer and designer of fortifications, Maréchal de France Vauban (1633–1707), with ditch and bossed walls. Facing out are two artillery batteries, the unmounted Batterie Trophée, and the Batterie Triomphale, whose salvoes announced victory at the end of the First World War. The Batterie Triomphale was removed by the Germans in 1940. Made for Frederick the Great in 1708, these pieces were captured in Vienna by Napoleon in 1805.

The interior of the Dôme des Invalides sheltering the tomb of Napoleon.

The main entrance

The dignified north façade is 200m long and four storeys high, with a pavilion at each end surmounted by stone trophies and flags. The remaining decoration is concentrated in the attic storey around the dormer windows. Flanking the main entrance are copies of the original statues of Mars and Minerva by Guillaume Coustou (1735). Above the central door, the equestrian bas-reliefs of Louis XIV accompanied by Justice and Prudence, replaced in 1815 the original designed by Coustou that was destroyed during the Revolution. The entrance leads to the vast Cour d'Honneur (102m by 64m) with 60 sculpted dormer windows and sundials. Either side are entrances to the Musée de l'Armée and opposite is the door of the church of St-Louis, above which stands Seurre's original bronze statue of Napoleon, which formerly topped the Vendôme Column (*see p. 239*), and an astronomical clock (1781).

EGLISE SAINT-LOUIS

The Eglise St-Louis (the chapel of Les Invalides or Soldiers' Church) was built c. 1679–1708 by Bruant and Hardouin-Mansart. The bare interior, with a gallery built at the same level as the dormitories of the disabled, is hung with captured regimental colours. In 1837 it resounded to the first performance of Berlioz's *Grande Messe des Morts*. The organ (1679–87) is by Alexandre Thierry, with a case possibly designed by Hardouin-Mansart. A sheet of plain glass behind the high altar separates the chapel from the very different Dôme des Invalides, where all is pomp and ceremony. There are memorials to those who fell on the field of battle and the coffin and pall used in the translation of Napoleon's remains in 1840. The graves of numerous French marshals and generals lie in vaults below (*no admission*). Outside is one of the legendary Renault cars or 'Marne taxis' which, commandeered by Général Gallieni, carried troops to the Marne Front in September 1914, so saving Paris from the advancing Germans.

Dôme des Invalides

The Dôme des Invalides, begun by J. Hardouin-Mansart in 1677 and finished in 1706, was added to the church of St-Louis as a chapel royal. In the niches on either side of the entrance are statues of Charlemagne and St Louis by Coysevox and Nicolas Coustou. The ribbed dome, the most splendid in France, is roofed with lead and stands on a balustraded base and attic storey. In each bay are trophies, regilded in 1989 with 12kg of gold, and it is crowned with a lantern and short spire rising to a height of 107m. The interior of the dome is decorated with allegorical paintings (1705) on the theme of *St Louis Presenting his Arms to Christ* by one of Le Brun's most talented disciples, Charles de la Fosse (1636–1716), who also worked at Versailles (*see p. 379*). The artist was recalled to Paris by Hardouin-Mansart from London, where King William III had been hoping that he would decorate Hampton Court Palace.

The 56 metre-square interior is in the form of a Greek cross with an ornate Baroque decoration of paintings, sculpture and mosaic paving. The main altar has a mid 19th-century baldaquin and there are paintings by N. Coypel in the vault. The chapels on the upper level, going in an anti-clockwise direction from the right of the entrance, contain the tombs (some enshrining only hearts) of Joseph Bonaparte (d. 1844); Vauban (d. 1707), with a tomb of 1847 by Antoine Etex; Ferdinand Foch, Marshal of France (d. 1929), by Landowski; Lyautey, soldier and colonial administrator (d. 1934), by Albert Laprade; La Tour d'Auvergne (d. 1800), the first grenadier of the Republic; and Turenne, soldier (d. 1675), first buried at St-Denis, his remains were saved from destruction, and his tomb is by Le Brun and Tuby with others. The last chapel, St-Jérome, stands empty. Relics of the 'King of Rome', the Duke of Reichstadt (1811–32), Bonaparte's only son, who died prematurely of tuberculosis and was originally buried in Vienna, were brought here by the Germans in 1940, but since 1969 have lain in the vaults of the crypt.

The Tomb of Napoleon

As you approach the circular gallery under the dome the seriously imposing Tomb of Napoleon, designed by Visconti, comes into view below. The Emperor's remains were placed here in April 1861, 40 years after his death on St Helena. They were brought to Les Invalides in December 1840 and lay in the Chapel St-Jérome while the sarcophagus was being prepared. Steps descend to the crypt where the proportions (4m by 2m and 4.5m high) and colours (dark red Finnish porphyry and green Vosges granite) make their full impact. The inscription at the entrance is taken from Napoleon's will: *Je désire que mes cendres reposent sur les bords de la Seine, au milieu de ce peuple français que j'ai tant aimé* ('I desire that my mortal remains should rest on the banks of the Seine, in the midst of the French people whom I have loved so dearly'). The sarcophagus is surrounded by a gallery with ten bas-reliefs after Pierre-Charles Simart (1806–57) representing the benefits conferred on France by the Emperor. Facing the sarcophagus are 12 figures by Pradier symbolising his greater victories, between which are six trophies of colours taken at Austerlitz. The statue *Napoleon in his Coronation Robes* is by Simart himself.

MUSEE DE L'ARMEE

The Musée de l'Armée comprises a vast collection of arms and armour, weapons, uniforms and military souvenirs up to the 20th century. The building also houses the Musée des Plans-Reliefs (see *p. 115 below*), a library and a small cinema. The collections of ancient arms and armour are among the best in Europe, with examples of all periods from the 13th to the 17th centuries. There are very impressive thematic displays of armour produced in the great workshops of the 16th century including suits used for jousting and tournaments, and weapons used for hunting. Many of them are masterpieces in the techniques of damascening and chasing, and there are diminutive 'sample' suits. The earliest pieces date from before the 9th century and the Pauilhac Collection contains the only remaining example of a 16th-century French painted harness. There is also an outstanding collection of firearms and suits of armour which belonged to Henri III, Louis XIII, Henri IV and Louis XIV and to their private armies. And there are also displays of Oriental arms and armour from Turkey, Persia, India and

China. Among individual helmets of interest is that of the Ottoman Sultan Bajazet II (1447–1512). On the exterior walls of the Cour d'Angoulème (north) is the Danube Chain, which the Turks used to hold their vessels in position during the Siege of Vienna in 1683. La Galerie de l'Arsenal recaptures the atmosphere of arsenals of the past.

Revolution and Empire: This collection extends from 1789 to the end of the Commune in 1871. There are sections concentrating on the Revolutionary, Directory and Consulate periods, with numerous Napoleonic souvenirs, including the order of the Légion d'Honneur, one of Bonaparte's grey coats, his hats, tent and furniture and the stuffed skin of his white horse, Vizir, which outlived the Emperor by eight years. Other displays show Napoleon at St Helena, and the period 1830–52 under the July Monarchy and Second Republic. Sections are devoted to the Crimean War (1854–56), the Second Empire and Franco-Prussian War of 1870, with early photographs, and paintings by Alphonse de Neuville and Edouard Detaille.

Artillery: The Artillery Department brings together huge canons and small firearms. There is also a section devoted to regimental and national emblems, standards, pennants and colours, including those of the Irish Clancarthy regiment (1642). A remarkable collection of around 150,000 historic toy soldiers from the 18th to the mid-20th centuries has been undergoing restoration and identification since 1987, made of lead, tin, cardboard or paper. The 18th-century examples in card represent cavaliers of the Maison du Roi, and others from Strasbourg are of Napoleon's troops and allies in military parade formation. The print room contains works on paper from the second half of the 16th century through to the end of the 20th, with paintings, sculptures, drawings and prints. The museum also contains a relief floor plan of the Hôtel des Invalides before 1757 and macabre curiosities such as the cannon-ball that killed Turenne in 1675 and the perforated back-plate of his cuirass.

Contemporary: This period spans the decades following the Franco-Prussian war of 1870–71, through the World Wars of 1914–18 and 1939–45, up to the V2 missiles and Atomic bomb. Illustrative records include documents of propaganda, maps and photos, as well as uniforms and scale models. The battle of the Pacific and the African campaigns are also covered, with films describing the movements of troops during the principal campaigns. There is an important section dedicated to General de Gaulle. Occupied France and the sad history of deportations are recorded, as are the Normandy Landings and France during the Liberation.

MUSEE DES PLANS-RELIEFS

The autonomous Musée des Plans-Reliefs on the attic floor is a fascinating collection of some 100 relief models of fortified sites, built to the scale 1:600, which were created for practical military purposes. Begun from 1668 onwards, at the time of Vauban, the practice ended after the Franco-Prussian War (1870–71). The original idea is attributed to Louvois (1641–91), Louis XIV's minister of war. Secreted until 1776 in the Louvre, they were then moved to Les Invalides. The display is divided between fortifications along the Channel, the Atlantic and Mediterranean coasts and the Pyrenees.

MUSEE DE L'ORDRE DE LA LIBERATION ET DU GENERAL DE GAULLE

The Musée de l'Ordre de la Libération et du Général de Gaulle is in the Robert de Cotte wing, headquarters of the Chancellerie de l'Ordre (entrance 15bis Blvd Latour-Maubourg). It is a repository of memorabilia connected with the fighters for France Libre and the Resistance, between 18th June 1940 and 8th May 1945. It is also a memorial to the 1,036 companions who received the Cross of the Liberation created by de Gaulle in 1940 and to those deported. In six rooms are 3,700 objects and documents.

ESPLANADE DES INVALIDES

Esplanade des Invalides, between Place des Invalides and the Seine, was laid out in 1704–20 by Robert de Cotte, who became in 1709 *premier architecte* (1709) to the Crown. The esplanade was planted with rows of elms but a gradual deterioration led, in 1978, to the replanting of the whole area with lawns and scented lime trees. To the west, Quai d'Orsay extends as far as Pont de l'Alma. The Gare des Invalides (1900), adapted in 1945 as the Air France Aérogare is the terminus for shuttle buses from Orly airport. At no. 65 on the quay is the neo-Gothic American Church in Paris (1927–31).

MUSEE RODIN
Map p. 474, B2

Open April–Sept 9.30–5.45, garden until 6.45; Oct–March 9.30–4.45, garden until 5; closed Mon; T: 01 44 18 61 10. Free first Sunday of month; garden café open March–Sept. Towards the end of his life, Auguste Rodin (1840–1917) worked for nine years in the Hôtel Biron, between Blvd des Invalides and Rue de Varenne. The mansion at 79 Rue de Varenne and its garden are now the Musée Rodin, the most popular museum in Paris dedicated to a single artist, containing works donated to the state by Rodin in 1916. The collection includes many original marbles and bronzes, plaster casts, maquettes, and 6,000 drawings and watercolours. Also his personal collection of art, antiquities and furniture, together with some 8,000 old photographs associated with the sculptor.

History of the Musée Rodin
Built 1728–30 by Jean Aubert to designs by Jacques-Ange Gabriel (1698–1782), the mansion was purchased by Gontaut, Duc de Biron, Governor of Languedoc, in 1753, who held sumptuous receptions here. In 1820 the Duchess of Charost, widow of the last owner, sold it to a religious community, les Dames du Sacré-Coeur de Jésus,

which was expelled in 1904. Their chapel of 1876 was built using the proceeds of the sale of painted and gilt panelling from the Hôtel Biron, some of which has been recovered or replaced. From 1908 Rodin rented a studio in the *hôtel* alongside other artists and writers including the Austrian Symbolist poet Rainer Maria Rilke (1875–1926), his secretary at that time. The sculptor gradually occupied more rooms and worked here until his death. The chapel has been adapted to make an improved space for temporary exhibitions and a new ticket office and boutique opened in 2005.

MEMORIAL TO HONORE DE BALZAC

In 1891 Rodin was commissioned to undertake the memorial to the eminent novelist Honoré de Balzac (1799–1850) by a committee presided over by Emile Zola. Balzac was an Olympian figure but did not have a Herculean physique. Rodin sought a way of describing the man within through multiple studies, but a version of Balzac in 1893, naked and ugly, was rejected. In 1898 the final draped figure was derided at the Salon and considered a travesty of the literary giant. Among Rodin's supporters were the sculptors Maillol (*see p. 122*) and Bourdelle (*see p. 108*). The statue was finally purchased for the city of Paris by public subscription. It stands in Montparnasse (*see p. 108*) as a monument to creative genius and is now considered one of Rodin's major achievements for its psychological insight and relative simplification. Among the preparatory works for the monument in the museum are both clothed (*pictured above*) and unclothed versions of Balzac.

The collections

Nearly 500 of Rodin's sculptures are on show in the museum, from early seminal works to his best-known masterpieces, grouped chronologically and thematically. Rodin opened new vistas in sculpture, which had stagnated in the 19th century, in much the same way as the Impressionists did in painting, although he was not as vigorously criticised. In fact by 1900 he was widely acclaimed. He trained as a sculptor-decorator for façades and to his great regret was rejected three times by the Ecole des Beaux-Arts. Throughout his career the major commissions were not always arrived at with any degree of ease. His technique was to model in clay—he was not a carver. Numerous assistants or *practiciens* copied the clays in plaster, from which bronzes were cast; others carved the marbles under the master's supervision. Scattered through the museum are the antiques that he collected from dealers who specialised in job lots for sculptors, and from which he drew inspiration. They range from Egyptian, Chinese and Indian to medieval European pieces. He greatly admired Michelangelo.

The gardens behind the house, which can be visited independently, were remodelled in 1993. The formal layout, which is flanked by mature trees, frames to advantage the elegant south façade of the *hôtel*. Scattered around are more Rodin works, including *Whistler's Muse*, *Cybele*, and statues of painters Bastien Lepage and Claude Lorrain; in the pool is *Ugolino and his Children*.

THE GATES OF HELL

The result of a commission of 1880 for the entrance to a new Musée des Arts Decoratifs (which never materialised), *The Gates of Hell* were based on Lorenzo Ghiberti's *Gates of Paradise* (1403–24) for the Bapistry in ·Florence, and the iconography on Dante Alighieri's *Divine Comedy* (1308–21) and Michelangelo's *Last Judgement* (1535–41) in the Sistine Chapel, Rome. Rodin modelled each figure separately in clay, experimenting with the composition on a wooden door frame. In the swirling cascade of the final version many figures are illegible and even faceless; some that stand out include the Three Shades at the entrance to Hell, the Thinker (who is Dante), two Falling Men, Ugolino, Paolo and Francesca and The Prodigal (slightly amended in *Fugit Amor*). Rodin described this project as his 'Noah's Ark' of inventions, as it provided him with an endless source of motifs which he re-used, in part or whole, in different positions, alone or in groups, amplified or reduced. The collection contains many examples: *The Thinker* in the garden, and the *Three Shades* on the staircase. The gates were cast only in 1926 and have stood in the forecourt of the Hôtel Biron since 1939.

The museum

The opening rooms contain portrait busts of Rodin by Bourdelle and others, and examples of the pretty potboilers Rodin produced to make a living. His first work accepted at the Salon was *The Man with the Broken Nose* in 1878. *The Age of Bronze* (1876–77) was Rodin's first freestanding figure and caused controversy at the time as it was erroneously reputed to have been cast from a living figure. In the late 1870s he systematically removed anything superfluous or distracting from his figures—the lance from the *Age of Bronze* or the cross from *St John the Baptist Preaching*—anything that added too

Detail from the *Gates of Hell* (1926) in the forecourt of the Musée Rodin.

precise an explanation. He would often reassemble anatomical elements from one work to create another: St John's vigorous legs became *The Walking Man* (1877–78); or reinterpret fragments of figures: *The Hand of God* is a blow-up of a hand from *The Burghers of Calais*. Sculptures of couples include *Paolo and Francesca*, the basis for *The Kiss* (1888). He also created a technique based on Michelangelo's unfinished works, although in this case the works were brought to a state of perfection, where a highly polished figure emerges from rough hewn marble or stone. Rodin's compositions modelled on Camille Claudel (*see p. 39*) include *La France* and *l'Aurore*. Works by Claudel herself which express her sensitivity and skill, are the bronze *L'Age Mûr* (1898), the onyx *Gossips* (1897), and *The Wave* (1897–1902) in onyx and bronze. Rodin sculpted many men, but he adored women and they were attracted to him. He made many female portraits some of which, like *Eve*, are symbolic. His affairs were legion, yet he married Rose Beuret, the mother of his son and life-long companion, just before her death. Both Rodin and Claudel were skilled draftsmen, and the museum's collection of works on paper are shown in rotation. Among Rodin's personal art collection are three glorious works by Van Gogh, a female nude by Renoir and a Monet landscape. There is an annexe to the museum at Meudon, Rodin's home (*see p. 370*).

THE BURGHERS OF CALAIS

This work was designed to commemorate an act of civic heroism in 1347 following a long siege by the English. It represents the group of six notables who elected to sacrifice themselves to Edward III in return for cessation of hostilities. In the event, so impressed was the king by their bravery that they, and the city, were spared. To commemorate this heroic act in the 19th century, the town commissioned a monument. The committee visualised something rather staid and allegorical in the style of the period. Rodin's conception, however, was based on the description of the event by the 14th-century chronicler Froissart. His ideas evolved as he worked on maquettes from 1884–89. The uncompromising realism was met with outrage, infuriating Rodin who considered his creativity compromised. Funding was slow and installation delayed until 1895. There followed disagreement on Rodin's outlandish suggestions for the plinth, either at ground level, or on a 4m high scaffold. The tomb-shaped compromise displeased Rodin. In the event though he had his way and the final version is a deeply moving portrait of six rugged men preparing to meet their death, huddled, heavy and agonised, expressing emotions of resignation, fear or despair. Two men, linked by their torment and by the ropes around their necks, carry the keys of the gates of Calais. The composition encourages the viewer to walk around the group. Some ten versions of the *Burghers* exist, including a cast of 1911 in Victoria Tower Gardens next to the Palace of Westminster in London. Room 10 in the Museum contains studies for the work.

RUE DE VARENNE & RUE DE GRENELLE
Map p. 474, B2

Streets such as Rue St-Dominique, Rue de Grenelle and Rue de Varenne—the latter two both deriving their names from *garenne*, or uncultivated land—have more examples of these fashionable and handsome 17th–19th-century *hôtels particuliers* in which the former elegance of Faubourg St-Germain is still apparent. Rue de Varenne opened in c. 1605. Just east of the Musée Rodin is one of the most beautiful *hôtels* in the faubourg, the Hôtel de Matignon (no. 57), graced with an unusually large garden. Built in 1721 and altered later, since 1935 it has been the residence of the *Président du Conseil* (Prime Minister). At no. 53, Edith Wharton, the American writer, spent 'rich years, crowded and happy…' from 1910–20. The Hôtel de Gallifet (no. 50) built 1775–96, is the Italian Institute and their embassy is at no. 47. The section of Rue du Bac (*see p. 92*), between Rue de Varenne and Rue de Sèvres is equally endowed. Rue du Bac meets Rue de Sevres at the only department store on the Left Bank, the elegant Bon Marché, with an excellent food hall.

Futher southwest, on Rue du Cherche-Midi, at no. 85, the Hôtel de Montmorency-Bours (1743) is an aristocratic mansion typical of the second half of the 19th century and the world of Proust, and contains the Musée Hébert (*see p. 420*). It was the home of Ernest Hébert, cousin of the writer Stendhal. Hébert was a painter of Italian landscapes and society portraits. Also on this street, at no. 8 is Boulangerie Poilâne, where the successful brown loaves were first baked. The bread is sold, but no longer made, here.

Rue de Grenelle was once a street of numerous embassies and ministries, but many have now moved out. The *Fontaine des Quatre-Saisons*, 57–59 Rue de Grenelle, the work of Bouchardon in 1739, is an exedral façade designed to maximize the limited space in this narrow street (Voltaire was critical of the choice of site) on a grand scale. Its objective was to feed the water supply of the quarter. The sculptures on the main section represent the City of Paris with the Seine and Marne at her feet, and there are bas-reliefs of the Seasons on the wings. The land once belonged to the Couvent des Récollets, and the poet and dramatist Alfred de Musset (1810–57) lived at no. 59 from 1824 to 1840. In the 20th century, jazz enthusiasts frequented the Cabaret de la Fontaine des Quatre Saisons. The building is now home to the Musée Maillol (*see below*). No. 127, the Hôtel du Chatelet, is one of the finest examples of the Louis-XV style, and was used as the Archbishop's Palace in 1849–1906.

MUSEE MAILLOL
Map p. 474, C2

Open Wed–Mon 11–6, closed Tues and public holidays; T: 01 42 22 59 58.
The Fondation Dina Vierny endowed the building at 59–61 Rue de Grenelle with the Musée Maillol which opened in 1995. Dina Vierny met Aristide Maillol (1861–1944; *see box overleaf*) in 1934, when she was 15 and he 73. In her Maillol recognised the

ideal figure he had been modelling all his life. Their association lasted for ten years, during which Vierny began collecting. She opened a gallery in St-Germain-des-Prés after the war and, as a native of Russia, launched avant-garde Russian artists such as Poliakoff. In 1964 she created the Foundation and the concept of the museum developed over 15 years with the skilful adaptation of the old buildings. The visit starts on the site of an old *poissonnerie*. Dina Vierny gave 18 of Maillol's bronzes to the Louvre in 1964–65, now in the Tuileries, and two more in 2001 to the Espace Tuileries.

Aristide Maillol (1861–1944)
Maillol rose to prominence as a sculptor in the early years of the 20th century with his first one-man exhibition at the Galerie Vollard, Paris, and the conspicuously good reception of *La Méditerranée* at the Salon d'Automne in 1905. He had turned to sculpture because of eye strain caused by working on tapestries. Maillol was a southerner, from Banuyls close to the Mediterranean border with Spain. Heavily influenced by Gauguin and the Nabis, but not strictly part of the group, he studied at the Beaux-Arts in Paris from 1887, but left in 1890 impatient with the outdated advice of Cabanel and Gérôme. The example of Gauguin, who remained a constant influence, and Emile Bernard, led him to experiment with pottery, wood-carving and painting, as well as decorative arts. His success in tapestry design was based heavily on the flat patterning and colours of the Nabis. By 1896 he abandoned tapestry weaving, and transferred his characteristic pure designs to sculpture. He restricted his output to reassuringly solid female nudes, refined and simplified, close to Renoir's late nude paintings. They present a timeless image, stripped of psychological insight, in contrast to Rodin's expressionistic work (*see p. 117*). Maillol's 'art for art's sake' condensations of form place him in an important position between the 19th century and Modernism.

The collections

Maillol's monumental works occupy a gallery with exposed original timbers. Among them is *La Rivière* (1938–43), and versions of those exhibited in the Tuileries. A spiral staircase takes you to the upper floor, to rooms mainly devoted to different aspects of Maillol's work. The first room contains the bronze sculpture, *La Méditerranée* (1902–05), pensive and serene, which established him among the great Modern sculptors. A painter initially, his works in crayon, pastel, chalk and charcoal and paintings in oils are exhibited in the upper rooms, and include *Portrait of Dina* (1940) and *Dina with a Scarf* (1941). Examples of Maillol's diverse talents—ceramics, wood and stone carvings—are often displayed including earlier works such as the Impressionistic painting, *Seated Woman with Sunshade* (1895), and tapestry designs. And in a bright white space are nine bronzes of between 1900 and 1931 including *Pomone* (1910).

Dina Vierny's collection of modern and contemporary art is included in the museum. Works by artists from whom Maillol drew inspiration include Renoir, Maurice Denis, as well as Gauguin, represented here with carvings and watercolours. There is also a gallery of Matisse drawings; and drawings and watercolours by Dufy.

The collection includes a vast number of drawings which are exhibited in the intimate setting of an 18th-century panelled room. They include *Noir* by Odilon Redon, and prints by Degas, Picasso, Bonnard, Ingres, Cézanne, Suzanne Valadon, Foujita, and others. Vierny was an early supporter of naïve artists, here represented by Douanier Rousseau, Louis Vivin and Camille Bombois among others. The collection also brings together works by each of the Duchamp brothers: Marcel Duchamp, one of the original Dadaists; Raymond Duchamp-Villon, who died of typhoid fever during the First World War; and the cubist Jacques Villon.

Russian non-figurative art includes works by Poliakoff, Kandinsky, Charchoune, Boulatov, Yankilevski and Oscar Rabin, and the Constructivist Jean Pougny. Ilya Kabakov, one of the first proponents of Installations, built for the museum *The Communal Kitchen* which is located below the ground floor.

QUAI BRANLY
& THE EIFFEL TOWER

MUSEE DU QUAI BRANLY
Map p. 473, E1

Open Tues–Sun 10–6.30, Thur 10–9.30, closed Mon; T: 01 56 61 70 00; reservations T: 01 56 61 71 72; www.quaibranly.fr. Enter from Quai Branly or from Rue de l'Université; ticket office beneath the building; bookshop and restaurant Les Ombres (T: 01 47 53 68 00) at garden level. A footbridge, Passerelle Debilly, links Quai Branly to the Right Bank across the river.
The new museum of ethnography and ethnology on the banks of the Seine at Quai Branly, between Pont d'Alma and the Eiffel Tower, opened in June 2006. The project was announced by President Chirac in 1995; in 2000 a flagship collection was deposited at the Louvre (*see p. 140*), and work started on Quai Branly in 2001.

The building
Eye-catching and ingenious, this is architect Jean Nouvel's most revolutionary work to date. A horizontal, undulating edifice on stilts, it is a darkly colourful building with earth-coloured cubes containing small exhibition spaces jutting out from the Seine façade. The museum emerges from sloping gardens, with a *mur végétal* or 'plant wall' covering part of the administrative section. Protecting the site from the noise of the traffic on the quays is a high transparent screen. Aboriginal artists have decorated the ceiling of the boutique. Tickets are sold under the building, and in the large entrance hall is the first object, a large totem pole. A ramp winds upwards around a glass tower stretching the full height of the building, containing the reserves of musical instruments. The main floor is wreathed in dramatic obscurity (partly for conservation purposes) and the exhibition space flows freely from one section to the next around a central 'river', in no specific sequence, dispelling any notion of a hierarchy of cultures. Each section is introduced by a representative group of objects. On the south side, in the Asian and Africa sectors, some 30 'boxes' contain special exhibits, and two boxes at each end of the building are reserved for music. The two spaces on the upper levels are dedicated to temporary exhibitions. Although the individual captions for each object are not always easy to read, information is widely diffused through audio guides, maps, texts, pictures, and interactive multimedia installations.

The collections
The Musée du Quai Branly is devoted to non-European arts and civilisations, namely Oceania, Africa, Asia, and the Americas. The objective is to illustrate the lifestyle of cultural and ethnic groups through the objects associated with them. The core of the collection comes from the Musée de l'Homme and the Musée National des Arts d'Afrique et d'Océanie. Of the 300,000 objects in the collection, some 3,500 objects are on permanent exhibition. The majority date from the 19th or 20th centuries, but

follow the tradition of their cultural heritage. A particular emphasis is put on recent Australian aboriginal art. The museum is also a research and education centre, with a media library open to the general public. Other activities include theatre, music, dance, cinema and talks.

Oceania

Melanesia: The objects from several islands of Melanesia, in the Southern Pacific, demonstrate not only the differences but also the similarities in cultures divided by great distances. Important in these cultures is ancestor worship. From Papua New Guinea and West Guinea are ceremonial house posts, roof sculptures and masks associated with the ancestor house; ancestor skulls are preserved and transformed with seeds and feathers while carved headrests establish a personal link between owner and ancestors. Objects which are used in male initiation rites range from secret musical instruments to a Bisj pole carved from new wood following ritual murder. The canoe and canoe sheds held a special role in the Solomon Islands in relation to head-hunting practised until the end of the 19th century. Reliquaries, some taking the form of a dug-out canoe, were beautifully carved for the remains of chiefs. The many and varied symbols of hierarchy might include a finely carved wooden dish or a disturbing Rambaramp funerary effigy with the remodelled features of the deceased's skull.

Masks cover a great diversity of forms, both animal or human. Some represent just one element of a costume, some cover the whole head or just the face, and others are not worn. Made from a combination of materials, most are painted, and each is linked to key points in public, spiritual or political life. Hemlour masks of the Sulka people, New Britain, are rare as they are normally burned at the end of a ceremony. Decorated Tapa cloth, made from beaten bark, is found throughout Oceania, in particular in Melanesia and Polynesia. Made by women, there is evidence of its use in clothing both mortals and gods.

Polynesia: This section gives an insight into the relations between man and his gods. Figurative or abstract, divine receptacles were used as containers for the breath of gods and ancestors, and placed on ceremonial platforms. Sacred materials enhanced the spirituality of these images. In Tahiti these are red feathers; in the Cook Islands stick gods come to life when covered with feathers and bark cloth; in the Fiji Islands coconut fibres cover miniatures of houses to attract spirits. Tiki, who begat the first human beings, is the most important god. Images of divinities are made in lasting materials so that they can be handed down. The refinement of body art, permanent or ephemeral, continues this relationship with the divine. Tatooing was carried out on girls from the ages of 8 to 10, and on boys at 15, starting on the face, and continuing in stages. Equal elegance is found in insignia of rank, notably the dishes for *kava*, the ceremonial drink. Other emblems of prestige might include a decorated club in blackened hard wood in the Marquesas or a finely inlaid head-rest in Fiji where the head could not be touched without permission. Art from the Maoris of New Zealand demonstrates their superb skill in carving, such as the Korere feeding funnel used during painful facial tattooing, and a Hei Tiki jade pendant.

Australia: The section devoted to Australia concentrates on vital, contemporary Aboriginal art from Northern and Western Australia. This is based on an adaptation of ancient forms which is the plastic expression of 'Dreaming', which refers to all that is known and all that is understood according to the Aboriginal explanation of life and is central to their existence. A modern version of sacred or body decoration has developed into acrylic paintings consisting of brilliant dots, straight or curved lines and circles. A series of shields and spear-throwers, whose motifs are connected with the modern works, are exhibited nearby. The Bark Chamber contains eucalyptus bark paintings using natural pigments, from Arnhem Land, Northern Australia, that elaborate on motifs of rock painting, both abstract and representational.

Insulindia: Exhibits from Insulindia, an archipelago of around 20,000 islands, including Indonesia, Malaysia and the Philippines, highlight the wide cultural and ethnic diversity of this region which forms a crossroads between continental South-East Asia and Oceania. The pre-history and protohistory of Insulindia is presented through recurring forms of metal artefacts and decorative items fashioned from gold, silver, brass and other alloys; megalithism in Sumba, Sumatra and Nias where ceremonial seats of honour were carved in the form of mythical animals. The spread of the Dong Son civilisation from China to Insulindia is represented by bronze drums traditionally buried with their owner and include a 4th–1st century BC Dongsonian drum from Java. The largest example of a bronze funeral drum is from Vietnam (18th–19th centuries).

Asia

The collections from the Asian continent cover a geographic area from Siberia to the Middle East, but the greatest number and variety of objects are from Southeast Asia, the former territories of French Indo-China. The objects are arranged thematically focusing on specific themes through representative items. These themes include village and minority cultures, popular religion, and communities living by oral tradition, in recent and even contemporary contexts. The survival of Shamanism in Siberia, for example, is evoked by a leather-fringed costume and headdress with metal antlers.

Costumes and textiles: The backbone of the section is a colourful array of costumes and textiles representing the diversity of lifestyles, cultures and climates on the Asian continent along with the cross-fertilisation of cultures. The collection illustrates the ways in which raw materials, techniques of weaving and sewing, dyes and decorative elements, are applied in individual communities. In Russia and far eastern Siberia, birch-tree bark is a basic raw material, as is reindeer hide; a bride's coat from Nivkh is made from fish skin and embroidered with a bear-head design for protection against evil spirits. Costumes play a major role in art and symbolism, and in exchange and movement, and the role of women and girls is highly developed in association with textiles, dress and adornment in many Asian communities. Some 300 examples of textiles and jewellery represent the minority Miao groups who migrated to the Southeast Asian peninsula. The largest ethnic group, who speak the Tai languages, is represented by many different weaving techniques including *Ikat*, where the thread goes through a tie-and-dye process. The most elaborate jackets were embroidered in Laos from memory, taking nearly a year to complete. The beautifully decorated Akha bonnet worn by the Yao and Tibeto-Burmese indicates age group, from birth to old age. According to Hindu ideology, flat lengths of cloth are used for the sari in India, but the costumes of Northwestern India and Pakistan were influenced by the Mughal Empire. The identifying dress of Western Asian civilisations includes face veils which go back to c. 1000; the Assyrians were the first to insist that married women cover their heads outside the home and this custom spread to Greece and Rome. It was adopted successively by Judaism, by Christianity for women at prayer, and by Islam as a sacred duty. An elaborate Burqa face veil from Gaza displays the wearer's wealth in the form of coins, silver, cornelian and agate.

Aboriginal *mimi* men painted on eucalyptus bark (1963) by the Gunwiggu tribe from Arnhem Land, Northern Australia, in the Musée Branly.

Southeast Asia: The agricultural communities of Southeast Asia live in close harmony with nature. Early 20th-century artefacts provide information on these civilisations such as a decorative mask from Myanmar for the lead bull in a caravan, or the machete essential for survival in the central highlands of Indochina, and an elaborate naga snake sickle from Cambodia. Religious practises included Buddhism in the plains, but did not reach the mountain people who believed in a multiplicity of spirits involving rituals in which tomb sculptures, such as the wooden image of a seated *bram* (from Vietnam) were carved. Beliefs among ethnic groups of the Himalayas are represented by an 11th-century Shâkyaumini Buddha and a Nepalese anthropomorphic mask in wood with goat's hair, thought to represent a forest spirit.

Central Asia: The two nomadic populations of Central Asia were Indo-Iranians who lived in goatskin tents and travelled on foot; and Turko-Mongolian yurt dwellers, who followed their stock on horseback. In these societies, jewellery and harnesses, such as the horse's saddle from Uzbekistan, acquired more value than coins. Felt, an ancient fabric made with layer upon layer of compacted fleece, is widely used as waterproof or protective clothing.

Africa

Nearly 1,000 works are on display in this section, from sub-Saharan and North Africa to the South and East. The department opens with the huge megalithic Lyre stone (1000 BC–AD 1000) from West Africa. The displays are by region and by three main themes: textiles, musical instruments, and sculpted representations of the body. The 'boxes' on the north wall each address a particular thematic or cultural focus. Interaction between maker and user is important, and the objects evoke nomadic life, dancing masks, concern with the metaphysical, body ornament, and so on.

North Africa: Examples of the spread of the written word in North Africa include a 10th-century parchment extract from the *Koran*, an 11th-century illuminated page from *The Guide of Blessings*, and silver Torah Shield (18th century). Caravan routes across the Sahara from the 3rd century BC facilitated trade in salt and other produce: from the Tuareg Berber north, slaves; gold, ivory and indigo from the Negro south.

West Africa: From West Africa is the huge Megalithic stone in the form of a lyre that introduces the continent in the museum. Similar objects are found in Mali and South Nigeria. From South of Mali, in the Mande region (Guinea), remarkable masks were produced for male initiation societies, such as the N'tomo mask in wood, brass and aluminium from Malinke. Statues associated with the ancestor include a wood carving of a mother suckling a child from Cameroon, and an anthropomorphic figure from Sierra Leone. Trade with Europe developed in Coastal West Africa in the 15th century, including slaves, but also valuable commodities like ivory horns, salt cellars and spoons.

The display of musical instruments highlights the skillful use of available materials and adaptation to the circumstances, as well as the decorative aspect. Gold was invested with considerable powers, and skilled goldsmiths created objects such as the appliqué jewel in the image of two facing crocodiles, and a *Hunting Scene* used as a weight. The lost-wax technique was developed in Ghana for containers including the finely worked and modeled Kuduo offerings jar. The first known figurative sculpture in West Africa, modeled by hand with extreme skill, was produced by the ancient Nok culture (1st millennium BC) in Nigeria. The 12th–15th-century Classical period of the Ife and Benin kingdoms includes objects, sometimes horrific, associated with court traditions. A typical *Head of a royal ancestor* marks an artistic high spot during the Benin kingdom's expansion. Ethnic groups from south-west Nigeria are represented by numerous carved wooden objects including a colourful Egungun cloth mask. Communities in the Niger Delta pay homage to water spirits with masks in the shape of fish or crocodiles.

Equitorial Africa: Equitorial Africa includes many ethnic groups creating an outstanding range and variety of sculptures of the type discovered by Western artists early in the 20th century. Striking examples of Kota reliquary figures are the *Mvoudi* mask, coloured in ochres, and the *Mboumba bwete* reliquary basket. Metal objects carry the ultimate symbolic value, represented by a Ngulu reliquary guardian incorporating brass and copper. Typical of the Kongo region is the *Nkisi nkondi*, a magical male image from Angola, made of wood with iron nails embedded in it. Fertility or fecundity images of women are frequent in Kongo art, often featuring children. The Kuba from the centre of Congo claim great ancestry and participate in lengthy rites of passage to adulthood. Related objects include the *Ndeemba* or anthropomorphic mask and the *Bwooom* helmet-mask imbued with regal power.

South and East Africa: In South and East Africa similar rites and rituals to Central Africa determine many of the arts. The anthropomorphic staff signifying adulthood is representative of Zulu art, traditionally featuring a male image on the handle, and pairs of figures representing the couple. Headrests from Zimbabwe and Mozambique often have a stylised zoomorphic design. Women have long been involved in bead work, first using natural materials, but glass beads became important after they were introduced in the 19th century. Madagascar has absorbed traditions from the peoples of the Indian Ocean and Insulindia. The Malgache protect themselves against spirits and supernatural beings with an amulet or *ody*, while the talisman case, or *sampy*, attracts success.

Harter collection: Art from Cameroon, donated by Dr Pierre Harter (1928–91).

The Americas

This collection is the richest, and is divided into three sequences: America from the 17th century to the present; the thematic transversal sequence which highlights the trans-continental unity of native American people through their objects; and Pre-Columbian or Pre-Hispanic America.

Pre-Columbian America: Pre-Columbian or Pre-Hispanic America refers to the indigenous Indian populations who lived undisturbed before the 'New World' was discovered by Christopher Columbus in 1492. The archaeological collections give an overview of the countless cultures that succeeded one another over 2,500 years in the three major cultural areas: Mesoamerica (a cultural zone between the North Mexican deserts and Central America), Central America, and the Andes. Pre-Hispanic Mesoamerica was dominated by the Olmecs between 1200 and 300 BC. They were replaced by the Mayas who created even more impressively monumental sites and developed a calendar and complex writing system. They made superb ceramics, such as the spherical bowl in the shape of a deathshead from Guatemala (300–600). The El Tajín, from the Gulf of Mexico, are represented by hollow ceramic statues, while the Huastecs sculpted unusual figures in limestone such as the *Old Man leaning on a Stick*. A fragment of paving stone (800–1200) is an example of Zapotec culture. The sophisticated Teotihuacán culture (150–650) on the central Mexican plateau made terracotta objects such as the Butterfly vase with a lid, and an anthropomorphic statue carved in green rock. The Aztecs (1350–1521) dominated central Mexico and much of the Pacific coast for 150 years before the arrival of the Conquistadors. Aztec divinities such as Tlaloc, God of rain and personification of the earth, or Huizilopochtli, god of war and guiding deity, were carved in stone or green rock. The Pre-Hispanic Andes, from Colombia to northern Chile, along the Pacific coast west of the Andes, benefited from deposits of gold and silver, but also produced terracotta objects, such as the Mosquito culture funeral urn with a seated figure on the cover, and the Cauca culture statuette of a warrior seated on a bench. The small elegant metal *Pectoral* (Boyaca Highland)

was an insignia of power for the Muisca culture (1200–1500) in the central high plateau. The earliest recognised culture in Ecuador (c. 4000–3000 BC) carved in soft stone. By 500–300 BC different styles had developed, such as the Jama Coaque culture in Manabi province who produced the seated statuette of a chief or priest, with elaborate headdress and piercings.

The great civilisations of the Central Andes, notably Peru, are represented by ceramics from c. 1800 BC. Following a succession of powerful societies which dominated the area, were regional developments, such as the Moche (c. 100 BC–c. AD 700) on the north Peruvian coast who worked gold and silver, and decorated terracotta vases with scenes of humans in their environment and rituals: a vase represents a mythical fight. The Paracas produced funerary fabrics of great quality; the Nasca are identified by their polychrome terracottas; and the Recuay by a novel piece, a vase representing a warrior and a cat, the cat definitely overpowering the warrior. The Chimú kingdom (1100–1450) on the north coast of Peru, who built great sites and irrigated the desert, produced the Ceremonial gauntlet decorated with stylised human figures and birds in silver. From 1438 the Incas (1200–1500) became the largest Pre-Columbian empire, their capital at Cuzco, and encouraged the worship of their foremost god, Inti, the sun god. Examples of their craftsmanship include a Male figurine in silver with coloured inlays.

A remarkable collection of textiles from the Pre-Hispanic Andes (2000 BC–AD 1532) is mainly from burial sites in the coastal deserts of Peru and Chile, including knotted cords used by Incas for counting; materials used in the production of cloth; and examples of embroidery and weaving. Regional variation in applied decoration is highlighted, many carrying important symbolic significance. Examples from Peru in llama wool and cotton include an embroidered textile edging from the Nasca culture, Peru (100–300), and a tapestry, with a figure carried on a litter (1100–1450). Textiles and clothing made from hides and bark demonstrate the importance of colour for the American Indians, also obvious in the feather-based artefacts from the Pre-Columbian period. The collections of clothing (19th–20th centuries) covers the whole of America from Canada to Patagonia and highlights their diversity.

Pan-American Transformations: The thematic sequence Pan-American Transformations brings together artefacts which relate to common themes and myths from all over the continent and from all eras, emphasising the influence of the collective unconscious throughout the American continent. This is highlighted in anthropomorphic objects, utensils in the form of animals, weapons from as far afield as Guyana and Canada, and bead work and basket work from North and South America.

Colonial and Contemporary America (16th–21st centuries): This period saw unprecedented contact and mingling of peoples and cultures. Here is a series of feather-based artefacts from Amazonia (the low-lying lands of South America) such as a Munduruku head-dress from Brazil with neck covering made from feathers and cotton. From the North American plains is a collection of 18th-century painted hides, once belonging to French royal collections, such as a Bison dance coat, as well as a series of paintings by George Catlin, commissioned by Louis-Philippe. The Northwest Canadian coast and the Inuits who relied on seal farming are represented by walrus ivory carvings, such as a harpoon support and an Ulu woman's knife. The indigenous people of the Northwest coast participated in important ceremonies, such as *potlache*, the distribution of food and gifts to guarantee power and status, and engaged in long winter ceremonials involving masks. One such that is particularly remarkable is the articulated mask made by the Haida people. Totem poles represent native clan kinships and stood in front of houses. The art of the Indians of the Plains—Sioux, Cheyenne and Blackfoot—divides into figurative for men, and abstract for women.

EGOUTS DE PARIS
Map p. 473, E1

Open May–Sept 11–5; Oct–April 11–4; restricted entry after heavy rain; closed Thur, Fri and 2 weeks in mid-Jan; T: 01 53 68 27 81.

The Egouts de Paris (sewers), adjacent to Pont de l'Alma, opposite 93 Quai d'Orsay, are of dubious appeal but very popular, romanticised by Victor Hugo's *Les Miserables*. Paris' water system began very modestly during the 14th century with a vaulted drain which carried waste via the Ménilmontant stream into the Seine. By 1740 the Grand Egout de Ceinture had been built (it served as the route for Jean Valjean carrying Marius in *Les Miserables*). Progress on further construction was slow until Haussmann's project (*see p. 223*) which included the cleaning up of the streets of the city and providing a wider network of drains and fresh water, carried out 1857–61. Engineer Eugène Belgrand (1810–78) was in charge, and by his death 600km had been completed. Now the network stretches over 2100km. The first public visits from the Châtelet area were introduced during the Universal Exhibition of 1867, first by small cart, then by boat. Today about 200m are covered on foot, enlivened by numerous maquettes and machinery and an audiovisual display.

THE EIFFEL TOWER & CHAMP DE MARS
Map p. 473, D2

From most parts of Paris there is a view of the familiar outline of the Eiffel Tower (Tour Eiffel) which stands close to the river on Quai Branly. Its looming presence is the main focus of one of the great vistas of Paris which stretches from the Ecole Militaire down the kilometre-long gardens of the Champ de Mars and across the Seine, spanned by Pont d'Iéna, to the Palais de Chaillot (*see p. 347*). This district is now doubly worth the visit since the Musée du Quai Branly (*see above p. 124*) opened in 2006.

HISTORY OF THE CHAMP DE MARS

Between the Ecole Militaire (*see p. 134*) and the Seine, the Champ de Mars was laid out in 1765–67 as a parade ground on the market-gardens of the old Plaine de Grenelle. Several early aeronautical experiments were carried out from here by J.-P. Blanchard in 1783–84 and others. It became the theatre of the celebration to mark the first anniversary of the storming of the Bastille, the *Fête de la Fédération* (14th July 1790), and of Napoleon's *Champ de Mai* on his return from Elba. Used as a racecourse after the Restoration, the parade ground was transformed and reduced in 1860 and became the site of five universal exhibitions. In 1908, work that continued for 20 years was initiated to create the park that exists today, with central lawns, avenues of trees and less formal areas either side. There is a bandstand, marionette theatre, and other entertainment. Among the sculptures is the *Monument of the Rights of Man*, near the Rue de Belgrade (southeast) commemorating the bicentenary of the Revolution. Captain Alfred Dreyfus, a promising young Jewish artillery officer from Alsace, was publicly degraded here in December 1894, the start of the Dreyfus affair in which he was falsely accused of delivering documents concerned with the national defence to a foreign government (*see p. 20*).

THE EIFFEL TOWER

Three lifts, from the North, East and West piers, go to levels 1 and 2 (115m); for Level 3, change at Level 2 (276m). Open mid-June–Aug 9–midnight, Level 3 last departure 11; Jan–mid-June and Sept–Dec 9.30–11, Level 3 last departure 10.30. Ascent on foot daily to Level 2 only, mid-June–Aug 9–midnight; Jan–mid-June and Sept–Dec 9.30–6. There can be a long wait for the lift to Level 3 at peak times. www.tour-eiffel.fr

The Eiffel Tower is a masterpiece of 19th-century engineering. At the beginning of the 21st century, its audacious proportions (318m high including the television installation) are still breathtaking. Long an inseparable part of the Parisian landscape, it remains the most emblematic monument of the city and continues to inspire painters, poets and film makers. As well as several snack bars, there are two restaurants: the Jules Verne on Level 2 (*T: 01 45 55 61 44; direct lift*) is the giddy heights where chef Alain Reix has brought the cooking up to Michelin star standard; and Altitude 95 on Level 1 (*T: 01 45 55 20 04*) serving brasserie food priced within reason, with Zeppelin décor and great views.

HISTORY OF THE EIFFEL TOWER

Opened in 1889 for the Universal Exhibition marking the centenary of the Revolution, the Eiffel Tower aroused as much controversy then as the Pompidou Centre or the Louvre Pyramid do today. Originally granted only 20 years of life, its new use in radio-telegraphy in 1909 saved it from demolition. Erected by the contracting company owned by the engineer Gustave Eiffel (1832–1923), the tapering lattice-work tower is composed of 18,000 pieces of metal weighing over 7,000 tonnes (total weight 10,100 tonnes), while its four feet are supported by masonry piers sunk 9–14m into the ground. The design was mainly due to the engineers Maurice Koechlin and Emile Nouguier and the architect Stephen Sauvestre. It is repainted every seven years in Eiffel-Tower bronze. The colour is exclusive to the monument and almost imperceptibly changes from a lighter tone at the summit to a darker one at the base to enhance the impression of perspective.

Visiting the tower

On a clear day, particularly about one hour before sunset, the tower is the ultimate place to view Paris. On the vast Level 1 there are two lighthearted, interactive presentations called Feroscope and Cineiffel providing information on the history and technology of the structure and a laser system that measures the oscillations of the summit. The old hydraulic pump and a section of the original spiral staircase can also be seen. There's even a post office where you can get a Tour Eiffel postmark on your postcard. On Level 2 is a 'virtual tower', and information on the working of the original hydraulic elevator as well as glazed portholes for an unusual view directly to ground level. At the top level, as well as the splendid panorama of Paris, is a reconstruction of Gustave Eiffel's office.

ECOLE MILITAIRE
Map p, 473; E3

The Ecole Militaire is a handsome structure covering part of the former farm and château of Grenelle, built by J.-A. Gabriel, and enlarged in 1856. Eighteenth-century railings separate the Pl. de Fontenoy from the elegant Cour d'Honneur, profusely embellished with Corinthian columns and pilasters. The figure of Victory on the entablature is in fact modelled on Louis XV, but this seemingly went unnoticed by Revolutionary iconoclasts. Officer cadet Bonaparte was confirmed in the chapel (1768–73), which is decorated with nine paintings of the *Life of St Louis*. The school was founded in 1751 by Louis XV for the training of noblemen as army officers. Opened in 1756, it was completed in 1773. In 1777 its rigid rules for entry were modified to accept the élite of provincial military academies. Thus in 1784 Bonaparte was chosen from the Collège de Brienne. It is now a staff college training the upper echelons of the armed services.

UNESCO
Map p. 474, E3

Visits by reservation only Tues and Wed at 3; apply to UNESCO Visitors Service, 7 Pl. de Fontenoy, 75352 Paris 07 SP, T: 01 45 68 03 59/01 45 68 16 42; tucker@unesco.org Identification is required.
The main UNESCO Building, headquarters of the UN's Organisation for Education, Science and Culture, is on Place de Fontenoy. The building was designed by an international team of French and American architects, Bernard Zehrfuss and Marcel Breuer and the Italian engineer, Pier Luigi Nervi, begun in 1954 and inaugurated four years later. The number of member states of UNESCO has increased from the original 37 to 186, and its multi-national character is reflected in all aspects of its design.

The buildings
This large complex consists of three major buildings. The main part is the Y-shaped concrete and glass Secretariat on seven floors, where the Ségur façade is enlivened by an extraordinary spiral fire escape.

The square building to the west has a mosaic by Jean René Bazaine on one exterior wall, next to which is the Japanese Garden of Peace designed by Noguchi (1904–88). It contains the *Nagasaki Angel* and a cylindrical Meditation Space with a pond of granite exposed to the bombing of Hiroshima.

The Conference Building has fluted concrete walls and an accordion-pleated concrete roof covered in copper. On the vast piazza, between Avenues Lowendal and Suffren, are works by Alexander Calder, Henry Moore, Giacometti, *Symbolic Globe* (1995) by Erik Reitzel, and *Birth of a New Man* by Zurab Tsereteli, marking the 500th anniversary of the discovery of America.

VAUGIRARD
Map p. 473, E4

15 Square de Vergennes
Open Tues–Sat 12–7; T: 01 56 23 00 22.
Close to Vaugirard Metro, 15 Square de Vergennes is an interesting 1930s' house used as an exhibition centre. It was designed by Rob Mallet-Stevens (1886–1945) as a workshop and home for master glazier and engraver, Louis Barillet (1896–1987), and is the only Mallet-Stevens house that can be visited in Paris. A window the height of the building incorporates the white or opalescent 'stained' glass that Barillet invented, combined with a geometric pattern. On the third floor there is another example of Barillet's work. The building, which had been radically altered, was restored by Yvon Poullain to display the ingenious modern design work of Yonel Lebovici (1937–98). There is also a Materials Library, and regular temporary exhibitions are mounted.

PARC GEORGES-BRASSENS

Parc Georges-Brassens was laid out 1977–85 and is one of the city's most successful new gardens, named after the legendary poet-singer who lived nearby. This was the former hamlet of Vaugirard and was until the end of the 18th century an important vineyard. The vineyards became market gardens in the 19th century, and abattoirs until 1974. Some vestiges of the old buildings have been integrated into the gardens. Among the attractions of the park are a pond and fountain, aromatic and medicinal gardens, and vines.

ALONG THE SEINE

At 101bis Quai Branly, between the Eiffel Tower and Pont de Bir-Hakeim, is the **Maison de la Culture du Japon à Paris** (*open Tues–Sat 12–7, Thur to 8; closed Sun, Mon; T: 01 44 37 95 01*). Designed by Masayuki Yamanaka and inaugurated in 1997, this provides a permanent centre where Japanese culture can be presented in all its aspects through exhibitions, concerts, and other events.

Pont Bir-Hakeim, which commemorates the resistance of the Free French against Rommel in Libya in 1942, is crossed by the Metro, and from it Blvd de Grenelle leads southeast. At no. 8 a plaque records the round-up of thousands of Parisian Jews in the *vélodrome* (cycle-track) here in July 1942 before their deportation. Quai de Grenelle continues southwest past Sq. Bela Bartok, a little planted valley created in 1981 among the high-rise buildings flanking the Seine. On the opposite bank is the Maison de la Radio. Stretching between Pont de Bir-Hakeim and Pont de Grenelle is an artificial island, the **Allée des Cygnes**, with a pleasant, tree-lined walk. At the western extremity is a scale replica in bronze of Bartholdi's *Statue of Liberty* (*see p. 96*), a gift from the Parisian community in the United States in 1885 in return for the original presented by France to New York. Further still is Pont Mirabeau (1895–97), leading to Auteuil (*see p. 356*). To the southeast, at 25–35 Rue de la Convention, is the Imprimerie Nationale (founded 1640), the state printing works (*visits in French by written application one month ahead, Mon–Thur 1pm; T: 01 40 58 34 31*) which moved here in 1925 from the Hôtel de Rohan (*see p. 299*).

PARC ANDRE-CITROEN
Map p. 472, B4

Open Mon–Fri 8am until dusk; Sat, Sun and public holidays 9am until dusk.
On the riverside beyond Pont Mirabeau the site of the former car factory was transformed 1992–99 into the Parc André-Citroën. Rigorous, architectonic and modernist, it is the creation of Alain Provost and Gilles Clément working in association with three architects, Patrick Berger, Jean-Paul Viguier and François Jodry. Four themes prevail: artifice, architecture, movement and nature. There are three principal sections: the White Garden to the east, the Black Garden to the south, and the main park dominated by two huge rectangular greenhouses. The principal perspective descending towards the Seine is flanked by banks of evergreen magnolias and beech hedges, with box and yew, trimmed into disciplined shapes. Water is a determining element of the park—a large fountain, canals, lily-ponds, water courses and *jets d'eau* account for about a hectare of the total. In the northeast side is a series of parallel rectangular gardens each planted to a different colour scheme. Opposite each is a small high greenhouse. The plants in the Jardin des Métamorphoses, on the other side, evoke alchemical transmutations. In contrast to the formal gardens, closer to the river there are stretches of wild gardens described as Jardin des Roches and Jardin en Mouvement.

THE RIGHT BANK

The greater part of Paris, encompassing 14 of the 20 arrondissements, is north of the arc of the Seine. The Right Bank or Rive Droite does not have one unifying characteristic, but the *quartiers* closest to the Seine are redolent of luxury and wealth. In the Middle Ages, the protective fortifications encompassed a far greater extent here than on the Left Bank, and the area was associated with royalty early on, evoked by the size and splendour of the Louvre Palace and by the remains of the great mansions of the Marais, the oldest inhabited part of the Right Bank. The Champs-Elysées and Place Vendôme laid out in the 17th century, and Place de la Concorde in the 18th, bear witness to the grandeur of those times, and they remain affluent districts, while finance is centred around the Bourse. The municipal authorities have been based on Place de l'Hôtel de Ville since the 13th century. As Paris expanded in the 19th century, landmarks were created such as the remarkable Place de l'Etoile (Pl. General de Gaulle) with avenues radiating out from the Arc de Triomphe, along with other wide boulevards. Garnier's opera house epitomised mid-century opulence, and a multitude of theatres, hotels and mansions accommodated a fun-loving population. The memory of the infamous prison of the Bastille lingers on, though now the name is more associated with opera and ballet. As the villages surrounding the capital were absorbed, Montmartre, La Villette, Belleville and Bercy became working-class districts of Paris, whereas Neuilly, Passy and Auteuil, between the Seine and the Bois de Boulogne, have, since the late 19th and early 20th centuries, been home to the rich bourgeoisie.

THE LOUVRE

THE PALAIS DU LOUVRE
Map p. 475, D1

The Palais du Louvre occupies an extensive site between the Rue de Rivoli and the Seine and was one of the world's most magnificent palaces. It is now home to the Musée du Louvre (*see p. 141 below*) and Les Arts Décoratifs (*see p. 196*). Despite its apparent homogeneity, the palace is the result of many phases of building, modifications and restoration. It is made up of two main parts, the Old Louvre, comprising the buildings surrounding the Cour Carrée to the east and along the bank of the Seine; and the New Louvre, the 19th-century buildings north and south of the Cour Napoléon, with their extensions to the west which were originally part of the Tuileries Palace (*see p. 194*).

History of the Palais du Louvre
The derivation of the name is unclear, but it was already used in relation to Philippe-Auguste's fortress (1190–1202) at the southwest corner of the Cour Carrée (*see p. 143*). Charles V (1364–80) carried out improvements to the castle, including new buildings and a handsome staircase, which became an official royal residence endowed with a library. Subsequent monarchs preferred other palaces until François I (1515–47) planned the total demolition and reconstruction of all the west and south sides of the fortress. The west side of the Cour Carrée, south of Pavillon Sully, part of the early 16th-century palace, is the oldest elevation above ground. The work, begun by Pierre Lescot shortly before the king's death, was continued under Henri II. Jean Goujon was responsible for the elegant Classical sculptural decorations which set the tone for all later additions.

Under Charles IX, the Petite Galerie (later the Apollo Gallery) was begun in 1566, the first part of a plan to build a long gallery to connect the Louvre with the Tuileries Palace (*see p. 193*), his mother Catherine de Médicis' new residence. At the time of Henri IV, Luis Métezeau and Jacques II Androuet du Cerceau built the Grande Galerie (1595–1610), or Galerie du Bord de l'Eau, on the Seine side, extending to the Pavillon de Flore which was part of the Grand Dessein (royal design) to enlarge the Louvre. The monumental Pavillon de l'Horloge (1639–42; later Pavillon Sully) and the north half of the west façade were the work of Lemercier.

From 1654, during the minority of Louis XIV, Lemercier supervised work on the court apartment of the queen mother, Anne of Austria. Fire destroyed the second floor of the Petite Galerie in 1661, and the royal decision to renew the Grand Dessein of Henri IV resulted in the Apollo Gallery, and new buildings to the west. The Pavillon de Marsan was built 1660–65 by Louis Le Vau and François d'Orbay. The quadrangle (now the Cour Carrée) was extended and several architects, including Bernini and Le

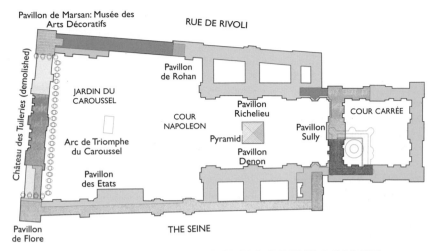

HISTORICAL GROUNDPLAN OF THE LOUVRE

DATES OF CONSTRUCTION		ARCHITECTS	DATES OF CONSTRUCTION		ARCHITECTS
	XII & XIII centuries	Philippe-Auguste Saint Louis		1624–1654	Louis XII	
	XIV century	Charles IV		1653–1670 1667–1670	Louis XIV	Lemercier Le Vau Perrault Le Brun
	1882–1883	Demolition of Château des Tuileries				
	1546–1549 1559–1574	François I, Henri II, François II, Charles IX, Henri III	Pierre Lescot		1806–1811	Napoleon	Percier & Fontaine
				1816–1824	Louis XVIII	Fontaine
	1564–1570 1566 1570–1572	Catherine de Médicis	Philibert de l'Orme Pierre Lescot Jean Bullant		1852–1870	Napoléon III	Visconti & Lefuel
				1874–1880	3rd Republic	
	1595–1610	Henri IV	Louis Métezeau J.A. du Cerceau		1981–1993	5th Republic	Ieoh Ming Pei

Vau, submitted projects for the main façade to the east. However, the great colonnade of 52 Corinthian columns and pilasters that now forms the exterior east façade was the work of Claude Perrault and Le Vau. (The decorations of the Cour Carrée were not completed until the 19th century.) Louis XIV, preoccupied with his new palace at Versailles, soon lost interest and these buildings were abandoned in a state of disrepair, to be occupied by the academies. It was not until 1754 that Louis XV commissioned Gabriel to renovate and restore the palace.

Under Napoleon part of the North Gallery along Rue de Rivoli was begun and in 1810, the wedding feast of Napoleon and Marie-Louise of Austria was celebrated in the Salon Carré. The building was attacked during the revolutions of 1830 and 1848. Under Napoléon III, Visconti and then Hector-Martin Lefuel (1810–80) finished the Grande Galerie (1861–68) linking the Louvre and the Tuileries, as well as new buildings on Rue de Rivoli extending the existing wings (*see p. 186*). Cour Napoléon was completed in 1857 and the interior decoration in 1861. After 1871, when the Tuileries was fired by the Communards, the damaged Pavillon de Marsan (now the Musée des Arts Décoratifs) of the Tuileries Palace, was rebuilt by Lefuel.

On 10th August, 1793, the Musée de la République was opened in the Louvre, and has remained the national art gallery and museum ever since. By 1981 the museum lacked sufficient space for both visitors and workshops, so the north wing, occupied by the Ministry of Finance since 1871, was handed back in 1989 and became the Richelieu wing. The Ministry transferred to Bercy (*see p. 310*). The ambitious Grand Projet du Louvre began in 1983 when President Mitterrand approved the plan proposed by the Chinese-born American architect, Ieoh Ming Pei, to construct a glazed pyramid as the new entrance to the museum. The Cour Carrée was excavated, and the foundations of the medieval fortress were exposed, now known as the Medieval Louvre.

The Grand Projet du Louvre

The finishing touches are still being made to President Mitterrand's Grand Projet du Louvre. On 18th November, 1993, President Mitterrand dedicated the whole Palais du Louvre to the museum, almost doubling the exhibition surfaces, from 31,000 to 60,000 square metres, allowing for greatly improved presentation of the works and more use of natural light. The number of works exhibited increased from 20,600 to 34,000, and the collections have been reorganised into more coherent themes or schools and a logical chronological order. The final gesture, at the initiative of President Chirac, was the installation in 2000 of a selection of the primitive arts of Africa, Asia, Oceania (Pacific and Australia) and the Americas, the flagship for the Musée du Quai Branly which opened in 2006 (*see p. 124*).

The Pyramid

The Pyramid, elegant and innovative, is almost as well known as the Eiffel Tower. It sits in the centre of Cour Napoléon, between the Pavillon Richelieu and the Pavillon Denon. The structure is 30m square by 20m high, with transparent walls supported by a trussed steel frame, and takes up less space than conventional building shapes. Designed to overcome problems of light and space, the glass reflects and refracts light as well as permitting uninterrupted views of the mellow façades of the palace. It shelters the hub of the Louvre Museum, the Napoleon Hall, and is flanked by three subsidiary pyramids and seven fountains with triangular basins of Brittany granite. The Napoleon Hall is increasingly busy—a project to ease congestion should take effect after 2010. Between the Pyramid and the Carrousel Arch (*see p. 194*) is an equestrian statue of Louis XIV, a lead copy of 1988 after Bernini's original at Versailles. The statue, but not the Pyramid, is on the same axis as the Tuileries, the Champs-Elysées and the Arc de Triomphe.

Carrousel du Louvre

The Carrousel du Louvre is a smart and popular underground shopping mall with a smaller inverted glass pyramid providing daylight for the area (accessed directly from the Metro station Palais Royal-Musée du Louvre, or via escalators from 99 Rue de Rivoli, or from the Napoleon Hall under the Pyramid). A section of Charles V's fortifications, rebuilt at the beginning of the 16th century, can be seen here. The mall has specialist boutiques and a large food hall with a variety of cafés. Between the Carrousel du Louvre and Napoleon Hall are sales outlets for objects connected with the Museum, including replicas of objects from national collections and the Chalcographie du Musée with an extensive range of prints. At CyberLouvre (*open 9–5.45*) the museum's multimedia products may be accessed free of charge.

THE MUSEE DU LOUVRE
Map p. 475, D1

The Musée du Louvre is one of the largest museums and art galleries in the world receiving some five million visitors a year. The eight departments of the museum are housed in three wings or *pavillons* around Cour Napoléon, the main courtyard. Pavillon Sully, to the east, extends around the four sides of the Cour Carrée; Pavillon Denon is to the south and Pavillon Richelieu to the north. In the centre of Cour Napoléon is the Pyramid (*see plans pp. 144–145*). Many of the rooms of the former royal palace still have their original décor, of great interest in itself; the remains of the medieval Louvre and Napoléon III's apartments in Richelieu are also part of the museum.

Opening times
The museum is open Wed–Mon 9–6; (Porte des Lions closes 5.30); evening openings on Wed and Fri until 9.45pm (except public holidays); it is closed on Tuesdays, and on 1st Jan, 1st May, 15th Aug, and 25th Dec. The main entrance is on the west side of the Pyramid (lift for disabled visitors). Other entrances: Carrousel du Louvre; Porte des Lions—Denon Pavilion (tickets sales); Passage Richelieu—Richelieu Pavilion (ticket holders only). Gallery openings: a weekly chart in the Napoleon Hall specifies which galleries are open/closed each day.

Tickets
Free admission for under-18s; free for everyone on the first Sunday of every month and for under 26s on Fridays after 6 pm. Reduced admission after 6pm on Wed and Fri. Combined tickets: evenings, to include permanent and temporary exhibitions; Louvre and Delacroix Museums (see p. 70) on the same day. At peak times there can be a long wait to enter the Pyramid because of security; other entrances (see opening times above) may be less crowded. A long wait to buy tickets can be avoided with the Paris Museum Pass (see p. 442), or by purchasing tickets in advance online (www.louvre.fr) or from stores in France (e.g. FNAC, Galeries Lafayette, Printemps Haussmann, Virgin). Combined transport-entrance tickets are available with RATP-Louvre from Paris Convention and Visitors Bureau.

Information
Switchboard T: 01 40 20 50 50; information desk T: 01 40 20 53 17; www.louvre.fr

also spent most of his working life in Rome. Claude created his own brand of classical landscapes, often based on atmospheric scenes of the Roman countryside, or of seaports, and an idealisation of nature. Typical are the U-shaped compositions that recede into a misty distance such as *Seaport in the Setting Sun*, *View of a Port with the Capitol*, and *Arrival of Cleopatra at Tarsa*. Room 17 next door is reserved for the Painting of the Month.

Sully second floor

Room 19: This room presents large-scale altar paintings (17th century) by the founders of the Académie Royale in 1648, including Eustache le Sueur and Laurent de La Hyre.

Rooms 20–27: In Rooms 20–23 French Graphic Arts (drawings, cartoons, engravings) are exhibited in rotation, changing every three to six months. Beyond, in Rooms A, B, C, are three collections: Beistegui, Lyon and Cröy (*see p. 151*). Next door to Room 19, in Room 24, is the series of 22 paintings of the *Life of St Bruno*, founder of the Carthusian order, by Eustache le Sueur, completed in 1648. Beyond, Room 25 evokes the decoration of 17th-century Parisian houses. In Rooms 26 and 27 are small-scale (*du cabinet*) religious paintings and still lifes.

Room 28: Works by Georges de la Tour who, like Claude, came from Lorraine. Famed for night-time scenes dramatically lit by candlelight, the richly painted and anecdotal *Cheat with the Ace of Diamonds* is one of only two works of his in the Louvre painted in direct light (the other is *St Thomas*). A favourite theme from Caravaggio to Cézanne, the card game provided an ideal opportunity to create a mood, study inter-relationships and moralise,

according to 17th-century standards, on the three major temptations: gambling, wine and lust. The elegantly dressed young man on the right is being set up by the other three whose body-language indicates what is about to happen, directing the viewer's focus to the hand of the card-sharp on the left. More typical of de la Tour perhaps are *The Adoration of the Shepherds* and *Mary Magdalen Watching a Candle*.

Room 29: Genre scenes here by the Le Nain brothers with titles like *The Travellers' Rest* and *The Peasant Family* range from the subdued colours and quiet dignity associated with the work of Louis (c. 1600–48), to the more Baroque Mathieu (c. 1607–77). The third brother was Antoine (c. 1588–1648).

Rooms 31–35: Portraits and religious works of the 17th century include Philippe de Champaigne's *The Prévôt des Marchands*. One of the founders of the Académie, Champaigne's earlier Baroque style was abandoned after 1643 as he became more involved in the ascetic Jansenist sect (*see p. 99*). An austere and rigorous masterpiece of 1662, *The Artist's daughter with Mère Catherine-Agnès Arnauld*, was painted in thanksgiving for the miraculous cure of his daughter, nursed by Jansenist nuns at Port-Royal.

Georges de la Tour: *The Cheat with the Ace of Diamonds* (c.1635–40).

Charles Le Brun, painter at the Court of Louis XIV, remained faithful to the Baroque style in the sumptuous equestrian portrait of Chancellor Séguier (c. 1661). Further works by Le Brun can be seen in Room 32, while Room 33 has religious paintings by Jean Jouvenet (1644–1717), a pupil of Le Brun, who in the last three years of his life, following paralysis in his right hand, taught himself to paint with his left. In Rooms 34 and 35 are examples of work by another Court painter, Hyacinthe Rigaud, who produced the quintessential Baroque portrait of absolute monarchy, the celebrated full-length likeness of Louis XIV in 1701. The talented Nicolas de Largillière, represented here by *The Artist with his Wife and Daughter*, was particularly popular with the *haute bourgeoisie*.

Rooms 36–40, 43, 46, 47: Eighteenth-century French paintings are displayed in this wing, starting with the Louvre's collection of around a dozen paintings by Antoine Watteau, who died young of tuberculosis. He began as a decorative painter and his works have a certain wistfulness, including the monumental but enigmatic *Pierrot* (also known as *Gilles*), a Pierrot from Italian or French comedy, and *Pilgrimage to Cythera* (1717) Watteau's vision of a lazy melancholic day of late summer, for which the term *fête galante* was coined. There are more gems of 18th-century elegance from the La Caze Collection of 1869. Still lifes by Jean-Baptiste-Siméon Chardin such as *The Ray* were made for the domestic market. In *Le Buffet*, perilously perched dishes and fruit form a pyramid of reds and greys. Typical paintings of pure pleasure by François Boucher include frothy nudes such as *Diana getting out of her Bath*—including the crescent moon, the shaft of arrows, and the hound, attributes of the Goddess of the Moon and of hunting. Room 43 contains large, mid-18th-century works. Rooms 46 and 47 contain Boucher landscapes, and portraits of Louis XV's queen, Marie Leszczynska (1740) by Louis Tocqué (1696–1772) and the encyclopedist Denis Diderot (1767) by Louis-Michel Van Loo (1707–71).

Rooms 41, 42, 44: Eighteenth-century Graphic Arts, including pastels and miniatures, are shown here in rotation.

Rooms 48 and 49: The work that made Jean-Honoré Fragonard's name in Paris was *The High Priest Croesus Sacrificing Himself to Save Callirhoe* (1765), but he soon turned to lighter themes dashed off with rapid, vibrant brushstrokes. Fantasy figures, of which the Louvre owns eight, include *Music* or *Man Playing an Instrument* (1769) and *Portrait of Marie-Madeleine Guimard*, a well-known Parisian dancer; *Adoration of the Shepherds* (c. 1775) and *Le Verrou* (c. 1777) are pendant pieces which symbolise sacred and profane love, the latter ('The Bolt') a masterpiece of eroticism. Hubert Robert painted large picturesque ruins in France such as *Le Pont du Gard* (1787).

Room 51: Here are portraits and examples of the moralistic and senti-mental work of Jean-Baptiste Greuze (1725–1805). Much admired by Denis Diderot and one of the most important

of French 18th-century painters, Greuze was enormously popular in his own day and is now being re-evaluated.

Rooms 52 and 53: One of the most successful portrait artists of her time, Elisabeth Vigée-Lebrun was encouraged to paint by Vernet, whom she painted in 1778 (in Room 51); also here are some of her celebrated portraits of women and children. The work of two other women, Anne Vallayer-Coster (1744–1818), and Adélaïde Labille-Guiard (1749–1803) is also exhibited here. Room 53, the Salle Vien, has large-format Classical and religious themes. The butterfly above Psyche's head in François Gérard's superficially classical *Psyche and Cupid* (1798) symbolises inconstancy.

Rooms 54–63: Central to the Louvre's collection of 19th-century French paintings, displayed in this wing, are the rigorous Neoclassical works of Jacques-Louis David, shown here along-side those of his pupils Gros, Gérard and Ingres. Room 60 is devoted entirely to Jean-Auguste-Dominique Ingres, a consummate draughtsman who painted great portraits of L.-F. Bertin, senior, and the composer Cherubini. Throughout his long career his style barely altered, but he was especially famous for his voluptuous scenes inspired by North Africa such as *The Turkish Bath* and *La Baigneuse de Valpinçon*. In Rooms 61–63 are grouped works by the great Romantic painters, such as Théodore Géricault's *The Mad Woman*, and Eugène Delacroix's *Self-por-trait* and *Algerian Women in their Apartments*. North Africa was a fashionable source of ideas for a group of painters known as 'Orientalists' such as Théodore Chassériau.

Rooms 64–72: Two major collections here, the Moreau-Nélaton, donated in 1906, and the Thomy-Thiery, in 1902, contain a number of Corot's, including exceptions to his usual silvery landscapes, such as the gentle *Souvenir of Castelgandolfo* (c. 1865), and *La Femme à la Perle*. There are works by Delacroix and Jean-François Millet, and several landscapes by Barbizon artists who worked in Fontainebleau Forest. (Impressionist works from the Moreau-Nélaton collection are at the Musée d'Orsay, *see p. 78*).

Room A: The works, mainly 18th–19th-century, of the Beistegui Collection, donated in 1953, have to be kept together. They range from a Flemish 14th-century *Virgin and Child* and a late 15th-century *Portrait of the Dauphin Charles Orlando* (son of Charles VIII and Anne of Brittany) by the Maître de Moulins, to numerous portraits by Fragonard, Largillière, Thomas Lawrence (1769–1830) and others. The most accomplished and eye-catching work here is Goya's powerful *Marquesa de la Solana* (c. 1795). It depicts Maria Rita Barranchea, educated aristocrat and

playwright, who married a friend of one of Goya's patrons, Jovellanos. She was 38 when this portrait was made, but gravely unwell, and she knew that she had little time to live.

Rooms B and C: Two further collections, the Cröy and the Lyon, were donated 1930–32 and in 1971 respectively. Princess Louis de Cröy's bequest of 3,800 drawings and paintings consists mainly of Northern school works and landscapes by Pierre Henri de Valenciennes (1750–1819), responsible for re-invigorating the *paysage historique* with his oil sketches done *en plein-air*. The Hélène and Victor Lyon donation, of 17th–18th-century Northern and Venetian paintings includes landscapes by Bernardo Strozzi (1581–1644) a Genoese Capuchin friar, also known as 'il Cappuccino', who moved to Venice in 1631 and whose style has been compared to Rubens and Van Dyck; by Canaletto (1686–1768), whose views of Venice were particularly popular with English Grand Tourists; the Venetian Gian Domenico Tiepolo (1727–1804), noted for the powerful simplicity of his compositions; and a cross-section of late 19th-century French works by Cézanne, Degas, Jongkind, Monet, Pissarro, Renoir and Toulouse-Lautrec.

Denon first floor

Rooms 75–77: These rooms contain the most famous large 19th-century French paintings of the Empire period. The theatrical works of J.-L. David, inspired by antiquity, include *The Sabine Women* (1799) and *The Oath of the*

Horatii (1784), widely seen as extolling Republican virtues although commissioned for the Crown. There is also the brilliant historical record of *The Coronation of Napoléon I by Pope Pius VII in Notre-Dame, 2nd December 1804*.

Albrecht Dürer: *Self-Portrait with a Thistle* (1493).

David's genius as a portrait painter is amply demonstrated, the most famous work being *Madame Récamier*. Jean-

Auguste-Dominique Ingres' three main themes are found here: portraits, such as the *Rivière Family* (1805); odalisques, such as *The Large Bather* (1814); and Classical history, *The Apotheosis of Homer*. A lighter note is Vigée-Lebrun's *Self Portrait with Daughter*. Great Romantic epics include Baron Gros' *Bonaparte visiting the Plague-stricken at Jaffa* (1804); Prud'hon's rather wistful *Empress Joséphine at Malmaison* (1805); by Delacroix are *Death of Sardanapalus*, from the poem by Baudelaire, and the battle-cry of the Republic, *Liberty leading the People* (1831). Géricault offers high drama in *Raft of the Medusa* (1818–19), based on a true event, the catastrophic shipwreck of the French frigate *Medusa* off Senegal in 1816.

English School

There are no paintings from the English school on display at time of writing; room 74 where they are normally housed having been temporarily given over to the *Venus de Milo* (*see box on p. 167*). The English collection is modest, but contains works by Constable, Gainsborough, Turner, and Richard Parkes Bonington among others.

Northern Schools

The Northern Paintings Department is a comprehensive collection of works by Flemish, Dutch and German artists from the 14th to the 19th centuries, along with some Scandinavian 19th-century works. The 36 rooms were designed by I.M. Pei as part of the Grand Projet (*see p. 140*). Rooms A–F were the most recent to open. The first three rooms are devoted to International Gothic (*see p. 146*).

Richelieu second floor

Rooms 4 and 5: Fifteenth-century Dutch and Flemish paintings show the result of a deliberate break by Robert Campin and Jan van Eyck in the southern Netherlands, c. 1420–25, from the brilliant but superficial qualities of International Gothic. By a pupil of Campin, Rogier van der Weyden (1399/1400–64), are the *Braque Family Triptych* (c. 1450), a work of intense colour and feeling, and the *Annunciation* with sparkling details. Another exceptional work of the period is Jan van Eyck's *Virgin with Chancellor Nicolas Rolin*. Rolin, the donor of this painting who kneels in prayer before the Madonna, was the rich and powerful Chancellor of Philip the Good of Burgundy. Among Bruges artists who followed Van Eyck's lead were Hans Memling, represented by several works including *The Virgin between St James and St Dominic*. The Louvre has only one painting by Brueghel the Elder, *Beggars* (1568), a curious group of five cripples; and one by Bosch, a fragment of an allegorical work depicting avarice, greed and drunkenness, *The Ship of Fools* (1490–1500), both disturbing images.

Room 6: Here is a series of 28 portraits of illustrious or wise men, including Dante, commissioned by Federico da Montefeltro for the Ducal Palace at Urbino.

Rooms 7 and 8: Representing 15th–16th-century German works is a dramatic and sensual oeuvre of the Master of the St Bartholomew Altarpiece (active c. 1500), *Descent from the Cross*, painted for an Antonite community in Paris, which was seized at the Revolution from the Church of Val-de-Grâce (*see p. 98*). Renaissance works between c. 1495 and 1550 are a fusion of German, Netherlandish and Italian art. The finely drawn *Self-Portrait with a Thistle* (1493; *pictured on p. 152*) by Albrecht Dürer from Nuremberg, was one of the first individual self-portraits in Western painting, although artists had previously included themselves in groups. Dürer painted this at the end of a guild tour through Southern Germany. He holds a thistle, possibly a symbol of fidelity to his betrothed, Agnes Frey. The Louvre also owns five portraits by Hans Holbein the Younger, which belonged to Louis XIV. These include three Humanists, the Dutch scholar Erasmus (painted for Sir Thomas More), Thomas Moore, author of *Utopia*, and friend of them both, and the Archbishop of Canterbury, William of Warham (c. 1430–1522), which was the first work made in England (1526–28), and is considered to be the original version of a copy in London.

Rooms 9–11: Netherlandish painters of the first half of the 16th century from Bruges and Antwerp are represented by a number of small works. A popular work is Quentin Metsys' (1465–1530) *Moneylender and his Wife*, which shows the couple at a table surrounded by a variety of objects including a small round mirror. It can be read as a record of an honest couple at work, and as an allegorical piece with references to vanity and avarice, and Christianity symbolised in the scales, an element of the Last Judgement. Jan Gossaert (Mabuse) fuses Italian Renaissance ideas with those of van Eyck and Dürer to create the beautiful object of private devotion the *Diptych of Jean Carondelet*, representing the Chancellor of Flanders and the Virgin and Child.

Room 12: Examples of the Graphic Arts of the Northern Schools.

Rooms 13–16: Rooms 14 and 16 contain small-scale landscapes and still lifes from the end of the 16th to the beginning of the 17th century, while Rooms 13 and 15 contain Dutch and Flemish Mannerist works from the same period, demonstrating the exaggeration of the style that spread from Italy.

Rooms 17–26: Seventeenth-century Flemish painting was dominated by Peter-Paul Rubens (1577–1640) and Van Dyck (1599–1641). Against the light-green walls of the specially created Medici Gallery (Room 18) are Rubens' 24 huge, resplendent allegorical works depicting the *Life of Marie de Médicis*. Designed 1622–25 to decorate the Luxembourg Palace this series, the painter's greatest single achievement, glorifies the life and achievements of the Queen in an appropriately exuberant and eulogistic manner. Running in chronological sequence from left to right, each canvas represents a major event of Marie's life, starting with her birth in April 1575. Other scenes include her *Arrival at Marseilles* on 3rd November 1600 to become Henri IV's second wife; the *Birth of her Son*, Louis;

the *Apotheosis of Henri IV*; and *Proclamation of the Regency of the Queen*, the key moment in the cycle. The sequence ends with the *Reconciliation* with her son, Louis XIII, in 1619. Above the door, between portraits of her parents, is Marie de Médicis as *Reine Triomphante*. This great series influenced later French artists as wide ranging as Watteau and David.

Beyond the Medici gallery are huge, mainly religious, paintings (Room 19), several here (and in other galleries) by Jacob Jordaens (1593–1678) who worked with Rubens and yet was also influenced by Caravaggio. Further works by Rubens (Rooms 21–22) include a tenderly executed portrait of his wife Hélène Fourment with two of her children, and *Baron Henri de Vicq* (c. 1625), a portrait of the ambassador who obtained for the artist the commission to paint the Medici canvases; among landscapes by Rubens is the unforgettable *Kermesse—the village wedding*, a rustic scene superbly observed and peopled.

Rooms 24 and 26: Several of the works by Van Dyck here were in Louis XIV's collection. They include mythological scenes, such as *Venus and Vulcan* (1626–32) painted just before the painter's departure for England, and two beautifully composed and elegant portraits executed in Antwerp, *A Lady of Quality and her Child* and its counterpart *A Gentleman and his Child*. The full-length portrait of Marchesa Spinola-Doria, was made during his stay in Italy (before 1632). From his English period is *Portrait of James Stewart* (1612–55), a private work which introduces an element of mythology with the apple in his

hand, possibly an allusion to the Judgement of Paris. *Charles I at the Hunt* (c. 1637) was paid for by the king in 1635 although not kept by him. It presents him as an aristocratic gentleman rather than monarch. The work was already in France by 1738, and was purchased by Louis XVI from Madame du Barry in 1785. Jan Davidsz de Heem's (1606–1683/84) *The Dessert* is an opulent still life, of which Matisse made a version in 1893.

Rooms 23 and 25: Here are several works by David Teniers the Younger, who married Jan Breughel's daughter Anna, and small 17th-century Flemish genre paintings by his contemporaries.

Room 27–30: The last 12 rooms are devoted to Dutch paintings arranged by genre, rather than around a single artist, with the exception of Rembrandt. The paintings are displayed more or less chronologically, emphasising the variety and wealth of the Dutch School. Rooms 27–30 have works from the first half of the 17th century, and work by Frans Hals, including the majestic portrait of Paulus van Berestyn, and the later *Old Woman* which demonstrates his growing preference for restrained colours. Landscape is dominated by Van Goyen's *Two large Sailing Boats* and Solomon van Ruysdael's *The Landing-stage*, often with brilliantly observed sky. One of several architecture specialists was Saenredam, represented here by *Interior of a Church Haarlem*. Dutch genre scenes are typified by Adam van Breen's *Skaters*. Still life also has a particularly privileged place in Dutch painting. Fine examples of large history or genre painting typical of

Caravaggist artists are Gerard van Honthorst's *The Concert* and *The Lute Player*. More sober is the work of Ter Brugghen from Utrecht.

Room 31: Rembrandt van Rijn (1606–69) painted himself through every stage of his life. Of the four in the collection, two date from 1633, the introspective *Self-Portrait Bareheaded*, and *Self-Portrait Wearing a Toque and Chain* which uses a rich palette and play of light. A third of 1660 is the even more self-reflective *Artist in his Old Age at his Easel* (1660). Saskia van Uylenborch, whom he married in 1634, brought a considerable dowry. In the period up to her death in 1642 he lived in grand style and beyond his means. During those years he painted *The Philosopher in Meditation* and the *Holy Family*. From his more mature and mystical period is *Christ at Emmaus* (1648). *Portrait of Hendrickje Stoffels with a Velvet Beret* (c. 1654) is a loving painting of the nursemaid to Rembrandt's son, who became his mistress after his wife died. Hendrickje posed for one of the best known of Rembrandt's works in the Louvre, the monumental copper-toned *Bathsheba Bathing*. Rembrandt records Bathsheba's dilemma when she receives the note from King David, who had fallen passionately in love with her. To meet his ends, the king banishes Uriah, her husband and general in the army, to certain death on the battlefield. There are also many works by the pupils, imitators and followers of Rembrandt.

Rooms 33–39: Dutch paintings from the mid- to late 17th century include scenes of everyday life, such as *The Fish Market* by Adriaen Van Ostade (1610–85), a typically bucolic landscape by Cuyp, *Landscape near Rhenen*, and works by Gerard Dou. *Flowers in a Crystal Jug* is representative of luscious Dutch flower paintings by Abraham Mignon. There are two works by Jan Vermeer (Room 38): the *Lacemaker* (c. 1679) is the smallest he ever painted (24cm by 21cm), showing an intensely concentrated domestic scene and a masterful use of colour and light. The book in the foreground, which appears to be the Bible, adds moral and religious overtones. The second painting here by Vermeer, by whom only 35 paintings are known, is *The Astronomer*. It uses cool blue tones in an intimate interior with a small group of figures. Pieter de Hooch painted *The Drinker* (1658) during his stay in Delft. Also here are his *Courtyard of a Dutch House* and *Card Players in an Opulent Interior in Amsterdam* (c. 1663–65). In both he makes great play of indirect light and the careful orchestration of figures in perspective, the latter painting apparently set in a brothel.

Italian Schools

The richly endowed Department of Italian Paintings dates back to the reign of François I and constitutes the oldest collection in the Louvre. It also contains the most famous painting in the museum, the *Mona Lisa*. The collection embraces works of the 14th–18th-centuries, Renaissance works being displayed in the Grande Galerie, part of the old Louvre Palace. This room was used in the 18th century as a repository for military relief plans (*see p. 115*), and in Louis XVI's time the intention was to make it the Musée Royal. In fact the museum was only to open during the Revolutionary period, on 10th August, 1793.

Denon first floor

Rooms 1 and 2: The first two rooms, Salle Percier et Fontaine and Salle Duchâtel, contain elegant and refined works by Florentine masters of the 13th–15th centuries. *Madonna and Child in Majesty with Six Angels* by Cimabue (c. 1240–1302) is an early attempt to bring a certain naturalism and depth to a fundamentally Byzantine composition. In the painted frame are 26 medallions of Christ, angels, prophets and saints. Freer and more lifelike figures are achieved by Giotto (c. 1266–1337) in *St Francis Receiving the Stigmata*.

Room 3: The Salon Carré contains works typical of the Quattrocento, the 15th century, by great masters. Fra Angelico (c. 1387–1455) handles a traditional religious subject with a novel use of perspective in his triumphant *Coronation of the Virgin*. Botticelli (c. 1445–1510) painted a delicate youthful virgin and fresh-faced adolescent in *Madonna and Child Surrounded by Angels*. The colourful and charmingly wooden battle scene *The Battle of San Romano* (c. 1438), by Paolo Uccello, is one of three panels on the same theme (the others being in Florence and London). Much admired by Lorenzo de Medici, it depicts the Florentine victory over the Sienese in 1432 (*see box overleaf*).

Room 4: In the Salle des Sept Metres are 13th–15th-century works from Siena and Northern Italy. Artists include Pisanello (c. 1395–1454), and Gentile

da Fabriano (c. 1370–1427) whose *Presentation at the Temple* shows detailed attention to the architectural setting and materials. The Sienese Sano di Pietro's (c. 1405–81) *Five Episodes from the Life of St Jerome* includes the episode in which the saint extracts a thorn from the lion's paw. *The Portrait of Sigismondo Malatesta* by Piero della Francesca (c. 1416–92) is a fine example of the artist's intellectually rigorous style and predilection for sharp profiles. Smaller works include *Christ bearing the Cross* (c. 1342), a small vivid section of a polyptych of the Passion by Simone Martini, an artist from Siena who worked for a time in Avignon (France).

The Grande Galerie, Room 5: Along the great length of the Grande Galerie (which includes Rooms 8 and 12) the paintings are arranged to set up dialogues facing each other across the room. The first section has 15th–16th-century paintings from Tuscany and northern Italy. The precise draughtsmanship of Andrea Mantegna can be appreciated in the *Crucifixion*, and his fully developed interest in antiquity in *St Sebastian* painted for the Church of Aigueperse in the Auvergne for the wedding of Chiara Gonzaga to the Count of Monpensier. The exaggerated perspective of the *Virgin of Victory* (1496), made for Francis II Gonzaga, suggests it was intended to be viewed from below. Ghirlandaio (1449–94) from Florence painted the tender *Old*

FOUR PAINTINGS IN THE ITALIAN RENAISSANCE COLLECTION

The *Entombment* (c. 1530) is one of Titian's greatest pictures, one of the most powerful of all Renaissance paintings, and one of the jewels of the Louvre's collection—dramatic, moving, and ground-breaking in its time, both in tone and technique. Commissioned for the Gonzaga Dukes of Mantua, and bought by Charles I of England in 1627 when their collection was broken up, it was then purchased (for £120) just over 20 years later for Louis XIV by Cardinal Mazarin's agents following the execution of the English king, passing thereby into the French national collection. Much of the core of the Louvre's Italian collection followed this same route from Mantua, via London to Paris, passing through the hands of some of the most important collectors in European history.

Others came by a different route: the richly poetic *Concert Champêtre* (c. 1510) by Titian and Giorgione, in the same room, came first into the possession of the Kings of Spain for whom Titian was working, and moved to the Louvre only after it had been severely damaged in a conflagration, which claimed a number of other important paintings by Titian, in the Palace of El Pardo, north of Madrid, in March 1604. Scholars have debated endlessly whether this is the work of Titian or Giorgione, or both, or even of other artists in their circle, although to little purpose, since so much of the picture is inevitably restoration. Nonetheless, the exquisite passage on the left of the painting, depicting the nymph filling a water jug at the fountain (one of the areas least damaged in the fire; *pictured opposite*), does have much of the precocious flair of the young Titian. Few paintings of the collection have in fact survived unaltered: greatest of all, the *Mona Lisa* (left among Leonardo's possessions at his death in the Château de Cloux, now Clos-Lucé, in Amboise, southwest of Paris) has been cut down and its colours would now be unrecognisable to him. The Louvre's outstanding collection of Leonardo's works contains almost one third of the small corpus of paintings which can be indisputably attributed to his hand: but the chromatic variation and tone of all these masterworks has darkened dramatically because of the experimental oil-technique Leonardo used (*see box on p. 162 below*).

Something similar has occurred, but for different reasons, with another of the museum's greatest works, Paolo Uccello's *Battle of San Romano* (c. 1455), which was one of a triptych of grand panels depicting this costly battle of dubious outcome between Florence and Siena (the other two being in the National Gallery, London, and Uffizi Gallery, Florence). Representing the counter-attack of Michelotto da Cotignola, the picture once shone with the arresting glitter of military armour, executed in silver-leaf gilding; but nothing that Uccello could have done has stopped the inevitable process of oxidation of the silver, which has darkened and dimmed the armour so that it now recedes into the background.

Across the gallery from Uccello's masterpiece is the tiny *Portrait of an Old Man with a Young Boy* (c. 1490) by Domenico Ghirlandaio, the early Florentine master who taught painting and drawing to the young Michelangelo. The picture is a brilliant and naturalistic study of a sitter, painted literally 'warts and all'; the looseness of the hair and the dermatological condition of the nose are observed with an attention to detail that could only possibly derive from life-drawing. Unusually, in this case, we do in fact still possess one of Ghirlandaio's preparatory drawings (now in the National Museum, Stockholm). But, in vivid contrast, the wooden quality of the child's face, the curls of his hair painted as if by rote and his whole puppet-like appearance must surely be the work of another, far inferior hand. Not even the gaze of the eyes of the two figures meets. The picture may originally have featured an old man, seated alone, reading a book, and was later altered to give it greater appeal by the addition of a little boy. The Louvre's collection of Italian paintings is one of the most wide-ranging

Detail from *Le Concert Champêtre* (c. 1510) by Titian in the Italian Renaissance collection of the Louvre.

in Europe. To us it is of incomparable value: but to the great painters represented here, many of their own works would now simply be unrecognisable to them, were they ever to return to see them.   **N.McG.**

Man and Young Boy, of a bottle-nosed old man suffering from *rhinophyma* and his grandson (*see box on previous page*). Giovanni Bellini, the greatest artist of his family, raised Venetian art to the level of that of Florence. The development of his personal vision is represented in several works including *Crucifixion* (c. 1465–70) and *Virgin and Child with Saints* (c. 1487). Pietro di Cristoforo Vannucci, from Perugia, called Perugino (1445–1523), who strongly influenced his pupil Raphael, frequently painted St Sebastian, the plague saint, and here the saint is placed in an architectural setting with a delicately painted landscape in the distance.

The end of the Quattrocento and first quarter of the Cinquecento (16th century), the Italian High Renaissance, was the moment that produced some of the greatest Italian painters. One of them was Leonardo da Vinci (1452–1519). There are five works by him in the Louvre. *The Virgin of the Rocks* (1482), which shows the Virgin Mary and Jesus with the orphaned St John sheltering in a grotto under the protection of the Archangel Uriel, was the result of a commission from the confraternity of the Conception de San Francisco Grande, but considered unfinished when Leonardo left Milan in 1499 and replaced by the later version, now in London. The *Madonna and Child with St Anne* is a vital, closely knit group of three generations expressing tenderness and compassion. The painting was undoubtedly brought to France by Leonardo, but did not enter the Royal collections until the time of Louis XIII. Also by Leonardo is the late painting, *St John the Baptist* (1513–16), depicting an eloquent androgynous figure whose smile is almost as enigmatic as that of Mona Lisa.

Salle de la Joconde, Rooms 6 and 7: Here is Leonardo's *Mona Lisa* (*see box on pp. 162 and 163*) in a new specially protected free-standing display, in the middle of the gallery. In the same gallery are works by Venetian artists, celebrated for their dynamic use of colour. The most accomplished was Titian (c. 1485–1576) represented by a number of paintings, including the *Concert Champêtre* (c. 1509; *see box on previous page*), the first in the tradition of *fêtes champêtres*. Previously attributed to Giorgione, who heavily influenced Titian, the work is now considered to be an early Titian and it was also a strong influence on Manet (*see p. 85*). It is suggested that the female nudes are allegories, existing only in the imagination of the two seated figures. Titian's flair for colour and technical prowess are fully exploited in the charming *Lady at her Toilet*, and *Man with a Glove* is a deeply expressive portrait carried to perfection by the force of dramatic tonal contrasts. From Louis XIV's collection is *Carrying of Christ to the Tomb*, which encapsulates a moment of dramatic pathos, heavy with the weight of the dead Christ and the burden of sorrow. Tintoretto (1518–94) combined the 'colour of Titian and the drawing of Michelangelo' to produce a highly personal style found in *Paradise*, a preparatory work for the Doge's Palace. Opposite the *Mona Lisa* is the huge painting by Paolo Veronese, *Marriage at Cana*, which was painted for the refectory built by Palladio at San

Giorgio Maggiore, Venice. A religious subject packed with secular detail, the intensity of its colours were rediscovered when it was restored in 1989–92.

The Grande Galerie, Room 8: The greatest of the Roman School artists grouped here is Raffaello Sanzio, called Raphael (1483–1520), who was 30 years younger than Leonardo, and the most eclectic of the great masters of the High Renaissance. The type of Madonna for which he became so famous is La Belle Jardinière (1507), a work heavy with religious symbolism, and one of several such versions of the Holy Family using the pyramidal composition pioneered by Leonardo. The Portrait of Baldassare Castiglione, a straightforward but remarkably effective likeness of the poet and diplomat, was purchased by Louis XIV from the heirs of Cardinal Mazarin in 1661. Works commissioned by Pope Leo X for François I include The Large St Michael, as a diplomatic gift when the countries were allied in conflict against the Turks, and the monumental Holy Family of François I. Giulio Romano (c. 1499–1546) who trained with Raphael and also practised architecture has been described as a pioneer of the Mannerist style. Typical of Correggio (1489?–1534), who is associated with an extreme use of sfumato and a tenderly voluptuous quality, is The Mystic Marriage of St Catherine of Alexandria. Among other Mannerist works are those by the exceptionally accomplished Florentine eccentric Jacopo Pontormo (1494–1556).

Rooms 9 and 10: Reserved for 16th- and 17th-century Italian cartoons and drawings from the Louvre's extensive collection, exhibited in rotation.

The Grande Galerie, Room 12: The greatest Italian painter of the 17th century was Caravaggio (c. 1499–1546), who threw himself passionately into both life and work, and whose artistic influence spread throughout Europe. The message in The Fortune-Teller is clearly legible, and Death of the Virgin (1605–06) was considered scandalous at the time because of the earthy realism of the figures and the dramatic contrasts of light and shade. The Carracci family from Bologna is also represented here, notably Annibale, and also Guido Reni, who was influenced by the Carracci, fell out of fashion in the 19th century but is now admired as a great colourist.

Room 13–22: This series of rooms at the end of the Grande Galerie contains 17th-century works by artists from Genoa, Naples, Bologna and Rome, including Sassoferrato (1609–85). Giuseppe-Maria Crespi was the most individual 18th-century Bolognese artist, best known for his genre scenes.

Rooms 23–25: Eighteenth-century Venetian artists are represented by Canaletto (1697–1768), with typical scenes such as The Molo (c. 1730), of which there are about 10 versions. Francesco Guardi painted in a freer and more expressive mood than Canaletto, obvious in eight scenes depicting festivities for the coronation of the Doge Alvise IV Mocenigo. Giambattista (Giovanni Battista) Tiepolo, was the last in a line of fresco artists and produced Rococo pieces such as The Last Supper.

MONA LISA

Carefully lit, this innovative and enigmatic portrait employing soft tonal modelling positively glows (*see p. 160*). The facts surrounding it are almost as mysterious as the painting itself. It is traditionally assumed to be a portrait of Mona Lisa Gherardini (correctly 'Monna', a variant of *mia donna* the Italian for 'my lady'), third wife of Francesco di Zanobi del Giocondo, the Florentine merchant who commissioned the work. 'Giocondo' is the same word as the English 'jocund'. The famous half-smile of the sitter is probably a visual pun on this name: and it is for this reason that she is also known as *La Gioconda* and in French, *La Joconde*. Leonardo probably began work on the painting in Florence in 1503, taking it to Milan in 1506, and then to France when he arrived at the behest of François I in 1517. One of his favourite pieces, he kept it with him when he returned to Italy, and it is probable that the French king purchased the work for a considerable sum in 1518 from one of Leonardo's two heirs. It was to become the most valued piece in the royal collection and was moved between royal residences—Fontainebleau, Louvre and Versailles. In 1798 the painting was transferred to the Museum Central des Arts, but was purloined in 1800 by Napoleon for his apartments in the Tuileries Palace. It returned permanently to the Louvre in 1804 and has been here ever since, except for a couple of gaps: in August 1911 the painting was stolen, but recovered in Florence in December 1913; during the Second World War it was moved around provincial France for safety.

At some point, probably in the 17th century, the painting was trimmed in size apparently in order to fit a required frame or hanging space: between two and three centimetres were taken off each of the sides and probably a smaller width from top and bottom. In the process the pillared window-frame in which Mona Lisa was originally seen sitting was lost: the bases of the two columns which framed her to each side can still just be perceived at the edges of the panel. This loss has inevitably distorted the effect of the painting, and explains the apparently abrupt passage from foreground to background, which would have been more logical in the original, complete design. As a consequence it is now a small portrait (77 x 53cm), but with tremendous and arresting power and magnetism. It is a seminal work in portrait painting of the 16th century and brings together all of Leonardo's highly experimental skills. It demands more than a brief glimpse to appreciate its beauty and complexity.

Mona Lisa's gaze is benign but elusive. She slightly averts her tawny-coloured eyes, as if something has caught her attention to her left. The smile, which appears to be the clue to her mood, is gentle, but her expression seems to shift from contentment to irony, or from nostalgia to self-satisfaction. She is relaxed, her hands demurely placed on the arm of the chair in which she is seated, dressed in the Florentine fashion of the day, including a lightly draped veil over her hair.

In the background is an aerial view of water and mountains in a misty dawn. The glow of her skin is offset by the dark blue of her dress with yellow sleeves, and complemented by the light sky. There is no hiatus between the tones of foreground and background which are all bathed in a mutable luminosity. Her features and long curled hair are hinted in the facial types in the *Madonna of the Rocks* (c. 1483 and c. 1506) and *Virgin and Child with St Anne* (c. 1483). Leonardo's experience and technical range is concentrated in this small work with a naturalism not practised by his predecessors. Crucial in obtaining the extraordinary effects of the portrait is his use of *sfumato*, the

soft-edged effect which he perfected, managing the natural transition between light and dark in almost imperceptible degrees. The fluidity of the composition and delicacy of the image was achieved by building up layer upon layer of glazes heightened with tiny amounts of pigment on a medium ground. This proportion of an exceedingly small amount of pigment to a substantial thickness of medium (walnut-oil), accounts for the considerable change in colour in the picture: the much brighter Reanaissance colours—the reds and highlights in her face which Vasari (1550) repeatedly mentions—have all been overwhelmed by the oxidation and darkening of the oil, giving the portrait its predominantly greenish hue 500 years on. Leonardo's *Notebooks* document his tireless experimentation with this new and difficult oil-technique, and the degree to which it obsessed and eluded him. The shifts in level in the background force the observer to keep refocusing on the face giving the illusion that the features are in flux. The mobility of Mona Lisa's face is enhanced further by the indistinct definition of the corners of the eyes and mouth. In contrast, hard edges pin the image to the picture surface, such as the border of the transparent veil, and the virtuoso draughtsmanship displayed in her clothes—the pattern on the bodice, the pleats in the sleeves. Arguably the most reproduced image in the world, it has inspired endless copies and alternative versions.

Stone stele (2590–2565 BC) of Princess Nefertiabet from her tomb at Giza.

end. Egyptians believed that Osiris had reigned in the world before becoming sovereign of the dead, and all deceased kings were revered as gods.

Rooms 14–16: On the way out of the Crypt of Osiris is the oldest sarcophagus in the collections, the *Sarcophagus of Abou Roash* (c. 2300 BC), carved in a single block of limestone. The coffin has a number of functions: it is the protective covering of the body; the new home of the deceased; it reproduces the universe in miniature; and stands in for the life beyond. Its shape and decoration reflect the social position of the owner and the art of the period. It also illustrates religious concepts with regard to survival after death. These rooms

illustrate these procedures and equipment with a standing display of wooden mummy cases and embalming and burial rites including a mummy of the Ptolemaic period, with an intricately painted *cartonnage* (moulded linen and plaster) protection. Objects from burial chambers of four different periods describe the evolution in funerary customs over more than 1,000 years. It continues with the full extent, more than 25m, of the papyrus *Book of the Dead* of Hornedjitef, a priest in the Temple of Amun at Thebes c. 220 BC.

Rooms 18 and 19: These final rooms, on the themes of Gods and Magic, bring together animals, sacred and mummified, and the contents of the

Serapeum (a temple to the god Serapis) of Memphis. A procession of animals associated with Egyptian gods includes the goose of Amon, the bull of Montou, Bastet, the cat-faced goddess of Bubastis, and an astonishing collection of mummified animals. There is also the magnificent statue of the bull Apis.

Chronological Circuit: Sully first floor

The north stairs (or the lift in Room 16, or escalator near room 18) lead up to the first floor. An illustrated chronology consisting of panels, each representing 1,000 years, introduces the Circuit which covers some 3,000 years of Egyptian history and art.

Rooms 20 and 21: The highlight of the Nagada period (c. 4000–3100 BC), the end of the Predynastic era, is a dagger from Gebel-el-Arak with a hippopotamus-tooth handle carved with a battle scene, a very early example of relief sculpture. From the Thinite period (c. 3100–2700 BC), the 1st and 2nd Dynasties, is the stele of King Zet Ouadji, the Serpent King, which epitomises the two great phenomena of this period: the unification of Egypt under a single crown, and the birth of writing. The name of the king is written with the hieroglyphic of the serpent. The art of bas-relief was perfected, and luxury objects in ivory and fine vases of coloured stone appeared.

Rooms 22–28: The Old Kingdom (c. 2700–2200 BC) was the time of the great pyramids. The individuality of the king and his funerary monument reached its peak in the 3rd Dynasty and the majority of the objects surviving from this period are funerary. A remarkable find from the pyramid of Didoufri, son of Cheops, is one of the most popular works in the Egyptian department, a small highly coloured limestone figure called the Seated Scribe (c. 2620–2500 BC), sitting cross-legged, with eyes of white quartz and rock crystal. The stone stele of Nefertiabet (Room 22), sister of King Cheops, reflects the degree of refinement reached during this period, showing her seated before a funerary banquet guaranteeing her sustenance in the afterlife.

The Middle Kingdom (c. 2033–1710 BC) marks the classical period of Egyptian civilisation when the kings re-united their kingdom previously carved up by invaders. Among the oustanding statues is the elegant female Libation Carrier, carrying food and water to a departed soul, and remarkable portrait statues of Sesostris III and of his son, Amenemhat III. A small corridor contains the most beautiful stelae of this period.

The New Kingdom spanned the period c. 1550 to 1069 BC. The glorious age when gigantic temples such as Karnac and Luxor were built, c. 1550–1353 BC, is represented here by the statue of Prince Iahmes and the more sensual portraits of the King Amenophis III and Touy.

The time of Akhenaton and Nefertiti (c. 1353–1337 BC) left an outstanding artistic legacy. The famous heretic Akhenaton (Amenophis IV) built the huge open courtyard near Karnac, with massive sculptures in a revolutionary robes and wearing the Ordre du St-Esprit. The work was modelled on the triple portrait of Richelieu by Philippe de Champaigne in London. Antonio

Canova's *Cupid and Psyche* (1787–93) is an idealised representation of young love and a technically perfect and harmonious composition of interlocking forms.

Spanish sculpture

Denon lower ground floor; Room 3: The small collection of 12th–18th-century Spanish sculpture contains examples of capitals from the Visigothic and Mozarab periods, and pieces in alabaster from royal tombs of the Catalan Monastery of Poblet. There is a monumental Gothic doorway, richly decorated with vegetal motifs and an *Annunciation* group. A fairly typical Spanish work is that illustrating a Franciscan legend, the *Dead St Francis* (probably mid-17th century), in polychrome wood, with cord of hemp, eyes of glass and teeth of bone.

Northern European sculpture

Denon lower ground floor; Rooms A–C: Northern European sculpture is a small collection from the 12th–16th centuries. From England are 15th-century alabasters typical of Nottingham production. The most beautiful of the northern *Virgins* (12th–15th centuries) in International Gothic style, is the *Virgin and Child* (c. 1510) from Isenheim, near Colmar (Lorraine), originally the central part of retable carved in lime wood, a material that lends itself well to complicated drapery. Among German and Dutch later-Gothic reliefs and sculptures is a kneeling *Virgin of the Annunciation*, in painted alabaster, by Riemenschneider; and a naked *St Mary Magdalen* (1510), in painted lime wood, made by Gregor Erhart (d. c. 1540) of Augsburg. Her nakedness refers to the legend of the Magdalen living as a mystic ascetic in a cave in Sainte-Baume (Provence) clothed only in her hair.

Renaissance sculpture is represented by the Tombstone of Jean de Coronmeuse, Abbot of St Jacques de Liège (c. 1525–30). There is a bronze *Mercury and Pschye* (1593) by Adriaan de Vries from Prague, and a spirited model of a sculpture by the Swedish artist Johan Tobias Sergel (1740–1814), *Othryades the Spartan, Dying* (1779) in preparation for the plaster maquette to gain admission to the Paris Academy.

ARTS OF AFRICA, ASIA, OCEANIA & THE AMERICAS

West pavilion, Denon ground floor (entry via Portes des Lions)

This collection is a sample of some 120 key works belonging to the Musée du Quai Branly (*see p. 124*). The visit is organised around the four main cultural regions, Africa, Asia, Oceania (Pacific and Australia) and the Americas. The visitor is greeted by an ancient African *Statue of a Man* of the Nagada II period, from pre-dynastic Egypt (5000–4000 BC). A stone sculpture, which once belonged to André Breton, from the Island of Nias, opens the Asiatic sector, while a c. 2000-year old sculpture from Chupicuaro, Mexico, is at the centre of the room devoted to the Americas.

TUILERIES PALACE & ARC DU CARROUSEL

Map p. 474, C1

The former Château des Tuileries has completely disappeared, leaving only fragments at the western extremities of the Palais du Louvre (*see plan on p. 139*): to the north is the Pavillon de Flore and to the south, the Pavillon de Marsan. Both have been restored or rebuilt, and the latter houses the Musée des Arts Décoratifs (*see p. 196*).

History of the Tuileries Palace

The Tuileries Palace, at right angles to the Seine and 500m west of the Louvre, was begun in 1564 by Philibert de l'Orme for Catherine de Médicis as a more comfortable alternative to the Louvre, but she left in 1570 for the Hôtel de Soissons in the Marais (*see p. 261*). The two palaces were eventually linked (*see p. 138*) and the Tuileries became the residence of the ruling monarch. Louis XVI was confined here after being brought from Versailles, until 10th August, 1792, and it became the headquarters of the Convention. The Tuileries then became the main residence of Napoleon (when the Arc du Carrousel was erected as the main entrance to the courtyard), Louis XVIII (who died here), Charles X, Louis-Philippe and Napoléon III. In May 1871 the *communards* set fire to the building which, like the Hôtel de Ville, was completely

The Arc du Carrousel (1806) in the Carrousel Gardens, a scaled-down version of the triumphal arch of Septimus Severus in Rome.

waisted, multi-drawed chiffonier in shark skin for the bedroom of the Ambassadress is by André Groult.

Modernity and Tradition highlights different trends across the period. The couturier Jacques Doucet, major collector of contemporary art, commissioned Pierre Legrain, Marcel Coard and Paul Mergier in the 1920s to design the furnishings, inspired by Cubism and African art, to accompany his collection of contemporary paintings. Also here are pieces made 1916–33 by Emile-Jacques Ruhlmann, and the contents of Robert Mallet-Stevens' studio. The Union des Artistes Modernes in the 1930s, formed by Mallet-Stevens and other leading designers in 1929, was responsible for the first Salon of the UAM at the Musée des Arts Décoratifs in 1930. This period produced rigorous designs typical of Le Corbusier, and the eclectic pieces by Pierre Legrain, but as time went on, the group as a whole took an increasingly rational approach to interiors, especially the use of tubular steel which was pioneered by Marcel Bruer at the Dessau Bauhaus in the 1920s, and revolutionised furniture design.

Ninth to fifth floors

Modern and Contemporary Rooms 54–67: This section occupies the five upper floors at the western end of the Pavillon de Marsan, a unique section of the building characterised by the use of metal and glass from its rebuilding in 1873. From here are magnificent views over the Tuileries. Chronologically the exhibits start on the 9th Floor, with the 1940s, and end on the 5th Floor with 2000. Access is by lift on the 4th Floor north, near Room 48.

The 1940s and 50s: The Vitrine of Objects is a tribute to the wealth of decorative arts from the 1930s to the 1950s. Experimentation with new forms, materials and techniques, and inspiration drawn from diverse sources, was expressed in ceramics, glass, enamels and metalwork. Works exhibited at the 1937 Exhibition show the diverging trends of Modernist artists such as René Herbst, André Hermant and René Coulon, whereas private and public commissions carried out by André Arbus remained more traditional. The influence of Surrealism and the study of dreams is evident in the spectacular table by Gilbert Poillerat, and in elements from the studio of Diego and Alberto Giacometti. The 1950s are dominated by three architect-designers: Jean Prouvé, illustrated by his work for the Cité Universitaire; Jean Royère, who freely reinvented traditional knowledge to create furniture such as the banana sofa; and Charlotte Perriand, who spent time in Japan, hence her bamboo chaise longue. Other new generation objects adapt to the new technology, such as the TV and record player.

Ambassador's Office Library designed by Pierre Chareau for the Pavilion of the French Embassy at the Internationl Exhibition of Decorative Arts in 1925.

The 1960s and '70s: Here the chair reigns supreme (*see p. 199*), with a display of around 100 examples which can be followed in strictly chronological evolution and include artists' designs such as the Nikki de Saint Phalle chair. The 1970 Exhibition *A Table* is evoked by a long trestle with experimental tableware. A large vitrine contains around 120 examples of ceramics and glass of 1981 and 1982. Not to be missed (in a corner room) are a range of contemporary chairs from which to watch a film of clips featuring iconic furniture of the period.

The 1980s and '90s: Fun, funky, outrageous—the avant garde of these years have become the household names of today: Philippe Starck designs are found all over Paris, including the Café de la Musique at La Villette (*see p. 320*); Olivier Gagnère was responsible for the interior of Café Marly (*see p. 436*); and Roger Tallon designed the seating for the TGV. Marc Newson's curvy three-legged *Pod of Drawers*, laminated in rivetted aluminium, contrasts with Alessandro Mendini's elaborate post-modernist *Proust* chair. At other extremes are Gaetano Pesce's *Samson* table and *Delilha* chairs, and *Collection Pi*, by Martin Szekely, in steel and aluminium.

The 2000s: A group of architectonic pieces, some classic, some extreme, addresses the new concepts such as the Bouroullec brothers' *Cabane* or the *Line of furniture* by Frédéric Ruyant. Sculptures in glass or ceramic are impressive and innovative, such as Bernard Déjonghe's *Meules Vives*.

Second floor south

Toys Gallery and Jean Dubuffet Gallery

The museum has over 12,000 objects in its collection of toys, which will be rotated in these galleries twice a year. The oldest pieces are pre-Revolution pieces, but the majority date from the mid-19th century onwards; the first acquisition was a collection of 19th-century furniture but the museum's pieces are no longer exclusively of French production. The evolution of Jean Dubuffet's work can be followed from the 1940s in his large personal collection, donated to the museum in 1967.

Jewellery Gallery

The oldest pieces in this veritable Aladdin's cave are Merovingian (5th century) and Byzantine rings. Jewellery from the Middle Ages through to the 17th century normally carried religious themes, such as the remarkable pendant of the Pascal Lamb (16th century). By the 17th century, decorative pendants became ever more elaborate and by the 18th production boomed with the increased availability of precious stones, including diamonds, and wealthier customers. By the 19th century, sets of jewellery became the fashion for women. The museum also owns the Nissim de Camondo collection of tie-pins. The delicate and elaborate French Art Nouveau pieces, many from the Vever collection, include several by Lalique. The more rigorous Art Deco jewellery includes examples by Georges Fouquet,

Jean Lambert Rucki, and Maison Boucheron. The Modern collection includes work by Line Vautrin and Jean Schulmberger, also by Alexander Calder, Georges Braque, Jean Lurçat and Henri Laurens. Contemporary artists employ a wider range of materials and have revolutionised designs. Representative are the *Hinged Loop Neckpiece* (1976) by David Watkins in acrylic, aluminium and gold, or the filigree silver *Col-Collier Mains* (1994) by Jacomijn van der Donk.

Rohan wing first and second floors

Musée de la Mode et du Textile

The Musée de la Mode et du Textile (Fashion and Textiles) occupies the first and second floors of the Rohan wing. It conserves some 19,000 costumes, dating from the 17th century to the present, along with 36,000 accessories (such as umbrellas, Second Empire hats, fans, shoes, handbags and gloves) and 31,000 samples of textiles (prints, tapestries, laces, embroideries, braids) since the 14th century, and patterns and pattern-books. The 20th-century fashion houses are well represented, including Paul Poiret, Jeanne Lanvin, Elsa Schiaparelli, Chanel, Balmain, Dior, Courreges, through to Alexander McQueen and Hedi Slimane. To complete the museum, there is a photographic library, a slide library, commercial catalogues of the second half of the 20th century to the present day, books, periodicals, drawings and engravings.

Rohan wing third floor

Musée de la Publicité

The space for the Musée de la Publicité (advertising), which opened in 1999, was designed by Jean Nouvel. This museum mounts temporary exhibitions twice a year on specific themes drawn from the remarkable collection of around 100,000 posters from the 18th century to the present. In addition the museum has over 20,000 publicity films (French and foreign) from the 1930s to today, as well as many other items of promotional material. There is also a multimedia library with free public access, and a reading room.

MUSEE DE L'ORANGERIE
Map p. 474, B1

Open Wed–Mon 12.30–7, Fri 12.30–9; closed Tues; T: 01 44 77 80 07; excellent audio-guides; free audio-visual; disabled facilities; well-stocked bookshop and boutique.
The Musée de l'Orangerie stands above Place de la Concorde, between the Tuileries and the Seine. Always a popular small gallery, it reopened in 2006 after a long closure. It contains Monet's series of painted panels, *The Water Lilies*, and the Jean Walter and Paul Guillaume Collection of early 20th-century art featuring work by many of the most famous names in French art. (*Cont'd overleaf*)

The Water Lilies

Claude Monet offered his sensational series *The Water Lilies* (1914–26) to the State in 1918. The eight compositions (a total of 22 panels) were installed in 1927 in two oval rooms specially designed with the approval of the painter. At the time Impressionism was not fashionable and Monet's paintings did not draw in the crowds. In 1960 the Orangerie received the Walter-Guillaume Collection. To house this donation an extra floor was constructed above the Monet rooms, depriving *The Water Lilies* of natural light. As part of the recent alterations, this floor has been removed, and the series, an integral part of the structure, are flooded with daylight again. The walls of *The Water Lilies'* galleries are transformed into the lily ponds of Monet's gardens at Giverny, drenched in colour and reflected light. The first cycle is orientated with the clear blue of *Morning* to the east and the hazy pinks and golds of *Setting Sun* to the west. *Clouds* and *Green Reflections* are self descriptive. The view is directly into the water, and the mood is calm. From a distance the tones and staining create a shimmering surface, while up close the energetic commas of paint reveal Monet's expertise—and sheer joy—in putting colour on canvas. The second cycle is based on ever deeper and richer blues and greens. The trunks and branches of weeping willows frame the ponds and add some degree of spatial depth. The longest continuous panel on the east wall is acutely curved, and standing close to it creates an effect of almost total emersion.

Walter-Guillaume Collection

The collection does not set out to be a representative cross-section of art in Paris during the first decades of the 20th century, but reflects the personal taste of one visionary individual, Paul Guillaume (1892–1934). Guillaume had no artistic background, but he had enough instinctive appreciation of talent and native skill in making the right contacts to become a successful dealer and collector of modern art. He found African masks in a consignment of rubber and exhibited them, catching the attention of the 'pope' of Modernism, Guillaume Apollinaire. The painter and writer Max Jacob (1876–1944) introduced him to many rising stars in the art world. In 1914, Guillaume opened a gallery and went on to found the review, *Les Arts à Paris*. Such was his reputation that Dr Albert C. Barnes, the American patron of the arts who established the Barnes Foundation in Philadelphia, called on him for advice. After he died at the age of 42 his widow, Juliette Lacaze, known as Domenica, married Jean Walter. She sold some 144 works by ten major artists to the state in 1959 and 1963.

The new Lower Ground Floor galleries have been specially created for this collection. During excavation, a section of an old wall, the *enceinte des Fossés jaunes* (c. 1566) was revealed and can be viewed. The first room provides information on Paul Guillaume through photographs, documents, and other memorabilia, and there are portrait tributes to him by Modigliani, van Dongen and Derain. A reconstruction of an interior from Domenica Walter's home includes paintings by Rousseau and Derain and photographs show the rooms in which Paul Guillaume originally exhibited his collection in the 1930s.

Renoir

Impressionism is represented by Monet and Sisley and some earlier works by Pierre-Auguste Renoir. From the 1880s, Renoir moved away from Impressionism and in the 1890s captured the innocence and prettiness of youth in studies of girls at the piano. The 1892 study, a major work of the period, was in response to a State commission, and he made four more versions. Renoir's delight in fancy dress, in the manner of Van Dyck or Veronese, is revealed in his portrait of his youngest son Claude (b. 1901), known as 'Coco', as *The Clown* (1909). Renoir was by then in poor health but continued to paint for pleasure, and to give pleasure, returning constantly to the female nude, voluptuous and passive.

Cézanne

The 14 superb works by Paul Cézanne include two versions of *Still Life with Apples*, ten years apart. The earlier is a carefully balanced composition, while the tipped perspective of the later results in a more dynamic work. Typically Cézanne returned time and time again to the same subjects—the apples, the ginger jar, the rustic tabletop—in order to explore structure, and the relationships of parts to the whole; the same applies to bathers, family portraits such as the long-suffering Madame Cézanne (1885), and landscapes around his hometown, Aix-en-Provence.

Rousseau, Modigliani and Laurencin

The museum owns the largest group of works in France by Henri 'le Douanier' Rousseau

Claude Monet: *The Water Lilies* (1914–26) in the Musée de l'Orangerie.

(1844–1910) including *The Wedding* (c. 1908), and *Père Junier's Cart* (1910), of his neighbour. The static figures, flat and detailed painting, strong colours and outlines, were a refreshing contrast to ethereal Impressionist paintings but not so far removed from the monumentality of Seurat, or the flat colours of the Symbolists. Picasso admired le Douanier's work, and gave a dinner in his honour in 1908. Naïve or Primitive paintings also delighted the Surrealists for their imaginative, story-telling content and the artists' lack of formal training.

Paul Guillaume was the first and possibly the only real patron of Amedeo Modigliani (1884–1920). The apparent simplification of Modigliani's style is the result of influences ranging through the Italian masters, Toulouse-Lautrec, and Cézanne, as well as African primitive art. He was charming but self-destructive and his paintings frequently evoke both isolation and tenderness. The portrait of Guillaume stands out vividly.

Marie Laurencin (1883–1956), Apollinaire's lover, friend of the Cubists and designer of ballet sets, produced wistful paintings, mainly elegant and evanescent studies of women, which carry a fleeting reference to Orphic Cubism. She painted a portrait of Madame Paul Guillaume.

Picasso and Matisse

Picasso and Matisse, the two great rivals, stand out from the crowd. Picasso's blue and pink periods are represented in a rare large pastel *L'Etreinte* (1903) and *Les Adolescents* (1906) which was painted in Spain. *Nude on Red Background* (1905–06) just pre-dates *Demoiselles d'Avignon* (1907) and shows the influence of African masks in the schematisation of the features. The tonally modelled, monumental *Large Bather* (1921) stands out in contrast to the flat planes and colour of *Woman with Tambourine* (1925).

All the paintings by Matisse are of women in interiors. In the earliest, *The Three Sisters* (1916–17), Matisse is still organising forms with great clarity, colours are vivid, and contours flattened. The decorative interiors with *odalisques*, painted during the 1920s in Nice, are more atmospheric, evoking the indolence of warm afternoons, and introduce Matisse's deep involvement with fabrics and costumes.

Derain, Utrillo and Soutine

The 28 examples of works by André Derain include the elegant *Portrait of Mme Guillaume* (c. 1929). The solemn realism of these works of 1920–30 reveal explicitly the 'return to order' in art after the First World War, and the reaction against the pre-1914 abstract and cubist experiments. *Le Beau Modèle* (1923) and *Nude with Pitcher* (1924–30) are both monumental nudes, but show a marked change in brushwork, and there are reassuring still lifes such as *Nature Morte au Panier* (1927) using a limited palette, and landscapes.

Less reassuring is the large collection of works by Maurice Utrillo (1883–1955), alcoholic son of the painter Suzanne Valadon, who lived on La Butte Montmartre. Like Laurencin and Modigilani, he belonged to no particular group or school. His thickly painted and scraped pictures were often taken from postcards or photographs, and show a technical affinity with the subjects that he painted such as the desolate, almost monochromatic, urban landscapes of Paris including *L'Eglise de Clignancourt* and *Berlioz's House* (both 1914).

The disturbing Expressionist paintings of the Lithuanian Chaïm Soutine, on whom van Gogh was an early influence, are painted in thick impasto. Distortions, acrid colours, and a very personal and emotional approach brought him instant fame and concomitant self-doubt. He painted raw flesh in abattoirs, and young people who served, almost to the point of caricature, as for example *The Choirboy* (1928).

THE GALERIE DU JEU-DE-PAUME

Open Tues 12–9, Wed–Fri 12–7, Sat, Sun 10–7, closed Mon; T: 01 47 03 12 50.
On the opposite side of the Tuileries gardens to L'Orangerie, the Jeu-de-Paume is so named because it was originally a real (royal) tennis-court built in 1851. The building once contained the Impressionist collections that were transferred to the Musée d'Orsay in 1986. It reopened in 1991 for exhibitions of modern and contemporary photography.

SAINT-GERMAIN-L'AUXERROIS
Map p. 475, D1

Open daily 8–7; T: 01 42 60 13 96.
On Place du Louvre, Rue de l'Amiral de Coligny, the area where reputedly Caesar's legions encamped in 52 BC, is the church of St-Germain-l'Auxerrois, a Gothic church (13th–16th centuries) but much altered. It stands opposite the eastern façade of the Louvre and was the parish church of the Palace.

History of St-Germain-l'Auxerrois
The church, dedicated to the 5th-century St Germanus, Bishop of Auxerre, stands on the site of a Merovingian sanctuary which was replaced in the 11th century. The present building was begun in the 13th century at the time of Philippe-Auguste and the only remains of the earlier church are the foundations of the belfry south of the choir. On 24th August, 1572, the church bell, *la Marie*, signalled the start of the Massacre of St Bartholomew, the wholesale slaughter of Huguenots on the occasion of the marriage of Protestant Henri de Navarre (Henri IV) to Catholic Marguerite de Valois during the Wars of Religion. The church was drastically altered in the 18th century, and after desecration during the Revolution and ransacking in 1831 was in need of serious restoration when it reopened in 1837. Under the direction of Jean-Baptiste Lassus an attempt was made to recreate the Gothic church (1838–55). According to Viollet-le-Duc, the adjacent *Mairie* (Town Hall; 1859) of the 1st Arrondissement was intended as a caricature of the adjoining church. The conspicuous neo-Gothic north tower was added the following year. Many royal artists and architects of the Valois Court were buried here including Lemercier, Gabriel and Le Vau, all of whom worked

on the Louvre, and De Cotte who worked at Versailles. Among painters were Coypel, Boucher and Chardin and sculptors Coysevox, N. and G. Coustou (1658–1733) , all of whose work is represented in the Musée du Louvre. The most striking exterior feature is the porch, by Jean Gaussel (1435–39), with a rose window, and above, a balustrade which encircles the building.

The interior

The interior (78m by 39m) is double-aisled. The alterations in 1745 mingle 18th-century classicism with Gothic by converting piers into fluted columns and heightening their capitals as well as removing some of the stained glass. The organ case from the Sainte-Chapelle was designed by Pierre-Noël Roussel and made by Lavergne in 1756. Opposite the entrance are two 17th-century white marble holy water stoups. The brass pendant chandeliers are 18th-century. To the right of the door is a 12th- or 13th-century *St Germanus* (Germain) which, with the 15th-century *St Mary of Egypt*, was originally in the porch. In the adjacent chapel is a wooden *Crucifix*. The Chapel of the Holy Sacrement (late 13th-century) reserved for silent prayer, has a *Tree of Jesse* designed by Viollet-le-Duc and above it a 14th-century *Virgin* of the Champagne School. The royal pew (1682–84), in the north aisle, a *tour-de-force* of wood carving, was designed by Le Brun and executed by François Mercier. The wood is worked to represent a baldaquin with draperies above fretworked panels and supported by Ionic columns and pilasters. The pulpit is 17th-century and the wooden *Christ* is by Bouchardon (18th century). Fragments of the destroyed rood-screen, sculpted by Jean Goujon, are preserved in the Louvre. The wrought-iron choir-railings date from 1767. At the choir entrance is a wooden statue of St Germanus, seated, and a stone figure of St Vincent (both 15th century). Only the transepts have their original 15th–16th-century stained-glass, *Pentecost* to the south, and the *Life of Christ* opposite. The font was designed by Mme de Lamartine.

Above a small door in the south ambulatory is a late 15th-century polychrome *Virgin* and on the left is a French triptych (1530). The first inner bay, the oldest part of the church, is the base of the 12th-century belfry. In the 4th chapel are marble statues of Etienne d'Aligre and his son, both Chancellors of France (d. 1635 and 1677).

Environs of St-Germain-l'Auxerrois

On Rue St-Honoré is the classical-Mannerist **Temple de l'Oratoire** (1621–30), with an 18th-century façade. It was designed by Clément Métezeau the younger, and Jacques Lemercier and François Mansart also had a hand. Originally the French mother church for the Congregation of the Oratory, it was assigned by Napoleon in 1811 to the Calvinists.

In Rue de Rivoli is a monument of 1889 by Crauk to the Huguenot Admiral Coligny (1519–72), the chief victim of the massacre of St. Bartholomew's Eve (*see p. 209 above*), initially wounded nearby. At the angle of Rue-St-Honoré and Rue de l'Abre Sec is the *Fontaine du Trahoir*, its stalactites and shells surrounding a nymph sculpted by Boziot. The fountain was rebuilt by Soufflot in 1778, replacing one by Goujon.

THE CHAMPS-ELYSEES

PLACE DE LA CONCORDE
Map p. 469, E4

Place de la Concorde is one of the world's most impressive squares, situated next to the Seine between the Etoile and the Ile de la Cité, at the east end of the Avenue des Champs-Elysées. Even the constantly swirling traffic does not detract from the superb perspectives and skilful landscaping of this huge open space, devoid of buildings on three sides. The design dates from the First Empire, but its present appearance dates from 1852, when Jacques-Ignace Hittorff (1792–1867) redesigned the square. In 1995, the 18 green-bronze and gilded *colonnes rostrales* (rostral columns) made for the July festivities of 1838, were renovated and reinstalled. They are decorated to resemble the prow of a ship, and symbolise, like the city's coat of arms, the importance of the river in the history of the Paris.

HISTORY OF PLACE DE LA CONCORDE

In 1757 the empty site to the west of Paris was chosen to receive a bronze statue of Louis XV commissioned by the *echevins* (magistrates, *see p. 281*, Hôtel de Ville). The statue by Bouchardon and Pigalle (model in the Louvre) was unveiled in 1763 and the surrounding square, the creation of Jacques-Ange Gabriel, named Place Louis XV. The celebrations with fireworks to mark the marriage of the Dauphin Louis and Marie-Antoinette in 1770 resulted in 133 onlookers being crushed to death in a ditch. In 1792 the statue was replaced by a huge figure of Liberty, designed by Lemot and the square was renamed Pl. de la Révolution. In the same year the perpetrators of the theft of the crown jewels (*see below p. 212*) were executed here by guillotine. On 21st January 1793 the same fate befell Louis XVI on the site now occupied by the fountain nearest the river, and between May 1793 and May 1795 the blade claimed 1,119 victims. The square received its present name in 1795 at the end of the Terror, but it was subsequently renamed Place Louis XV at the Restoration (1815) before it finally reverted to Concorde under Louis-Philippe (1830).

Monuments and buildings of Place de la Concorde

In the centre, on the site of first Louis XV's statue and then *Liberty*, rises the *Obelisk of Luxor*, a monolith of pink syenite, almost 23m high. It originally stood before a temple at Thebes in Upper Egypt and commemorates in its hieroglyphics the deeds of Rameses II (13th century BC). It was presented to Louis-Philippe in 1831 by

Mohammed Ali (the donor of Cleopatra's Needle in London). The pedestal, of Breton granite, bears representations of the apparatus used in its erection in 1836 (*see p. 292*). The two fountains, by Hittorf, copies of those in the piazza of St. Peter's at Rome, are embellished with figures symbolising inland and marine navigation.

On the north side of the square are two handsome colonnaded mansions designed by Gabriel in 1763–72, originally intended as official residences, with pediment sculptures by M.-A. Slodtz and G. Coustou the younger. The one on the right, from which the crown jewels were stolen, is now the Naval Ministry whereas before that it has served as the Garde-Meuble de la Couronne, or royal furniture store. At that time the public was allowed to see the furniture which royalty changed according to the season. The left-hand building has long been shared between the Automobile Club and the prestigious Hôtel Crillon. Between these buildings Rue Royale leads to the church of the Madeleine (*see p. 237*) and the Palais-Bourbon (National Assembly) can be seen to the south (*see p. 91*) across the Seine.

Pont de la Concorde, on the south side of the square, with magnificent views up and down river, was built in 1788–90 and widened in 1932. Stone from the Bastille was used in the construction of the upper part (so that Parisians could feel they were treading upon the relics of tyranny).

Eight 18th-century stone pavilions around the square, by Gabriel, support statues (restored in 1989) by Caillonette, Cortot and Pradier personifying the eight provincial capitals. Strasbourg (as capital of Alsace, lost to France in 1871) was hung with crêpe and wreaths until 1918.

The pillars of the gateway opening from the Pl. de la Concorde to the Tuileries Gardens (*see p. 194*) are crowned by replicas of equestrian statues of Fame and Mercury, by Coysevox (brought from Marly in 1719; *see p. 190*). Balancing these equestrian groups, on the west of Pl. de la Concorde, the dramatic sweep of the Av. des Champs-Elysées towards the Arc de Triomphe is framed by replicas of the *Horses of Marly* (originals in the Louvre), two groups by G. Coustou, which were brought from the Château de Marly (*see p. 402*) in 1794.

THE CHAMPS-ELYSEES
Map p. 469, D4

To the west of Place de la Concorde extend the Champs-Elysées, through which the Avenue des Champs-Elysées, the most famous avenue in the world, gently ascends northwest for nearly 2km to the striking silhouette of the Arc de Triomphe. Parisians and visitors alike still flock there, although time has taken its toll on the 'Elysian Fields' and its former elegance is a little faded. Three hundred additional trees, which are now maturing, help to redress the balance and when lit up at night, especially at Christmas, the old magic returns. This is the focus for numerous state occasions and commemorations, as wide-ranging as the celebration of Liberation in 1944 and France's soccer triumph in the 1998 World Cup.

The Champs-Elysées has two distinct parts. The smaller section, from Pl. de la Concorde to the Rond-Point des Champs-Elysées, has museums (notably the Musée du Petit Palais, *see below*) and theatres among the Jardins des Champs-Elysées created in 1838. In the gardens are several restaurants (Ledoyen, *1 Av. Dutuit, T: 01 53 05 10 01*, and Carré des Champs Elysées, *T :01 53 05 10 02*; Laurent, *41 Av. Gabriel, T: 01 42 25 00 39*, and Pavillon de l'Elysées, *10 Av. Des Champs- Elysées, T: 01 42 65 85 10*). At no. 25 Av. des Champs-Elysées is the former Hôtel de la Païva (1866), in florid neo-Renaissance style, built for the Marquise de Païva (*see p. 253*) where artists and writers were entertained. It is now home to the Travellers' Club.

The more commercialised section of the Avenue, between the Rond-Point and the Arc de Triomphe, is flanked by offices and showrooms, cinemas and banks, expensive restaurants and fast-food outlets.

HISTORY OF THE CHAMPS-ELYSEES

At the beginning of the 17th century, this low-lying area was still marshland, but after a decree issued in 1667 to create a promenade in the same perspective as the Tuileries Gardens, it was drained and in 1670 laid out to designs by Le Nôtre. The name was changed from Grand-Cours to Champs-Elysées early in the 18th century. The Marquis de Marigny, brother of Madame de Pompadour, had it replanted in 1765 and the avenue was extended to the Pont de Neuilly in 1774. It was used from 1814–16 as a military encampment for allied troops and the gardens consequently suffered. The area became fashionable during the Second Empire and in 1858 the gardens were re-landscaped in the less-formal English style, remaining virtually unchanged since then.

MUSEE DU PETIT PALAIS
Map p. 469, D4

Open Tues–Sun 10–6; Tues, during temporary exhibitions 10–8; closed Mon and holidays. Entrance on Av. Winston Churchill; T: 01 53 43 40 00, www.petitpalais.paris.fr
The Musée du Petit Palais is the fine arts museum of the City of Paris with collections of a rare diversity housed in a municipal palace of 1900. Frequent temporary exhibitions (free for under-13s) are mounted and the permanent collections are free to all. There is a garden café-restaurant, a bookshop-boutique, and a tactile visit for the visually impaired.

History of the Petit Palais
The Musée des Beaux-Arts de la Ville de Paris opened its doors on 11th December, 1902, in a fine building echoing Les Invalides designed by Charles Girault (1851–1932) for the Universal Exhibition of 1900. It is now a prime example of a

building of the period whose grandiose Neoclassical public face is a veneer disguising the thoroughly 'modern' aspects of the interior spaces achieved by the use of materials such as cast iron, concrete and quantities of glass. The entrance hall and main galleries are palatial. Among the stone, stucco, mosaic and paint are two statues in gilded zinc, *Renommées* and *Enfants musicians*, but by the time Albert Besnard was working on the painted décor of the entrance hall (1903–10), Cubism had arrived. The renovations carried out from 2001 to December 2005 have returned the museum to its original aspect, re-establishing the interplay between interior and exterior space and re-introducing natural light. In addition, new spaces have been created and the number of works on display has increased by more than a half, from 850 to 1,300.

The collections

The origins of the collections in the Musée du Petit Palais are responsible for the peculiar diversity of the exhibits. In 1870 the City of Paris began to purchase and commission work in the *Salons* or directly from artists, and also acquired the contents of workshops, resulting in an interesting cross-section of French fine and decorative arts, from Rococo to Impressionism. At the same time, the museum was enriched by donations of personal collections, some more or less contemporary whereas others introduced new themes and periods. The four major bequests were Dutuit, Tuck, Ocampo and Marie, plus a collection of icons from Roger Cabal in 1998. The Museum's permanent collections, exhibited on two levels facing the Champs-Elysées, are presented to create visual interactions between the different arts on display. Temporary exhibitions are on the first floor galleries on the Seine side.

First floor

Rooms 1–8: Taking their cue from the date of the building itself, these rooms contain art works and artefacts from the late 19th century and Paris in 1900. The emphasis in the first two rooms is on hand-crafted ceramics, glassware, enamels and metalwork, illustrating the reaction against increasing mass-production encouraged by the Universal Exhibitions. A unique piece by Emile Gallé (1846–1904), Art Nouveau glass-maker from Nancy, *Vase Cypripedium* (1898), is based on a wild French orchid commonly known as the *Sabot-de-Venus* (Lady's Slipper), and is a pioneering example of the complicated procedure of glass marquetry; it stands on a carved wooden plinth.

Representative of the eclectic taste of the period are Armand Point's (1861–1932) *Small Coffer* (1898) inspired by medieval enamels, a studiously nonchalant *Portrait of Sarah Bernhardt* (1876) by Georges Clarin (1843–1919), and an extravagant piece of polychrome ceramic sculpture, the *Jardinière des Titans*, inspired by Rodin.

In Room 3, the finely executed Naturalist or Realist works by Alfred Roll (1846–1919) and Fernand Pelez (1848–1913) describe different aspects of Parisian life at the turn of the century: the Belle Epoque for some but misery for many others. They are the

PETIT PALAIS

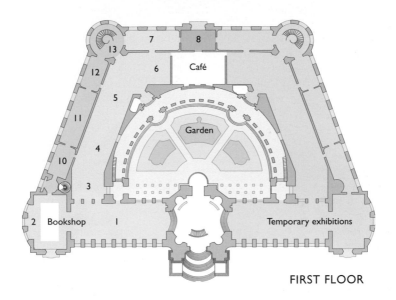

FIRST FLOOR

visual arts' equivalent of Zola's literary observations of man in his environment. In Room 4, two major Realist works by Courbet, *Girls on the Banks of the Seine* (1857; *pictured overleaf*) and *Sleep* (1866), demonstrate his remarkable skills of observation, possibly influenced by photography. They were donated by his sister Juliette. In the following two rooms the Third Republic is celebrated in a plaster model by Dalou, while a return to religious themes is heralded by *The Valley of Tears* by Gustave Doré (1832–83) and *The First Funeral* (1883) by Louis-Ernest Barrias (1841–1905). The latter also indicates the growing interest in pre-history.

In Rooms 7 and 8 the portable painting equipment on display is a reminder of how crucial these innovations were for developments in painting *en plein air*. Works here by masters of the outdoors include *Sunset at Lavacourt* (1880) painted by Monet, just at the moment when the ice on the river was melting. Other pioneering *plein-air* painters represented include Boudin, Sisley, and the father of them all, Pissarro. Work in the round is represented by Rodin (*see p. 116*) who furthered the art of sculpture much as the Impressionists did that of painting. In stylistic contrast is Bourdelle's *Penelope*. Portraits of the art dealer and supporter of avant-garde artists, Ambroise Vollard, were painted by Cézanne in 1899, Renoir c. 1911, and Bonnard c. 1924. Vollard owned the vase decorated by the American, Mary Cassatt, that can be seen here. The museum also has a collection of pastels by Berthe Morisot and others.

Gustave Courbet: *Girls on the Banks of the Seine* (1857).

Henri Matisse purchased Cézanne's *Three Bathers* (c. 1879–82) from Vollard in 1899 and kept it for 36 years, until he and his wife donated it to the Petit Palais, when he wrote: '...it has provided me with moral support in critical moments in my adventure as an artist; I have drawn from it my faith and my perseverance...' This almost-square composition, one example of many *Bathers* painted by Cézanne, has a concentrated vitality. The paint handling is rapid and dense, and the figures, which are neither monumental nor especially lyrical, appear self-absorbed, enveloped by the landscape.

Rooms 9–13: These rooms contain examples of 18th-century decorative arts, mainly from the Edouard and Julia Tuck collection (*see p. 367*), and include a beautiful Sedan chair (c. 1700). French Regency *rocaille* furniture is characterised by the use of exotic wood veneers, intricate marquetry and lacquer. Beauvais tapestries include Rococo and Chinoiserie designs. An elaborate clock with a metal and porcelain case, *The Orchestra of Monkeys,* comes from Germany. From Room 13 the north staircase, with a very fine wrought iron balustrade, sweeps down to the ground floor.

Ground floor

Rooms 14–17: Here are 19th-century Romantic and Classical works of portraiture. The leading sculptor of the period, Jean-Baptiste Carpeaux (1827–75), pre-empted Rodin in the use of dramatic light and shade in sculpture and came to prominence with the Ugolin (plaster) group in 1861. Several of his major public commissions led to controversy, and at the end of his career he was wracked by increasing persecution mania. Contrasting studies among a collection of portrait paintings are *Roman Odalisque* (1843), a beautifully balanced nude by Corot, and Manet's portrait of the dandified Cognac merchant, Théodore Duret, in which Manet includes an impeccable still-life.

Rooms 18–20: The mysteries of Symbolism, the antidote to Realism or Naturalism, permeate all the arts, with

Bartholomé's *femme fatale*, Symbolist landscapes by Ménard and Brokman, experimental works by Henry Cros (1840–1907), and pastels by Odilon Redon (1840–1916), illustrating the range of Symbolist paintings, while bizarre creations by Jean Carriès (1855–94) include experiments with different materials and the maquette for a gateway. In Room 20, the sinuous lines of Art Nouveau are equally present in the dining room designed by Hector Guimard (1867–1942) for his home, and in superb jewellery by Georges Fouquet. Like Lalique, Fouquet preferred to use semi-precious stones on the basis of their colour and shapes.

Room 21: This room displays decorative panels commissioned from Edouard Vuillard (1868–1940) to decorate a room in a private home around 1900.

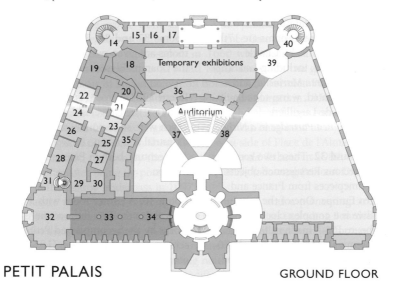

PETIT PALAIS   GROUND FLOOR

THE ARC DE TRIOMPHE
Map p. 496, B3

Open April–Sept 10am–11pm; Oct–March 10am–10.30pm; and after ceremonies on 8 May, 14 July, 11 Nov; T: 01 55 37 73 77. Most easily accessible via the tunnel from Champs-Elysées. Twelve avenues radiate starwise from Pl. Charles-de-Gaulle, formerly Pl. de l'Etoile, and still commonly known as such, around which traffic roars at an alarming rate. In the midst of this traffic chaos stands the serene and grandiose Arc de Triomphe, the largest triumphal arch in the world (almost 50m high, and 45m wide), erected to the glory of the French army and a monument to Napoleon's megalomania.

HISTORY OF THE ARC DE TRIOMPHE

Napoleon's desire to raise a triumphal arch to the Imperial armies began to take shape in 1806 after their victory at Austerlitz. Designed by Chalgrin, the arch was completed only in 1836. At the time of the Emperor's marriage to Marie-Louise of Austria (1810), it was necessary to build a mock arch for the wedding procession. Still unfinished by the time of the fall of the Empire in 1814, it was not until 1823, when Louis XVIII dedicated it to his armies returning victorious from Spain, that work began again under Huyot. The project was finally brought to a close at the time of Louis-Philippe when Blouet took over in 1832, remaining faithful to Chalgrin's ideas, and Blouet also supervised the decoration, carried out by several of the best sculptors of the day. On an intensely cold day in 1840 the funeral cortège bearing Napoleon's ashes passed under the Arch. The Pl. de l'Etoile was designed by Haussmann after the Arch was built, and the uniform façades between each avenue by Hittorff in 1854–57. These have no access from the square but are reached from the encircling Rues de Tilsitt (north) and de Presbourg (south).

The arch and its sculpture

The arch contains a museum of the history of the monument, but the greatest attraction is the observation platform at the top. From here, until late into the evening, there are spectacular views down to the star pattern of the street below, along the great vista of the Champs-Elysées or towards the huge Grande Arche de la La Défense. The sculptures at ground level, especially the colossal groups in high relief on the main façades, are impressive. Facing the Champs-Elysées are (on the right) the *Departure of the Army in 1792* or *La Marseillaise* by Rude, undoubtedly the most dynamic composition of the four, and (on the left) the *Triumph of Napoléon in 1810*, by Cortot. Facing the Av. de la Grande-Armée are (right) the *Resistance of the French in 1814*, and (left) the *Peace of 1815*, both by Etex. The four spandrels of the main archway contain figures of Fame by

La Marseillaise by François Rude on the east façade of the Arc de Triomphe.

Pradier, and those of the smaller archways have sculptures by Nicholas François Vallois (south side) and Théophile Bra. Above the groups are relief panels of the campaigns of 1792–1805 including (north) the Battle of Austerlitz. On the row of shields in the attic storey are inscribed the names of battles of the Republic and the Empire, although not all were French victories. Below the side arches are the names of some hundreds of generals who took part in these campaigns with the names of those killed in action underlined. Beneath the arch is the Tomb of the Unknown Soldier, victim of the 1914–18 War. The flame has burnt constantly since 11th November, 1923. At its foot is a bronze plaque representing the shoulder-flash of SHAEF (Supreme Headquarters Allied Expeditionary Force), dated 25th August 1944, the day of the Liberation of Paris.

Along Avenue Foch

From the Etoile (Place Charles de Gaulle) two avenues lead directly to the Bois de Boulogne: Av. Victor-Hugo, where Victor Hugo (1802–85) died in a house on the site of no. 124, leads to Porte de la Muette; and the majestic Av. Foch, the widest avenue in Paris, created by Napoléon III and Haussmann, ends at Porte Dauphine. From its inception in 1855, Av. Foch had a succession of names before the death of the illustrious general in 1929. The **Musée d'Ennery** (*open Thur, Sun 2–6, T: 01 45 53 57 96.*) at no. 59 Av. Foch, has a small personal Asian art collection formed by the dramatist Adolphe d'Ennery (1811–99), containing Ming vases, porcelains and furniture. The building also houses a collection covering 3,000 years of Armenian history through a variety of objects. No. 80 Avenue Foch was the home of Claude Debussy (1862–1918). Southwest of the park entrance is a huge building (1955–59) constructed for NATO but now housing university faculties. At Porte Dauphine there is one of the two surviving complete Art Nouveau Metro station entrances of 1900 by Hector Guimard. Nearby is a monument (between nos. 17 and 22) to Adolphe Alphand (1817–91) by Dalou and Formigéz, who laid out Av. Foch, the Bois and many other parks in Paris.

RUE DU FAUBOURG ST-HONORE
Map p. 468, B3–p. 469, D3

Rue du Faubourg St-Honoré runs from from Rue Royale (*see p. 212*), to Pl. des Ternes, parallel with the Champs-Elysées. It follows the course of the medieval road from Paris to the village of Roule and became fashionable at the end of Louis XIV's reign. In the 18th century its grand mansions rivalled the prestige of Faubourg St-Germain. Today the district includes the Elysées Palace, along with the British Embassy and the American Embassy, and is one of the most chic and expensive in Paris. Liberally graced with smart hotels and restaurants, the section up to and around Avenue Montaigne is lined with fashion houses, designer boutiques and jewellers.

The American Embassy is at no. 2 Ávenue Gabriel, north of Place de la Concorde, and Rue Boissy d'Anglas runs alongside, past the shopping arcade, the Galerie Royale.

At no. 35 Rue du Faubourg St-Honoré is the British Embassy. The building goes

BARON HAUSSMANN

Baron Haussmann, Prefect of the Seine (1853–70), was responsible for altering the face of Paris in just 16 years during the Second Empire. He demolished slums, drove major routes through the city, created grand vistas, and put in place an efficient infrastructure which largely improved living conditions. It could also be argued that Haussmann's heavy hand was responsible for creating a windy city with tedious boulevards fronted by uniform buildings. Urban regeneration was already an issue in the Age of Enlightenment. Urbanist Edmé Verniquet (1727–1804; *see p. 58*) and philosopher and economist Saint-Simon (1760–1825; *see p. 326*) contributed to the impulse. Napoleon's grandiose ideas were partly realised under Louis-Philippe (1830–48), but it was Napoleon's nephew, Louis-Napoléon Bonaparte, who put into action the strong views on the subject that he had developed during his exile in England. As Emperor Napoléon III, he appointed Baron Haussmann to take charge of the overall plan. A formidable, ambitious, hard-working, artful man of dubious taste, whose career had started in Bordeaux, the Baron carried out the Emperor's plans with the solid support of Eugène Belgrand, hydraulic engineer, and Jean-Charles Alphand, Director of Public Works with responsibility for landscape architecture. The scheme included a new network of some 135km of major roads across medieval Paris, beginning with the north–south artery of Boulevards de Sebastopol, du Palais (crossing and almost obliterating the Ile de la Citè) and St-Michel. The area west of the Madeleine was breached by Boulevards Malesherbes and Haussmann, and the Left Bank was riven by the creation of Rue des Ecoles and the initial section of Blvd St-Germain. Blvd Magenta, Blvd de Strasbourg and Rue de Rennes serviced the train stations. Streets were asphalted, pavements laid, trees planted, handsome apartment blocks of prescribed height with uniform stone façades were built on requisitioned land at the cost of many fine *hôtels particuliers* and picturesque older buildings. There was no control over what was built behind the grand frontages. The Louvre Palace was extended by another wing on the north as far as the Tuileries, becoming Louis-Napoleon's residence. The rivers Dhuis and Vanne were harnessed for drinking water, and the sewers were hugely extended (from 150 to 500km) using the course of the Bièvre River to carry effluent into the Seine. The Bois de Boulogne, the Bois de Vincennes and the parks Monceau, Montsouris and Buttes-Chaumont were created on requisitioned land. To realise his plans for modern Paris, Haussmann obtained from the Emperor a law authorising the expropriation of land by simple decree of executive power. His daring methods of raising money ultimately came to grief when he was forced to request a loan from the Legislative Body. In 1868 the statesman Jules Ferry (1832–93) issued a violently critical pamphlet *Les Comptes fantastiques d'Haussmann*, which led to the Baron's resignation, while the war of 1870 brutally ended further 'Haussmannising'.

back to 1722, when it was built for the Fourth Duc de Charost. During the tenancy of the Comte de la Marck from 1785, much of its interior decoration was completed and the English-style garden laid out. It was bought in 1803 by Pauline Bonaparte (later Princess Borghese), much of whose furniture remains. She sold the house to the Duke of Wellington for £32,000, complete with numerous clocks, chandeliers, candelabras and chimneypieces and it became the Embassy in 1815. In the chapel, the marriage of Berlioz and Harriet Smithson took place in 1833, with Liszt as best man, and that of Thackeray and Isabella Shawe in 1836. Either side of the British Embassy are the exclusive Cercle Interallié (1714), at no. 33, the Russian Embassy during the Second Empire, and the Hôtel Pontalba (no. 41), designed by Louis Visconti. The British Embassy church of St Michael is in Rue d'Aguessau opposite. There is a plaque on no. 11 Rue des Saussaies in memory of victims of the Gestapo, which had its headquarters here during 1940–44.

Palais de l'Elysée

The Palais de l'Elysée (no. 55; *no admission*), the official residence of the President of the French Republic since 1873, stands at the corner of Av. de Marigny. This heavily guarded mansion was built for the Comte d'Évreux in 1718 and later became the Parisian residence of Madame de Pompadour, who commissioned the architect Jean Cailleteau, known as Lassurance the Younger, to make alterations. It was also occupied by Joachim Murat, brother-in-law of Napoleon who himself signed his second abdication here in 1815, and by Wellington. Napoléon III lived here as President from 1848 until he moved, as Emperor, to the Tuileries in 1852. It then reverted to its use as a residence for visiting heads of state, including Queen Victoria in 1855 and Elizabeth II in 1957. Opposite the Elysée Palace, behind a gilded wrought iron gate flanking Pl. Beauvau, is the Ministère de l'Intérieur (Home Office), built 1769–84.

Beyond Avenue Matignon

West of the Elysée Palace, beyond Av. Matignon, stands St-Philippe-du-Roule, built 1774–84 by Chalgrin and added to in the 19th century, on the site of the parish church of Roule. The sculpted *Religion* on the pediment is by Duret, and the basilica style interior contains Chassériau's ceiling painting, *Descent from the Cross*.

One of the more important concert-halls in Paris, Salle Gaveau (*T: 01 49 53 05 07*), built 1906–07, is nearby at 45 Rue La Boétie. At no. 208 Rue du Faubourg St-Honoré, beyond Av. Friedland, are the buildings of the old Hôpital Beaujon (1784). The writer Honoré de Balzac (1744–1850) died where no. 12 Rue Balzac now stands. A statue of him stands at the intersection with Av. de Friedland. At no. 252 Rue du Fbg. St-Honoré is Salle Pleyel (*T: 01 45 61 53 00*), the premier concert hall in Paris, which re-opened after extensive renovations in September 2006. It was built in 1927 by Camille, son of Ignace Pleyel (1757–1831), friend of Hayden, who manufactured pianos from 1807.

Round the corner in Rue Daru is the neo-Byzantine Russian Orthodox Cathedral (1860) of St-Alexander-Nevsky (1859–61). It has five gilded domes, and an elaborate interior with frescoes and icons. Several Russian restaurants are in the vicinity.

SAINT-LAZARE QUARTER

The interior of Gare St-Lazare, a terminus of the western region of the SNCF, was famously the subject of paintings by Monet in 1877 (*see p. 84*). To the west of the station, the Rue de Rome leads northwest past the Pl. de l'Europe, painted by Caillebotte in 1877. At no. 8 Rue du Havre, the Lycée Condorcet, founded in 1804, occupies the former buildings (with a Doric cloister court) of a Capuchin convent; on the site of its chapel (in the street to the east) is the church of St-Louis d'Antin by Brongniart (1782).

CHAPELLE EXPIATOIRE
Map p. 469, E3

Open Thur, Fri, Sat 1–5, closed Sun-Wed, 1st Nov and 11th Nov; T: 01 44 32 18 00.
The Chapelle Expiatoire stands in Sq. Louis XVI, formerly the Cimetière de la Madeleine. Here lie the bodies of the victims of the panic of 1770 in the Pl. de la Concorde (*see p. 211*), together with the Swiss guards massacred on 10th August 1792 and all those guillotined between 26th August 1792 and 24th March 1794. The chapel was erected in 1815–26 from the plans of Fontaine in the style of a classical funeral *temenos*. Built by order of Louis XVIII, it was dedicated to the memory of Louis XVI and Marie-Antoinette, whose remains, first interred in the graveyard on this site, were removed to St-Denis in 1815 (*see p. 407*). Inside are two marble groups: *Louis XVI and his confessor Abbé Henry Essex Edgeworth* (1745–1807) by Bosio, below which is inscribed the king's will, dated 25th December 1792, and *Marie-Antoinette supported by Religion*, by Cortot, the latter figure bearing the features of her sister-in-law Mme Elisabeth. Below is inscribed a letter said to have been written by the queen to Elisabeth from the Conciergerie on 16th October 1793. The bas-relief by Gérard above the doorway represents the removal of their remains.

MUSEE JACQUEMART-ANDRE
Map p. 468, C3

Open 10–6; T: 01 45 62 11 59; entrance at no. 158 Blvd Haussmann.
One of the city's more intimate museums, the Jacquemart-André holds a remarkable collection of predominantly Italian Renaissance and French 18th-century art and furnishings, in the almost unchanged setting designed and inhabited by the collectors. The *salon de thé* in the former dining room has a Tiepolo fresco. The house was built c. 1870 for Edouard André (1833–94) who married the painter Nélie Jacquemart in 1881. She bequeathed the collection to the Institut de France in 1912. Over two floors are 16 rooms containing objets d'art and paintings of great beauty and value. (*Cont'd overleaf*)

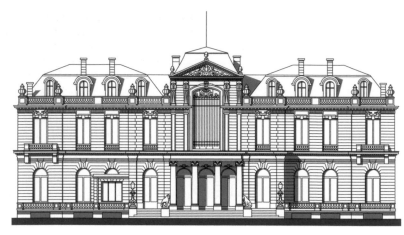

MUSEE JACQUEMART-ANDRE: THE FRONT FAÇADE

The Salon des Peintures: The collector, Edouard André, who came from a rich Protestant banking family is introduced in the lobby on the ground floor in a portrait of him in the uniform of the Imperial Guard by Winterhalter. In the Salon des Peintures, against red damask, are charming 18th-century French works by some of the best artists of the period. They include two oval canvases of typically frivolous subjects by Boucher, *Toilette of Venus* and the *Sleep of Venus*. These are balanced by two more sober still lifes by Chardin, *The Attributes of the Sciences* and *The Attributes of the Arts*. The furniture and Sèvres porcelain is also French 18th-century, complemented by *St Mark's Square* and *The Rialto, Venice* by Canaletto.

Grand Salon: This spacious room has a curved bay lined with gilded 18th-century wood panelling and mirrors, and contains busts by Coysevox, Houdon, Lemoyne and others.

The Private Rooms: The suite of smaller private rooms starts with the sumptuous Tapestry Room, built to house the three exceptional Beauvais tapestries called *Russian Games*, which had been purchased before the house was built, and a Savonnerie carpet (1663), combined with upholstered furnishings and fine cabinets, the only painting being the Guardi gouache, *Venetian Portico*.

The couple's Office is much as it was in their time with their favourite works including the risqué *The Model's Debut* by Fragonard and, on the desk, a portrait of Nélie Jacquemart, who painted Edouard André's portrait in 1872.

The Boudoir has some very fine portraits by Vigée-Lebrun, at her best when painting women, of Countess Skravonska, and David's magnificent and realistic *Portrait of Count Antoine Français de Nantes*, member of the Council of State. The Library contains Egyptian antiquities as well as works by 17th-century Flemish and Dutch masters much admired by later French painters. Among them are Van Dyck, Ruysdael and three paintings by Rembrandt including the dramatic *Pilgrims at Emmaus*. The *Boucicaut Book of Hours* belonged to Diane de Poitiers, mentor and mistress of Henri II.

The Music Room: The second large reception room beyond the Grand Salon was used as a Music Room. It has opulent Second Empire-style red damask walls and ebony furniture. Paintings here include a picturesque *Ruined Archway* by Hubert Robert. A Beauvais tapestry from a cartoon by Boucher adorns the end of the room.

The Winter Garden and Smoking Room: The most unusual and successful feature of this house, designed by Henri Parent, is the Winter Garden, an unusual oval space at one end of the building, with a beautiful curved double staircase.

The Smoking Room is the repository of souvenirs of travels by Madame André, including a 14th-century mosque lamp. In this male preserve are portraits from England by Joshua Reynolds, of Captain Torryn, and by Sir Thomas Lawrence (1769–1830) of the Count of Buckingham. The staircase is decorated with an illusionistic fresco by Tiepolo, *Henri III welcomed by Federigo Contarini to the Villa de Mira*. (*Cont'd overleaf*)

The Winter Garden in the Musée Jacquemart-André.

First floor

The Italian Museum: Three rooms adapted in 1892 became the Italian Museum: a prodigious collection with more than 80 Renaissance paintings. The first rooms contain sculptures and reliefs, such as the fine marble bust of Isabelle of Aragon by Francesco Laurana, a sculptor whose work was only re-discovered in the 19th century; a pair of lamp holders in the form of angels; and a bronze panel of *Martyrdom of St Sebastian* by Donatello. A number of 15th-century marble door surrounds have been re-erected, and terracottas from the della Robbia workshops include a serene *Virgin and Child*. The Florentine Room has a handsome coffered ceiling. Here are four elegant Cinquecento versions of the *Virgin and Child* by different artists: Botticelli, Perugino, Francesco Botticini, and Baldovinetti. Attributed to Uccello is a Quatrocento style *St George and the Dragon* purchased in London. Prime examples among the Venetian works, reflecting the taste of Edouard André, are Mantegna's powerful and poignant *Mocking of Christ* and *The Virgin and Child between St Jerome and St Louis of Toulouse*, as well as a strong and dignified *Virgin and Child* by Giovanni [?] Bellini.

MUSEE NISSIM DE CAMONDO
Map p. 469, D2

Open Wed–Sun 10–5.30; closed Mon, Tues; T: 01 53 89 06 50. Entrance at no. 63 Rue de Monceau. Guided visits on Sun at 11.

An annexe to the Les Arts Décoratifs (*see p. 196*), the Musée Nissim de Camondo was bequeathed by Count Moïse de Camondo (d. 1935), as a memorial to his son Nissim, killed in 1917. His daughter and grandchildren died at Auschwitz. The count, descended from a Turkish banking family, demolished his parents' house to build (1911–14) more fitting surroundings for his 18th-century collections. He commissioned René Sergent (1865–1927) who modelled the façades on the Petit Trianon at Versailles, and used panelling or reproductions to create an appropriate interior. It was also designed to be a comfortable home where the collector could live among the outstanding examples of furniture, carpets, tapestries and tableware that distinguish his taste. Moïse de Camondo stipulated in the bequest that nothing should be altered, and nothing lent, though the house has been much restored and fabrics remade to replicate originals. The most recent refurbishment, of the bathrooms and kitchens, evinces the functional design of the building. The living quarters are mainly on the first floor.

First floor

The Grand Bureau: This room has unpainted wood panels which were unusual in the 18th century, but much sought after later. The room contains two low chairs known as *voyeuses*, designed for women in voluminous dresses to watch the gaming tables, made by J.-P.-C. Séné for Madame Elisabeth, sister of Louis XVI. An important piece is the speckled mahogany roll-top desk by Claude-Charles Saunier, which is occasionally displayed open, and there are fine Aubusson tapestries depicting six of the *Fables* of La Fontaine, after Oudry. There is also a writing desk to stand at, such as Victor Hugo used (*see p. 283*).

The Grand Salon: Overlooking the garden, the large drawing room has white and gold panelling from 9 Rue Royale which does not precisely fit the space. Above the marquetry cabinet and tables by Riesener is Elisabeth Vigée-Lebrun's *Portrait of Madame Le Coulteux du Molay*, painted just before the Revolution. The Le Coulteux owned the Château de Malmaison before Josephine moved in (*see p. 364*). The six-leaved screen, designed by François Desportes, belonged to the Duvivier family who directed the Savonnerie works where the carpet now here was woven for the Grande Galerie of the Louvre (1678). Moïse de Camondo was among the few who appreciated the value of pieces decorated with Sèvres porcelain such as the lady's desk by Carlin.

Salon Huet: This room is named after the painter of the seven panels within,

along with the three *dessus de portes* of *Scènes pastorals* (1776), who was a designer for Toile de Jouy. There is a little table with porcelain plaques, by Roger Vandercruse (called Lacroix, RVLC), and another superb marquetry roll-top desk by Oeben, who taught Riesener and Leleu and worked for Louis XV. The *Chaises à Chassis* were made so that the upholstery could be changed depending on the season. There are several objects originally in royal collections.

Other rooms: With a view of Parc Monceau, the Dining Room has silverware by Roettiers which was ordered by Catherine the Great of Russia for her favourite, Gregory Orloff, part of a set of 3,000 pieces for 60 people. She took it back when Orloff was no longer in favour, and much of the set stayed in Russia. In the Porcelain Room is Sèvres porcelain known as the *Buffon* set, each piece decorated with a different bird, and named. The Butler's Pantry (Petit Bureau) with 'dumb waiter', its walls in crimson, contains numerous paintings, several depicting hunts such as sketches for Gobelins tapestries of *The Hunts of Louis XV* by Oudry; here also are the *Porte de St-Denis* by Hubert Robert, and four *Views of Venice* by Francesco Guardi (1712–93).

Second floor and Basement

On the second floor were the private apartments used by Moïse de Camondo, Nissim and his daughter Béatrice, each with a bathroom. Overlooking Parc Monceau, the Blue Room became his living room, and is

less grandly furnished than the floor below. Here are *Views of Paris* by Jean-Baptiste Raguenet and a red morocco casket embossed with the arms of Marie-Antoinette. The Library is an oak-panelled round room, with Sèvres

biscuit candelabras by Blondeau after Boucher. The Bedroom retains an 18th-century allure, with painted panels from a house in Bordeaux, while the bathroom is resolutely 20th-century. The white-tiled Kitchen, in the basement, has an impressive free-standing stove dating from 1912 and a huge furnace. There would have been a staff of around 12 to run the house.

MUSEE CERNUSCHI
Map p. 469, D2

Open Tues–Sun 10–6; closed Mon; T: 01 53 96 21 50. Regular temporary exhibitions.

Enrico Cernuschi (1821–96) bequeathed his collections and the building at no. 7 Avenue Velasquez to the City of Paris, and the museum opened in 1898. Born in Italy, ardent republican and follower of Garibaldi, Cernuschi fled to Paris in 1850 and then became embroiled with Gambetta and the events leading to the Third Republic. Following the uprisings of the Commune de Paris, he undertook a world voyage in 1871–73, during which he used his considerable wealth derived from banking to acquire some 5,000 works of art in Japan and China. He then commissioned William Bowens de Boijen (1834–1907) to design a museum-mansion next to the Parc Monceau. The Cernuschi owns over 12,000 works and is the second most important museum of Eastern antiquities in France after the Guimet. Entirely renovated, it re-opened in June 2005 with alterations that take full advantage of natural light and the views over the park. The permanent collections, from the Neolithic period to the 13th century, are displayed chronologically, starting on the first floor, reached via the grand staircase with a portrait of the wildly bearded Cernuschi (1890) by Léon Bonnat, and a Coromandel lacquered screen (17th–18th centuries).

First floor

The Neolithic collection: Dating from the 8th to 1st millennia BC, the Neolithic collection comes mainly from the provinces of Gansu and Qinghai, and is not a complete picture. Most objects are of the Majiayao period (c. 3500–c. 2200 BC), which divides into three phases. Banshan is represented by terracotta jars with swirling designs; the Dawenkou produced remarkable wafer-thin, turned, black ceramics; and the Longshan culture made delicately carved jade (nephrite) pieces including a disk decorated with birds.

Representative of Shang dynasty bronzes (c. 1550–c. 1030 BC) are a number of ritual containers such as the Fanglei vase with a lid. The most outstanding object in the museum is the bronze vase or *You* (1st half 11th century BC) from Hunan province, designed for fermented drinks. Known as *The Tigress*, it takes the shape of a small feline (35.2cm tall) propped on

The Tigress: a bronze vase of the Shang dynasty (11th century BC) in the Musée Cernuschi.

graceful Corinthian colonnade, which may have come from either the Château du Raincy or from the projected Valois chapel at St-Denis. To the east of the lake is a Renaissance arcade from the old Hôtel de Ville. When Paris was enclosed in the Farmers General wall in the 18th century, Ledoux (*see p. 318*) built a toll-house to the west, which was known as the Rotonde de Chartres as the Duke had part of it adapted for his use. It later became a keeper's lodge, and was disfigured in 1861 when the columns were fluted and a dome added. The four monumental gates are by Gabriel Davioud (1824–81), and scattered among the ornamental trees, shrubs and colourful flowerbeds are several statues, including *Ambroise Thomas* by Falguière (1902), and *Guy de Maupassant* by Verlet (1897). It has not changed a great deal since Marcel Proust (1871–1922) lived with his mother from 1901–05 at no. 45 Rue de Courcelles in a cork-lined sound-proof room (*see p. 294*), before moving to 102 Blvd Haussmann where he remained until 1919. Dickens lodged at no. 38 (then 48) in 1846. The Galerie Ching Tsai Loo at no. 48 is a unique red building in Chinese style commissioned in 1926 for an Asian art dealer.

BATIGNOLLES
Map p. 469, D1

This quarter gave its name to a school of Impressionist painters under the leadership of Manet remembered in a painting by Fantin-Latour in the Musée d'Orsay (*see pp. 82 and 83*). In the Cimetière des Batignolles (best approached by the Av. de Clichy, and some distance northwest of the Cimetière de Montmartre) lie Verlaine, André Breton and the Russian Art Deco designer Léon Bakst. Musée Henner (*closed for renovation at time of writing; T: 01 47 63 42 73*), at 43 Av. de Villiers, is devoted to the work of the Alsace-born French Academic painter Jean-Jacques Henner (1829–1905). The small Art Deco concert hall, Salle Cortot, at 78 Rue Cardinet, was designed by Auguste Perret, also responsible for the Théâtre Champs-Elysées, and opened in 1930.

OPERA
& THE GRAND BOULEVARDS

OPERA GARNIER
Map p. 470, A3

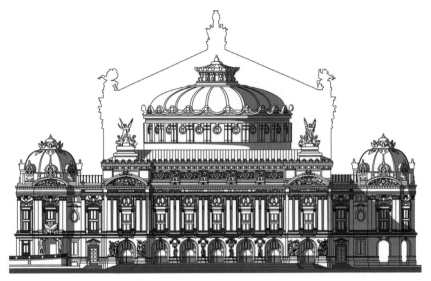

OPERA GARNIER: THE MAIN FAÇADE

Ticket purchase: box office at no. 1 Place de l'Opéra, Mon–Sat 10.30–6.30; T: 0892 89 90 90; from outside France T: 33 1 72 29 35 35; or www.operadeparis.fr

The façade, flanked by a flight of steps, is grandly adorned with coloured marbles and sculpture. On either side of the arcade opening into the vestibule are allegorical groups, including (right) *The Dance* by Carpeaux (a copy by Paul Belmondo, the original being in the Musée d'Orsay). Above are medallions of composers; and bronze-gilt statues of other composers and librettists are seen between the monolithic columns of the loggia. Behind the low dome of the auditorium is a triangular pediment crowned by a statue of Apollo of the Golden Lyre.

The interior

The public areas may be visited, including the auditorium when not in use. The second vestibule contains the box office, beyond which is the Grand Staircase, with its white marble stairs 10m wide and a balustrade of onyx and *rosso* and *verde antico* lit by elaborate chandeliers. On the first floor, where the staircase divides, is the entrance to the stalls and the amphitheatre, flanked by caryatids, and on each floor are arcades of monolithic marble columns. The Avant-Foyer leads to the Grand Foyer; glass doors communicate with the Loggia overlooking the Pl. de l'Opéra. By the middle door is a bust of Garnier by Carpeaux. The auditorium is resplendent in red plush and gilt, and has five tiers of boxes. The dome, resting on eight pillars of scagliola, was painted in disturbing contrast to the rest of the décor in 1964 by Chagall with murals inspired by nine operas. The huge stage is 60m high, 52m wide and 37m deep, behind which is the Foyer de la Dance (the scene of many paintings of ballet dancers by Degas; *see Musée d'Orsay p. 78*), with a mirror measuring 7m by 10m.

HISTORY OF THE OPERA GARNIER

The first opera house in Paris was established in 1669 by Perrin, Cambert and the Marquis de Sourdéac on the Left Bank, between the Rue de Seine and the Rue Mazarine. The first director was Lully (from 1674), under whom it acquired its secondary title of Académie Royale de Musique. Opéra Garnier, an appropriately lavish monument to the grandiose period of the Second Empire, was built in 1861–75 to the designs of Charles Garnier (1825–98), inspired by the 18th-century Bordeaux Opera, but intended to gratify a more opulent clientele than the rich upper-class Bordelais. The opera house should have been one of the more splendid symbols of the Second Empire, but it was not completed until 1875.

Museum of the Opéra

Open daily 10–5, except Sun afternoons when there is a performance.
The museum (a department of the Bibliothèque Nationale de France; *see p. 66*) is in the Rotonde de l'Empereur to the left of the Grand Staircase. This charming museum displays in rotation its collection of the scores of all operas and ballets performed here since its foundation, over 100,000 drawings of costumes, scenery and photographs and paintings of *artistes* as well as memorabilia including objects that belonged to Diaghilev.

Vicinity of the Opéra

In the immediate vicinity of Opéra Garnier is the Musée Fragonard, a museum of perfume (*see p. 420*). Av. de l'Opéra leads southeast towards Pl. André-Malraux (*see p. 247*). Napoleon and Josephine Beauharnais were married in 1796 at no. 3 Rue d'Antin, which was then the *Mairie* of the 2nd arrondissement. The *Fontaine Gaillon* (1828), just to the east in the Rue St-Augustin, is by Visconti. Mozart in 1778, and Chopin in 1833–36, both stayed at no. 5 Rue de la Chaussée-d'Antin. At no. 37 is Librairie Brentano's, which sells both English and French books (*T: 01 42 61 52 50*). Immediately behind the Opéra, on Blvd Haussmann, are two famous department stores: Galeries Lafayette (1898), facing Pl. Diaghilev, has three levels of balconies overlooking the main hall covered with a glazed dome; Printemps (1889; remodelled since) has a panoramic view on Level 9.

LA MADELEINE
Map p. 469, E4

La Madeleine, or the church of Ste-Marie-Madeleine, was built in the style of a Greco-Roman temple and surrounded by a majestic Corinthian colonnade, which is visually counterbalanced by the Assemblée Nationale building (*see p. 91*) across the river. Two earlier churches had been demolished unfinished, in 1777 and 1789, before Pierre-Alexandre Vignon (1763–1828) started work in 1806 on the orders of Napoleon, who, before coming up with the Arc de Triomphe, intended it as a Temple of Glory for the Grande Armée. It was finished by Huvé in 1842. In the pediment is a relief of the *Last Judgement* by Henri Lemaire; the bronze doors are adorned with bas-reliefs of the *Decalogue* by Baron Henri de Triqueti (1838), a commission awarded by the July Monarchy of 1830–48. The memorial service was held here for the 113 who died when Concorde crashed in the summer of 2000.

The interior

The interior abounds in gold leaf and coloured marble, paintings, mosaics and sculptures, and has a fine Cavaillé-Coll organ. The nave is covered by three coffered domes and the east end by a half-dome, with an enfilade of columns around the sanctuary. In chapels on either side of the entrance are the *Marriage of the Virgin* by Pradier, and the *Baptism of Christ* by Rude; the group of the *Ascension of the Magdalen* (1837), on the high-altar, by Marochetti, adds a touch of high drama.

Relief by Lemaire of the *Last Judgement* in the pediment of the west front of La Madeleine.

Detail of the bas-relief in bronze by Bergeret depicting Napoleon's Austerlitz campaign, on the Colonne de la Grande Armée in the Place Vendôme.

foot of which is in the Musée Carnavalet). Spiralling up the 43.50m high column is a band of bronze bas-reliefs, designed by Bergeret, which was hammered out of the metal of 1,250 Russian and Austrian cannon captured at the Battle of Austerlitz in 1805, the three-month campaign depicted in a chronological sequence. The statue of Napoleon at the summit is a copy by Dumont (1863) of the original by Chaudet torn down by the royalists in 1814. Dumont's sculpture replaced the one by Gabriel Seurre (*see p. 113*) that had been commissioned by the July Monarchy in 1833. The present statue narrowly escaped destruction in 1871 when a group of *Communards*, allegedly encouraged by the artist Gustave Courbet, demolished the column. Courbet fled to Switzerland after being condemned to finance the re-erection of the column in 1875 and died there in 1877.

ST-ROCH
Map p. 467, F4

Steps ascend from the Rue St-Honoré to the monumental façade of St-Roch, one of the largest churches in Paris, rich in paintings and monuments. When it was built, this was already a wealthy and elegant quarter. The façade has recently been cleaned, although the impact of the fine Baroque exterior is hampered by its confined position.

History of St-Roch
The body of the church, which has a classical layout, was begun 1653–90 to plans by Jacques Lemercier but only completed in 1719 thanks to a generous donation from John Law, a Scottish entrepreneur financier, also credited with the initial development of New Orleans. In the meantime, from 1706–10 Jules Hardouin-Mansart added the

circular Chapel of the Virgin to the north. The elegant façade was the work of Robert de Cotte in 1736–38. The church was consecrated in 1740, later to be further extended by the Chapel of the Calvary (c. 1750) to produce a dramatic sequence of Baroque spaces. Between 1750 and 1770, at the initiative of Curé Jean-Baptiste Marduel, St-Roch was endowed with a grandiose ensemble of painted and sculpted decoration. Many of the original works were lost at the Revolution but replacements were commissioned in the 19th century and others were acquired from defunct churches. The organ case dates from 1752 although the instrument has been modified several times. The stalls and the upper part of the pulpit are 18th-century. The total length of the interior is 126m.

The interior

To the left of the entrance is a medallion memorial to the dramatist Corneille (1606–84), who is buried in the church. In the first chapel in the right aisle (east) are a bust of François de Créquy (d. 1687) by Coysevox, the Spanish sculptor to the court of King Louis XIV who also worked at Versailles, and the tomb of the Comte d'Harcourt (d. 1666) by Renard. The second chapel contains a statue of Cardinal Dubois (d. 1723) by G. Coustou and a monument, by J-B. Huez, to the astronomer and Newtonian mathematician Maupertuis (1698–1759). In the dome of the Chapel of the Virgin is a restored painting of the *Assumption* (1756), by Jean-Baptiste Pierre, a forerunner in his style to J-L. David. The stucco *Glory* (1756), by Mme de Pompadour's favourite Rococo sculptor, Etienne Maurice Falconet, against the arcade, was part of a group replaced by the marble *Nativity* by Michel Anguier, from Val-de-Grâce (*see p. 98*). There are also 17th-century paintings by E. Le Sueur and Claude Vignon, and 18th-century works by Germain Drouais and Jean Restout. The Communion Chapel has a curious tabernacle inspired by the temple in Jerusalem (c. 1840), and some fine stained glass depicting St Denis the Areopagite (1849). Continuing around the church, on the last pillar on the west side of the ambulatory, is a bust of Le Nôtre (d. 1707) by Coysevox and in the transept a plaster of St Andrew by Pradier (1823), and a statue of St Augustin by Huez (1766); also a canvas of *St Denis Preaching* (1767) by Joseph-Marie Vien, and 19th-century murals. The next chapel contains a monument to the Abbé de l'Epée (*see p. 57*). The third chapel (beyond the transept) contains the remains of a monument to the Baroque artist Pierre Mignard (1610–95) by Jean-Baptiste II Lemoyne, 1744. And in the last chapel is a painting by Théodore Chassériau, a gifted disciple of Ingres.

BIBLIOTHEQUE NATIONALE DE FRANCE
CARDINAL DE RICHELIEU
Map p. 470, B4

Open Tues–Sat 10–7, Sun 12–7; closed Mon, public holidays and the first two weeks in Sept; T: 01 53 79 59 59; www.bnf.fr

The Bibliothèque Nationale de France (National Library of France or BNF) was established at this site in the 17th century and, with the British Library, is one of the two largest in Europe. However, in 1998 the collections were split between this site, known as the Bibliothèque Nationale de France-Cardinal de Richelieu, and the new Bibliothèque National de France-François Mitterrand (*see p. 66*) to which were transferred printed materials and audio visuals. This changed the emphasis of the attractive Richelieu site with the creation of the Institut National d'Histoire d'Art, which brings together here various national collections, among them manuscripts, prints, photographs, maps and plans, music, coins, medals, antiquities, and the performing arts.

HISTORY OF THE BIBLIOTHEQUE NATIONALE DE FRANCE

The buildings of the Bibliothèque Nationale de France consist of a group of 17th-century *hôtels particuliers* added to and amended until the end of the 19th century. In 1666 Colbert installed the Bibliothèque du Roi in one of his houses on Rue Vivienne, next to the Hôtel Mazarin. It was first opened to the public for two days a week in 1692. In 1724 the buildings were extended by Robert de Cotte and in 1826 the library spread into Galerie Mazarin, the former Hôtel Chevry and Hôtel Tubeuf, built by Le Muet in 1635, up to Rue des Petits-Champs. Between 1857 and 1873, Henri Labrouste carried out a number of modifications to the building, including the delicate cast and wrought iron frame supporting a cluster of faïence cupolas suspended over the Main Reading Room, which seats 259 readers as against the 2,000 in the new Bibliothèque Nationale-F. Mitterrand.

Formerly known as the Bibliothèque Royale and the Bibliothèque Impériale, the library originated in the private collections of the French kings. Largely dispersed at the end of the Hundred Years War, it was refounded by Louis XII and moved to Blois. During the next two centuries the library was at Fontainebleau, and then Paris, before finding its present home in Rue de Richelieu. Guillaume Budé (c. 1468–1540) had earlier been appointed the first Royal Librarian. It was enriched by the purchase or gift of many famous private libraries and smaller collections (including that of Colbert), and at the Revolution its range was extended with the confiscation of books from numerous convents and châteaux. In 1793 an act was passed that a copy of every publication printed in France should be deposited by the publishers in the Bibliothèque Nationale.

Visiting the library

The main gate is at 58 Rue de Richelieu, and the entrance vestibule is on the right of the Cour d'Honneur. On entering, the Labrouste's Reading Room is opposite and can be viewed through the glass doors. Areas open to the public include the Musée du Cabinet des Médailles et Antiques (*see below*) and, during temporary exhibitions, Galerie Mansart and Galerie Mazarine. Galerie Mansart, to the right at the foot of the stairs, was formerly Mazarin's sculpture gallery and the Cardinal's coat of arms can be seen above the door. The Cabinet des Estampes beyond contains about 11 million items varying from master prints to postcards, posters and wallpaper samples. The Department of Music contains two million works including collections of musical scores, books on music, and MSS (among them Mozart's *Don Giovanni*) previously in the Library of the Conservatoire de Musique. The Manuscripts department has an awesome collection, with more than 530,000 MSS, of which some 10,000 are illuminated, ranging from the oldest book, an Egyptian manuscript, c. 2000 BC, to manuscripts by authors such as Marcel Proust and Jean-Paul Sartre. The Department of Maps and Plans has 90,000 items, including 104 globes.

MUSEE DU CABINET DES MONNAIES, MEDAILLES & ANTIQUES

Open Mon–Fri 1–5.45; Sat 1–4.45, Sun 12–6; T: 01 40 46 55 53; www.bnf.fr
This collection is the permanent showcase of the Department of Coins and Antiques, built up around the royal collections of antiquities and enriched in the 19th and 20th centuries. It consists of precious objects, coins and medals of outstanding quality from Antiquity to the present day. The four rooms of the museum are laid out in the manner of a cabinet of curiosities, rather than chronologically. One room reveals different techniques involved in working with precious metals, enamels, glass, ceramics and ivories, and another is dedicated to the history of coins.

The collection

The brilliant collection of precious objects is very varied. There is a fabulous emerald which Catherine de Médicis had mounted in gold, and the oldest fan in France which is purported to have belonged to Diane de Poitiers (1499–1566), favourite courtesan of François I. There is also the so-called Throne of Dagobert, on which the kings of France were crowned, as well as treasures from the tomb of Childeric I at Tournai, and a Merovingian chalice and oblong paten (6th century) from Gourdon, in the Charollais. A rock crystal bowl, known as the *Coup de Chosroes*, is studded with garnets, the central medallion representing the victory of the king, a celebrated Iranian warrior. The largest antique cameo known, the *Grand Camée*, represents the Apotheosis of Germanicus, with Tiberius and Livia, which Louis XVI ordered to be moved from the Sainte-Chapelle to the Cabinet des Medailles; and an aquamarine intaglio (engraving) of Julia, daughter of Titus, is a particularly fine carved portrait. A series of ivory chessmen is dated from the 11th century, but was once reputed to have belonged to Charlemagne (d. 814).

Other objects include Egyptian terracottas and painted limestone statuettes, Roman bronze statuettes, ancient arms and armour, and domestic utensils; Greek and Etruscan vases, including a red-figured amphora, signed Amasis; Renaissance medals and bronzes; and gold *bullae* of Charles II of Anjou, King of Naples (1285–1309), of Baldwin I, Emperor of Constantinople in 1204–06, and of Edmund, Earl of Lancaster, titular King of Sicily, 1255–63.

THE GRANDS BOULEVARDS

Map p. 469, F4–p. 470, C4

The once fashionable Grands Boulevards are a succession of wide thoroughfares extending in a curve from Pl. de la Madeleine to the Bastille. They were laid out in 1670–85 on the site of the inner ramparts built by Charles V in the 14th century and fortifications built by Louis XIII in 1633–37 already demolished some decades earlier. Although not quite the debonair district of the dashing *boulevardiers* who frequented it in the 19th century, the boulevards support a combination of banking and commerce with entertainment—opera, theatre, cabaret and cinema. There are also historic links with developments in art and cinema in the 19th and early 20th centuries. The Grands Boulevards are now in fact rather staid, nightlife for the young now being centred further east around République and Bastille.

Boulevard des Capucines

Blvd de la Madeleine, the westernmost of the Grands Boulevards, becomes Blvd des Capucines, at which point is Rue Edouard-VII, built in 1911. It widens out into a circular area with an equestrian statue by Paul Landowski (1875–1961) of Edward VII (1913), who was a frequent visitor to Paris as Prince of Wales and king, and a promoter of the Entente Cordiale which was established between Britain and France in 1904. At 19 Blvd des Capucines a tablet records the first exhibition of a cinema film given by the brothers Lumière (28th December, 1895). A few days later the first demonstration of X-rays, a discovery of Dr Roentgen, took place in the same room. No. 35 was once the studio of Nadar (Félix Tournachon, 1820–1910), the portrait-photographer and aeronaut. The first Impressionist Exhibition was held here in 1874, where Monet's *Impression Sunrise* (1872; *see p. 352*) depicting the port of Le Havre in the mist, gave the group its name. On the corner of Place de l'Opéra and Blvd des Capucines is Café de la Paix (*see p. 441*).

Boulevard des Italiens

Boulevard des Italiens, whose once famous cafés have been replaced by cinemas and commercial buildings, derived its name from the Théâtre des Italiens (1783), where Donizetti's *Don Pasquale* was first performed in 1843. Sir Richard Wallace (1819–90), who collected many of the works of art now in the Wallace Collection, London (*see p. 36*) had a home in Rue Taitbout.

Blvd des Italiens and the eastern extremity of Blvd Haussmann, a mainly banking and commercial district, are linked by Rue Laffitte which was named after financier and politician, Jacques Laffitte (1767–1844) who played a role in the 1830 Revolution. From here is an almost uninterrupted view of Sacré-Coeur (*see p. 256*). Napoléon III was born on 20th April, 1808, at no. 17, where his mother, the Queen of Holland, held brilliant *salons*. On 14th November, 1840, Claude Monet (*see p. 352*) was born at no. 19, and art dealer and publisher Ambroise Vollard (1868–1939) opened his first gallery at no. 39 in 1893, and then moved to no. 6. It was Vollard who introduced the work of Gauguin and Cézanne to the public and organised the first exhibitions in Paris of works by Picasso and Matisse (1901 and 1904 respectively).

In the parallel Rue Le Peletier Napoléon III narrowly escaped death in 1858, when Orsini attempted to assassinate him, killing or injuring 156 others instead. No. 3 was the Café du Divan, frequented by writers and poets, and Degas painted at the predecessor of the Opéra Comique, no. 6, until 1873. And it was in this street that the Second and Third Impressionist exhibitions were held.

Boulevard Haussmann, named after the man responsible for transforming Paris in the mid-19th century (*see p. 223*), was begun in 1857 to create an unbroken thoroughfare from Blvd Montmartre to the Arc de Triomphe, only finally completed in 1926.

South of the Blvd des Italiens in Rue de Marivaux stands the **Opéra-Comique-Salle Favart** (entrance at 2 Rue Boïeldieu) with a bijou auditorium built 1894–96 and practically no backstage, thus excluding modern opera productions. The Opéra-Comique originated in a company that produced pieces during local fairs, and in 1715 purchased from the Opéra the right of playing vaudevilles interspersed with ariettas. Discord between the two theatres continued until in 1757 Charles Favart (1710–92) finally established the rights of the Opéra-Comique, which moved to this somewhat confined site in 1783, replacing an 18th-century château.

Boulevard Montmartre

In Rue Drouot is the Hôtel des Ventes de Paris, or Nouveau Drouot (named after Napoleon's aide-de-camp) at no. 9, rebuilt in the 1980s. This is the main auction-rooms of Paris, the French equivalent of Christie's or Sotheby's, where important sales are held from February to June. Pissarro painted 13 views of Blvd Montmartre from a window of the Grand Hôtel de Russie, which stood at 1 Rue Drouot. The short section which is Blvd Montmartre was very fashionable from its creation in 1676 until 1860 and Haussmann's alterations. At no. 10 is the Musée Grévin (*see p. 420*), a waxwork collection, and opposite is the pretty Théâtre des Variétés (*T: 01 42 33 09 92*) built in 1807, for the Comédie-Française (*see p. 246*). It still has its original façade, and in the 1860s it was the scene of several of Offenbach's successes. In the block on the right between Blvd Montmartre and Rue St-Marc is a labyrinth of 19th-century arcades, leading off Passage des Panoramas (gaslit in 1817), where the first Académie Julien was established in 1868.

Rue du Faubourg-Montmartre curving northwest towards the former suburb of Montmartre, recalls the time when the boulevard formed the city boundary, and was traditionally a Jewish quarter with several synagogues. The famous Restaurant Chartier, originally a workmen's canteen or *bouillon*, is at no. 7 and has its original 19th-century décor. At no. 32 Rue Richer is the Folies-Bergère music hall founded in 1869, with Art Deco interior (*T: 0892 681 650, www.foliesberger.com*). Manet's *Bar at the Folies-Bergère* (Courtauld Gallery, London) was indeed painted here in 1881.

Boulevard Poissonnière

Boulevard Poissonnière is crossed by Rue Poissonnière (south) and its northern extension, the Rue du Faubourg-Poissonnière, which was the route taken by fishmongers of old on their way to Les Halles.

Beyond this junction is Blvd de Bonne-Nouvelle, on the northern side of which is the façade (1887) of the Théâtre du Gymnase (*T: 01 42 46 79 79 / 0892 68 36 22*), an institution with a formidable reputation on the French comedy circuit. South are steps leading to the church of N.-D. de Bonne-Nouvelle, rebuilt in 1824 with an earlier belfry. A plaque within records that the foundation stone was laid by Anne of Austria, Louis XIII's queen. At no. 34 is the popular De La Ville Café (*see p. 438*).

WALK TWO

PALAIS ROYAL & THE BOURSE

The area of the Palais Royal is very central yet discreet, and was laid out in the 17th century. Close to the financial district of Paris, the old palace now encompasses government institutions, shops and restaurants, and elegant old apartment blocks with galleries around a formal Parisian garden. The Bourse (Stock Exchange) and the Banque de France are grand buildings which befit their role.

The Théâtre Français, better known as the **Comédie-Française** (*tickets: from abroad T: 00 33 1 44 58 15 15; from France T: 0825 10 1680; or on www.comedie-francaise.fr. Guided visits in French given by CMN at 10.30am on 3rd Sunday of month; reservations T: 01 44 54 19 30*), part of the Palais Royal, presents a profusion of Tuscan columns to Place André Malraux and Place Colette. Built from 1786–90 by Victor Louis for the Théâtre des Variétés, it was remodelled in 1900 after a serious fire, and much restored. The company originated in the Comédiens-Français created by Louis XIV in 1680, seven years after Molière's death, which brought together two rival troops: l'Hôtel de Guénégaud, Molière's former company, and the actors of the Hôtel de Bourgogne. The company had

many homes before settling here in 1799, led by the great actor François-Joseph Talma. In 1812 Napoleon signed a decree (when he happened to be in Moscow) reorganising the Comédie-Française, which is still a private company with 37 shareholding member actors and 20 contracted actors. In the foyer is the seated statue of Voltaire by Houdon. The chair in which Molière was sitting when acting in *Le Malade Imaginaire* and taken fatally ill can only be seen in the upper foyer during performances or on guided tours. The theatre also owns various statues of actors and dramatists, including *Talma* by David d'Angers, *Dumas fils* by Carpeaux, *Mirabeau* by Rodin, and a statue of George Sand by Clésinger; also the portrait of Talma by Delacroix, and other paintings; the auditorium ceiling was painted by Albert Besnard (1913).

First take Rue de Richelieu north out of Place André-Malraux passing at the corner of Rue Molière the *Fontaine Molière* by the architect Visconti (1844) with a bronze statue of the playwright by Gabriel Seurre and supporting marbles by James Pradier. A miniscule restaurant called L'Incroyable (*T: 01 42 96 24 64*), at no. 26 Rue de Richelieu, claims to have existed since 1793. A board outside explains that the *incroyables* were the male version of the *merveilleuses*, the post-Terror generation of fops who dressed and behaved outrageously.

Slip through the tiny alley into **Rue de Montpensier** where there are more restaurants. Au Trois Oliviers (*T: 01 40 20 03 02*) at no. 37bis, offers a selection of six different Provençale specialities,

and *Bouride de Marseille*, a version of bouillabaisse. Pierre au Palais Royal (*T: 01 42 96 09 17*) at 10 Rue de Richelieu/7 Rue de Montpensier, serves updated traditional French cuisine, an elegant option long popular with patrons of the Comédie Française.

A number of passageways connect the surrounding streets with the large rectangle of the **Jardin du Palais Royal**, a calm and decorous oasis giving the lie to the turbulence and notoriety of its past. The buildings on three sides create a harmonious ensemble and under their arcades are specialist shops and varied restaurants; the garden is closed to the south by the Cour d'Honneur (*see below*). Enfilades of limes planted in 1970 flank a formal parterre enlivened by colourful flowers, and a fountain. The houses and galleries were the work

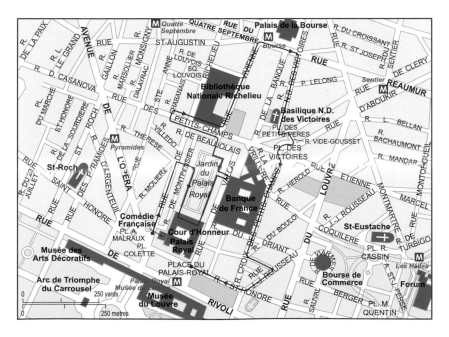

of the architect Victor Louis and built as a speculative venture in 1781–86 by Philippe-Egalité (so called because of his democratic views), descendant of the Orléans side of the royal family. At the time he was heavily in debt, and shops and cafés were let out. Over the years they became at different times a rendezvous for political activists, literati and, since the police were excluded from entry, various insalubrious activities especially prostitution. On 13th July 1789 Camille Desmoulins delivered from the garden the fiery harangue which precipitated the fall of the Bastille the following day. Charlotte Corday purchased the knife to kill Marat from one of the boutiques.

During the 18th century this was a fashionable place to be seen, and smart restaurants opened, including the **Grand Véfour** (*T: 01 42 96 56 27; see p. 434*) at 17 Rue du Beaujolais, which resides under the north-western arcades. A favoured rendezvous of writers in the Second Empire, it is still a restaurant of high repute (and prices). In the plush red 18th-century interior you can study the lists of the late and great who dined here. In the northeast corner is Restaurant au Palais Royal (*T: 01 40 20 00 27*) at 110 Galerie de Valois, a serious place with impeccable white tablecloths patronised by local civil servants. A terrace stretches into the gardens.

Close by is the **Théâtre du Palais-Royal**, designed by Victor Louis. In 1785, there was a museum of waxworks at no. 17 Galerie de Montpensier, founded by Curtius, Mme Tussaud's uncle. The Café du Caveau (nos. 89–92) was the meeting place of the partisans of the Resistance. The effete

and multi-talented Jean Cocteau (1889–1963), author of *Les Enfants Terribles* (1929) who also made the films *Orphée* (1950) and *Testament d'Orphée* (1959), spent the latter part of his life at no. 36. The earthy female writer Colette (1873–1954), author of *Le Blé en Herbe* (1923) and *Gigi* (1945), among many other novels, lived in Palais Royal from 1927–29 and again from 1932 until her death.

The **Cour d'Honneur**, the main courtyard of the old palace which is open to the public, is separated from the gardens by the Galerie d'Orléans, a double Doric colonnade by Fontaine (1829–31), which was restored and cleared of its shops in 1935. The pools of the Galerie are decorated by Pol Bury's mobile steel spheres. In 1985–86 the Cour d'Honneur received Daniel Buren's 250 puzzling truncated black-and-white fluted marble columns of differing heights, installed above and below ground. The minimalist brevity of this work is undoubtedly all the more controversial in these surroundings. The north façade of the courtyard was completed by Fontaine, who also restored the east and west wings.

The palace, originally known as the Palais-Cardinal, was designed by Jacques Lemercier in 1634–39 for Richelieu, Louis XIII's chief minister, to be near the Louvre. The Cardinal (d. 1642) bequeathed it to the king, who died the following year. Anne of Austria (d. 1666) then queen regent, took up residence with her sons Louis XIV and Philippe d'Orléans, and called it **Palais-Royal**. They had to beat a hasty retreat during the Fronde in 1648 and when Louis XIV returned he preferred to live at Versailles.

Queen Henrietta Maria, widow of Charles I of England and sister of Louis XIII, moved in. When her daughter married Monsieur, brother of Louis XIV, the palace passed to him and his male heirs until 1848, and was altered by Mansart. Up until 1723 was the most brilliant period of the palace, when constant improvements were made. In 1763 the southeast wing, including Richelieu's theatre, burned down and the buildings of the Cour de l'Horloge, facing Pl. du Palais-Royal, were rebuilt by Constant d'Ivry, with sculptures by Pajou and Franceschi. The so-called Galerie des Proues (prows) on the east, is the only relic of Lemercier's 17th-century building. After the Revolution the name changed to Palais-Egalité and it became government offices only to return, in 1814, to the Orléans family and its earlier name. It was the residence of King Louis-Philippe until 1832, when the seedier joints were closed down, but in 1848 it was plundered by revolutionaries. The palace was rebuilt by Chabrol in 1872–76 after it was fired during the Commune. Occupied by the Conseil d'Etat and the Ministère de la Culture et de la Communication, it is not open to the public.

Immediately east of the Palais-Royal is the **Rue de Valois**, with (at nos. 1–3) the Pavillon du Palais-Royal (1766); at nos. 6–8, once the Hôtel Melusine, the first meetings of the French Academy took place in 1638–43. The ox sculptured above the door recalls its period as the restaurant Boeuf à la Mode from 1792 to 1936. An inscription high up on the corner of Rue de Valois marks the site of the Salle de Spectacle du Palais-Cardinal, occupied

by Molière's company from 1661–73, and by the Académie Royale de Musique from 1673 until the fire in 1763.

Leaving the Jardin du Palais Royal by the north, cross Rue de Beaujolais and **Rue des Petits-Champs**. To the left, at no. 12 Rue Chabanais, was the setting of Toulouse-Lautrec's painting *Au Salon* (1894). Among the bars and restaurants around here are English run Willi's Wine Bar (*T: 01 42 61 05 09; see p. 441*) at no. 13 Rue des Petits-Champs, with interesting food, and Restaurant le Grand Colbert (*T: 01 42 86 87 88*) at 2–4 Rue Vivienne, an attractive brasserie which was a workmen's café in a former draper's shop and is not too expensive.

Galerie Colbert, which opened in 1826 when shopping arcades became all the rage, on the site of a *hôtel particulier*, is a handsome structure with a rotunda in the middle. It adjoins the livelier and smarter **Galerie Vivienne**, which opened at the same time as Galerie Colbert. First called Galerie Marchoux, after its owner who was Président de la Chambre de Notaires, it is wonderfully decorated with scenes of commerce. It has always benefited from being in a banking and stockbroking area and has luxury boutiques specialising in fashion, flowers and interiors, and the popular tea shop A Priori Thé (*T: 01 42 97 48 75, closes 6pm*).

Rue Vivienne continues north past the Galeries to the **Palais de la Bourse** or Stock Exchange (*occasional visits in French with CMN; T: 01 44 54 19 30*), also known as the Palais Brongniart after the architect, Alexandre Brongniart (1739–1813). Built by Brongniart and Labarre in 1808–27, it is a typical Neoclassical building of the period with a grandiose Corinthian peristyle. The north and south wings were added in 1903. Rue du Quatre-Septembre was driven, in 1864, through an old district which can still be seen to have kept some interesting houses around Rue Feydeau, built on Louis XIII's fortifications, and the Rue des Colonnes.

Rue Notre-Dame des Victoires runs south (parallel to Rue de la Banque) past the church of **Notre-Dame-des-Victoires**, which stands on the surprisingly provincial-looking Place des Petits-Pères. The church was dedicated in 1629 by Louis XIII to commemorate the capture of La Rochelle from the Huguenots in the previous year. On the site of a former chapel, it was begun by Pierre Le Muet in 1629–32; Libéral Bruant designed the transept and last bay of the nave 1642–66, and it was completed only in 1740 by Sylvain Cartault. The plan of the interior derives from the Gesù in Rome, with communicating chapels around the nave. Every interior wall is plastered with *ex-voto* tablets; the organ case and carved stalls date from 1740. The second chapel on the left contains the tomb of the composer Jean-Baptiste Lully (1633–87) by Pierre Cotton, with a bust by Gaspard Collignon; in the choir are seven paintings (1746–55) by Carle van Loo, Boucher's great rival as court painter to Louis XV.

From here Rue Vide-Gousset leads southeast into the impressive, circular **Place des Victoires**, laid out by Jules Hardouin-Mansart in 1685; the surrounding houses were designed by Pradot. The equestrian statue of Louis XIV by Bosio (1822) replaces the original, destroyed in 1792; the bas-reliefs on the pedestal depict the *Passage of the Rhine*, and *Louis XIV Distributing Decorations*.

In Rue Croix des Petits-Champs is the entrance to the **Banque de France** (*occasional visits in French with CMN; T: 01 44 54 19 30, www.monum.fr*), founded in 1800 and relocated here in 1811. The buildings incorporate the former Hôtel de la Vrillière, built by Mansart in 1635–38 and restored by Robert de Cotte in 1713–19, later occupied by the Comte de Toulouse, son of Louis XIV and Mme de Montespan. Within the bank is the profusely decorated 17th-century Galerie Dorée, one of the first of its kind.

Further on, between Rue Croix des Petits-Champs and Rue Jean-Jacques-Rousseau is the once elegant **Véro-Dodat** arcade (1822), now rather seedy, which was named after Messieurs Véro and Dodat, two *charcutiers*, and was lit by gas lamps. The building opposite, on the corner of Rue St-Honoré, is part of the Ministère de la Culture et de la Communication. It is in fact two buildings, one of 1960 and 1989, which were enveloped in a metal fretwork mantle designed by architect Francis Soler to unify the structure in 2002–04.

Returning west to the Place du Palais-Royal, along Rue St-Honoré, on your left is the Louvre des Antiquaires (*open Tues–Sun 11–7; closed Mon; and also closed Sun mid-July–mid-September; T: 01 42 97 27 27*). This building of 1852, formerly the department store of the Grands Magasins du Louvre, was acquired in 1975 by the British Post Office Staff Superannuation Fund as an investment, then gutted. Since 1978 it has accommodated, on three floors, some 250 professional antique dealers' stalls.

WALK THREE

RUE DES MARTYRS & MONTMARTRE

This walk is a gradual progression uphill towards Montmartre, through a remarkable cross-section of Paris. Rue des Martyrs, with many tempting small shops and independent businesses, runs through a mainly residential and lesser-known district, with several interesting twists, while the bohemian reputation of the village on the Butte Montmartre continues to draw the tourist crowds. Despite its popularity the village has retained a distinct atmosphere, best discovered on foot or sitting in a café.

Start from **Notre-Dame-de-Lorette** (1823–36), a landmark although not very exciting basilican church built by Hippolyte Lebas, characteristic of the July Monarchy, with a Corinthian portico and coffered vaults inside. The story of its name is perhaps more beguiling. *Lorettes* were girls of easy virtue who inhabited the newly constructed area in the mid-19th century. They were tolerated by property owners seeking a quick return on their investment and *lorettes* were frequently depicted by writers and painters at the time. In Rue Bourdaloue next to the church, is an adorable tea shop Les Cakes de Bertrand (*open Mon–Fri 12–3.30, Sat 9–7, Sun 12–6, T: 01 40 16 16 28*) at no. 7, and next door a beautiful *boulangerie* Nature et Pains sells organic bread and sandwiches.

For a worthwhile detour before Rue des Martyrs itself, head left down the casual Rue St-Lazare (past an animal bookshop—for pets who like to curl up with a book?). Among the many places to eat here are Chez Jean (*T: 01 48 78 62 73; see p. 435*) at no. 8, with a quirky menu that might feature *Juste pour Rire*, and *Rougebaiser* (try them if you dare). On **Rue St-Georges** is the unmissable Restaurant Georgette (*see p. 437*), at no.

29; on Rue St-Lazare, at no. 40, Restaurant Romain (*T: 01 48 24 58 94*), with paintings, and also Casa Olympe (*T: 01 42 85 26 01*) at no. 48, are two recommended Italian restaurants.

In **Rue Taitbout** the atmosphere changes. This area was dubbed *la Nouvelle Athènes* by Dureau de la Malle in the *Journal des débats* in 1823 for its luxury Greek-Revival buildings, designed by Auguste Constantin among others. Businessmen and bankers were attracted, but importantly it became an intellectual mecca favoured by artists, musicians and writers who met up at the Café de la Nouvelle Athènes on Pl. Pigalle. Typical is Square d'Orléans at no. 80 Rue Taitbout (through a smart passageway), built in 1829 'in the manner of English squares' by English architect Edward Crecy, the fountain added in 1836. Always a highly desirable address, this was where George Sand and her lover Chopin had apartments in 1842–47, as well as Alexandre Dumas Père whose home was decorated by well-known artists. Round the corner in Rue d'Aumale, Richard Wagner lived for a while at no. 3.

At the top of Rue St-Georges is a small theatre of the same name, the façade

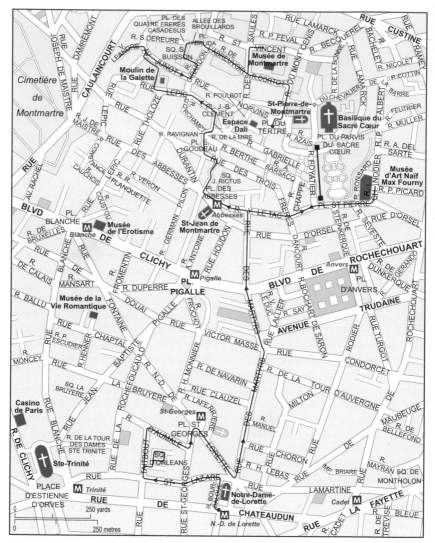

decorated in *trompe l'oeil* and next door
is a friendly café A la Place St-Georges
(*T: 01 42 80 39 32*). The Goncourt
brothers lived at no. 43 (1849–63), and
Renoir had a studio at no. 35. The circular Pl. St-Georges revolves around a
fountain-monument to the caricaturist

Gavarni (1801–66) who frequently portrayed the *demi-mondaines* or *lorettes* of
the area, represented here in a sculpture
by Denys Puech. The Fondation Dosne-
Thiers at no. 27 contains the
Bibliothèque Thiers, which specialises
in Napoleonic and 19th-century French

history and is part of the Institut de France. From 1822–71, this was the residence of President Thiers (1797–1877), responsible for ordering the massacre of thousands of *Communards* in 1871, and his wife Elise Dosne. The original house (1840) was destroyed by the *Communards* in 1871 and rebuilt in 1873. Opposite, at no. 28, is an over-ornate 19th-century Renaissance pastiche, briefly home to the notorious socialite, the Marquise de Païva, before her house on the Champs-Elysées was completed (*see p. 213*). West on Rue N.-D. de Lorette, is the Théâtre la Bruyère, while on Rue Laferrière is the church of St-Constantin-Ste-Hélène and the discreet Hôtel Arvor (*see p. 430*).

Return to **Rue des Martyrs** via Rue N.-D. de Lorette, to admire the shops and the distant view of Sacré Coeur. Well known for its cabarets in the 18th century, the name refers to the legend of the martyr Denis, and his companions, Rusticus and Eleutherius, who took this route c. 258 to the foot of Montmartre, where they were beheaded. The lower end of Rue des Martyrs is the archetypal Parisian neighbourhood street, nothing fancy and with no pretensions, where locals do their shopping; on Sunday there is a morning market. As well as the long-term population, incomers include young bourgeois families and an increasing number of artists. Among many cafés and restaurants, at no. 46 is Rose Bakery, small and unsophisticated, but fragrant and also resolutely organic.

The street forks left at Av. Trudaine (at 10 Rue Lailler is Phonogalerie with an array of old phonographs), and continues the other side of the southern boundary of Montmartre, at the meeting point of Blvd Clichy and Blvd de Rochechouart. This is **Pigalle**, the old red-light district. After decades of seediness, the foot of the Butte, from here to Abbesses, is now experiencing a strong revival as a happening district. While the Moulin Rouge (founded 1889) grinds on, the most up-beat night club is the **Divan du Monde** at 75 Rue des Martyrs (*T: 01 44 92 77 66*). Opposite is La Fourmi Café, a local meeting place, while the designer boutique Antoine & Lilli is installed at no. 90.

Rue Yvonne le Tac, traditionally the site of the martyrdom of St Denis, is marked by the **Chapelle du Martyr** in the convent at no. 9. It was in the crypt that Ignatius de Loyola and his six companions, including Francisco Xavier, founded the Jesuits Society (1534). Among several suggestions for the origin of the name Montmartre, the most likely is *Mons Martyrum*, referring to St Denis' martyrdom. According to tradition, Denis walked from here northwards to the site of his burial, now called St-Denis (*see p. 407*), carrying his severed head. Taking a straight line, he would have gone over the **Butte Montmartre** which is 130m at the summit with an east-west spine of about 500m. A strategic vantage point, its history is characterised by sieges and battles. Henri of Navarre occupied the hill in 1589 when besieging Paris (*see p. 13*); the final struggle between the French and the Allies took place here in 1814; and on 18th March 1871, to the northeast of the Butte, two generals were murdered by insurgents, precipitating ever more drastic government action against the *Communards*. In more distant times it was covered with vines and watered by numerous springs, its rocky cliffs dotted with windmills and gypsum quarries. Until the late 18th century, only one route led south, and one to the north, but as more were built, the Butte attracted poor artists, being both picturesque and cheap, and it remained an artistic centre for about 30 years until the artists gradually retreated towards the Left Bank (*see p. 105*).

At the foot of the Butte Montmartre, in the old Halle St-Pierre (1868) on Rue Ronsard is the **Musée d'Art d'Art Naïf Max Fourny** (*open 10–6: T: 01 42 58 72 89*) a cultural centre which holds the Fourny collection of *naïf*, outsider and folk art and puts on regular events.

Back on Place des Abbesses is one of only two surviving complete Art-Nouveau Metro entrances by Guimard in cast iron and still glazed. Here also stands the brick-clad **St-Jean de Montmartre** (1894–1904), one of the first churches in reinforced concrete, by Anatole de Baudot. The nave is covered by two cupolas, and the interior, which should glitter, is dark from grime. Rectangular windows with arched tracery have a variety of glass, dating from 1914 to Max Ingrand windows of 1954.

At no. 39 Rue André Antoine, downhill from the church, the *pointilliste* Georges Seurat died of diptheria in 1891, aged 31. Behind the church, in Sq. J. Rictus is an interesting art work, *Le Mur des je t'aime*.

Passage des Abbesses opens onto Rue des Trois-Frères, across which is Place Emile-Goudeau, the site of the **Bateau-Lavoir**. Only no. 13A survived a fire in 1970, the rest has been rebuilt. Around 1910 this was the ramshackle residence at different times of Picasso, Modigliani, Van Dongen, Derain, Gris, and Max Jacob, where Picasso conceived his ground-breaking *Demoiselles d'Avignon* and where a banquet was held in honour of Henri 'Le Douanier' Rousseau in 1908.

Until the 1780s, the only access to the summit was Rue Ravignan (formerly Chemin Vieux); close by in Rue d'Orchampt, was the home of singer Dalida (*see facing page*). Steps climb up Rue de la Mire to arrive in Pl. Jean-Baptiste Clement, named after the hero of the Commune de Paris, and author of the refrain *Le Temps des Cerises* (1868), music by Antoine Renard, which was adopted as the hymn of the Commune of 1871 (often found today as the name of a shop or café). Clement (1836–1903) dedicated the song to Louise, an ambulance driver he met on the barricades.

La Folie Sandrin (1774), at no. 22 Rue Norvins was a mental clinic whose most famous patient was the schizophrenic poet Gérard de Nerval (1808–55), in 1841, who eventually committed suicide. The Espace Montmartre Salvador Dali (*open 10–6; T: 01 42 64 40 10*) with over 300 works by the Surrealist artist is close by in Rue Poulbot.

In **Rue Lepic**, built in 1852, are the only two remaining (rebuilt) windmills of Montmartre, the Moulin Radet and the Blute-fin. Confusingly, the Radet was once known as the Moulin de la Galette, a working-class dance hall in the 19th century, where wine and *galettes* (small round rye cakes) were sold. It was the subject of the painting by Renoir (Musée d'Orsay) in 1876.

The Blute-fin (no. 83) is now the Moulin de la Galette Restaurant (*T: 01 46 06 84 77*). Van Gogh lived with his brother Theo at no. 54 in 1886–88. Just beyond the Moulin Radet, at no. 65, is an unnamed passage with 62 steps. This almost becomes a grotto as it passes the Rocher de la Sorcière before opening into 23 Av. Junot, a pleasant, bourgeois street built 1910–12. To the left is Villa Léandre (1926), with bijou brick houses and immaculate front yards.

Retrace your steps to pass the Modern Movement house at no. 15 Av. Junot, built in 1926 by Adolphe Loos, the Viennese purist, for the Dadaist writer, Tristan Tzara, and no. 13, home of Francisque Poulbot (1879–1946), famed for drawings of local children. The painter-engraver Eugène Paul lived 1917–75 on Impasse Girardon.

Sq. S. Buisson, a small public garden with a statue of St-Denis, typically carrying his head in his hands, leads into Pl. des Quatres-Frères Casadesus at the end of **Rue Simon Dereure** (where between nos. 15 and 16 the Paris meridian is marked). Steps lead to the Allée des Brouillards alongside the 18th-century Château des Brouillards (restored 1922–26) built on the site of the Moulin des Brouillards (mists). Pierre-Auguste Renoir's final residence in Montmartre was at no. 6. On Place Dalida is a statue to the hugely successful singer, actress and Miss Egypt who was born Yolanda Gigliotti (1933–87).

Where Rue de l'Abreuvoir meets Rue des Saules is **La Maison Rose** (now a restaurant) painted by Maurice Utrillo,

who was born in Rue du Poteau, and buried in the nearby Cimetière St-Vincent. Rue des Saules turns downhill, past the Clos Montmartre, planted in 1933 with vines which are harvested each October and vinified in the Mairie du 18ème Arrondissement. No. 4 in this street is **Au Lapin Agile** (*T: 01 46 06 85 87*) named after the rabbit belonging to André Gill who commissioned the sign, a place originally made famous by its artistic clientele (such as Modigliani, Picasso and Utrillo) and which is still a *cabaret-chansonnier*.

Old Montmartre is recaptured in the **Musée de Montmartre** (*open Tues–Sun, 10–6; closed Mon; T: 01 49 25 89 37*) at no. 12 Rue Cortot, a 17th-century house in a garden, which belonged to one of Molière's troupe. Occupants over the years included Renoir in 1875, Suzanne Valadon and Utrillo. The museum records the history of the district, and contains ephemera and material of local interest ranging from Clignancourt porcelain to a reconstruction of a Montmartrois Bistrot. Exhibits evoke local cabarets, notably the Chat Noir, theatre of shadows.

Return to Rue R. Cortot, and Rue du Mont Cenis, which opens into the legendary, commercialised and crowded **Place du Tertre** where rapid-portrait artists constantly tout for business. In summer or winter it has a holiday atmosphere (and pickpockets). From here is a short hop to the church of St-Pierre (*see p. 256*), and Rue R. Azais leads to Sacré-Coeur.

BASILICA OF SACRE-COEUR
Map p. 470, B1

The funicular runs every five minutes from Pl. Valadon (one metro ticket) and there is also the Montmartrobus (no. 18) from Pigalle and the Mairie du 18ème every 12 minutes.

History of Sacré-Coeur

In 1873 the National Assembly decreed the building of a basilica here as an expiatory offering after the Franco-Prussian War of 1870–71. It was dedicated to Sacré-Coeur, the cult of the Sacred-Heart, which became popular after the first pilgrimage in 1873 to Paray-le-Monial in Burgundy, the site of a 17th-century revelation. This conspicuous Romanesque-Byzantine edifice, built in Château-Landon stone which whitens with age, is visible from almost every part of Paris. Work on the church began in 1876 after plans by Paul Abadie (1812–84), who derived inspiration from St-Front at Périgueux in the Dordogne, which he had recently restored. Consecrated in 1891, it was elevated to basilica status in 1919. The square campanile contains the Savoyarde, one of the world's heaviest bells at 19 tons.

Visiting the basilica

The two statues at the front of the basilica depicting Joan of Arc and St Louis are by Hippolyte Lefebvre. Bronze doors with a delicate vegetal design welcome visitors, but it is hard to reconcile the radiant white exterior with the unremitting gloom of the interior. On a monumental scale and always crowded, the nave is in the form of a Greek cross surmounted by an 83m high dome on pendentives and the huge choir has eleven tall round arches, seemingly squeezed together. The high altar is a bronze reproduction of the altar at Cluny (Burgundy). The surfaces of the interior are extensively decorated with mosaics, by Luc-Olivier Merson, including the largest in the world above the high altar depicting *Christ and the Sacred Heart worshipped by the Virgin, Joan of Arc* and *St Michael.* The 20th-century glass is an interesting contrast with the rest of the décor. It is possible to climb up into the dome for the best views—inside and out. From the external gallery, the 80 columns, each with a different capital, can be seen close-up.

ST-PIERRE-DE-MONTMARTRE
Map p. 470, B1

St-Pierre-de-Montmartre, the successor of an earlier church built to commemorate the martyrdom of St Denis, is a relic of a Benedictine nunnery founded in 1134 by Adélaïde de Savoie (d. 1154). It was consecrated in the presence of her son Louis VII

The Basilica of Sacré-Coeur.

A J Lamme: *Le Jardin de la rue Chaptal* depicting the garden of the Musée de la Vie Romantique.

by Pope Eugenius III in 1147 and is one of the oldest churches in Paris. The severe façade dates from the late 17th century. The bronze doors (1980) were made by T. Gismondi. Inside, against the west wall, are two ancient columns with 7th-century capitals. There are two more of the same date at the apse entrance and in the north aisle. The Romanesque nave has 15th-century vaulting; the north aisle dates from 1765 and the south c. 1838, vaulted 1900–05. The transept and the choir retain Romanesque elements with, over the choir, one of the earliest examples in Paris of a ribbed vault (1147). The apse was rebuilt in the late 12th century. The tomb of the foundress lies behind the altar.

In the adjacent Jardin du Calvaire (*closed*) are Stations of the Cross executed for Richelieu. Foundations of a Roman temple have been discovered to the north of the church, while in the graveyard (*rarely open*) is the tomb of the circumnavigator Louis Bougainville (1729–1811); also buried here is the sculptor Pigalle (1714–85).

PLACE DE CLICHY
Map p. 469, E2

Place de Clichy was the site of the Barrière de Clichy which on 30th March, 1814, was defended against the approaching Prussian troops by pupils from the Ecole Polytechnique and the Garde Nationale under Marshal Moncey. The action is commemorated by a bronze group by Doublemard (1869). The Place and Blvd de Clichy were frequently painted by Renoir, Van Gogh (in 1887), Signac and other artists working and living in the vicinity during the 19th century and into the 20th. Rue de Douai was particularly popular with painters and writers including Charles Dickens. Henri de Toulouse-Lautrec, who kept studios at no. 21 Rue Caulaincourt and 5 Av. Frochot, also vividly brought this bohemian *quartier* to life. Renoir had studios at 73 Rue Caulaincourt c. 1910, and Degas died at no. 6 Blvd de Clichy, where Mary Cassatt had painted. Seurat and Signac worked for a while on Blvd Clichy. Picasso in 1909 lived at no. 130. Reminders of the era are the museums dedicated to Gustave Moreau and also to La Vie Romantique.

MUSEE DE LA VIE ROMANTIQUE
Map p. 469, F2

Open Tues–Sun 10–6, T: 01 55 31 95 67. Tearoom open May–Sept
Tucked away at the end of a cobbled courtyard with a small garden at no. 16 Rue Chaptal is the delightful Musée de la Vie Romantique, in the Maison Renan-Scheffer, with collections devoted to George Sand and Ary Scheffer; it is also used for temporary exhibitions. Scheffer brought together here the artistic glitterati of the era and the area. His great-niece, daughter of the philosopher Ernest Renan, carried on the tradition. The house remained in the family for about 150 years. As well as the house, the studios built by Scheffer for teaching and receiving guests contain paintings and memorabilia. George Sand (1804–76), the aristocratic, prolific and unorthodox novelist and writer famous for wearing men's clothes, taking radical political stances and many lovers (de Musset, Liszt, and Chopin among others), was an occasional guest of Scheffer's, who introduced her here to the likes of Delacroix and Gericault. Celebrity

designer Jacques Garcia had a hand in the look of the museum, which was founded in the 1980s as an outpost of the Musée Carnavalet.

MUSEE GUSTAVE MOREAU
Map p. 470, A2

Open 10–12.45 & 2-5.15, closed Tues; T: 01 48 74 38 50.
The Musée Gustave Moreau at 14 Rue de la Rochefoucauld contains a collection of some 18,000 paintings and drawings left by Moreau (1826–98) to the State. The walls of the creaking, evocative studio on two floors are covered with paintings by this leading Symbolist whose use of colour and surprisingly liberal teaching methods profoundly influenced the next generation of artists. A former pupil, George Rouault, was the first curator of this museum. Among the works on display are *The Apparition* and *Salomé*, of 1874–76, *Mystic Flower* (1890), *Hésiode et la Muse, Jupiter and Sémélé* (1895). A picturesque spiral staircase leads to the upper floor where watercolours are exhibited by rotation and drawings can be viewed in cases with movable panels. Degas' *Portrait of the Artist*, dated 1867, also hangs here. On the first floor it is possible to see the tiny apartment in which Moreau and his parents lived, full of family souvenirs.

LA TRINITE

Further south, at no. 16 Rue de Clichy is the Casino de Paris (*T: 08 926 98 926*), where Josephine Baker once starred. It originated in 1880, the successor of a disreputable Cabaret, which was demolished in 1851 to be replaced by La Trinité, identifiable by its 63m-high tower. The church was built 1863–67 by Théodore Ballu (1817–85) in a hybrid 'historic' style characteristic of the Second Empire with a heavy interior. Olivier Messiaën (1908–92) was organist here for some years in the 1930s. In front of the church is a welcome patch of greenery, with fountains and sculptures.

CIMETIERE DE MONTMARTRE

The Cimetière de Montmartre is one of the three great cemeteries of Paris, along with Père Lachaise (*see p. 327*) and Montparnasse (*see p. 108*). The main entrance is on Av. Rachel. Built on old quarries in 1798 and enlarged in 1825, it now covers over 11 hectares, and has around 750 trees. Plans indicating where the illustrious are buried are available at the main entrance. It is fascinating both for its tombstone art (by Bartholdi, David d'Angers, Falguière, Rodin and Rude among others) and the names of those buried here. Zola was entombed in a red marble monstrosity before his remains were translated to the Panthéon (*see p. 43*). Among others buried here are the comedy artiste, La Goulue, immortalised by Toulouse-Lautrec; writers as varied as Stendhal and Feydeau; great French composers such as Berlioz, Delibes and Offenbach; painters including Fragonard and Degas; and also the dancer Nijinsky, Mme Récamier (*see pp. 183 and 292*), and Marie Duplessis (*La Dame aux Camélias*).

LES HALLES, BEAUBOURG & THE MARAIS

LES HALLES
Map p. 475, E1

Les Halles Centrales of Paris, the central markets memorably described by Zola as *Le Ventre de Paris* (the belly of Paris), are no more, now likely to be referred to as *le trou* or 'the hole'. Markets were held here from the early 12th century; in 1969 they were moved out of central Paris to extensive modern markets at Rungis, about 11km south, near Orly airport. The ten huge pavilions constructed by Victor Baltard (1805–74) in the 1850s, plus two more completed in 1936, were demolished by 1974; number 8 was re-erected at Nogent-sur-Marne. The redevelopment of the whole area of Les Halles encountered technical problems, such as the Metro-RER intersection at the bottom of the hole, as well as underground parking. A number of architects took part in the project, including for a time the postmodernist Ricardo Bofill.

Bourse du Commerce

The Bourse du Commerce, at Pl. des Deux-Ecus, is the only remaining evidence in Paris of the old markets. A circular mid-18th-century building, formerly the Corn Exchange, it received its metal-framed dome in 1811 and was remodelled in 1888. Inside is a fresco representing international commerce around the upper part of the hall covered by a glass dome. Adjoining its southeast side is a fragment of the Hôtel de la Reine, built by Bullant for Catherine de Médicis in 1572 (*see p. 193*). It was later known as the Hôtel de Soissons and from 1720 stock-jobbing or brokering took place in the garden. Rue Coquillière, which runs into Rue Rambuteau, is lined with shops and restaurants, including Au Pied de Cochon where all-night revellers used to eat oysters for breakfast when the old market was in full swing.

Jardins des Halles

The Jardins des Halles, covering nearly five hectares, more laid out in place of the market, with 850 trees, plants trailing over metal structures, 11 fountains, alleys named after poets lined with limes and chestnuts, green sculptures and stepped flower beds around the large tropical greenhouse identified by four small glass pyramids. One alley leads to a hollow, beside the church of St-Eustache, with a large sandstone sculpture of a head, *l'Ecoute* (1986) by Henri de Miller (1953–99), with its ear to the ground. Most fun is the children's play garden which contains six fantasy worlds designed by the sculptor, Claude Lalanne. The **Forum des Halles**, its ribbed and glazed courtyard forming the sunken lid to the *trou*, and embellished by curious pink marble statuary entitled *Pyègemalion* (sic), by the Argentinian sculptor Julio Silva, has had a very mixed reception since it was inaugurated in September 1979 and the underground shopping malls are now somewhat run down.

SAINT-EUSTACHE
Map p. 475, E1

Keeping watch over the Jardins des Halles is the church of St-Eustache. Begun in 1532, perhaps by Pierre Lemercier, it was consecrated in 1637. On first sight it appears to be a thoroughly Gothic structure with supporting flying buttresses but, typically for this transitional period, it has Renaissance details and decorations. The Neoclassical colonnade of the west front, completed only in 1754–88, is strangely out of keeping with the rest of the church. The open-work bell-tower, known as the *Plomb de St-Eustache*, above the crossing, has lost its spire, and above the Lady Chapel in the east is a small tower built in 1640 and rebuilt in 1875. Molière was baptised in the church and lived in the district. The church was the scene of the riotous Festival of Reason in 1793, when revellers drank themselves senseless in the square outside around bonfires stoked with the choir stalls, and in 1795 it became the Temple of Agriculture. Here Berlioz conducted the first performance of his *Te Deum* (1855) and Liszt his *Messe Solenelle* (1866). St-Eustache has always been noted for its music and holds an organ festival in June and July.

The interior
The interior is a striking combination of Gothic plan and Renaissance decoration. The nave is short and the double aisles and chapels continue round the choir, while the wide transepts do not extend beyond the chapel walls. The square piers are decorated with

The church of St-Eustache seen from Les Halles.

squared shafts in three storeys of superimposed orders, and the vaulting is Flamboyant with heavy pendant bosses. Above the high arcades there is a small gallery. The chapels contain restored paintings from the time of Louis XIII, and the 11 lofty windows of the apse were executed by Soulignac (1631), possibly from cartoons by Philippe de Champaigne. The churchwardens' pew was designed by Pierre le Pautre and carved by Carteaux, c. 1720 and the unadorned stalls were acquired from the convent of Picpus (*see p. 309*). The organ, with an ornate case by Victor Baltard (1854), was rebuilt by the Dutch firm van den Heuvel in 1986–89, and is one of the most important in Paris.

The second chapel on the south, the Musicians' Chapel, commemorates Rameau, Franz Liszt and Mozart's mother. On the trumeau of the transept doorway is a 16th-century statue of St John and the second choir chapel has a *Pietà* attributed to Luca Giordano. The glass of the fifth chapel, which features St Anthony, was given by the Société de la Charcuterie de France—one of St Anthony's attributes being a pig. On the altar of the Lady Chapel is a *Virgin* by Pigalle (1748) accompanied by murals by the great historicist Thomas Couture (1856).

In the north aisle, in the first choir chapel is the very fine but incomplete tomb of Colbert (d. 1683), designed by Le Brun, with statues of Colbert and Fidelity by Coysevox, and of Abundance by Tuby. In the next chapel is a painting of the *Supper at Emmaus*, school of Rubens, and a 17th-century French painting of the *Burial of a Martyr*. *The Ecstasy of the Virgin* (c. 1627) is by Rutilio Manetti. In the west chapel is an *Adoration of the Magi* after Rubens, and above the northwest door is the *Martyrdom of St Eustace* by the early 17th-century French master of Italian Baroque, Simon Vouet.

RUE SAINT-DENIS

Rue de Turbigo leads northeast from St-Eustache towards Pl. de la République (*see p. 321*), soon reaching Rue Etienne-Marcel, in which, to the left (at no. 20), rises the **Tour de Jean-sans-Peur**, a graceful defensive tower c. 1400 once incorporated in the Hôtel de Bourgogne. Part of this mansion (see no. 29) was used from 1548 until the turn of the 18th century as a theatre, where plays by Corneille and Racine were performed.

Rue St-Denis, crossing Rue de Turbigo north-south, is one of the oldest routes in Paris. Parallel to the old Roman road, now Rue St-Martin, it runs north from Pl. du Châtelet and leads eventually to the Royal necropolis of St-Denis (*see p. 408*). Partly pedestrianised, near Les Halles this narrow, bustling street is lined with sandwich bars and seedy shops. At no. 135, in its northern section, an inscription indicates the former position of the Porte St-Denis or Porte aux Peintres, a gateway in the walls of Philippe-Auguste. No. 142 is the *Fontaine de la Reine* (1730). On no. 133 are statues from the medieval Hôpital de St-Jacques, once on this site.

To the south, at no. 92 Rue St-Denis, the church of **St-Leu-St-Gilles**, was built in 1235, the nave reconstructed after 1319. The aisles were added in the 16th century and the choir, still partly Gothic, in 1611 (but reconstructed in 1858–61 to make way for the adjacent boulevard). The façade and windows were remodelled in 1727 and a crypt excavated in 1780. The church contains three alabaster reliefs (in the sacristy entrance) and a sculptured group *St Anne and the Virgin* by Jean Bullant (second chapel south). The organ gallery is by Nicolas Raimbert (1659).

Further south, the small Pl. Joachim du Bellay stands on part of the site of the medieval Cimetière des Innocents, the main burial ground of Paris until 1785, when the remains, probably including those of La Fontaine, were transferred to the catacombs (*see p. 109*). Traces of the arches of the cemetery galleries are still to be seen on nos. 11 and 13 in the Rue des Innocents off Rue St-Denis. The restored Renaissance *Fontaine des Innocents* in the middle of the square was originally erected in 1548 in the neighbouring Rue St-Denis by Pierre Lescot, with bas-reliefs by Jean Goujon (now in the Louvre). It was remodelled and set up here by Payet c. 1788; the south side was decorated by Pajou.

BEAUBOURG
Map p. 475, F1

The Beaubourg is an old quarter on the other side of Blvd de Sébastopol from Les Halles, best known for the outrageously modern 1960s' edifice of the Pompidou Centre. The building famously collides aesthetically with its immediate surroundings. Just south of the Pompidou is Place Igor-Stravinsky, flanked by relics of the Rue Brisemiche. A novel installation is the fantasy fountain with amusing coloured mobile sculptures by Niki de St Phalle and Jean Tinguely, in keeping with the Pompidou

Detail of *Fontaine des Automates* (1983), a collaborative mobile water sculpture by Niki de St Phalle and Jean Tinguely in the Pompidou Centre's Place Igor-Stravinsky .

Centre but also setting up a cruel visual contrast with its neighbour, the church of St-Merri (or St-Merry; *see p. 274*). Literally translated as 'beautiful market town', the Beaubourg was once a small rural community outside Paris, surrounded by vineyards. It was gathered within the boundaries of the city when Philippe-Auguste's walls were built in the 13th century. The main artery was originally Rue Beaubourg, and the focus the church of St-Merri. This ancient quarter was carved up in the 19th century when Rue Rambuteau and Blvd Sébastopol were cut, and by the 1930s it had fallen into neglect and been partially demolished. Its character was radically altered when the Centre Georges Pompidou opened in 1977. Bounded to the west by the frankly unlovely Blvd de Sébastopol and Rue du Renard, relics of the old Beaubourg can be found in narrow streets such as Rue Quincampoix, with houses from the 17th–18th centuries.

THE POMPIDOU CENTRE
Map p. 475, F1

Open Wed–Mon 11–9 (last admission at 8), Thurs until 11pm for certain exhibitions; closed Tues; Atelier Brancusi open 2–6, closed Tues; T: 01 44 78 12 33; www.centrepompidou.fr. Restaurant Georges, T: 01 44 78 47 99, has a panoramic terrace (priority lift to Level 6).
The Centre National d'Art et de Culture Georges-Pompidou, known as the Centre Georges Pompidou for short, is the multicultural home of the Musée National d'Art Moderne (MNAM), one of the most important collections of 20th-century art in the world. The Paris City Museum of Modern Art (*see p. 338*) complements the Pompidou.

History of the Pompidou Centre
The Centre was named after the former president, Georges Pompidou, whose idea it was in 1969 to establish a centre focussed on modern creation, including the collections of the Musée National d'Art Moderne, built up through the generosity of artists and donations and previously exhibited in the Palais de Tokyo (*see p. 338*). As well as the modern and contemporary collections of visual arts, the centre also embraces theatre, music, cinema, literature and the spoken work. It houses a public reference library, general documentation centre on 20th-century art, two cinemas, performance halls, a Music Research Institute and educational activity areas. The centre holds around 30 public exhibitions a year as well as other public events.

The building had to answer the inter-disciplinary needs of the centre. The winning design by Anglo-Italian team of architects Richard Rogers and Renzo Piano, in association with G. Franchini and the Ove Arup group, was the first great project of its kind. It was inaugurated on 31st January, 1977. It introduced innovatory ideas to release maximum free-flowing space which could be adapted to the variety of uses. It is, in fact, a 15,000 ton metal box, 166m long, 60m wide, and 42m high with a glazed surface of 11,000 square metres with its functional elements—air conditioning, elevators, and so on—mainly on the exterior, picked out in primary colours. The interior space over seven floors (five above ground) totals 70,000 square metres. One of the most daring features of the building is the external escalator encased in a glazed tube which writhes up the façade. The Centre turned out to be one of the most controversial buildings constructed in Paris since the Eiffel Tower, and the hype surrounding it tended to overshadow the importance of the collections that it was built to house. Only part of the available two hectares was built upon, allowing space for the lively Piazza Beaubourg which slopes down from Rue St-Martin to the main entrance. This has become the theatre for a variety of street entertainment, bridging the gap between the neighbourhood and the more formal events inside the Centre. Despite the controversies, the building was hugely successful, to the extent that by 1997 it was suffering from excessive wear and tear inflicted by a far greater number of visitors than anticipated. A complete overhaul of the building and adjacent areas was carried out 1997–99, under the direction of Renzo Piano, for its reopening on 1st January, 2000. The galleries underwent further improvements in 2005–06, with another reopening on the 31st January, 2007, to coincide with the 30th anniversary of the Pompidou Centre itself.

Musée National d'Art Moderne

The National Museum of Modern Art encompasses all the creative arts, from painting to architecture, through photography, cinema, new media, sculpture and design and includes around 57,000 works by some 5,200 artists, architects and designers representative of artistic creation in the 20th and 21st centuries. The permanent collections are exhibited in vast exhibition halls on two whole levels of the centre and are backed up by substantial documentary information texts in each room. There is a study room providing further information in a variety of formats. Modern Art (1905–50) is on Level 5; Contemporary Art (1950 to the present) is on Level 4. The permanent collections are rotated annually with an emphasis on particular aspects of the collections, taking for example the theme of 'The Studio'. For the re-opening the collections were rehung chronologically, drawing from all the major holdings and returning the Centre to its customary depth and range of display.

Historic or Modern Collections 1905–50

Level 5

Works by all major artists of the first half of the 20th century, from Matisse to Germaine Richier, are in the collections, representing the major movements of the period from Fauvism to Art Brut. There are also extensive collections of architecture and design.

Fauvism: The collections contain beautiful examples of the first great 20th-century art movement, Fauvism, which was short-lived but nevertheless important in liberating the palette of many artists such as Georges Braque (*L'Estaque* c. 1906), Raoul Dufy (*Posters at Trouville* 1906), de Vlaminck (*Red Trees* 1906) and André Derain (*Two Barges* 1905-06). Georges Rouault

(1871–1958; *see p. 260*) adopted the Fauve manner in *Girl at the Mirror* (1906). On no one was the effect of the Fauves more emphatic than on Henri Matisse, illustrated in *Algerian Woman* (1909). Windows, such as *Window at Collioure* (1914), and *odalisques* became two constant motifs in Matisse's work during the period 1925–26, a key example being *Decorative Figure against an Ornamental Background*. *Large Red Interior* (1948) experimented further with the expressive qualities of colour. Sculpture helped Matisse organise his form: the collections have a large group of his bronzes. In the 1930s, his cut-outs developed as a technique for working directly with colour (*see p. 339*), and were used for the publication *Jazz* (Tériade; 1947).

Henri Matisse: *Large Red Interior* (1948).

Cubism: The development of Cubism, between 1907 and 1914, is followed through its creators, Braque and Picasso, through the Analytic phase (until c. 1911), broadly monochromatic, dividing objects up into their constituent planes, and Synthetic phase, bringing objects together, often in collages. Masks and carvings from Gabon and the Ivory Coast which deeply influenced the Cubist vision are displayed. Superb examples of Cubist work during the period 1907–13 such as Picasso's *Study for one of the Demoiselles d'Avignon* and *Woman Seated in an Armchair*, and Braque's *Still Life with a Violin* (*Le Gueridon*) demonstrate their parallel development. Mature, subtle still lifes by Braque are *The Duo*

(1937), and prizewinner at the Venice Biennale in 1948, *Le Billard* (1944). Works by the third great Cubist, Juan Gris, include *Breakfast* (1915). Cubist sculpture includes *The Bottle of Beaune* (1918) by Henri Laurens; the dynamic *The Horse* (1914–61) by Raymond Duchamp-Villon (1876–1918); and *Head of Gertrude Stein* (1920) by Jacques Lipchitz (1891–1973). Also represented here is Alexander Archipenko (1887–1964), one of the most notable Cubist sculptors. Robert Delaunay (*Joie de Vivre* 1930) and his wife Sonia Delaunay (*Electrical Prisms* 1914), were first characterised by Apollinaire as Orphic Cubists for their lyrical way with colour. Fernand Léger (*see p. 341*) shifted from Orphic forms in *The Wedding* (c. 1911), to Purism, in *Contraste de Formes* (1913), a rigorous geometrically ordered form of Cubism introduced by Amédée Ozenfant and the architect Jeanneret (Le Corbusier). He later painted monumental figures such as *Composition with Three Figures* (1932) and *Composition with Two Parrots* (1935–39) intended to appeal to the proletariat.

School of Paris: The School of Paris brings together stylistically individual international artists who gravitated to Paris between the wars: Picasso was among them and the Pompidou Centre is particularly well endowed with his works. From the post-Cubist period is *Portrait of a Young Girl* (1917), Neoclassical works of the 1920s and '30s include *Girl Reading* (1920), and *Still Life with Antique Head* (1925), and Surrealism features briefly in *Figure* (c. 1927). Picasso's mature works include a grating female figure in *Women with Pigeons* (1930) and the brightly coloured *Muse* (1935), while in *Dawn Serenade* (1942) he experiments with a variety of materials. The Italian painter and sculptor Amedeo Modigliani, and painters Chaïm Soutine from Russia and Foujita from Japan, among others, were also members of the Paris School. Later arrivals included abstract painters such as Maria Elena Vieira da Silva from Portugal, represented here by *The Library* (1949), and Antoni Tàpies (b. 1923) from Spain. Marc Chagall developed a very personal, poetic imagery in a blend of memories of his native Russia with borrowings from Orphic Cubism in works such as *To Russia, Donkeys and Others* (1911) and *Death* (1908).

Dada and Surrealism: Dada was born in 1916 in Zurich out of the horrors of the First World War. Anti-art, provocative and funny, even obscene, among its leaders were Marcel Duchamp, George Grosz (*Remember Uncle August, the Unhappy Inventor*; 1919) and Kurt Schwitters who created his own movement embracing a variety of the arts which he called *Merz*. Marcel Duchamp broke through the accepted boundaries of art with the enigmatic *Nine Malic Moulds* (part of *The Bride Stripped Bare by her Bachelors, even*; 1914–15), and especially *Fountain* (1917–64). This famous 'readymade', a urinal signed 'R. Mutt', was one of the most controversial works of the era and the jumping off point for future generations of artists.

Surrealism, which developed in the 1920s, was a synthesis of conscious and unconscious experience to create a new reality. Its roots were in Dada, literature, Freud's theories, and the hallucinatory paintings of Giorgio di Chirico, such as *Melancholy of an Afternoon* (1914). Its poet-painters, led by André Breton, had a far-reaching effect on all aspects of the visual arts, and are well-represented in the collections. Some of the best known Surrealist works include Max Ernst's *Ubu Imperateur* (1923), an assemblage of unrelated elements which create a new reality in the shape of a spinning top-man based on Alfred Jarry's character Ubu. *Loplop Presents a Young Girl* (1930) refers to an imaginary bird which inhabits many of Ernst's works, and *La Femme Cent Têtes* (1929) is a page from a collage 'novel'. The slick style and hallucinatory quality of Salvador Dali's work is more acceptable in *Putrified Donkey* (1928) than in many others. Other important Surrealists in the collections include René Magritte and Bataille's collaborator, André Masson. The American, Man Ray (1890–1977) settled in France in 1921, and participated in Dada activities before joining the Surrealists. Diverse artists who remained with Surrealism, or passed through it, include Hans Bellmer, Hans Arp, Wilfredo Lam, Victor Brauner, as well as Yves Tanguy (1900–55), and the sculptor Julio Gonzalez (1876–1942). Francis Picabia (1879–1953) embraced Cubism for a while (*Udnie*; 1913) before moving on to more aggressive anti-Salon-art tendencies as in *L'Oeil Cacodylate* (1921) and *Animal Trainer* (1923). In Luis Buñuel's *L'Age d'Or* (1930), Surrealism spread to the cinema. The poetic Catalan artist Joan Miró's earlier style is typified by *Interior, The Farmer's Wife* (1922–23). He was profoundly influenced by Surrealism, and shaped from it his own particular brand of imagery. *Blue I, II and III* (1961) is typical of his later work, with detached floating shapes on flat colour planes. Always close to the tenets of Surrealism, Miró also assembled derelict objects out of which might evolve monumental sculpture, either playful or threatening. The sometimes chilling earlier works of Alberto Giacometti such as *Sharp Point in the Eye* (1931) were replaced by the pared down, skeletal figures of *Venetian Woman V* (1956). Germaine Richier (1904–59), one of France's greatest 20th-century sculptors, who studied with Bourdelle and was influenced by

Giacometti and Marino Marini, was considered 'existentialist': among her works here is *The Storm* (1947–48).

Abstraction: Abstraction in fine and applied arts was born in the second decade of the 20th century, of the fertile breeding ground of the Bauhaus, and cross-pollinated with movements throughout Europe, notably Orphism in France, De Stijl in Holland, Futurism in Italy and Constructivism in Russia, all of which are represented in the collections. Dynamic abstract works by Russian-born Wassily Kandinsky (1866–1944) demonstrate one artist's progression from early Fauve-type landscapes to abstract shapes in *Yellow Red Blue* (1925). A colleague of Kandinsky at the Bauhaus (1922–33) was Paul Klee, whose gentle works here include *Villas at Florence* (1926) and *Arrow in the Garden* (1929). Constructivism, described as hovering between utopia and utilitarianism, is represented by Oskar Schlemmer (also ex-Bauhaus), Antoine Pevsner (1884–1962), who produced finely balanced geometric works such as *Construction in Space* (1923–25), and the Ukrainian Kasimir Malevich (1879–1935), whose *Black Cross* (1915) influenced the Minimalists. The De Stijl group of Dutch abstract artists included Piet Mondrian, represented here by his famous *New York City I* (1942), Van Doesburg, and Georges Vantongerloo (*S x R3*; 1933–34). The American sculptor Alexander Calder (1898–1976) bent wire into witty sculptures, including an evocation of *Josephine Baker* (1926), but later made his name, inspired by a visit to Mondrian's studio and also influenced by Miró, with delicate abstract mobiles such as *White Disk, Black Disk* (1940–41).

French Art Movements: Art movements in France in the mid-20th century included Art Informel, non-geometric abstraction practised by such as Jean Fautrier (*see p. 342*), with his series of *Hostages* (1945) fired by the brutality and agony he observed during the Second World War. The main exponent of Art Brut was Jean Dubuffet (1901–85), with dark, primitive, graffiti-like works including *Dhôtel Tinted in Apricot* (1947), and *Winter Garden* (1968–70) a painted architectural environment. Cobra, a group of northern painters including Pierre Alechinsky (b. 1927), Karel Appel (1895–1981) and Bram Van Velde (1921–2006), focused on unconsious spontaneous creation. Individualists include the pure abstract painter described as 'poet of space and musician of line', Hans Hartung

(1904–89), and Nicolas de Staël (1914–55), hovering between figuration and abstraction, tension and fluidity in *The Hard Life* (1946), and *The Musicians, Souvenir of Sydney Bechet* (1953).

Expressionism: The exaggerated forms and colour of Expressionism, as a movement, developed out of the symbolic use of colour by the Fauves in France and the de Brücke and Blaue Reiter groups in northern Europe. European pioneers were Frantisek Kupka, *Autour d'un Point* (1911), and Ernst-Ludwig Kirchner, *The Toilette–Woman in Front of a Mirror* (1912–13). Francis Bacon, who is well represented, pays tribute to an early Expressionist in *Van Gogh in a Landscape* (1957). Abstract Expressionists in the USA (1940–50) in the collections include Jackson Pollock, whose drip technique produced beautiful, subtle paintings such as *Silver, over Black white Yellow and Red* (1948) and also especially *The Deep* (1953).

Contemporary Collections 1960–Present

Level 4

The works in the collections are representative of the variety and innovation of mediums used in the second half of the 20th century and early years of the 21st: painting, sculpture, casting, photomontage, photography, video, drawing, recycling, performance art, kinetics and so forth. On the outside terrace are monumental sculptures by Laurens, Calder, Takis, Richier and Miró.

Nouveau Réalisme: Yves Klein (1928–62) was the driving force behind Nouveau Réalisme founded in Paris in 1960, the name coined by the critic Pierre Restany. This new perception of reality re-interpreted the ready-mades of Marcel Duchamp (*see above p. 268*).

Among leading New Realist artists were Arman (1928–2005) whose *Home Sweet Home*, an 'accumulation' of rubbish, is a criticism of 20th-century consumerism. Others were François Dufrêne (1930–82), Daniel Spoerri (b. 1930), and Gérard Deschamps (b. 1937). The early death of Yves Klein, in 1962, shook the autonomy of the group which dissolved in 1970 in Milan. Klein is best known for monochromatic works in deep ultramarine that he patented as *IKB* (International Klein Blue) in the belief that blue has no tangible reality and that by painting in monochrome, colour is deprived of subjective associations. Between 1955 and 1962, he produced 194 *IKB*s: on canvas, *Monochrome Blue (IBK 3)* (1960), and the assemblage *Tree–Large Blue Sponge* (1962). He caused an uproar by using 'human brushes' to create such works as *Big Blue Anthropophagy, Homage to Tennesee Williams* (1960). Martial Raysse (b. 1936) moved on from Nouveau Réalisme to become a brilliant interpreter of European Pop, illustrated by *America, America*, a huge neon-lighted metal hand, and *Made in Japan, La Grande*

Odalisque (both 1964). Jesus Rafael Soto (1923–2005) who exhibited with them, became a leading light of Kinetic Art.

The 1960s: César (b. 1921) is famous for *Compressions* of discarded objects, prompted initially by lack of money: *Compression Ricard* (1962) is a car reduced to a rectangle. He later made *Expansions*. Raymond Hains (1926–2005) and Jacques de la Villeglé (b. 1926) worked together making inventive *Décollages* from peeled and torn-up posters, such as *Ach Alma Manetro* (1949).

A major artist of the 20th century, Joseph Beuys was associated with the group Fluxus. His mysterious work (made for a 'happening') is *Infiltration for Grand Piano* (1964–66) reminiscent of a rhinoceros; *Skin* (1984) is the felt that was discarded when the artist

Joseph Beuys: *Infiltration for Grand Piano* (1964–66).

changed the piano's wrapping. *Plight* (1958–85) is a padded room with a piano. Other Fluxus members were Ben (Ben Vautrier; b. 1935), Robert Filliou, and Erik Dietman who is represented here with a diptych *Body Art* (1962).

The museum also has a representative selection of British and American Pop Art, including Andy Warhol's *Ten Lizes* (1963), Claes Oldenburg's (b. 1929) *Ghost Drum Set* (1972), Robert Rauschenberg's (b. 1925) *Oracle* (1962), Christo's (b. 1935) *Package and Wrapped Floor* (1968), and James Rosenquist's (b. 1933) *President Elect* (1960–61).

Abstract Expressionists in France are headed by Pierre Soulages (b. 1919), the grand old man of French abstract painting who has remained constant to the possibilities of black, or black on white, and sometimes sombre browns, on huge canvases, with designs which trace a form in space and are often reminiscent of hugely magnified Chinese characters. The works, which are frequently monochromatic, depend on paint textures and the absorption or reflection of light, as for example, *All-black Painting* (1979). The objectivity of titles such as *Painting 1985, 324 x 362 cm*, or *Polyptych C*, avoids any figurative reference.

Arte Povera, impoverished art, is a mainly Italian movement which appeared in 1967 to confront the materialism of the established art world by employing the most simple and worthless materials. The main movers were Giuseppe Penone (b. 1947), with *Albero* (1973), Annis Kounellis (b. 1936) represented by enigmatic untitled installations of the 1960s, and Mario Merz (1925–2003) *Che fare* (c. 1968–69). Antiforme is a sub-group of

Arte Povera, whose temporary forms and 'soft non-fixed sculptures' were developed in the work of Eva Hesse (1936–70) *Seven Poles* (1970), and the curious yet eloquent felt *Wall Hanging* (1969–70) by Robert Morris (b. 1931).

Conceptual Art, the art of ideas which began with Marcel Duchamp, gave its name to a wide-ranging movement in the 1960s. Joseph Kosuth (b. 1945) opined that art should only be conceptual and therefore must break with aesthetics, epitomised in *One and three Chairs* (1965) and *The First investigation (Art as Idea as Idea)* of 1968.

Installations and Special Works:
Large, playful fantasies of mechanised sculpture in the collections focus on 'representation'. Wide-ranging, some of the best-loved are Jean Tinguely's (1925–91) mechanical mobiles, such as *Requiem for a Dead Leaf* (1970). Claes Oldenburg's *Giant Ice Bag* (1969–70) is marginally threatening. *Shop* (1958–73) by Ben (Ben Vautrier; b. 1935) is a monumental montage of disparate objects making a Dadaistic anti-art statement. Niki de Saint-Phalle was influenced by Art Brut, Tinguely and Klein. Her assemblages, such as *The Bride* (1963), are an extraordinary comment on life, both disturbing and humorous. Annette Messager (b. 1943) specialises in series (*see p. 344*) such as *Les Pensionnaires* (1971–72) a sequence of 14 vitrines. Christian Boltanski, *The Archives of Christian Boltanski* (1965–88), is an installation of 644 biscuit boxes containing around 1,200 photographs and 800 documents. Other installations include *While Visions of Sugar Plumbs Danced in their Heads* (1964) by Edward Kienholz

(1927–1994); and *Container Zéro* (1988) by Jean-Pierre Raynaud (b. 1939).

1970–90: The period 1970–90 was a time of crisis, questioning and reaffirmation, represented in France by the Support/Surfaces group. Typical are the striped installations *Jamais Deux Fois la Même* (1967–2000) by Daniel Buren (b. 1938) and two monoliths in polyester and wood, *Double Column* (1982) by Toni Grand (1935–2005). Also representative are the neo-Expressionist violence of Markus Lüpertz (b. 1941), *Untitled MLZ 2546/00* (1992), of a firing squad, as well as Malcolm Morley (b. 1931), who shifted from photo-realism to a painterly style combining two scenes, a beachscape and the horse of Troy in *Cradle of Civilisation with American Woman* (1982). *Ralf III* (1965), and also *Die Mädchen von Olmo* (1981), designed to be hung upside-down, are typical of the controversial work of Georg Baselitz (b. 1938).

1990–present: Works from 1990 to the present frequently involve cross-disciplinary observations of the human figure incorporating casting, sculpture, photography, video, and mechanical installations by artists such as Claude Closky (b. 1963), Thomas Schütte (b. 1954), Valérie Jouve (b. 1964) and Marie-Ange Guilleminot (b. 1960).

Photography: The Pompidou Centre is well endowed with a collection of over 17,000 prints representing more than 700 artists, considered a vital document in the history of photography, including images by Man Ray, Dora Maar, Brassaï, and László Moholy-Nagy.

Architecture and Design: Rotated are examples of drawings, models, furniture and other aids to design. In the Modern period, these range from Russian villages to the work of Le Corbusier (*see p. 356*), Jean Prouvé (pre-fabricated buildings), Robert Mallet-Stevens (1886–1945; *see p. 135*), the influence of the Bauhaus and De Stijl in furniture design, the resolutely progressive ideas of the Union of Modern Artists, Pierre Jeanneret (1896–1967) and the Finnish designer, Alvar Aalto (1898–1976). Architecture from 1940–60 concentrates on industrial and urban design. Megastructures and utopias as well as Pop Art designs are characteristic of the 1960s.

Representative of the period 1970–80 are French architects Christian de Portzamparc, Jean Nouvel, Norman Foster, Richard Rogers, and Frank Gehry, plus designers Gaetano Pesce and Martin Sezakely. Architecture of the 1990s' features the work of Dominique Perrault, Rem Koolhaas, Toya Ito and designers Marc Newson and Jonathan Ive.

Atelier Brancusi

On the north of the Piazza Beaubourg in a separate building designed by Renzo Piano is the Atelier Brancusi, a small and dignified haven of monumental sculptures. Constantin Brancusi reacted against the dynamism of Rodin to create taut, coherent shapes. The four studios of Atelier Brancusi from his workshop at 11 Impasse Ronsin have been exactly reconstructed here, complete with works such as *Le Coq* (1935), as well as models, plinths, and memorabilia. It is designed so that visitors can circulate around the exterior of the studios viewing them through glass from different angles.

SAINT-MERRI
Map p. 475, E1

South of the Pompidou Centre, the church of St-Merri (1515–52) stands at the intersection of the two major Roman roads, the present Rue St-Martin and Rue de la Verrerie. The dingy exterior of the church belies a noble interior which has retained many original furnishings. It replaced at least two older churches that covered the grave of St Médéric of Autun (d. c. 700), and was built in Flamboyant Gothic at a time when Renaissance styles were taking over. The porch, although damaged, is carved with pinnacles and friezes. In the 18th century the interior was given Baroque décor. From 1796–1801 it became the Temple of Commerce. The west front is notable for its rich decoration, but the statues are mostly poor replacements of 1842. The northwest turret claims the oldest bell in Paris (1331); the southwest tower lost its top storey in a fire.

The interior

The nave and choir are of equal length and have simple quadripartite vaults except over the crossing which has lierne vaults and a pendant boss. A frieze of animals, leaves and figures runs around the nave above the arcades and the window tracery has flame-like curves. There is a double aisle on the right (south)—one for the canons and one for the public—and a single on the left. The church lost its 16th-century wooden *jubé* early in the 18th century. The Slodtz brothers were responsible for the sculptured embellishments in the 18th century: Michel-Ange Slodtz designed the pulpit (1753) and the gilded *Glory* above the main altar, and added marble veneer and stucco to the choir chapels. The dark oak organ case dates from 1647, modified in the 18th century and in 1857. Saint-Saëns was organist here.

Immediately to the right of the entrance is a Renaissance screen, and in the first outer chapel of the south aisle are the remains of the 13th-century church. Further on is a large chapel by Boffrand (1743–44), with three oval cupolas, beautiful bas-reliefs by Paul-Ambroise Slodtz (1758), and a *Supper at Emmaus* by A. Coypel. The 17th-century painting above the choir's south entrance of the *Virgin and Child* was one of a pair by C. Van Loo, but its opposite number was stolen. In the left aisle, the first chapel contains a 15th-century tabernacle; the third a *Pietà* (c. 1670) attributed to Nicolas Legendre from Etampes; the fourth, a painting by Coypel (1661). From the fifth chapel a staircase descends to the crypt (1515), which has grotesque corbels and the tombstone of Guillaume le Sueur (d. 1530). The church was decorated with murals in the 19th century, some by Théodore Chassériau, in the third chapel north of the choir. The painting of *St Merri Liberating Prisoners* in the north transept is by Simon Vouet. There is some good stained-glass contemporary with the church in the upper windows, although much was taken out in the 18th century, and the lower windows are mainly 19th century. The nave windows belong to the early 16th century; outstanding are the two west windows, depicting the life of St Nicholas of Myra ('Santa Claus') and of St Agnes. The stained glass of the choir and transept is attributed to Pinaigrier and dated c. 1540.

Environs of St-Merri

The quarter around St-Merri, with its narrow and picturesque alleys, retains several characteristic old houses that survived the rage for demolition during the Halles-Beaubourg redevelopment scheme. Rue des Lombards, named after the Italian bankers and moneychangers active in the Middle Ages, continues to the east by the Rue de la Verrerie. It is said that the writer Boccaccio (1313–75), whose mother was French, was born near the junction of Rue des Lombards and Rue St-Martin.

MUSEE NATIONAL DES ARTS & METIERS
Map p. 471, D4

Open Tues–Sun 10–6; Thur 10–9.30; closed Mon and holidays; T: 01 53 01 82 00 / 60. Included in the entrance ticket are guided visits (45 mins or 1hr30) and demonstrations, including Foucault's pendulum and the Theatre of Automata; www.arts-et-metiers.net
North of Beaubourg, in Rue Réaumur, the Musée National des Arts et Métiers is described as the museum of technical innovation. Incorporated in the museum is the Abbey Church of St-Martin-des-Champs. At the northwest corner of the building is the *Fontaine du Vertbois* (1712) which, with the adjoining tower, has been restored.

HISTORY OF ST-MARTIN-DES-CHAMPS

The priory of St-Martin-des-Champs, founded in 1060 by Henri I and presented to the Abbey of Cluny by Philippe I in 1079, stood outside the city walls until the early 14th century. After the Revolution it became an educational institution and its dependencies were later used as a small-arms factory. In 1798 the buildings were assigned to the Conservatoire des Arts et Métiers, founded in 1794. The collections of Vaucanson and other scientists were assembled here and in 1802 it opened as the Musée des Techniques. The library (42.80m by 11.70m) is now installed in the former refectory, a 13th-century masterpiece, probably built by Pierre de Montreuil (possible architect of the Sainte-Chapelle, *see p. 32*), its vaulting supported by a central row of columns, and with a reader's pulpit at the east end. The external side of the southern doorway is a good example of decorated Gothic, and the sole relic of the original cloisters. Further south is the restored 13th-century doorway of the church (enter from the museum). The turret is a comparatively recent addition, restored in 1854–80. The choir has perhaps the earliest Gothic vault in Paris (1130–40), while the aisleless nave dates from the 13th century.

The collections

The museum is arranged over three floors and divided into seven themes (Scientific Instruments, Materials, Construction, Communication, Energy, Mechanics and

Transport, each sub-divided chronologically into pre-1750, 1750–1850, 1850–1950, and 1950 onwards. From the 80,000 objects in the collection (it also has some 20,000 works on paper), exhibits demonstrate the evolution of major inventions since the 16th century, not only the technically and scientifically brilliant ones but also the beautiful, skilful or curious. The suggested sequence is to begin the visit on the Second floor (lifts).

Second floor

Scientific Instruments: In the extensive collection of Scientific Instruments are astronomical and surveying instruments for calculating time, distance, weight, temperature and so forth including Arsenius's great astrolabe of 1569; Pascal's calculating machine of 1642; and time-pieces and clocks by Berthoud, Lepaute, Bréguet, Janvier and other famous 18th-century horologists. There are also Abbe Nollet's instruments of natural philoso-phy (early electrostats), the laboratory of Jaques-César and Alexandre Charles, Buffon's circular mirror with variable focus, an anemometer (1734) for measur-ing the speed of wind—the oldest known instrument integrating a system of recording data—and Lavoisier's laboratory (1743–94). Exhibits range from Foucault's experiments with the measurement of speed of light (1862) in the Observatory (*see p. 97*) to the cyclotron of the Collège de France (1937) and a Cray-2 Super computer (1985).

Materials: Includes natural products—paper, ceramics, iron, linen, wool and glass such as that produced by Emile Gallé at the turn of the 20th century—and the development of plastics.

First floor

Construction: On the first floor the Cabinet de Dessins (Drawings) intro-duces Construction which addresses the development from traditional methods using wood and stone through to the greatest revolution in the 19th century: the introduction first of metal frames and then concrete, and finally their combination in the reinforced concrete such as that used in the Théatre du Champs-Elysées (1911–13) by Perret.

Communication: The large area devoted to Communication covers a multitude of techniques: writing, and printing, from Gutenberg (1438) to the mechanised printing press (1750–1850); the development of photographic equipment and the apparatus used by Daguerre, Niepce, Lumière and others in the pioneering days of photography and cinematography; historical equip-ment such as the optical telegraph invented by Chappe (*see p. 326*) and Edison's phonograph (1877); objects illustrating the development of recording, radio and television; discoveries by Bell; global satellites in the 20th century; and the various current means of communication.

Energy: Three main stages, from water- and windmills, including the Machine de Marly (*see p. 402*), to the invention of steam engines, with a model of Watt's steam engine, to electricity are covered. And there is also an example of energy economy with a model of a modern bioclimatic house (1999).

Mechanics: Automation, machine tools, levers and mills are among the subjects of this theme, with an example of the 18th-century sliding lathe by Vaucanson. Also, for children and the less mechanically minded, the utterly charming Theatre of Automata includes Marie-Antoinette's *Joueuse de Tympanon.*

Ground floor and chapel

Transport: On the ground floor level are various modes of transport demonstrating the development from wind and animal power, to steam then motorised vehicles. Among the museum's excellent collection are two prototypes of the motor car, Cugnot's steamcarriage of 1770 and one by Serpollet (1888) and early petrol-driven vehicles such as a Panhard (1896), Peugeots of 1893 and 1909, a Berliet phaeton (1898), a De Dion-Bouton (1899) and a Renault of 1900. Pioneering aeroplanes include those of Ader (1897), Esnault-Pelterie (1906), the plane in which Blériot made the first flight across the Channel (1909) and a Bréguet of 1911.

The chapel: This has become a shrine to technology and science. Foucault's pendulum has been returned to its original place in the chancel; there is Scott's steam engine; the first steam-powered bus, called *L'Obéissante*, made by Amédée Boillée; the model for the *Statue of Liberty* by Bartholdi; Ader and Blériot aircraft; and a model of the Vulcan engine from the Ariane rocket.

QUARTIER DU TEMPLE
Map p. 471, D4

East along Rue Réaumur is Square du Temple, one of the 24 squares created during the Second Empire. Until the late 12th century it was the site of the stronghold of the Knights Templar. The headquarters of their Order in Europe until 1313, it was then occupied by the Order of St John. The garden boasts many different trees, a lake and a cascade made with rocks from the Forest of Fontainebleau.

The area owned by the Templars lay for the most part between this point and Pl. de la République to the northeast (*see p. 321*). Before the Revolution it was occupied by wealthy families, artisans who did not belong to the corporations and therefore were free from many restrictions, and debtors who were protected here from legal action.

The palace of the Grand Prior of the Knights of St John was renowned for its luxuriousness but, with the Revolution, the Tour du Temple (1265) was transformed into a prison, and in August 1792 Louis XVI and the royal family were taken from the Tuileries and incarcerated here (objects from the prison are now in the Musée Carnavalet; *see p. 291*).

Environs of the Square du Temple

At 195 Rue du Temple is the church of Ste-Elisabeth, founded in 1628 by Marie de Médicis. The main feature is the woodwork, including, in the ambulatory, 17th-century carvings of scriptural scenes from the abbey of St-Vaast at Arras. There are interesting houses in the quarter, including no. 3 Rue de Volta (off Rue Réaumur) which, dating from c. 1300, is possibly the oldest surviving house in Paris, and also on Rue de Montmorency. The Hôtel de Montmorency (entrance at no. 5) was the residence of Fouquet (Louis XIV's Minister) in 1652. The Maison du Grand-Pignon, at no. 51 was built in 1407 by Nicolas Flamel, and restored in 1900. A number of early 17th-century houses have survived in Rue Michel-le-Comte.

MUSEE D'ART & D'HISTOIRE DU JUDAISME
Map p. 475, F1

Open Mon–Fri 11–6, Sun 10–6; closed Sat and Jewish holidays; T: 01 53 01 86 60.
On the west side of Rue du Temple is a charming ensemble of 17th-century houses, one of the best of which is Hôtel de St-Aignan (no. 71), home to the Museum of Jewish Art and History, with regular exhibitions, a media library and an auditorium.

HISTORY OF THE HOTEL DE ST-AIGNAN

The Hôtel de St-Aignan, designed by Pierre le Muet (1591–1669), was completed in 1650 for Cardinal Mazarin's Superintendent of Finances. An unprecedented example of civil architecture in Paris, the giant Corinthian order is deployed in the magnificent courtyard. On the south side, masking a section of Philippe-Auguste's boundary wall, is a *trompe l'oeil* façade creating an illusion of space and symmetry. The mansion was acquired by the Duc de St-Aignan in 1688, at which time the main staircase was installed and the garden façade enlarged. Le Nôtre was involved in the design of the original garden (under renovation). The Hôtel St-Aignan was later at the heart of the Jewish quarter known in Yiddish as the *Pletzl*. It was made available for a museum at the initiative of Jacques Chirac in 1986, then Mayor of Paris, and opened in 1999.

The museum

The building has been imaginatively adapted to fulfill the functions of a modern museum and now brings together collections from the former Musée d'Art Juif in Montmartre (now closed), and a collection that had been languishing in the reserves at the Hôtel de Cluny (*see p. 43*) including the Strauss-Rothschild collection. A main theme of the museum is Jewish communities that have congregated on French soil over the centuries, such as European Jews who migrated to France in the 19th century, or those from North Africa in the 20th century. Three sections are reserved for specifically French

Jewish history and art: the Middle Ages; the process of emancipation from the French Revolution to the Dreyfus Affair; and the 20th century. The identification of Jewish applied art generally adheres to different criteria according to historic period (although there are exceptions): from the Middle Ages to the 18th century it depends on the artist or craftsman, type of decoration, motif or iconography, and function. The more recent period is described by the title: the Jewish Presence in 20th-century Art. The entrance is beneath the St-Aignan family coat of arms. The main staircase leads to the permanent collections starting on the first floor with the Introductory Room. Here the antiquity of the Jewish people is evoked through its relationship to a text, a language, a homeland, and its particular destiny of exile, using handwritten Hebrew texts and translations.

Rooms 2–6: The displays on Medieval France contain gravestones, manuscripts and four rare objects: a Hanukkah lamp, a wedding ring, an alms box and a seal; Jews in Italy, from the Renaissance to the 18th century, are represented by synagogue furniture such as a Holy Ark from Modena, a marriage ring and illuminated marriage contracts; also here is a fascinating ensemble of Hanukkah lamps of all types, origins and periods, representing the diversity of Jewish customs worldwide; the meeting of two diaspora in Amsterdam in the 16th and 17th centuries is narrated through engravings; a *sukkah* decorated with a view of the Holy City serves as the focal point for a display concerning the central role of Jerusalem.

Rooms 7 and 8: These rooms are divided between the first and second floors, taking visitors past the Library on the mezzanine. They are devoted to the traditional Ashkenazi and Sefardi worlds, with models of synagogue architecture and silverware including a highly ornate 17th-century Torah case from Vienna.

Room 9: The next section enters the Era of Emancipation, which began with the French Revolution. Vital events in 19th-

century French Judaism are illustrated with documents, paintings and other objects. They include more than 3,000 items from archives donated by the grandchildren of Dreyfus (1859–1935).

Room 10: A transitional sequence on the important intellectual role of Jews in Europe at the turn of the century includes the emergence and spread of Zionism and Yiddish culture. Graphics are used to highlight the Jewish cultural renaissance in Germany and Russia at the beginning of the 20th century, focusing on folklore, ornament, biblical subjects and calligraphy, linking Jewish themes and identity.

Room 11: Arranged on several levels, the Jewish Presence in 20th-century Art features School of Paris artists, such as Lipchitz, Soutine, Marcoussis, Orloff, Modigliani, El Lissitsky, Zadkine and Chagall, all of whom absorbed contemporary artistic developments in a very personal manner, often breaking away from the exclusively religious iconography which had once dominated Jewish art.

Room 12: A documentary picture of European Judaism around the theme of the Jewish community which inhabited the Hôtel de St-Aignan in 1939 is built up here. The only reference in the museum to the Holocaust is very personal to this community: in a tiny courtyard is a low-key but moving installation by Christian Boltanski which consists of plaques naming former residents. During the round-up of Parisian Jews in 1942, seven were arrested and in all 13 were deported and died.

PLACE DU CHATELET
Map p. 475, E2

The hectic Place du Châtelet is named after the vanished Grand Châtelet, a fortified gate to the Cité, once the headquarters of the Provost of Paris and the Guild of Notaries, begun in 1130 and demolished 1802–1810. A plan of the fort can be seen on the front of the Chambres des Notaires to the north. To the south is the Pont au Change (*see p. 35*). On the east is the **Théâtre de la Ville** and opposite the **Théâtre du Châtelet** (1862), a vast Renaissance-style hall where *communards* were court-martialled in 1871. In the centre is the *Fontaine du Châtelet* (1808–59), once the site of the Parloir aux Bourgeois, seat of the municipality from the 13th century until 1357 (*see below*).

Just north is Sq. St-Jacques, a public garden since 1856, the first of a series of green areas created by Haussmann (*see p. 223*), with the Flamboyant Gothic **Tour St-Jacques** (1508–22) in the middle. Since 1797 this has been the only relic of a series of churches that stood on this site from the 9th century dedicated to St Jacques-la-Boucherie, a rallying point for pilgrims on the road to Santiago de Compostella in Spain. In the 17th century Blaise Pascal carried out experiments here. From 1836 it was used as a shot tower, where shot was made by pouring molten lead through a sieve at the top into water at the bottom, until it was creatively restored in 1858 by Ballu. At the end of the 19th century it became a meteorological station. It has long since been under wraps.

Av. Victoria, named in honour of Queen Victoria's visit to Paris in 1855, runs between Pl. de l'Hôtel-de-Ville and Pl. du Chatelet. To the north, the **Temple des Billettes**, at 22 Rue des Archives, was built in 1756 for Carmelites, but since 1812 used by Lutherans. On the north side is the only medieval cloister (1427) extant in Paris, a Flamboyant relic of an older convent constructed on the site of the anti-Semitic 'Miracle des Billettes' in 1290, where the Host was supposed to have bled upon being used by a Jew in his kitchen. Later, the miracle supported the Catholics' argument with the Protestants over transubstantiation. Temporary exhibitions are now sometimes held here.

HOTEL DE VILLE
Map p. 475, F2

For visits T: 01 42 76 43 43 or 01 42 76 50 49 or enquire at 29 Rue de Rivoli.
Place de l'Hôtel-de-Ville is a large pedestrianised square which is frequently used for - public gatherings. Until 1830 it was known as Pl. de Grève, as ships had moored on the

strand or *grève* in this area since the 11th century. It was the location for public executions, many incredibly barbarous, of Protestants, assassins, sorceresses, highwaymen, murderers, revolutionaries, and criminals. It was often a rendezvous for unemployed or dissatisfied workers, who were said to *faire grève*, which came to mean to go on strike. The Hôtel de Ville, on the eastern side of the square is the administrative centre of the City authorities and as such was frequently the centre of unrest. Crowds gather now for a variety of activities, such the ice rink in winter, big screens during major sporting events and exhibitions. Since 2005, it has been the beach games extension to Paris Plage, a 3km stretch of river bank between Quai des Tuileries and Quai Henri IV.

Central façade (1874–84) of the Hôtel de Ville.

History of the Hôtel de Ville

In 1264 Louis IX created the first municipal authority in Paris by allowing the merchants to elect magistrates (*échevins*), led by the Prévôt des Marchands, who was also head of the *Hanse des marchands de l'eau*. This merchant guild, which had the monopoly of the traffic on the Seine, Marne, Oise and Yonne, took as their emblem a ship, a device which still graces the arms of the city. They had two temporary meeting places. The Parloir aux Bourgeois and then the Grand-Châtelet (*see above*) until in 1357, the Provost Etienne Marcel (*see p. 11*) purchased a mansion in Pl. de Grève for their assemblies. In 1532 plans for an imposing new building had been drawn up but nothing was completed until 1628. In 1789 the 300 electors nominated by the districts of Paris met here and on 17th July, Louis XVI received the newly devised *tricolore* cockade from the hands of Jean Sylvain Bailly, the Mayor. However, on 10th August, 1792, the 172 commissaries elected by Paris gave the signal for a general insurrection. Robespierre took refuge here in 1794 but was arrested on 27th July and dragged, injured, to the Conciergerie (*see p. 34*). In 1805 it became the seat of the Préfet de la Seine and his council, and was the scene of numerous official celebrations. The Swiss Guards put up a stout defence of the building during the 1830 July

Revolution. In 1848 it became the seat of Louis Blanc's provisional government and witnessed the arrest of the revolutionary agitators Armand Barbès and Louis-Auguste Blanqui. The Third Republic was proclaimed here on 4th September, 1870 and, in the following March, the Commune. On 24th May, 1871 the building was evacuated before being set ablaze by its defenders. It was rebuilt from 1874–84 with elaborate façades, on a larger scale than before, in the style of the French Renaissance, to the plans of Ballu and Deperthes. The façades are embellished with statues of eminent Frenchmen and its interior lavishly adorned in accordance with the official taste in architecture of the period, including sculpture, elaborate carvings and murals by Puvis de Chavannes. In 1944 the Hôtel de Ville was a focus of opposition to the occupying forces by the Resistance movement who, by 19th August, had established themselves in the building, repelling German counter-attacks until relieved by the arrival of Général Leclerc's division five days later.

THE MARAIS
Map p. 476, B2

The Marais is one of the most interesting districts of old Paris. Despite past neglect, demolition and some rebuilding, it remains substantially as developed in the 17th century. It contains buildings of outstanding architectural interest, and a number of important and inviting museums.

HISTORY OF THE MARAIS

A marshland (*marais*) on the northern banks of the Seine, the district only became habitable with the arrival of the Knights Templar and other religious houses which settled here in the 13th century and drained the marshes for arable land. Royal patronage began with Charles V who, anxious to forget the associations of the Palais de la Cité with the rebellion of Etienne Marcel in 1358, built the Hôtel St-Paul here. The Hôtel de Lamoignon (*see p. 300*) and Hôtel Carnavalet (*see p. 284*) were built in the 16th century, but the seal of royal approval came with the construction of the Place Royale (1605), later known as Place des Vosges (*see below*). Courtiers built themselves houses in the district, and the Marais remained the most fashionable residential area of Paris until the Faubourg St-Germain took over in the early 18th century. At the Revolution, the State confiscated the property of the nobles for sale to craftsmen, mechanics and merchants. The grand buildings were neglected. Much of the Marais is still busy with trade and commerce and it is now one of the most animated parts of Paris on a Sunday, with shops and restaurants open. Once again it is a fashionable place to live.

PLACE DES VOSGES & HOTEL DE SULLY
Map p. 476, B2

Place des Vosges, built 1606–11 at the heart of the Marais, has a specific charm unlike any other square of Paris. This large quadrangle is surrounded by 39 houses built on a uniform plan with brick, stone and stucco façades, arcaded ground floors and simple dormers. Trees were not planted in the central gardens until 1783, damaging the overall symmetry: the ideal time to visit is in winter when the leaves have fallen. The main approach, from Rue St-Antoine, is by Rue de Birague, through the Pavillon du Roi.

History of Place des Vosges

The square occupies the site of the royal Palais des Tournelles, the residence of the Duke of Bedford, English regent of France in 1422 after the death of Henry V of England. Close to the royal house of St-Pol (*see p. 306*), in 1559, during the double marriage celebrations of Henri II's daughter Elisabeth de France to Philippe II of Spain, and his sister Marguerite to Emmanuel Philippe of Savoie, a tournament was held on the exceptionally large Cours St-Antoine near the square. Henri II was wounded during the last joust by Montgomery, Captain of the Scottish Guard, dying after ten days of agony. His widow, Catherine de Médicis, consequently abandoned the palace. The square in its present form was laid out for Henri IV, possibly by Louis Métezeau or Baptiste du Cerceau, and was inaugurated by Louis XIII in 1612. The slightly taller king's pavilion was built above the gateway in the centre of the south side, and the queen's was the corresponding building on the north (no. 28). In the earlier part of the reign of Louis XIV this was one of the most fashionable addresses in Paris, and the centre of the *Nouvelles Précieuses* satirised by Molière. It acquired its present name in 1799, after the department of the Vosges was first to discharge its liabilities for the Revolutionary Wars.

Exploring the square and Hôtel de Sully

No. 6 is the **Maison Victor Hugo** (*open Tues–Sun 10–6, closed Mon and holidays, T: 01 42 72 10 16*), in which Victor Hugo lived in 1832–48. It is of especial interest for his numerous pen and wash drawings (around 350). The upper rooms provide an

Victor Hugo's writing desk in the Maison Victor Hugo, Place des Vosges.

opportunity to enjoy the view over the square. Things to see include the bust of Hugo by Rodin; *Portrait of Juliette Drouet* by Bastien-Lepage; *The Première of Hernani* by Besnard; *Portrait of Adèle Foucher*, the poet's wife, by Louis Boulanger; *Hugo on his Death-bed* by Bonnat; and works by Célestin Nanteuil and Delacroix. There is also furniture, including the desk in the style of the time at which he stood to write, and woodwork designed or carved by Hugo.

Théophile Gautier (in 1831–34 writing *Mademoiselle de Maupin*) and later, the journalist and novelist Alphonse Daudet (*Letters from my Windmill*; 1866), lived at no. 8, the Hôtel de Fourcy (1605), and no. 21 was the mansion of Cardinal de Richelieu. At the corners of the square are fountains (1816), and in the centre an indifferent equestrian statue of Louis XIII (1825) set up to replace one destroyed in 1792.

There is a route through the gardens of the Petit-Hôtel de Sully (1634–41), at no. 7 Place des Vosges, to the most elegant and prestigious *hôtel particulier* in the Marais, the **Hôtel de Sully**. The main entrance is on Rue St-Antoine. The mansion (1624–30), thought to be by Jean du Cerceau, was acquired by Maximilien de Béthune, Duc de Sully (1560–1641), Henri IV's minister, in 1634. The courtyard, a fine example of Louis-XIII style, abounds in carved decorations, notably around the dormers and six bas-reliefs in niches, the females representing the Elements and the males Autumn and Winter. Spring and Summer are on the garden façade, a subdued echo of the courtyard. The entrance pavilions and the interior, extensively restored, still have 17th-century ceilings and panelling. The buildings are occupied by the Caisse Nationale des Monuments Historiques et des Sites (CNM), who can provide information about guided tours to the monuments of Paris (*booklet Visites Conférences available in most museums, T: 01 44 54 19 30/01 44 54 19 35. There is also an excellent bookshop, open Tues–Sun*).

MUSEE CARNAVALET
Map p. 476, B2

Open Tues–Sun 10–6, closed Mon and holidays; T: 01 44 59 58 58, www.carnavalet.paris.fr
Anyone passionate about Paris will at some time want to visit the Musée Carnavalet which illustrates the history of the city through works of art. Its collections are arranged across two of the most outstanding historic buildings in the Marais, the Hôtel Carnavalet and the Hôtel le Peletier de St-Fargeau. The main entrance (at the Hôtel Carnavalet) is on Rue de Sévigné. There is a second entrance into the gardens from Rue des Francs-Bourgeois. To the north is the Hôtel le Peletier de St-Fargeau, inherited in 1779 by Louis-Michel Le Peletier de St-Fargeau (*see p. 291*). The imposing Renaissance Hôtel Carnavalet was begun in 1548 for Jacques de Ligneris, President of the *Parlement*. It consisted of the main building overlooking the courtyard with two wings at right angles. Dating from this period are the four magnificent reliefs on the main facade opposite the entrance, representing *The Seasons* by Jean Goujon as were the four signs of the Zodiac: Aries, Libra, Cancer and Capricorn. In 1578 the building was acquired by the widow of a Breton gentleman, François de Kernevenoy, called

Portrait of Madame de Sévigné by Claude Lefebvre in the Musée Carnavalet.

Carnavalet by the Parisians. Claude Boislève, the new owner in 1660, commissioned François Mansart to make alterations and a new façade was built around the 16th-century gateway. Allegorical reliefs by Gérard van Obstal (1594–1668), were added to the Rue des Francs-Bourgeois façade. Obstal was also responsible for those on the right

MUSEE CARNAVALET

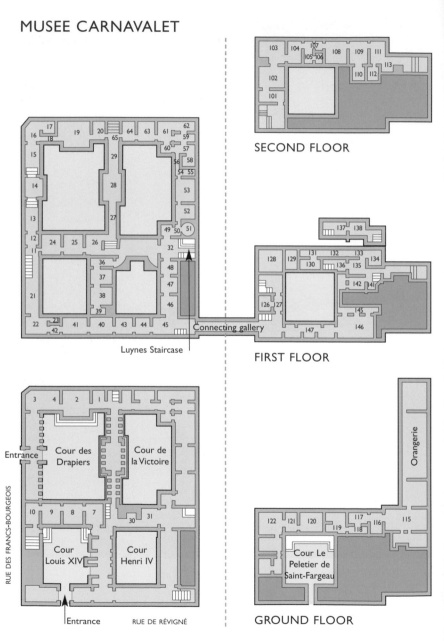

SECOND FLOOR

FIRST FLOOR

Luynes Staircase

Connecting gallery

RUE DES FRANCS-BOURGEOIS

Entrance

Cour des Drapiers

Cour de la Victoire

Cour Louis XIV

Cour Henri IV

Entrance

RUE DE RÉVIGNÉ

Orangerie

Cour Le Peletier de Saint-Fargeau

GROUND FLOOR

HOTEL CARNAVALET

HOTEL LE PELETIER

wing of the courtyard, Juno, Hebe, Diana and Flora. It is not certain who carved the allegories of the four Elements on the left. Some years later Mme de Sévigné rented the building and lived here until her death in 1696 (see p. 289).

The Carnavalet was acquired in 1866 by the City of Paris and it was renovated and adapted to open as a museum in 1880. The front courtyard became known as Cour Louis XIV after the bronze statue of the king by Coysevox which stood in the courtyard of the Hôtel de Ville, miraculously survived the Revolution, and was moved here in 1890. The museum soon outgrew the space and it was extended to the west using elements from three demolished Parisian buildings: on the Rue des Franc-Bourgeois side is the Arc de Nazareth (1552–56) from the Ile de la Cité; to the west, the façade of the Bureau des Marchands Drapiers (1660), from Rue des Déchargeurs; and north, the central part of the Hôtel de Marêts (c. 1710) from Rue St-Augustin, all creating the Cour des Drapiers. Further extensions were carried out early in the 20th century around the two courtyards: Cour de la Victoire, named after the original lead statue *Winged Victory* (1807) by Simon Boizot (1743–1809) for the Châtelet fountain (a copy replaced the original in 1898); and Cour Henri IV after the bronze relief (1834) of the king by Henri Lemaire (1798–1880) for the Hôtel de Ville and placed here in 1907.

In 1895 the museum acquired the Hôtel le Peletier de St-Fargeau, built by Pierre Bullet for Michel de Peletier in 1687–90 on Rue de Sévigné. A sober building, the Rue Payenne façade (around the gardens of Square Georges Cain) is less austere than those facing the courtyard. The Orangerie is decorated with an allegory of Truth, and on the main façade is a figure of Time. The building has retained only the main stairwell and one room with gilded panelling and mirrors on the first floor.

Paintings and sculpture collection

The Museum has a vast collection of art works which are distributed throughout the museum in the relevant rooms or in separate galleries. These important historic documents recording cityscapes and monuments, momentous events and people, are by well-known as well as lesser-known artists. There are views of medieval Paris on the Ile de la Cité and the Left Bank and many painters captured the Seine and the Quais on canvas. Gradually the emblematic buildings and monuments which still define Paris appear in the works, such as the Louvre and Tuileries, Pont Neuf a. 1633 when it was still new, Place Dauphine, Place Royale (the present Place des Vosges), the Hôpital St-Louis, Les Invalides, and the Eiffel Tower. The 'Parisian Canaletto', Nicolas Raguenet (1715–93), left a rich source of information on Paris during the the the Enlightenment (in Room 29) and the Romantic landscapist, Hubert Robert (1733–1808), painted many views including the Eiffel Tower and the Champ-de-Mars when brand new in 1889.

Visiting the museum

This is a complicated museum to get around, the two buildings being linked by a long gallery, and containing some 155 rooms. Since the museum belongs to the City of Paris, however, and is free of charge, it is possible to be selective and make several visits. Archaeological finds, paintings, sculpture, furniture, interiors and other objects, are displayed according to periods or themes. The reconstructions of 17th- and 18th-century rooms, the Revolutionary period, and the 20th-century section are all particularly popular. The visit starts in the Salles des Enseignes which are an evocation of old Parisian streets, with shop and tavern signs (15th–19th centuries), and maquettes of Paris during the 19th century. Beyond these rooms is the foot of the Escalier de Luynes (*see p. 292*) which leads up to the first floor of the Hôtel Carnavalet. The description that follows describes the museum's collections in chronological order; room numbers refer to the ground plans (*see p. 286*).

Le Peletier ground floor

Orangerie: Prehistoric to Gallo-Roman Paris collections occupy the 17th-century Orangerie, which is a rare survival of this type of building in Paris (and quite a difficult room to find). The most interesting objects here include mammoth molars, gold coins of the Parisii era, Gallo-Roman divinities and 7th-century damascened buckles. Especially exciting were the discovery in 1991, during archaeological digs in the Bercy, of two ancient pirogues or dug-out canoes (c. 2000–4000 BC), and other finds, providing new insights into the origins of Paris. Maquettes of Gallo-Roman *Lutetia* and Paris during the Merovingian period explain the evolution of the early city.

Carnavalet ground floor

The rooms covering **Medieval Paris** (Rooms 1–4) were closed for extensive refurbishment at the time of writing. **Sixteenth-century Paris** (Rooms 7–10) was a time of cultural expansion and religious and political conflict.

Rooms 7–10: These rooms contain a model of the Ile de la Cité, Renaissance fireplaces and pieces of furniture. There are two portraits from the School of Clouet: one shows Mary Stuart (1561), widow of François II, and later the Queen of Scots, wearing a white mourning veil; the other Catherine de Médicis (1519–89), widow of Henri II, who failed to find a solution to the religious problems that resulted in the St Bartholomew's Day Massacre; further portraits depict Diane de France, Duchesse d'Angoulème (1538–1619), who built the nearby Hôtel de Lamoignon (*see p. 300*) and was the natural daughter of Henri II by Diane de Poitiers, long Catherine's triumphant rival; and the Duc de Guise, known as Le Balafré because of a facial scar, who belonged to the hard-line Catholic dynasty opposed to the Huguenot supporters of Henri de Navarre. There is also a painting that depicts Ste-Geneviève, Patron of Paris (*see p. 49*), in front of the 17th-century Hôtel de Ville. Two huge 17th-century *mascarons* (grotesque masks) removed from the Pont Neuf when it was renovated in the 19th century can also be seen here. The foundation stone of the bridge, the design of which was considerably ahead of its time, was laid in 1578 by Henri III. It was most recently restored in 2006.

Carnavalet first floor

On this floor the history of Paris in the 17th and 18th centuries is illustrated through a series of reconstructed period interiors, including Madame de Sévigné's apartments, along with impressive collections of of topographical art and fine furniture.

Seventeenth-century Paris (Rooms 11–25), involving the transformation of the city during the reigns of Louis XIII and Louis XIV, is represented through paintings, sketches for decorative schemes inspired by Italy, and the interiors of grand town houses, including the Sévigné Rooms of the Hôtel Carnavalet itself.

Rooms 13–15: These rooms are dedicated to 17th-century painted views of Paris, including three of the Place Royale (later Place des Vosges).

Room 17: Here is the sumptuous reassembled drawing-room of the Hôtel Colbert de Villacerf (23 Rue de Turenne), dating from around 1655, with cream and gilt wood panelling decorated with polychrome grotesques.

Rooms 19 and 20: These rooms contain the most important early examples of integral decoration: the richly painted and gilded *boiseries* of c. 1656 of the *Grande chambre* and the *Cabinet doré* from the Hôtel de la Rivière, 14 Pl. des Vosges. Abbot La Rivière, Bishop of Langres, purchased the property in 1652 and called on architect François Le Vau (1612–76; *see p. 38*) and painter Le Brun to refurbish it. These rooms represent the most remarkable decorative ensembles of the Carnavalet and were the first to be reassembled here, from 1872. The project was one of Le Brun's first major decorative commissions which prompted Fouquet to engage him to work at Vaux-le-Vicomte and which ultimately led him on to work at the Château de Versailles.

Rooms 21–23: Mme de Sévigné's apartments contain memorabilia which belonged to the epistolary writer, Marie de Rabutin-Chantal, Marquise de Sévigné (1626–96) who occupied two wings of the *étage noble* of Carnavalet from 1677 until her death. Her daughter and main addressee, Mme de Grignon, lived on the ground floor in an apartment adapted by Liberal Bruant (c. 1636–97). Mme de Sévigné's *Lettres de la Marquise*, which spanned 30 years, are a brilliant and lively testament of the society of the day, written in an unusually informal style for the time. Her portrait (Room 21) by Claude Lefebvre (1632–1675) was reproduced in an engraving used as the frontispiece for the second edition of *Letters*, published in 1754. Her japanned desk from the Château des Rochers near Vitré, is below the portrait. There are also likenesses of contemporary literary figures, including *Jean de la Fontaine* by Rigaud and playwright Molière depicted in Corneille's *La Mort de Pompée* (c. 1657).

Rooms 24 and 25: An evocation of the City of Paris during the Ancien Régime with municipal paintings. The original grand fireplaces still grace these Madame de Sévigné's main rooms.

Decorative Arts in the Musée Carnavalet

The Decorative Arts are a key part of the collections. Painted and sculpted wood panels and ceilings saved from *hôtels particuliers* originally situated in smart *quartiers* such as the Faubourg St-Germain and Faubourg St-Honoré, many of them demolished during Haussmann's urban reconstruction in the mid-19th century (*see p. 223*), have been reassembled in the museum. Following scrupulous research, some of these décors have been meticulously restored using the original technique of *peinture à la colle* or distemper, using water-based pigments combined with animal glue or milk protein. The colour schemes, all of which are different, vary according to the period, as do the relief decoration of the panelling, which may be either wood or stucco. Rooms were also smaller then. Fabrics were specially woven to match the original decoration, carefully differentiating between what is authentic and what has been remade. The museum has around 800 examples of furnishings, and the rooms are brought to life with relevant objets d'art, tapestries, and pieces from the workshops of leading cabinet makers such as Migeon, Riesener, Weisweiller, and Roger Vandercruse (called Lacroix, RVLC).

Eighteenth-century Paris (Rooms 26–64) is divided into four different periods or styles of the century: Louis XIV, Regency of Louis XV, Louis XV, and Louis XVI.

Rooms 27–29: These rooms contain views of Paris in the 18th century, and Rococo panels colourfully painted with garlands of flowers, cameos and mirrors from a mansion that once stood in Rue de Varenne.

Room 32: This is a reconstruction of a stairwell from the Hôtel de Luynes, decorated with *trompe-l'oeil* paintings of peopled balconies, by P.A. Brunetti (1748).

Rooms 30 and 31: These two rooms (on the ground floor at the foot of the Luynes staircase) contain a room from the Café Militaire (1762), in Rue St-Honoré, which was reserved for officers, a rare survival of the decorative work of Claude-Nicolas Ledoux (1736–1809; *see*

p. 318) and his first commission in Paris. Cafés came into fashion at the end of the 17th century, the first being Le Procope, in 1675, which still exists on Rue de l'Ancienne Comedie (*see p. 77*). Also by Ledoux is the magnificent gold and white panelling from the Salon de Compagnie (1767) of the Hotel d'Uzès, with golden trees garlanded with musical instruments.

Rooms 37–41: The early 18th century, during the Regency of Philippe d'Orleans, demonstrates the wealth of invention of Rococo decoration. After Louis XIV's death in 1715, during the eight years that the young Louis XV spent at the Tuileries, high society was evolving to include financiers and intellectuals. Women also had a greater influence in defining tastes. Paris eclipsed Versailles, and architects, cabinet-makers, ornamentists, sculptors and haberdashers were hugely in demand in the city. Representative paintings of the period include Boucher's *Le Pied de Mlle O'Murphy* (Room 39), a tiny study for the odalisque *Mlle O'Murphy*, and Chardin's *Game of Billiards* (Room 41).

Rooms 46–58: The varied themes of these rooms are religious, theatrical (with statuettes from the Comédie Italienne), and literary (with a portrait of Voltaire aged 24 and the chair in which he wrote); the Blue Room has a variety of chairs, a harp of c. 1780, and a table by Adam Weisweiller who was patronised by Marie-Antoinette; an oval boudoir; and the superb painted decoration of Room 58, from the house of the engraver Gilles Demarteau in the Rue de la Pelleterie, the work of Boucher and Fragonard c. 1765.

Le Peletier second floor

French Revolution Collections (Rooms 101–113) hold a central place in the museum and vividly retrace this turbulent period in Parisian history.

Rooms 101–106: Paintings and engravings which record key moments include *The Tennis Court Oath* (1789), in the Jeu de Paume at Versailles (*see p. 386*), by Jacques-Louis David, *The Storming of the Bastille* (1793) by Charles Thévenin, and *Demolition of the Bastille* (1789) by Hubert Robert, *The Declaration of the Rights of Man* by Thévenin (in Room 103), and the huge *Fête de la Fédération*, on the Champs de Mars on 14th July, 1790, when the oath to the republic นาแ ฅบเซาท *Capital Punishment* (1793–94) by Pierre-Antoine Demachy shows an execution during the Terror declared on the 5th September, 1793, by Robespierre on Place de la Révolution (now Pl. de la Concorde). A major element of the revolutionary history on display here is the multitude of curiosities which have survived: the chest that carried letters from the Bastille; the keys of the Bastille; a model of the Bastille cut from one of its stones under the direction of Palloy, the demolition contractor; and Danton's toiletries case. Royal references include Louis XVI's shaving dish, a portrait of *Young Louis XVII*, and a reconstruction (in Room 106) of the room in the Temple where the royal family were imprisoned from 10th August, 1792.

Rooms 107–109: These are dedicated to the Convention, the Terror and the Thermidor. Immortalised on canvas or in sculpture are the key players of the time, such as Count Mirabeau (1749–91) constitutional monarchist as was the great orator and *beau* Barnave (1761–93), whose likeness was sculpted by Houdon. There is also a bust of the Jacobin demagogue, Marat, stabbed to death in his bath by Charlotte Corday in 1793. Le Peletier de St-Fargeau (1760–93) was himself a revolutionary aristocrat who voted for the death of the Louis XVI and was assassinated by one of the king's guard while dining in a restaurant of the Palais Royal. There are also portraits (anon.) of Robespierre (1758–94), dominant member of the Jacobins and chief architect of the Reign of Terror, who had Danton and Camille Desmoulins, also pictured here, 'eliminated' in 1794, though he too went to the guillotine the same year. Dr Guillotin is remembered in a portrait and in a model of the guillotine (Room 108) which was adopted in 1789.

Rooms 110–113: Later rooms address lesser known aspects of the Revolution such as the European wars, Patriotic fervour, and the Generals, including

Bonaparte (1759–1821) at the start of his rise to power. *Desecration of the Royal Vaults* (1793) by Hubert Robert is a reminder of the vandalism of the time. Conversely these acts engendered an interest in the safeguarding of the national heritage, in which Alexandre Lenoir (1762–1839) played a major role (*see p. 71*). Popular imagery of the period is recorded in around 50 gouaches by Pierre-Etienne le Sueur, and a gruesomely direct image shows a man whose arm has just been amputated (it lies on the table) declaring his devotion to *la patrie* (with his other arm).

Le Peletier ground floor

Early 19th-century Paris (Rooms 115–122) from Napoleon to 1848, is covered here in rooms next to the Orangerie (*see above p. 288*) that contain paintings and furnishings from the Consulate and First Empire.

Rooms 115–116: The *Portrait of Napoleon* (1809) in the uniform of Colonel des Chasseurs de la Garde was commissioned from Robert Lefèvre by the City for the Hôtel de Ville. Also here are Napoleon's preferred *Nécessaire de Campagne*, with 110 pieces, and his death-mask. The fine portrait, *Mme Récamier Seated* (1805) by Gérard, depicts the famous beauty of post-Revolutionary Paris, Juliette Récamier (1777–1849), who was credited with the introduction of the 'Empire' style, sparked by a general interest in Antiquity following new archaeological discoveries in Italy. The Restoration Period under Charles V is evoked in Room 116 by furnishings from the Duchesse de la Gaëte's home in Rue du Fbg St-Honoré, and a painting by Corot *The Pont St-Michel and Quai des Orfèvres*.

Rooms 117–118: These rooms display painted views of Paris in the first half of the 19th century.

Rooms 119–120: These two rooms are dedicated to events surrounding the Revolution of July 1830 and the July Monarchy. The three days when the barricades went up following Charles X's suppression of the freedom of the press on 27th July, *Les Trois Glorieuses*, lost him the throne. A maquette depicts the *Arrival of the Duc d'Orléans at the Hôtel de Ville, 31 July, 1830* to accept the Lieutenant-Generalcy of France. On 8th August Charles X abdicated and Louis-Philippe was acclaimed *Roi des Français*, the only member of the House of Orléans to reign. Two paintings here commemorate the erection of the Obelisk of Luxor in Pl. de la Concorde (*see p. 211*). Louis-Philippe's overthrow came in February 1848, with more barricades, depicted in the *Burning of Louis-Philippe's throne on Pl. de la Bastille*.

Room 122–127: Between 1830 and 1848 was the height of the Romantic Movement in France, embracing figures such as the historian Michelet, Victor Hugo, Rousseau, Mme de Stael represented by portraits, including *Franz Liszt* (1811–86) by Henri Lehmann, and a series of sculpted caricatures in bronze or plaster made by Jean-Pierre Dantan of famous artists and musicians and also the Duke of Wellington. The last two rooms (on the first floor) display paintings of the city during the Romantic era, several by visiting Englishmen.

Le Peletier first floor

Late 19th-century Paris (Rooms 128–138) and **early 20th-century Paris** (Rooms 141–148) are covered on this floor, tracing the story of the city during the Second Empire (1852–70), through the Belle Epoque up to 1900, to the years preceding the First World War.

Rooms 128 and 129: In the first room is the Prince Imperial's grand ceremonial cradle (1856), a gift from the City of Paris to Emperor Napoléon III and Empress Eugénie on the birth of prince Eugène-Louis-Joseph (1856–74). The large painting *Napoléon III handing over to Haussmann the Decree of Annexation of the Suburban Communes (16 June, 1859)* refers to the urban development of Paris under Baron Haussmann's direction (*see p. 223*) and also, in January 1860, the establishment of 11 *communes* within the boundary of Paris, doubling the size of the city, divided from that time into 20 arrondissements. Part of the scheme is shown in *The Building of Av. de l'Opéra* by Giuseppe de Nittis (1846–84). The portrait of Prosper Mérimée (1803–70) by Simon Rochard depicts the author of the novella *Carmen* (1845) on which Bizet's opera was based and also first Inspector of Historic Monuments, a post created in 1830 to protect and conserve the national heritage. This was also the time of Universal Exhibitions in 1855 and 1857, for which many foreign dignitaries, including Queen Victoria, visited Paris.

Rooms 130 and 131: *Gambetta Leaving Paris by Balloon*, and small sketches made by Puvis de Chavannes *The Pigeon* and *The Balloon* (finished works at the Musée d'Orsay), refer to episodes during the Siege of Paris at the time of the Franco-Prussian war (1870–71). The *Commune of 1871* illustrated by G. Boulanger and the tiny work *Paris Burning* by Corot depict the collapse of the Second Empire and the extremely violent repercussions summed up in the *Execution of a Trumpeter* by Alfred Roll (1846–1919) when Versaillais troops indiscriminately executed all suspects, officially numbered at 17,000. The 19th century ends with paintings of events and personalities of the Third Republic.

Rooms 133–136: Paris seen by the painters of the period includes two versions of the Moulin de la Galette (*see p. 254*) in Montmartre, one by Paul Signac in 1884, at a time that witnessed the gradual urbanisation of the villages around Paris. The mill was demolished in 1925, but its neighbour still stands. Other glimpses of Paris include *Views of the Seine* by Guillaumin, Jongkind's *Rue St-Séverin at Night* (1877) in the Latin Quarter, and the *Cité et Port St-Michel* by Maximillien Luce (1858–1941). Among portraits of literary figures are Félix Nadar (1820–1910), aeronaut, photographer, designer and writer by P.L. Mita, *Edmond de Goncourt* by Carrière, *Daudet Writing*, and so on. Less literary was the legendary music-hall performer Yvette Guilbert (1867–1944), captured in a sculpture by Leonetto Cappiello (1875–1942). Famous for her expressive gestures and mimicry, and identified by long black gloves and butterfly bows, she was happy to be portrayed by the Italian, Cappiello and by poster-maker Jules Cheret (1836–1932), but she had a love-hate relationship with Toulouse-Lautrec who made studies of her which she considered 'caricatures'.

Rooms 141–148: Paris into the 20th century covered here shows the radical changes in taste. Art Nouveau, or the new style which did not imitate the past, took off in the 1890s mainly in architecture and the decorative arts. In the collections are two remarkable Art Nouveau interiors: one is the décor of 1899 by Henri Sauvage of a private room from the Café de Paris, a famous restaurant at 39 Av. de l'Opéra until demolished in 1954; the other example of this short-lived fashion is Georges

Fouquet's jewellery shop (1900) in Rue Royale, a unique and complex piece entirely created by Alphonse Mucha (1860–1939), best known for poster design. By 1923 Fouquet decided to remodel his boutique: the old one was dismantled and stored until 1941 when it was donated to the Carnavalet, restored, and finally reassembled here in 1989. Slightly later is the Art Deco decoration of the Hôtel de Wendel ball-room (1925) by the Catalan artist José Maria Sert. This is an extraordinary example of the decorative arts during the Roaring Twenties, its theme the *Procession of the Queen of Sheba*.

Three alcoves in the gallery dedicated to the intellectual and society life of Paris at the beginning of the 20th century (Room 147) contain furniture and mementoes from the homes of three writers, Marcel Proust, Anna de Noailles and Paul Léautaud, who had little in common except for the fact that they each worked in their bedrooms, and in the case of the first two, in bed. Paul Léautaud (1872–1956), life-long author of the *Journal Littéraire*, was something of a marginal, indifferent to fame, who lived in run-down conditions at Fontenay-aux-Roses in the company of around 300 cats and 100 dogs. Very different is the room of Anna de Noailles (1876–1933), from 40 Rue Scheffer, where she moved in 1909. This is a pleasant, feminine retreat where she reclined on cushions on her bed to receive visitors and to compose poetry. The bedroom of Marcel Proust (1870–1922) is recreated from the three places he occupied as a recluse. The cork tiles are a reminder of their use to line the walls and ceiling at 102 Blvd

Haussmann, where he lived from 1906. The room also contains his childhood bed, a Chinese screen, and a portrait of his father.

The great variety of paintings in this section range from elegant Belle Epoque works to late 20th-century Parisian subjects. They include *Young Woman holding a Book* by Alfred Stevens

(1828–1906); *The Young Jean Cocteau In the Garden at Offranville* (1913) by J.E. Blanche; a portrait of the couturier who liberated women from the corset, *Paul Poiret* (1927); and *Princesse Jean de Broglie* (1914), depicted in a dress by Poiret. There are also works by Paul Signac, Marquet, Foujita, and Marcel Gromaire.

MUSEE PICASSO
Map p. 476, B1

Open April–Sept Wed–Sun 9.30–6; Oct–March 9.30–5.30, closed Tues; T: 01 42 71 25 21; www.musee-picasso.fr. Free guided visits in French Mon and Fri at 2.30.

The Hôtel Salé is an elegant 17th-century mansion on Rue de Thorigny which acquired its name on account of the huge profits its owner made from salt tax. The largest house in the Marais, it is a prime example of a *hôtel particulier* between court and garden. It was thoroughly restored before receiving the collection of works by Pablo Picasso (1881–1973), acquired by the State in lieu of death duties. The combination is wonderful, making the museum a favourite visit with anyone who loves seeing modern art in a fine house. Selections from the large collection of drawings and prints are displayed in galleries arranged in approximate chronological order to show Picasso's development from 1894–1972.

The collection

The collection includes works from Picasso's Blue Period, just after his first visit to Paris, a haunting *Self-portrait* (1901) painted when he was 20; and *Celestina* (1904). Between *The Two Brothers* (summer 1906) from his Rose Period, and *Self-Portrait* (autumn 1906), after his discovery of Iberian art, there is a change of direction. The culmination of this was his seminal work of 1906–07, now in New York, *Les Demoiselles d'Avignon*, for which the Museum has some preparatory works. Representative of his Cubist era (1907–15) are the well-known *Still-life with Chair Caning* (1912), his first collage, made with rope and oil-cloth printed with a design of chair caning, and also a three-dimensional interpretation of Cubism, *Sculpted Female Head* of his companion Fernande Olivier. The synthesis of collage and sculpture produced the witty construction of 1915, *Violin*. In total contrast is the Ingresque portrait *Olga Khoklova seated* (1917), of the Russian dancer who became his wife in 1918.

Among works collected by Picasso which now belong to the museum are Degas' *La Fête de la Patronne*; Cézanne's *Still Life with Oranges* and *Château Noir*; and Henri Rousseau's *Self-Portrait with Lamp*, *The Artist's Wife*, and *The Sovereigns*. Picasso's *Bathers* (Biarritz; 1918) recalls summer by the sea, and from his Classical Period come

Jug and apples; Women Running along a Beach (1922); and *The Pipes of Pan* (1923). *Paul as a Harlequin* and *Paul as a Pierrot* show his small son in fancy dress. Although Picasso was never part of the Surrealist group its influence, and the impact of his personal problems at the time, emerge in the aggression of *The Kiss* (1925), *Large Nude in a Red Armchair* (1929), and *Composition au Gant* (1930) of found objects reminiscent of Dali's paintings, as well as *Figures by the Sea* (1931).

Works of the 1930s include the voluptuous *Nude in the Garden* (1934) and the Boisegeloup studio plaster *Head* (1931), one of a series of sculptures that were inspired by his lover, Marie-Thérèse Walter. The mystery and sacrifice of the bull fight and the Minotaur recur throughout Picasso's art. In early 1930, this imagery is introduced into a scene of the *Crucifixion*, as well as a drawing *The Murder*. Towards the end of the 1930s the new woman in the painter's life is captured in *Portrait of Dora Maar* (1937); and in 1938, he painted his small daugher, *Maya and her Doll*. His political anguish in the same year is reflected in *Cat with a Bird* (1938).

During the war, Picasso assembled and sculpted the cryptic *Bull's Head*, from bicycle parts, and large *Man with a Sheep* (1943). *Woman with a Pushchair* (1950) is a reference to the birth of his two children, Claude and Paloma in 1947 and 1949. In 1946 he visited Antibes accompanied by Françoise Gilot whom he captured in a luxuriant drawing. The south of France inspired *Skull, Sea Urchins and Lamp on a Table* (1946) and a passionate interest in decorating ceramics, represented by a terracotta Spanish dish decorated with a *Bull's Eye* (1957). Animals and birds always played an important role in his work, as in *Nanny-Goat* (1951). Later works include *Massacre in Korea* (1951); *Déjeuner sur L'Herbe* (1960), a burlesque tribute to Manet (*see p. 85*); *Woman with Open Arms* (1961); and *The Young Artist* (1972).

MUSEE COGNACQ-JAY
Map p. 476, B2

Open 10–5.40; closed Mon and holidays; T: 01 40 27 07 21.
Since 1990 Musée Cognacq-Jay has been at 8 Rue Elzévir, in the intimate Hôtel de Donon, built c. 1575 but altered in the mid-17th century. The collection of 18th-century objects put together from 1900–25 by Ernest Cognacq (1835–1928), founder of the Magasins de la Samaritaine, and by his wife Marie-Louise Jay, was bequeathed to the Ville de Paris on his death. A profusion of objects is displayed in 20 small rooms on four floors and in the impressively beamed attic. Many rooms contain beautiful panelling with *rocaille* decoration, some removed from the Château d'Eu (Normandy), and some original to the house. A charming evocation of a luxurious 18th-century interior, the museum also reflects the tastes of a 20th-century collector.

The collection
Some of the best-known artists of the time are represented here, including Jean Siméon Chardin, the 18th-century master of the still life. His *Still Life with a Copper Cauldron,* a small painting on wood of simple kitchen utensils, is a simple yet deeply

Boucher: *Diana's Return from the Hunt* (c. 1745) in the Musée Cognacq-Jay.

satisfying work. Typically hedonistic Rococo paintings include Watteau's *Gilles à l'Orée du Bois* and Fragonard's *Perrette et le Pot au Lait*, which illustrates one of the Fontaine's *Fables*. And full of painterly virtuosity are François Boucher's *Mme Baudouin*, his daughter, and *Diana's Return from the Hunt* (c. 1745). Rare for a Parisian collection is the large collection of English works, including Thomas Lawrence's *Princess Clémentine de Metternich* and Wright of Derby's *Young Bird-Catchers*.

The portraitist Jean-Baptiste Lemoyne (1704–78), protected by Louis XV, was responsible for the remarkably lifelike yet unflattering terracotta portrait bust of the Count de Lowendal (1700–55), who became Maréchal de France in 1749. Among portraits by Maurice Quentin Delatour are a pastel of Mme la Présidente de Rieux (1742), dressed in a grey silk ballgown with blue taffeta frills and holding a mask, which is a masterpiece of light and textures. There is also an early work by Rembrandt. Among delicate pieces of furniture are a bureau in ebony by Boulle inlaid with a variety of materials, and a charming oval oak writing table on two levels (c. 1770) by La Croix (1727–99) which contains a sliding writing desk with compartments for ink and pens. Jean-François Oeben (1721–63), was probably responsible for the *Mechanical Table* (c. 1760) with a secret drawer and a pair of commodes by Martin Carlin (c. 1730–85) illustrates the transition between Louis XV and Louis XVI styles: the curved legs and the marquetry floral medallions are still Louis XV, but the overall shape and decorative elements such as the urn and acanthus leaves, medallion surmounted by a bow, are typical of the aesthetic of Louis XVI. The collection of ceramics and porcelain includes a pair of Kien-Lung cranes in white porcelain, which symbolise longevity, standing on a pine tree, symbol of happiness, two favourite images in Chinese art.

MUSEE DE L'HISTOIRE DE FRANCE
Map p. 476, A1

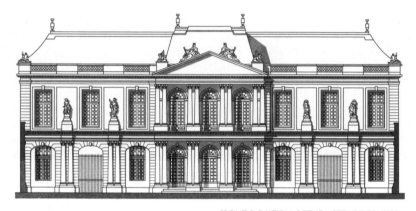

FRONT ELEVATION OF THE HOTEL DE SOUBISE

Open Mon, Wed–Fri 10–12.30 & 2–5.30; Sat and Sun 2–5.30; closed Tues and holidays; T: 01 40 27 60 96.

The Hôtel de Soubise, which can be visited at no. 60 Rue des Francs-Bourgeois, is the home of the Museum of the History of France, part of the National Archives of France that occupies the adjacent Hôtel de Rohan and other buildings. Frequent temporary exhibitions are held here.

History of the Hôtel de Soubise

The first mansion here was the Hôtel de Clisson, built in the 14th century by Constable Olivier de Clisson, supporter of Charles V against the English. The turret-ed Gothic gateway of 1380 (58 Rue des Archives), is a remnant of this building and a rare example of 14th-century architecture in Paris. Bolingbroke (later Henry IV) gave a farewell banquet here in 1399 before setting out for England. Purchased in 1553 by François de Lorraine, Duc de Guise and his wife Anna d'Este, as the Hôtel de Guise, it is possible that this was where the St Bartholomew's Day Massacre (1572) was planned. In 1700 the mansion was sold to François de Rohan-Soubise and Anne de Rohan-Chabot and became known as the Hôtel de Soubise. Between 1705 and

1712 the architect Delamair transformed the building and re-orientated it, making the main entrance on Rue des Francs-Bourgeois. The Hôtel de Rohan was begun in 1705 by Delamair and successively inhabited by four cardinals of the Rohan family, all bishops of Strasbourg. The National Archives, covering the 7th century to 1958, have used these buildings since 1808, and have five specialised centres on this site.

Visiting the museum

Inside the semi-circular entrance of the Hôtel de Soubise is an inspired colonnaded Cour d'Honneur with copies of *The Four Seasons* by Robert le Lorrain on the façade. Although the interior has been drastically altered in places, there are remnants of the original sumptuous stuccos, by Adam and Lemoyne, and a remarkable number of integral paintings by François Boucher, as well as Carle Van Loo and others. The Prince's Apartments consist of the Bedchamber, the Salon Oval and the Grand Cabinet, with remnants of the original décor and furniture of the period introduced from the national collections. A 19th-century staircase leads to the Princess's Apartments where the Antichambre, large and empty, was the Guard Room at the time of the Guise, but the Ceremonial Bedroom is a glorious and busy room decorated by Boffrand in 1735–36, with gilded stuccos and Boucher paintings, and a reproduction of the princess's bed. The oval Princess's Salon is one of the best Parisian Rococo interiors, by Boffrand and Natoire, in white and gold with large windows and mirrors. The chapel bears traces of the Chapelle de Clisson of 1375, transformed in 1533. There follow the small rooms of the Princess's Private Suite decorated with paintings, and the portrait of Anne de Rohan Chabot, Princesse de Soubise, who was favourite, for a time, of Louis XIV.

SMALLER MUSEUMS IN THE MARAIS

At no. 11 Rue Payenne, the Hôtel de Marle houses the Swedish Cultural Centre, the only one of its kind in the world, administered by the Swedish Institute in Stockholm. It contains the **Musée Tessin** (*open Tues–Fri 10–1 & 2–5; closed Sun–Mon except during temporary exhibitions; T: 01 44 78 80 20*), with paintings by the Swedish portrait painter Alexander Roslin (1718–93), much influenced by Nicolas de Largillièrre.

The Hôtel Libéral-Bruant, at no. 1 Pl. de Thorigny (off Rue de la Perle), is named after one of the architects of Les Invalides and was built in 1685 for his personal use. It has a perfectly harmonious pedimented elevation, decorated with four busts in niches. It houses the **Musée de la Serrure** (*open Mon–Fri 10–12 & 2–5; closed Sat and Sun, T: 01 42 77 79 62*), a splendid collection of decorative door-furniture, including locks, keys, handles and plaques of all periods, put together in the 19th century by Eugène Bricard, whose family firm is still a name among locksmiths.

The magnificent Hôtel de Guénégaud, designed by François Mansart (c. 1650), at 60 Rue des Archives, can be entered for a visit to the **Musée de la Chasse et de la Nature** (*open 11–6; closed Tues and holidays; T: 01 53 01 92 40*). The museum contains hunting weapons from France and elsewhere, decorative arts, furniture and paintings including Philip I of Spain in falconer's costume, and *La Chasse de Diane* by 'Velvet'

Christ in the Garden of Olives (1827) by Eugène Delacroix, in the church of St-Paul-St-Louis.

Brueghel, as well as by François Desportes (1661–1743), Chardin, Corot and others. No. 78 Rue des Archives was built c. 1660.

On the south side of Rue des Francs-Bourgeois, no. 31 is the Hôtel d'Albret, built c. 1640 by François Mansart, with an 18th-century street façade. At the end of the courtyard of no. 33 is a fragment of Philippe-Auguste's walls.

On the corner of Rue Pavée, no. 24 is the fine **Hôtel Lamoignon**, named after a 17th-century occupant, which was built in 1584 for Diane de France, legitimised daughter of Henri II. Possibly the work of J.-B. Androuet du Cerceau, it has colossal Corinthian pilasters and curved pediments. It now houses the **Bibliothèque Historique de la Ville de Paris**, containing over 400,000 volumes and 100,000 manuscripts relating to the history of the city, and to the Revolution. Rue Pavée, with an Art Nouveau synagogue designed by Hector Guimard, brings you to Rue des Rosiers, the old Jewish quarter (parallel with Rue des Francs-Bourgeois), atmospheric with interesting restaurants.

Notre-Dame des Blancs-Manteaux is on the street of the same name, and refers to the white habits of an order of mendicant monks established here in 1285 by Louis IX. Rebuilt in the late 17th century, the 18th-century door came from St-Barthélemy in the Ile de la Cité, demolished in 1863, and inside the church is a Flemish-style Rococo pulpit (1749).

SAINT-PAUL-SAINT-LOUIS
Map p. 476, B2

On Rue St-Antoine is the Church of St-Paul-St-Louis, or the Grands-Jésuites, built for that Society by Louis XIII in 1627–41, replacing a chapel of 1582. The Jesuits were suppressed in 1762, and St-Paul was added to the original name in 1796 to commemorate the demolished St-Paul-des-Champs.

HISTORY OF ST-PAUL-ST-LOUIS

Building work, including the handsome Baroque portal, was supervised by Martellange until 1629, and François Derrand saw it through to its completion in 1641, while Turmel was responsible for the interior decorations. Its florid style, inspired by 16th-century Italian churches, is a good example of French Jesuit architecture. The clock on the façade came from the church of St-Paul. The church was restored by Baltard in the 19th century and the statues on the façade are 19th-century (by Lequesne, Etex and Préault). Richelieu said the first mass here.

The interior

The ornate interior is imposing but light, retaining the original clear glass with floral friezes. The 55m high dome over the crossing, was the third to be built in Paris (after the Petits Augustins (now the Ecole des Beaux-Art; *see p. 70*) and the Carmelite Chapel on Rue de Vaugirard. In the pendentives are medallions of the four Evangelists and, in the drum, 19th-century *trompe l'oeil* paintings of saintly kings, Clovis, Charlemagne, Robert le Pieux and St-Louis. Most furnishings have been dispersed, some to the Louvre, and the tomb of Henri II to Chantilly. The suspended silver angels carrying the embalmed hearts of Louis XIII and XIV have, of course, long gone, but the church still contains some fine works: in the north transept is the beautiful painting *Christ in the Garden of Olives* by Delacroix, and opposite is *St Louis Receiving the Crown of Thorns*, by the school of Vouet (1639); in the south is *Louis XIII offering a Model of the Church to St Louis* by Vouet. There is also good woodcarving and 17th-century ironwork. Buried here are Bishop Huet of Avranches (d. 1721), and Louis Bourdaloue, confessor to Louis XIV.

Environs of St-Paul-St-Louis

East along Rue St-Antoine, on the corner with Rue Castex, is the circular Temple de Ste-Marie, originally the chapel of the Convent of the Visitation, and now a Protestant church. It was built by François Mansart in 1632–34. The unscrupulous Surintendant des Finances, Nicolas Fouquet (1615–80) and Henri de Sévigné (Mme de Sévigné's husband, killed in a duel in 1651) were buried here. Vincent de Paul was almoner of the convent for 28 years. A few paces to the west, at no. 21, is the Hôtel de Mayenne (or d'Ormesson), with a turret and charming staircase. Now the Ecole des Francs-

Bourgeois, it was built by Jean or Jacques II du Cerceau in 1613–17, and modified by Boffrand in 1709. To the east, a tablet on 5 Rue St-Antoine marks the position of the court of the Bastille, by which the Revolutionary mob gained access to the fortress. Near the junction of this street and the Pl. de la Bastille (*see p. 308*) was the site of the great barricade of 1848, and also the last stronghold of the *Communards* in 1871.

SAINT-GERVAIS-SAINT-PROTAIS
Map p. 476, A2

Dominating the eastern side of Pl. St-Gervais, near the Hôtel de Ville, is St-Gervais-St-Protais. The cult of Gervase and Protase was popular in the early Middle Ages and this was one of the oldest parishes on the Right Bank, going back to the 6th century. It is supposed that the sanctuary was rebuilt in the 13th century. Despite the Classical façade, the body of the present church is a late Gothic structure begun in the late 15th century.

History of St-Gervais-St-Protais

The original plans are attributed to Martin Chambiges, whose work was continued by his son Pierre. The lower stages of the tower are an early 15th-century survival. The façade (1616–21), by Clément II Métezeau, is posited as an early example in Paris of the received sequence of the three Classical orders: Doric, Ionic and Corinthian (*see p. 71*). The choir and transepts date from rebuildings of 1494–1578 and the nave was continued in Flamboyant Gothic c. 1600–20, with lierne and tierceron vaults, despite the strength of Italian Renaissance influence at this time. The painter Philippe de Champaigne (1602–74), the writer Paul Scarron (1610–60) and the dramatist Crébillon the Elder (1674–1762) are all buried here. François Couperin (1668–1733) and seven members of his family served as organists from 1653 to 1830. The organ (16th–17th century), known as the Couperin organ, survives, the case rebuilt in the 18th century.

The interior

The interior, impressively lofty and stylistically unified, has several works of art. The high windows of both nave and choir contain painted glass of c. 1610–20 by Robert Pinaigrier and Nicolas Chaumet. In the south aisle, the third chapel has an altar commemorating some 50 victims of the bombardment on Good Friday, 1918, when a German 'Big Bertha' shell struck the church. In the fourth are seven low 17th-century painted panels of the *Life of Christ*. Painted glass of 1531 by Pinaigrier, restored in the 19th century represents, in the fifth chapel, the *Martyrdom of St Gervais and St Protais*, and in the sixth the *Judgement of Solomon*. The eighth chapel contains the tomb of Chancellor Michel le Tellier (d. 1685), supported by bearded heads from the tomb of Jacques de Souvré (d. 1670), by François Anguier, the rest of which are in the Louvre. The Lady Chapel, a heady example of Flamboyant Gothic (1517) with complicated vaults and a bravura pendant boss, also retains fine original glass (restored in the 19th century) of the *Life of the Virgin*.

In the north aisle is a plaque commemorating the consecration of an earlier church, 1420. All that remains are the first two levels of the belfry above the sacristy, which retains a good iron grille of 1741. The next chapel is the Chapelle Dorée (1628) with its original decoration; in the adjacent chapel are a 13th-century high relief of the *Dormition of the Virgin* (below the altar), and a portrait by Pajou (1782) of Mme Palerme de Savy. In the choir, the first seven stalls in the upper row were remade in the 17th century; the rest are mid-16th century with interesting misericords. The 18th-century bronze-gilt candelabra and cross were designed by Soufflot. Against the north entry-pillar is a 14th-century *Virgin*, known as *Notre-Dame de Bonne-Délivrance*; and on either side of the altar, wooden statues of the patron saints, by Michel Bourdin (1625).

WALK FOUR

SOUTHERN MARAIS

The southern section of the Marais, a wedge-shaped zone cut off from the rest of the quarter when Rue de Rivoli was built in the mid-19th century, is bounded by the Seine and the Bastille. It has developed a rarefied character and discreet charm in its quiet streets with a number of fine old buildings, restaurants and specialist boutiques.

Place St-Gervais, in front of the church of St-Gervais and St-Protais (*see above*), is planted with a single elm, a reminder of the elm of St-Gervais, beneath which justice used to be administered, and from which comes the proverbial expression for waiting for Doomsday. *attendre sous l'orme.*

Rue François-Miron is part of the Roman road leading east from *Lutetia* to Melun which was paved above the marshes. Much later it was named after François Miron, Prévôt des Marchands from 1604–06, who carried out many improvements in the area, including the enhancement of the quays. The imposing stepped terrace on the south side of the street was built c. 1735; the wrought iron first-floor balconies carry an elm tree motif. The Couperin family, organists and composers for the church, lived in this terrace; François Couperin (1668–1733), prodigiously talented, was born on the site of no. 2.

Behind the gate at no. 15 **Rue de Barres**, a pretty street which descends towards the Seine, are the remains of the charnel house. On the left is a boutique selling objects produced in religious houses and at the end is a small garden with a Baroque pediment and sundial, and impressive view of the south flank of the church.

Among the well-preserved houses with stone façades and sagging timbers in **Rue de l'Hôtel de Ville** is the head office of the Compagnons du Devoir de la Tour de France (no. 82), which provides support

and training in many practical trades. At
the southern end of Rue du Pont Louis-
Philippe is a restaurant Chez Julien (*T: 01
42 78 37 64*), and an old dairy at no. 6
with prettily painted décor inside and
out; also specialist shops for paper and
calligraphy, artefacts, photography, framing and musical instruments.

Back on **Rue François-Miron**, two
medieval houses (at nos. 11 and 13),
were known to exist in the early 1500s;
the façade of no. 13 is leaning perilously
into the ancient Rue Cloche Perché.
Overhanging jetties were forbidden from
1508, and in 1607 wooden beams had
to be rendered with plaster to reduce fire
risk, but during restoration in 1967 the
old plaster was removed and the wooden
beams replaced. All along the street are
interesting details such as *mascarons*
(masks), wrought iron balconies and
shop signs. **La Maison d'Ourscamps**
(1585), at nos. 44–46, is an outstanding
structure built around a timbered and
jettied courtyard and over a vaulted
13th-century cellar (*open daily 11–6.30;*

T: 01 48 87 74 31). It was formerly the
townhouse of the Cistercian Abbey of
Ourscamps (near Noyon), and it is now
occupied by the l'Association de Paris
Historique, who organise guided walks.

In Rue Geoffroy-l'Asnier (to the right)
the Hôtel de Chalons-Luxembourg
(1608) at no. 26, has a magnificent
doorway (1659). The **Shoah Memorial**
(*at no. 17, open Sun–Fri 10–6; Thur
10–10; closed Sat; T: 01 42 77 44 72,
www.memorialdelashoah.org*) is a solemn
and moving location inaugurated in
1956, which combines the Memorial to
an Unknown Jewish Martyr, the
archives, photo library and library of
the Centre de Documentation Juive
Contemporaine (CDJC), and a museum.
The names of 76,000 Jews deported
from France are engraved on the Wall
of Names in the forecourt, and the Wall
of the Righteous carries the names of
those who, at great personal risk,
helped Jews to find safety.

Return to **Rue François-Miron** where
there is a prettily decorated bakers' shop

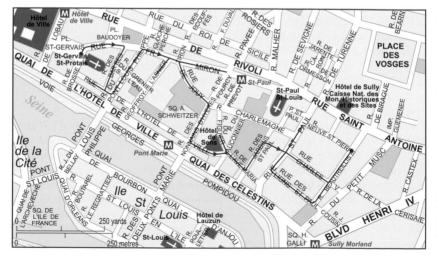

with a painted ceiling, and at no. 60 the Comptoir du Saumon & Cie (*open Mon–Sat 9–11.30, Sun 10–7; T: 01 42 77 23 08*) which specialises in all things salmon as well as caviar, champagne and vodka, to eat-in or take-away. The star of the street though is the **Hôtel de Beauvais** (no. 68). For many years drab and neglected, a huge restoration project in 2002–03 brought this superb Baroque building back to life. Now occupied by the Cour Administrative d'Appel de Paris, the courtyard can usually be visited. The building (1654–57), a tour de force by Antoine Lepautre (1621–81), was built on land purchased from the Cistercian Abbey of Châalis by Pierre de Beauvais and his wife, Catherine Bellier, first lady of the bedchamber to Anne of Austria. Lepautre's design was an ingenious solution for dealing with what were in fact two adjacent plots with no parallel lines between Rue François Miron and Rue de Jouy. The François-Miron wing is two rooms deep, with shops over the medieval cellars, pierced by a long *porte cochère* leading to a circular peristyle. The lobby on the left contains a grand stone staircase supported by four Corinthian columns and the main courtyard façades are a clever play of curves and counter-curves ending in an apse-like form. Cleverly disguised, the left is simply a curtain wall while on the right is a structure with depth, incorporating a corridor, stables and the Rue de Jouy entrance. Around the courtyard the *étage noble*, outlined by a beautiful balcony, was the level of the main living quarters, including a hanging garden, terrace and chapel. It was from this building in August 1660 that Cardinal Mazarin, Maréchal Turenne (1611–75), the Queen

Mother Anne of Austria, and Queen Henrietta Maria of England, watched the arrival in Paris of Louis XIV and Marie Thérèse of Austria on the occasion of their marriage. By 1686 Catherine Bellier had tired of her mansion and moved to the increasingly fashionable St-Germain. Mozart, with his father and sister, stayed here for five months in 1763 when Maximilien d'Eyck, Ambassador of Bavaria, was renting the *hôtel*. It was sold at the Revolution.

The early 18th-century **Hôtel Hénault de Cantobre** at 82 Rue François Miron, with a handsome wrought iron balcony supported by carved corbels, is home to the Maison Européenne de la Photographie (*entrance on Rue de Fourcy. Open Wed–Sun, 11–7.30; closed Mon, Tues and holidays; T: 01 44 78 75 00; www.mep-fr.org*), a centre for contemporary photography which holds regular exhibitions. The zen courtyard is designed to illustrate the significance of light to the medium.

The refined decoration and heavy door surround adorned with a grinning head at no. 7 Rue de Jouy announce the **Hôtel d'Aumont** (1648), a grand affair designed by Le Vau (*see p. 36*). It was altered by François Mansart in 1656, with the addition of the garden façade visible from Rue de Fourcy. The courtyard is usually open on weekdays.

On Rue Nonnains d'Hyères a sunken garden with parterres creates a romantic foreground to the turrets, ogees, dormer windows and steep roofs of the **Hôtel de Sens** (1475–1519, entrance at 1 Rue du Figuier). This was designed as the Paris base for the archbishops of Sens when the bishopric of Paris was suffragan to the metropolitan See of

13th June, 1794, the Commune of Paris requisitioned the garden and dug two ditches to receive the bodies of those executed on Pl. du Trône-Renversé (La Nation). Closed in 1795, the cemetery was secretly sold in 1797 to Princess Amélie de Salm de Hohenzollern-Sigmaringen whose brother was buried there. In 1803 the families of the deceased were able to purchase the old convent land with the right to be buried in an adjoining cemetery. A very simple chapel was built by the Congrégation des Sacrés-Coeurs et de l'Adoration. In it is a painting of the 16 Carmelites of Compiègne who were beheaded on 17th July, 1794, and beatified on 27th May, 1906. On the chapel walls the names of those buried here are engraved on marble plaques.

PROMENADE PLANTEE
Map p. 476, C3–p. 477, D4

Avenue Daumesnil is the site of two imaginative installations making use of the old elevated railway line. The 60 arches of the Viaduc des Arts are home to arty boutiques where around 50 different craftsmen and artists create traditional and contemporary objects, as varied as musical instruments, textiles, furniture and sculpture. Above the viaduct is a walkway called the Promenade Plantée, a series of planted areas and gardens leading from near Rue Ledru-Rollin to Vincennes (Rue Edouard-Lartet), created out of the old railway track, giving views of a little-known district of Paris including the unnerving repetition of a replica of Michelangelo's *Dying Slave* (*see p. 191*) on the police station façade. There are a number of access points and along the way it widens into four gardens, Hector-Malot, de Reuilly, de la Gare de Reuilly, and Charles-Péguy.

GARE DE LYON
Map p. 476, C4

The Gare de Lyon serves the southeast and south of France, and also Italy. It is recognisable by its tall belfry, and preserves a *fin-de-siècle* buffet called Le Train Bleu on the upper floor behind the Beaux-Arts façade. Opposite the station once stood the Mazas Prison, where 400 Communards were rounded up and massacred by Thiers' troops in 1871. In this redeveloped business area, the two sides of the Seine are linked by the Pont Charles-de-Gaulle (1995), and Pont d'Austerlitz (originally 1802–07), rebuilt in stone in 1855 and widened in 1886.

BERCY
Map p. 477, D4

Bercy was extensively redeveloped in the 1980s and is now a place where Parisians come to relax. It began with the hexagonal Palais Omnisports, which opened in 1984, a turf-clad stunted pyramid topped by a tubular platform supported by four cylindrical towers, which holds 17,000 spectators. The Ministère de Finances followed in 1989, when it vacated the Louvre (*see p. 140*), to occupy a specially designed building next to the Seine on Blvd de Bercy. The existing Pont de Bercy (1864) was widened at the time. Alongside the stadium, the Parc de Bercy, completed in 1997, covers 14 hectares parallel with the Seine where bonded wine warehouses once stood, opposite the Bibliothèque Nationale Mitterrand (*see p. 66*).

MUSEE DU CINEMA & CINEMATHEQUE FRANCAISE

Open Wed, Fri–Mon 12–7; Thurs 12–10; Sun 10–8; closed Tues. Film Library open Mon–Fri 10–7; closed Sat and Sun. Debates, lectures daily except Tues. Screenings daily; T: 01 71 19 33 33; www.cinematheque.fr

The former American Centre building (1994; Frank Gehry) in Parc de Bercy, at 51 Rue de Bercy, was adapted to become the new Cinémathèque Française and Musée du Cinéma in 2005. The aim of the Cinémathèque is to conserve and protect film and it continues to receive donations. At present it holds around 40,000 films, 4,000 pieces of equipment, 1,500 objects and 1,000 costumes. The first collector of film was the Englishman, Will Day (1873–1936), after whose death Henri Langlois (1914–77), with Lotte H. Eisner, continued the project. Langlois founded the Cinémathèque Française, which acquired Day's collection in 1959, and it has become the best of its kind in the world. Film Archives were created in 1969 by the engineer-technician and historian, Jean Vivié (1904–72), and the collecting and preservation of films continues. The Musée du Cinéma's permanent exhibits range from the *Head of the Dead Mrs. Bates* from Hitchcock's *Psycho* and the robot from Fritz Lang's *Metropolis*, to costumes among which is one worn by Vivienne Leigh in *Gone with the Wind*, as well as early cinematic equipment, sets and props.

PARC DE BERCY

Parc de Bercy occupies the site of the old bonded wine warehouses which in the 19th century were the largest of their kind anywhere. Trading in wine and spirits, they finally closed in the 1950s. Some of the old buildings have been preserved. The garden continues both sides of Rue Joseph-Kessel. Relics of the wine trade are the paved alleys with old rail tracks, and some old buildings. Next to the Palais Omnisports is a novel fountain, called *Canyoneaustrate* by Gérard Singer. Opposite the Cinémathèque is the *grande prairie*, an open grassy area. Then follows an area of intimate themed spaces with hedges, including a kitchen garden, a rose garden, and a token vineyard, as well as the **Maison du Jardin** (*T: 40 53 46 19 19*) which holds exhibitions for garden lovers. Then there is a small maze, a sunken garden and wisteria covered pergolas lining a canal. Protecting the garden from the embankment is a high terrace and steps leading up to a view of the Seine. The city's latest bridge, the light and transparent single span Simone de Beauvoir footbridge (304m) by Dietmar Feichtinger, opened here on 6th July, 2006. At the same time a new floating swimming pool, named after the singer Josephine Baker, using recycled water from the Seine, was inaugurated.

The hump-backed bridge over Rue Joseph-Kessel leads to the Romantic garden, with a variety of trees, a lake, and pleasant lawns. Here the **Maison du Lac** (*T: 01 40 71 75 60*) holds exhibitions with a gardening theme and also runs tours. Many mature trees are integrated into the landscape. The Chai de Bercy, the old bottling workshops, is another exhibition centre.

Beyond Rue François-Truffaut is the very popular Bercy Village (*shops open daily 11–9, restaurants until 2 am*), an attractive centre which has transformed 19th-century wine cellars into a large variety of boutiques and restaurants.

The **Musée des Arts Forains** (*see p. 419*) at no. 53 Av. des Terroirs de France, is a fairground museum in old mill warehouses, with traditional rides and stalls including a miniature racecourse and Japanese billiards.

VINCENNES
Map p. 3, F4

The Cours de Vincennes was once the scene in Easter Week of the *Foire aux Pains d'Épice*, a festival dating back to the 10th century, when bread made with honey and aniseed was distributed by the monks of the Abbey of St-Antoine. It leads directly east from Pl. de la Nation to Porte de Vincennes at the eastern extremity of Paris and is important for the Château de Vincennes, one of the glories of the French monarchy in the 14th and 15th centuries, and the Bois de Vincennes with the Parc Floral. Approximately 2km east of the Porte de Vincennes, it is easily reached by Metro, or RER.

CHATEAU DE VINCENNES

Open May–Aug 10–12 & 1.15–6; Sept–April 10–12 & 1.15–5; T: 01 48 08 31 20. Guided visits only to the ramparts, moat and Sainte-Chapelle (in French).
The impressive bulk of the former royal residence, the Château de Vincennes, a less familiar landmark for many visitors, played a very important role in French history.

History of the Château de Vincennes
A royal property since 1178 under Louis VII (1137–80), it became Louis IX's (1226–70) second residence after Paris and remained a royal stronghold until the 14th century. The keep or *donjon*, begun by Philippe VI, the first of the Valois, in 1337 at the beginning of the Hundred Years War, was completed by his grandson Charles V (1364–73) around 1370, who built the ramparts in about seven years and started work on the Chapel in 1379, replacing the one built by Louis IX. This great fortress was then the political capital of the kingdom, and the illustration *December* in the *Très Riches Heures du Duc de Berry* and Fouquet's panel for the *Hours of Etienne Chevalier* (both in the Musée Condé

December from the Très Riches Heures du Duc de Berry *(c. 1412–16), depicting in the background the towers of the Château de Vincennes in its 15th-century heyday.*

at the Château de Chantilly in Picardy, north of Paris) give an idea of its splendour and importance in the 15th century. By the 16th century this huge rectangular construction comprised nine square towers linked by fortified walls surrounded by a moat. Enclosed within were a keep, chapel and buildings of different periods.

The foundations of the Pavillon du Roi and the Pavillon de la Reine (the Queen Mother, Anne of Austria), to the southeast, were laid in the 16th century and completed nearly a century later when the château, then in Cardinal Mazarin's possession, was altered and decorated by Le Vau. It was used as a refuge for the court during the Wars of Religion and by Mazarin to protect his collection during the Fronde (*see p. 14*). Deserted by the court in favour of the palace at Versailles (c. 1680), Vincennes was gradually stripped of its furnishings and glory, to become first a porcelain manufactory, in 1745, until that transferred to Sèvres in 1756, then a cadet school, and finally, a year later, a small-arms factory. By 1788 it was put up for sale but found no purchaser. It was rescued by La Fayette from the destructive fervour of the Revolutionary mob in 1791. When, in 1808, Napoleon converted it into an arsenal, the surviving 13th-century buildings were demolished. Later in the 19th century, all the towers, except the Tour du Village (now the entrance), which lost only its statues, were reduced to the level of the walls. By 1840 it was being used as a fortress again, to the detriment of much of Le Vau's decoration. Degradation continued during the Second World War when German occupying forces installed a supply depot here, and the Pavillon de la Reine was partially destroyed by an explosion in 1944 when they evacuated.

There are many historical associations, some sombre, with Vincennes: Louis X died in the castle in 1316; Charles IV in 1328; and Charles V was born here in 1337. Both Charles IX (in 1574) and Cardinal Mazarin (in 1661) died here as well as Henry V of England in 1422, seven weeks before the death of Charles VI whom he should have succeeded as king of France. During the reign of Louis XIII, the keep was used as a state prison. The Duc d'Enghien (1772–1804) related to the Bourbon monarchs of France, was arrested on trumped-up charges on Napoleon's orders, was tried by court-martial and shot the same night in the château. Général Daumesnil, governor at different periods between 1809 and his death in 1832, famously retorted, when summoned to surrender to the Allies in 1814: 'First give me back my leg' (lost at the Battle of Wagram). It is not generally known that Mata Hari was shot here in 1917. The French historian Jules Michelet (1798–1874) described it as 'the Windsor of the Valois'. Part of the fortress is now occupied by the armed forces.

Visiting the château

The 48m-high Tour du Village stands over the entrance. The campanile on the tower was rebuilt in 2000 and reproduces the 14th-century clock installed by Charles V in the keep, an innovatory and costly undertaking at that time. The bell of 1369, which is struck from outside, still survives, and would originally have been used for liturgical purposes although, being semi-public, it also came to signify the hours of the working day. The visitor's route then passes between a range of buildings in military occupation.

The huge *donjon* or keep, a 52m tall square tower flanked with round turrets, rises above its free-standing turreted *enceinte*. The finest of its type still standing in France, the *donjon* is a sophisticated construction consisting of a series of superimposed vaulted chambers using iron girders to stabilise the upper floors. Charles V's quarters were on the second floor and a plaque records the death of Henry V of England here. His body was taken to Westminster for burial.

The areas dating from the time of Charles V (guided visit) include the ramparts and the Sainte Chapelle, founded in the 14th century and completed in 1552. This, like other chapels with the same dedication, was modelled on the royal chapel on the Ile de la Cité, but here there is no lower level. The Flamboyant façade has a magnificent rose-window surmounted by an ornamental gable filled with tracery. The bare interior contains graceful vaulting, tracery and sculptures and, at the east end, seven stained-glass windows by Beaurain (16th century) restored after an explosion in 1870. In the oratory is a monument to the Duc d'Enghien of 1816 by Deseine.

To the south, through a portico, the immense Cour d'Honneur opens out and, beyond, the monumental main entrance at the time of Mazarin, the Tour du Bois. On the right is the Pavillon du Roi (now containing military archives), and opposite, the Pavillon de la Reine where Mazarin died in 1661. Both were completed by Le Vau in 1654–60. The Pavillon de la Reine, where two rooms with their painted decor have survived, contains the Navy Insignia Museum (*open Wed 2–5*).

BOIS DE VINCENNES

The Bois de Vincennes which at 995 hectares is slightly larger than the Bois de Boulogne, has many attractions, both botanical and sporting. The forest was first enclosed in the 12th century and replanted in 1731 by Louis XV who converted it into a park for the citizens of Paris. In the 19th century there were many transformations and embellishments including three lakes. After further land was ceded to the Bois in 1860, more lakes and avenues were created. The **Parc Floral** (*open 9.30–7 or dusk if earlier*), a botanic garden with a collection of over 3,000 plants, was created in 1969 to the southeast of the château. The naturally flat terrain was given a contoured relief and two irregular-shaped lakes provide a focus. Within the 35 hectares are thematic gardens, rhododendrons and water plants plus a wealth of modern sculptures. The Lac des Minimes is a tropical garden with an Indo-Chinese pagoda. The **Parc Zoologique de Vincennes** (*open April–Oct 9–6.30; Nov–Dec 9–5; T: 01 44 75 20 10; Metro: Porte-Doree*) at 53 Av. de St-Maurice is the main zoo of Paris, close to the Lac Daumesnil with a Buddhist temple. To the south of the park, near the most popular trotting racecourse in Paris, is the **Ferme de Paris** (*open Tues–Sun; Summer 1.30–7; winter 1.30–5; closed Mon; T: 01 43 28 47 63*) covering 5 hectares and created from a genuine old farm that is still a working environment. Also something of a hidden gem, the **Musée de l'Histoire Vivante** (*open Wed–Fri 2–5, Sat and Sun 2–6; T: 01 48 70 61 62*), at 31 Blvd Théophile Sueur, Montreuil, holds temporary exhibitions largely devoted to the Socialist ethic and the history of Revolutions in France, the Paris *Commune* and so forth, up to 1960, in a charming house and garden.

WALK FIVE

CANAL SAINT-MARTIN

The Canal St-Martin, even 30 years ago, would hardly have been contemplated for a pleasant stroll or boat trip. Inaugurated in 1825, the canal was built to extend the Canals de l'Ourcq and St-Denis (*see pp. 405 and 408*), which run into the holding basin of La Villette. By thus linking two sections of the Seine, the journey was reduced by 12km. The Canal St-Martin covers the extent of the 10th arrondissement over some 4.5km, from La Villette to the Bassin de l'Arsenal (*see p. 307*). Over this stretch are nine locks, two swing bridges, and several arched iron footbridges. The disappearance of commercial shipping and its related industries, and a determined effort at regeneration, have now made this a fashionable and popular area. During the day or in the evening, and especially at weekends, it is well adapted to cyclists and roller-bladers. Old buildings have been transformed; shops, restaurants and a large cinema complex have sprung up along its banks; the proximity of water and trees is pleasant on a hot day. The area just beyond Place de la Bataille de Stalingrad at the start of the Bassin de la Villette benefited from a programme of landscaping in 2006.

To the east of **Place de la République** (*see p. 321*), the busy commercial Rue du Faubourg du Temple runs over the point where Canal St-Martin emerges from beneath Blvd Jules Ferry. In Square Jules Ferry is a modern fountain and a statue called *La Grisette* (1880), a coy interpretation of the young working-class girls who once frequented the quarter. On the bridge is the bust (1899) by Pierre Granet of Frédérick Lemaître (1800–76), the famous 19th-century entertainer who played the boulevards. Below, the canal appears between the green banks of **Square F. Lemaître.**

From here the canal heads north to Pl. Stalingrad (*see p. 320*), flanked by the **Quai de Valmy** on the west and **Quai de Jemmapes** on the east, which are linked by a succession of bridges, some moveable, some pretty arched footbridges. The Passerelle de la Douane, level with Rue Leon Jouhaux, is followed by the Pont Tournant de la Rue Dieu (1884–85), a lifting road bridge. The arched *passerelle* beside it makes an ideal vantage point to watch the procedure. Hortus Verde, 55bis Quai de Valmy, sells plants and flowers which, while not dried, have been stabilised to last without watering for up to five years.

A short detour from Quai de Jemmapes down Av. Richerand arrives at the **Hôpital St-Louis**. The hospital, built by Claude Vellefaux in 1607–12, is an excellent and rare example of the early Louis XIII style in brick and stone, announced by an entrance lodge with central archway leading to a courtyard and a second, taller pavilion with a clock in the high roof. The arched corridor opens into a large square garden court planted with a variety of trees and enclosed by identical facades each with a central pavilion reminiscent of Place des Vosges (*see p. 283*). The elevations are mainly in brick, with stone quoins and central pavilions with high slate roofs; the lower roofs have red tiles. The hospital was built at the orders of Henri IV and all the old buildings are still in use. Beyond are the newer wings.

The canal here veers to the northeast around the site of the old hospital. Since the 13th century and until 1790, the Gibet de Montfaucon, the Tyburn of Paris, stood near **Rue de la Grange aux Belles**. The gallows proved fatal to three Surintendants des Finances: Enguerrand de Marigny, who erected it; Jean de Montaigu, who repaired it; and Semblançay, who tried to avoid it.

Beyond the swing bridge is **Square des Recollets**, a tree-lined double lock (the 5th and 6th). The square and the Hôtel du Nord (T: 01 40 40 78 78), at 102 Quai de Jemmapes, was the setting for the novel *Hôtel du Nord* by Eugène Dabit (1898–1936) made famous in Marcel Carné's film of the same name in 1938, starring Louis Jouvet and Arletty. The bar-brasserie building has been revamped in retro-1930s' style (the floor is original and the plumbing in the loo also seems pretty 'authentic'), and is now an in-place to eat and drink. At this point, Quai de Jemmapes boasts eye-catching architecture. Opposite the bridge as you cross back over the canal is a mural depicting scullers. This section of **Quai de Valmy** is reserved for pedestrians, roller-bladers and cyclists on Sundays, between 10am and 8pm (10–6 in winter). Along here are a number of interesting stores and eating places, such as the Colombian Salon de thé Mukura (no. 79; T: 01 42 01 18 67) and

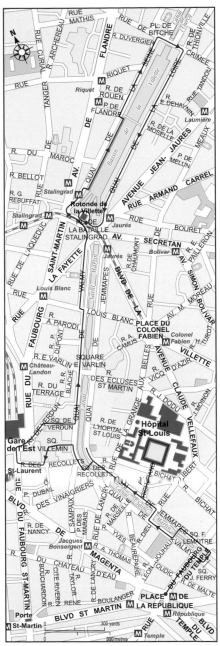

CLAUDE NICOLAS LEDOUX (1725–1806)

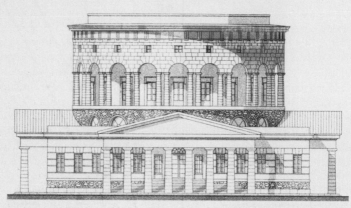

LA ROTONDE DE LA VILLETTE

Ledoux was a visionary and far-sighted architect of the Age of Enlightenment. Born in Champagne, he studied in J.-F. Blondel's *atelier* in Paris and became architect attached to the Département des Eaux et des Fôrets. His knowledge of antiquity was indirect, through engravings and Palladio, reinforced by a visit to England. In Paris he built mansions (1765–79) in the Chaussée-d'Antin and Poissonnière districts, but most were demolished by the creation of Rue Meyerbeer. Examples of Ledoux's decorative work survive in the Musée Carnavalet (*see p. 284*). When the Farmers General (collection of direct and indirect taxes) built a wall to surround Paris to prevent smuggling, they chose Ledoux to design the toll gates (*postes d'octroi*). The barrier, 24km long, nearly 4m high, fed public discontent: Paris wailed about being walled in: *le mur murant Paris rend Paris murmurant*. Ledoux's toll gates, of which there were over 50, were all different. Many were damaged at the Revolution; most were destroyed in the 19th-century reorganisation of Paris. There are four surviving examples (1785–88) of which La Villette is the finest (*see p. 320*). The most serious and imposing, appropriately monumental for this important entrance to Paris, it takes the very pure classical form of a Greek cross with peristyles, surmounted by a circular drum ending in a rotunda, using the Doric Order, square columns and heavy rustication. Ledoux's career ended with the Revolution and he spent his last years preparing the summary of his theories, published in 1804 as *L'architecture considérée sous le rapport de l'art des moeurs et de la legislation*. The book combined antique repertory, symbolism of geometric forms, and romantic anticipations. His interpretations of Neoclassical architecture were the most advanced in France, and his simple and functional shapes are the historic antecedents of the Modern Movement.

the Design Bookstore (*no. 83; T: 01 40 40 24 00*). Then there is Carré (since 1888), a smart purveyor of all types of tiles, followed by a series of acid-coloured shopfronts signalling two boutiques, Stella Cadente (*no. 93; T: 01 42 09 27 00*) and a branch of Antoine & Lili (*no. 95; T: 01 42 37 41 55*). Local bar-restaurants include L'Atmosphère, (*49 Rue Lucien Sampaix, T: 01 40 38 09 21*), serving the best *Croque Monsieur à la mousse de chèvre et basilique* in the business. In **Rue des Récollets** is Les Ateliers de Paris, both workshop and outlet for some unusual pieces of pottery; where it meets Rue du Fbg St-Martin is the Armurerie (gunsmiths) de la Gare de l'Est, with a formidable window display of firearms.

The most important public garden in the 10th arrondissement, **Square Villemin** has a wide variety of well-established trees and shrubs, a band-stand, playground, and an elaborate drinking fountain of 1848. A small area is made over to the local school, a yellow box-like construction, as a flower and vegetable plot. The square is built on the gardens of a military hospital dating from 1870, named after Dr. Jean-Antoine Villemin (1827–92), who demonstrated how easily tuberculosis can be transmitted. The hospital was an extension to the existing buildings of the **Convent of the Récollets**, entrance at 148 Rue du Faubourg St-Martin, since 2003 home to the Centre International d'Accueil et d'Echanges providing accommodation for researchers from all over the world, and the Ordre des Architectes en Ile-de-France. Inside, on the right are the café, old chapel and exhibition space, in the process of being

refurbished at the time of writing. In 1604, the Récollets, an offshoot of the Franciscan Order vowed to poverty, were authorised by Henri IV to establish their house on land given them by Jacques Cottard, a weaver, close to the church of St-Laurent. It amassed an important library, and many leading preachers were educated here. The convent, rebuilt in the 18th century, closed in 1790, and became a hospital for incurables. During the Second World War and the Algerian War (1954–62), it was used as a military hospital because of its proximity to the Gares du Nord and de l'Est.

Across from the Récollets Convent, **Gare de l'Est**, one of the oldest stations of Paris, built in 1849, extended and altered in 1930, is in good shape following a recent clean-up in readiness for a new TGV line. The forecourt occupies the site of the medieval St-Lawrence fair. Certain street names around recall that, serving the east, trains brought in people from Alsace and Lorraine.

At the intersection of Blvd de Magenta with Blvd de Strasbourg is the church of **St-Laurent**. On the site of a 6th-century basilica near the old Roman road, the building has been much altered. The present church dates from before 1429, with an older north tower. The nave was vaulted (with some splendid pendant bosses), and the choir remodelled, in 1655–59, with a high altar by Antoine Lepautre. The Lady Chapel dates from 1712. The 17th-century façade was demolished in 1862–65 in favour of a neo-Flamboyant one. Return via Sq. de Verdun, a tiny garden, to Quai de Valmy.

Square Eugène Varlin lines the sides of a lock with shady trees, and Opus Jazz and Soul Club (*T: 01 40 34 70 00*) is at 165 Quai de Valmy. The canal now widens into the **Bassin du Combat** and is crossed by Rue Louis-Blanc, the last bridge of the canal. On the corner of Rue Louis-Blanc and Quai de Jemmapes are handsome warehouses (1906) belonging to Société Clairefontaine. The contrasts in this area are summed up here, with vagrants sleeping under canvas on the canal-side and young business people bustling out of modern office-blocks. On Quai de Valmy water-side is a fire depot, and next door at no. 200, Point Ephemère, **Centre de Dynamiques Artistiques** (*T: 01 40 34 01 48*), which provides young artists with work spaces, as well as a concert hall and rudimentary exhibition spaces, and has a popular and inexpensive café.

Here the Canal St-Martin disappears under Rue Lafayette and its extension Av. Jean-Jaurès, named after the journalist, socialist politician and pacifist. The busy **Place de Stalingrad** can be daunting after the relative calm of the canal but the effort of crossing is rewarded by the older and wider Bassin de la Villette, inaugurated in 1808 by Napoleon. It boasts a fine example of 18th-century architecture in the shape of the **Rotonde de la Villette** (*see box on p. 318*). The Rotonde or toll house is the best of the four remaining toll gates designed by Ledoux for the barrier which surrounded Paris at the time when La Villette was still a village. It has lost the four sentry-boxes which con-trolled the Grande Rue de la Villette (now Av. de Flandre) and Route de Meaux (now Av. Jean-Jaures) and has had many uses since the Revolution. At time of writing, after recent restoration work, its future remains undecided.

The area between the Pl. Stanlingrad and the Quais has recently been landscaped. From the tree-lined terraces either side of La Rotonde is a panoramic view of the calm **Bassin de la Villette**, which flows between the **Quai de la Seine** on the northern side and **Quai de la Loire** opposite. The 19th-century building at 6 Quai de la Seine was home to the Services Généraux des Canaux de Paris but is destined for a new role. This quarter is gaining in popularity due in great part to the innovatory **MK2 Cinemas** (www.MK2.com), a major complex which spread to both sides of the canal in 2005, linked by ferries. Both have wide terraces and café/restaurants (Le Rendez-Vous des Quais and K Café, 14 Quai de la Seine; and K Café, 7 Quai de la Loire) and bars on boats. **Promenade Signoret-Montand**, named after Simone Signoret (1921–85) and Yves Montand (1921–91), runs alongside the canal. There are modest corner cafés along here, the most unusual being the café/bike-hire combination at No. 75, on the corner with Rue Riquet, Vélo et Chocolat (*open 10–7; closed Mon and Tues; T: 01 46 07 07 82*), which specialises in hot chocolate, chocolate cake, and brunch (not necessarily chocolate). Old warehouses across the basin are being converted into student accommodation. The basin narrows to become the Canal de l'Ourcq (*see p. 405*) with a lifting bridge (1884) carrying Rue de Crimée across, and a footbridge.

In the little garden which is Pl. de Bitche is a bandstand in front of the Neoclassical basilical style **St-Jacques et St-Christophe** (1901). Inside, the statue of St Peter has one very highly polished foot.

REPUBLIQUE

Place de la République (*on map p. 471, E4*), on the site of the Porte du Temple and the junction of seven important thoroughfares, is a popular centre for nightlife, especially with the young. It was laid out in 1856–62 by Haussmann as an anti-revolutionary planning scheme but continues to be the rallying point for demonstrations. It takes its name from the large central *Monument de la République* (1883), with an allegorical female figure. The bronze reliefs on the base by Dalou recount the history of the Republic from its inception to 1880.

At the corner of Rue Léon-Jouhaux, leading northeast from the Place, was the workshop from 1822–35 of Jacques Daguerre, one of the pioneers of photography who produced the first *daguerréotypes* in 1838. In the vicinity, Rue d'Oberkampf (between Rue de la République and Ménilmontant) and Rue St-Maur are particularly hot night-spots; the **Cirque d'hiver** (winter circus) at 110 Rue Amelot (off Blvd Voltaire) has existed since 1852, and there is a modern clothes market, Le Carreau du Temple, at 2 rue Perrée (between Rue du Temple and Blvd du Temple).

Two famous theatres in Blvd St-Martin, the **Théâtre de la Renaissance** (*T: 01 42 08 18 50*), managed by Sarah Bernhardt from 1893–99, and the **Théâtre de la Porte-St-Martin** (*T: 01 42 08 00 32*), were burnt down during the Commune and rebuilt. They are a reminder of the many theatres that opened in this area after 1791, with the emancipation of French theatre. In fact so frequent were performances of passionate and bloody melodramas that this street became known as the *Boulevard du Crime*.

The extension of Blvd St-Martin, the short Blvd St-Denis, lies between two triumphal arches, Porte St-Denis and the Porte St-Martin. Porte St-Denis, 23m high, designed by Blondel, was erected in 1674 to commemorate the victories of Louis XIV in Germany and Holland. The bas-reliefs were designed by Girardon. It faces Rue St-Denis, or Voie Royale, once the processional route of entry into Paris, and used on the occasion of Queen Victoria's visit in 1855. Porte St-Martin, also built in 1674 in honour of Louis XIV, is c. 18m high, and decorated with bas-reliefs of contemporary campaigns.

Blvd de Magenta runs northwest from Pl. de la République to the outer boulevards, linking Gare de l'Est (*see p. 319*) and Gare du Nord (1863), designed by Jacques Hittorff (1792–1867), with an iron and glass interior and Neoclassical façade.

The Hôpital St-Lazare was built on the site of the headquarters of the Lazarists or Priests of the Mission from 1632, founded in 1625 by Vincent de Paul (1576–1660). Also by Hittorff is the church of **St-Vincent-de-Paul** (1824–44). Two square towers dominate a pedimented portico of 12 Ionic columns approached by a cascade of steps. The interior frieze was painted by Hippolyte Flandrin (1809–64) and the dome by François-Edouard Picot (1786–1868). On the altar is a *Crucifixion* by Rude and there is a Cavaillé-Coll organ.

The **Petit Hôtel Bourrienne** (1789–98) at 58 Rue d'Hauteville (*guided visits first two weeks of July and all Sept daily 12–6; rest of year by appointment; T: 01 47 70 51 14*), is a rare example of *hôtel particulier* built at the time of Napoleon Bonaparte's Consulate immediately after the Revolution. It was occupied 1795–98 by Fortunée Hamelin (1776–1851). A *merveilleuse*, she was born in Martinique, like her friend the Empress Josephine, and notoriously paraded topless down the Champs-Elysées. A boudoir painted with detailed tropical birds was decorated for her, and the mansion contains an Egyptian-style bathroom.

PARC DES BUTTES CHAUMONT
Map p. 471, F2

Open June–mid-Aug 7–10.15; mid-Aug–Sept, May 7–9.15; Oct–April 7–8.15.
The Parc des Buttes Chaumont (southwest of La Villette) is one of the most picturesque but least known of Parisian parks. Entered via Rue Manin or Rue Botzaris, the 23-hectare park was created during Haussmann's régime in 1866–67 by Alphand and Barillet from decidedly unpromising terrain. The bare hills (*monts chauves*) of extensive gypsum (plaster of Paris) quarries, where rubbish was dumped, were transformed into craggy scenery. Lawns slope down to a lake spanned by a suspension bridge leading to a rocky promontory topped off with a tiny Classical temple. The landscaping was of Anglo-Chinese inspiration, and therefore less formal than typical French gardens. Among the well-tended flowerbeds are three restaurants and various entertainments for children. Outside the park, off Rue de Mouzaïa, is a delightful series of little cobbled streets with terraced houses.

WALK SIX

BELLEVILLE & MENILMONTANT

Belleville-Ménilmontant was once a village on a steep hill to the east of Paris, higher than Montmartre, with a rural community gathered around the church of St-Jean-Baptiste. Surrounded by vines, there were abundant springs which were a source of water for Paris in Gallo-Roman times, and again from the 12th century, when monks, Templars, and King Philippe-Auguste constructed aqueducts or channels to carry the water to Paris, a system that lasted for some five centuries. Today the only reminders are a few street names and four inspection chambers. Gypsum quarries were also known here, but the community began to change towards the late 18th century when the gypsum was seriously exploited but remained outside the Farmers General walls (1784–87; *see p. 318*), and therefore exempt from tolls. Consequently, it became a free and easy extra-mural location for *bals* and *guinguettes*. Until 1830, during *Mardi Gras* there was much merrymaking when the Courtille descended Rue de Bellemont. During the Second Empire's grand project for Paris (*see p. 223*), when the Parisian working-class were made homeless and insalubrious industries were banished from the centre, the suburbs became centres of political ferment, but were then forgotten and ignored. Belleville-Ménilmontant combines hints of its more recent past and obvious evidence of its shifting multicultural immigrant community, where Berbers and Jews have now been joined by Asians, Poles and Pakistanis. Improvements in housing were begun in the 1970s, and today there is a desire to protect the surviving 19th- and early 20th-century buildings while at the same time promoting urban regeneration. Over the last few decades the quarter has been evolving into a fashionable 'village', considered more authentic than its glamorous but touristic neighbour Montmartre, attracting younger newcomers, artists and intellectuals to the melting-pot of nationalities and classes. The *Ateliers de Ménilmontant* in October are open days at artists' studios.

The first stop, in **Rue de Belleville**, is something of a pilgrimage site for fans of Edith Piaf (1915–63). There's nothing much to see, but at no. 72 a plaque announces that this house was her birthplace. Piaf, known as *La Môme Piaf* (the little sparrow), was considered the archetypal Parisian singer after making her career debut in 1935. She became instantly recognisable for her distinctive, strident voice and the performance of emotive songs such as *Je ne regrette rien* and *Milord* (the Edith Piaf museum is at 11 Rue Créspin-du-Gast, 11th arr, Metro Ménilmontant, near Père Lachaise Cemetery).

Further down is **Place Fréhel**, a small neglected square created in 1972 on the corner of Rue Julien-Lacroix with Paris 3 Temps (1986) creations, including *Le passé* by Jean Le Gac, a mural by Ben, *Il faut se méfier des mots*, and Marie Bourget's *le Futur*, a modernist luminous cone evoking Paris—*Ville Lumière*.

On **Rue Julien-Lacroix**, at no. 85, is a small café/bar which has good food and model boats, Le Petit Navire (*T: 01 40 33 58 72*) which used to be a Berber

café, and further along the street is Lacroix Synagogue. Turn up **Rue Ferme de Savy** opposite the café, next to Les Ateliers du Tayrac, which is cut short by a triangular relief and mosaic and

A doorway in Belleville.

steps leading into Parc de Belleville. Bear right up a rising path to the belvedere with the most remarkable view of Paris.

Parc de Belleville, which opened in 1988, is an interesting modern garden designed by François Debulois that occupies a site eight metres higher than the Butte Montmartre. Under the terrace the Maison de l'Air is dedicated to the Parisian environment and air quality. The main feature of the gardens are the rocky grottos and the stepped water-feature as well as steep tree-lined paths and a flight of steps under wisteria arches. To the left of the viewpoint is shaded Sq. Alexandre-Luquet, and then a path that leads to a tiny vineyard, a token reminder of how the area was once used.

On the corner of Rue des Envierges is a pleasant bar serving light meals, La Mer à Boire (*No. 1; T: 01 43 58 29 43*), and opposite is a boulangerie-pâtisserie.

Descend **Rue du Transvaal**, passing no. 16, the gated 19th-century Villa Castel, where a scene from the film *Jules et Jim* (1962) was shot. Take Passage Plantin lined with pretty houses, and after the steps turn right (Rue des Couronnes), left into Passage Notre-Dame-de-la-Croix, and right again into **Rue de la Mare**. Here you are faced with the east end of the neo-Romanesque **Notre-Dame-de-la-Croix** (1860–69), by Héret, the third longest church in Paris after Notre-Dame and St-Sulpice, with a belfry of 78m. There have been churches on this site since the 15th century. Monumental steps lead up to the west

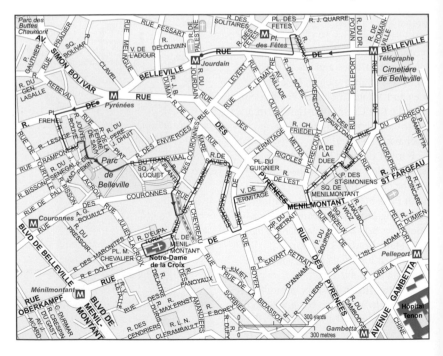

door from **Pl. Maurice-Chevalier**, which lies at the heart of Ménilmontant. Here is a Wallace fountain (*see p. 36*) and the cafés round about are where local men gather to smoke *chichas* (sold in the area), at the Casque d'Or for example on the corner of Rue Julien Lacroix (across Rue de Ménilmontant is La Boulangerie Restaurant on Rue des Panoyaux, *see p. 437*).

Return to Rue de la Mare, an old riverbed which ran into a *mare* (pool) where the church stands, and cross the Petite Ceinture railway line. The street climbs past Rue Henri Chevreau, where at no. 34 is a charming cul-de-sac, and continues up to Rue de Savies and the **Regard St-Martin** or **de Savies**, a small stone building with a pointed roof and an inscription giving its date as c. 1722. This was an inspection chamber over the collecting point of spring water which was carried to Paris via an aqueduct built by monks from St-Martin-des-Champs (*see p. 275*). In Rue des Cascades, are two more *regards*, de la Roquette (no. 37) and des Messiers (no. 17) which were part of Philippe-Auguste's Belleville aqueduct. The street has conserved much of its old character and was the background in 1952 for Jacques Becker's classic film starring Simone Signoret, *Casque d'Or*.

Follow a small section of Rue Ménilmontant to Rue de l'Ermitage where no. 19 has neo-Gothic touches. Further along are the paved and shady Impasse Louis Robert and the Villa de l'Ermitage, lined with low houses and flowered courtyards, which brings you to **Cité Leroy**, also a late 19th-century

Graffiti in Belleville.

development saved from demolition. In October in Ménilmontant, many artists' studios are opened up to the public.

Left on Rue des Pyrénées is Pl. du Guignier, with an early 20th-century covered market, and a street market on Sundays and Thursdays. At the corner of Rue des Pyrénées, at 119 Rue Ménilmontant, is an elegant Neoclassical *folie* or country retreat, built in 1770 by Moreau-Desproux and now called the **Pavillon de l'Asile des Petits-Orphelins** or the **Carré de Baudoin**. In the 19th century it was owned by an uncle of Edmund de Goncourt and plans are afoot to establish a local history museum here (*T: 01 40 33 46 73*). The

Saints-Simoniens, followers of the influential aristocrat, early socialist, industrial entrepreneur and mystic Claude Henri de Rouvroy, Comte de Saint-Simon (1760–1825), founded a community at no. 145 in 1831, and the garden Sq. de Ménilmontant (at 115m) was the site of their house, off which is Passage des St-Simoniens. Passage de la Duée (small spring) off Rue de la Duée is reputedly the narrowest street in Paris.

Continue up Rue de la Duée, making a detour around Rue Tarclet to enjoy the gardens of Villa Georgina, and along Rue du Borrégo and Rue du Télégraphe, to arrive at the highest part of Ménilmontant. The **Cimetière de Belleville**, at 128m, was created in 1880 in part of the old Château de Ménilmontant belonging to the St-Fargeau family. An inscription on the gatepost records that here in 1792 Claude Chappe experimented with the Tachygraphe. His first attempts were regarded by the mob as a plot to communicate with Louis XVI, imprisoned in the Temple below: the installation was burned and Chappe was imprisoned. The following year he was successful in using the aerial telegraph to announce the Republican Victory. By 1794 a communication link was established between Paris and Lille, taking three hours rather than three days. The tomb of Léon Gaumont, promoter of the cinema industry (d. 1946), can be found about 20m to the right on the central alley. South of the cemetery are the Reservoirs de Belleville.

Further down Rue de Belleville, the **Regard de la Lanterne**, the most monumental of the inspection chambers, is among the trees on Rue des Compans. King Philippe-Auguste channelled water from the hills above and this domed chamber was semi-submerged to allow access by underground steps to the Aqueduct de Belleville.

The **Place des Fêtes** was once the focal point of festivities in the area, but was engulfed in concrete in 1970. Further down the main road is the church of St-Jean-Baptiste (1854–59) by J.-P. Lassus (1807–57). Georges Rouault (1871–1958; *see p. 260*) was born at 51 Rue Fessart, east of the church.

PERE LACHAISE CEMETERY
Map p. 477, E1

Open mid-March–5th Nov Mon–Fri 8–6, Sat 8.30–6, Sun and holidays 9–6; 6th Nov–mid-March Mon–Fri 8–5.30, Sat 8.30–5.30, Sun and holidays 9–5.30. Main Entrance on Blvd de Menilmontant.

Père Lachaise, or Cimetière de l'Est, is the largest (47 hectares) and long the most fashionable necropolis in Paris. On a hill overlooking the city it is, however, much more than a burial ground. It is a park and meeting place; it is designed for quiet contemplation with green spaces and flowerbeds, trees and benches. It is not laid out entirely in rigid chequer-board order but has an extensive free-flowing central area *à l'anglaise*. The rows of sombre graves and mausoleums are visited by over a million people a year. Among the monuments are some fine works of art by leading 19th- and 20th-century French sculptors, but also some outrageous kitsch. It receives the greatest number of visitors on All Saints Day (1st November), the Day of the Dead, when it will be ablaze with chrysanthemums.

HISTORY OF PÈRE-LACHAISE CEMETERY

Père François de La Chaise (1624–1709) was confessor to Louis XIV and lived in the Jesuit house rebuilt in 1682 on the site of a chapel on the side of the hill. During the Fronde (uprisings against Mazarin during the minority of Louis XIV, 1649–53), the king watched the skirmishes between Condé and Turenne from here. The land was bought by the city in 1804 and laid out by Brongniart, but has been extended several times. The burial ground is not reserved for Roman Catholics, or even exclusively for Christians; buried here side-by-side are also Jews, Buddhists, Muslims and non-believers. The first to be interred were La Fontaine and Molière, whose remains were transferred here in 1804.

Visiting the cemetery

The main alley runs through the central sector (24 hectares) which is classed as a historic site. Among those buried alongside are Colette, Rossini, Alfred de Musset, and Baron Haussmann on the north-west, and opposite the history painter Thomas Couture. At the end of the alley is the large and deeply moving *Monument to the Dead* (1895) by Albert Bartholomé (1848–1928), who turned to sculpture on the advice of Degas after his wife's death and then specialised in funerary masks and tomb sculptures. Beyond the monument are the tombs of David, Delacroix, and Balzac. The eastern part of the central sector where Chopin and Géricault are buried, designated Secteur Romantique, contains the graves of La Fontaine and Molière, Alphonse Daudet and Benjamin Constant, as well as Champollion. In the southern corner is the monument to Abélard and Héloïse (*see p. 42*), first erected in 1779 at the Abbey of the

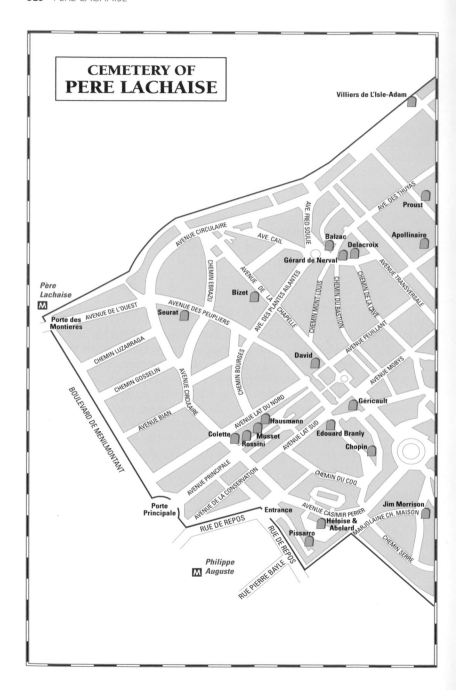

CEMETERY OF
PERE LACHAISE

Villiers de L'Isle-Adam

AVE. DES THUYAS

Proust

AVENUE CIRCULAIRE

AVE. CAIL

AVE. FRED SOULIE

Balzac

Apollinaire

Delacroix

Gérard de Nerval

AVENUE TRANSVERSALE

CHEMIN EBRAZU

AVENUE DE LA CHAPELLE

CHEMIN MONT-LOUIS

CHEMIN DU BASTION

CHEMIN DE LA CAVE

Père
Lachaise
Ⓜ

Bizet

AVE. DES PLANTES AILANTES

AVENUE DE L'OUEST

AVENUE DES PEUPLIERS

Porte des
Montières

Seurat

AVENUE FEUILLANT

CHEMIN LUZARRAGA

David

AVENUE MOBYS

CHEMIN BOURGES

CHEMIN GOSSELIN

BOULEVARD DE MENILMONTANT

AVENUE CIRCULAIRE

AVENUE BIAN

Géricault

AVENUE LAT DU NORD

Hausmann

Colette

Musset

Edouard Branly

Rossini

AVENUE LAT SUD

Chopin

AVENUE PRINCIPALE

CHEMIN DU COQ

AVENUE DE LA CONSERVATION

Porte
Principale

Entrance

AVENUE CASIMIR PERIER

Jim Morrison

Héloise &
Abelard

MARJOLAINE CH. MAISON

RUE DE REPOS

Pissarro

CHEMIN SERRE

RUE DE REPOS

Philippe
Ⓜ Auguste

RUE PIERRE BAYLE

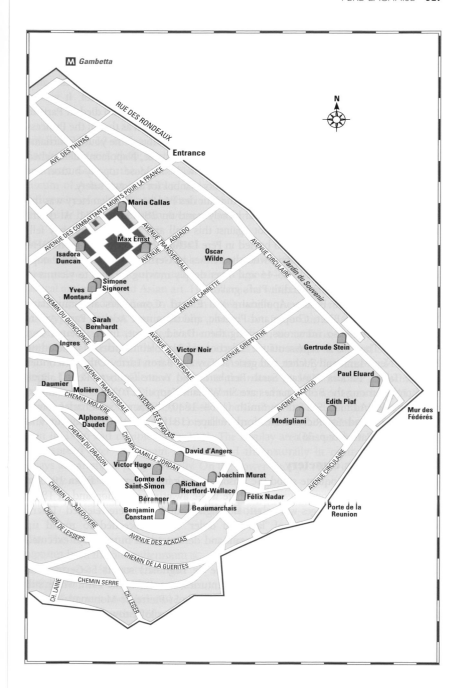

M *Gambetta*

N

RUE DES RONDEAUX

Entrance

AVE. DES THUYAS

AVENUE DES COMBATTANTS MORTS POUR LA FRANCE

Maria Callas

AVENUE AGUADO

AVENUE TRANSVERSALE

Max Ernst

AVENUE

Isadora
Duncan

Oscar
Wilde

AVENUE CIRCULAIRE

Jardin du Souvenir

Yves
Montand

Simone
Signoret

CHEMIN DU QUINCONCE

AVENUE CARRETTE

Sarah
Bernhardt

Ingres

AVENUE TRANSVERSALE

Victor Noir

AVENUE GREFFUTHE

Gertrude Stein

Daumier

AVENUE TRANSVERSALE

AVENUE PACHTOD

Paul Eluard

Molière

CHEMIN MOLIERE

AVENUE DES ANGLAIS

Edith Piaf

Alphonse
Daudet

Modigliani

Mur des
Fédérés

CHEMIN DU DRAGON

CHEMIN CAMILLE JORDAN

David d'Angers

Victor Hugo

AVENUE CIRCULAIRE

Comte de
Saint-Simon

Joachim Murat

CHEMIN DE L'ABEDOYERE

Richard
Hertford-Wallace

Béranger

Félix Nadar

CHEMIN DE LESSEPS

Benjamin
Constant

Beaumarchais

Porte de la
Reunion

AVENUE DES ACACIAS

CHEMIN DE LA GUERITES

CH. LAINE

CHEMIN SERRE

CH. LEGER

the Indianised Kingdoms of Southeast Asia. The *Nagaraja* or *Serpent King* of the 2nd century, from the Mathura region in Northern India, is distinctive for its red sandstone. The Mathura School flourished from the 3rd century until the Gupta period (4th–6th centuries) which was considered the Golden Age of Indian Art. The style is demonstrated by the Buddha torso (early 6th century) from the Mathura region, dressed in fine monastic robes that seem to cling to the body. The *Female Bust* from Madhya Pradesh (10th–11th centuries), also known as a female tree spirit or *shalabhanjika*, is representative of sculptures which embellished the walls of many Indian shrines. Seventeenth-century Indian miniatures from the Mughal Court are also on display.

Southeast Asia: This section comprises part of the Asian mainland, and the islands of Indonesia, Malaysia and the Philippines. Three groups on the mainland dominated in the 1st millennium: the Cham along the east coast of Vietnam; the Khmer in the Central Mekong valley; and the Mon to the west (Thailand and Burma). The Cambodian department contains some of the most beautiful Khmer sculptures outside Cambodia. It is divided into three periods: Pre-Angkorian (1st–8th centuries); from the Foundation of Angkor to Angkor Wat (9th–11th centuries); and the apotheosis and the end of Angkor (12th–15th centuries). The first temple at Angkor, capital of the kingdom, built c. 900, was dedicated to Shiva and called the Bakheng. It had five terraces and 109 sanctuary towers. The Banteah Srei *Pediment* (c. 967), in pink sandstone,

was part of a *gopura* or tower. It features a high-relief carving of Krishna in an animated struggle during an episode from the Sanskrit epic the *Mahabharata* and reflects the emergence of the style of Banteah Srei. The *Head of Jayavarman VII* (r. 1181–1219) is typical of the Bayon style, with downcast eyes and an enigmatic smile. The *Buddha Protected by the Naga Mucilinda* is very typical of the Angkor Wat style (1st half 12th century), with the hieratic figure of the Enlightened One seated on the serpent's coiled body and protected by its many heads. A section of the huge Giants' Causeway, Preah Kahn, Angkor Wat (12th or early 13th centuries) is part of a serpent balustrade on the bridge that crossed the temple moat, alluding to the passage from one world to another.

The Kingdom of Champa, east Vietnam, was Indianised from the 7th century. A rare group of Cham sculptures includes the iconic figure of *Shiva of the Silver Tower* (11th–12th centuries) which displays classic iconography of Shiva, with a central eye, a crescent moon in his matted hair, and a snake across the torso.

The influence of India was felt in Burma from the 1st century AD, represented by a huge number of temples and stupas. Delicate Buddhas finely carved in teak with traces of polychrome and lacquered include the *Crowned Buddha* (14th century, Myanmar). Indian culture also shaped Javanese development via the trade routes through the region, and inspired the astounding temple of Borobudur, erected in the 8th century, with over 500 lifesize Buddhist images, and nearly 3km of relief carvings.

Objects from Thailand and Laos from

the period of Mon Dvaravati, which emerged by the 5th century, include the *Wheel of the Law* (8th or 9th centuries), emblem of the Buddha's *First Sermon*. The bronze *Head of Buddha* (14th century), of the Ayutthaya period, displays classic features, such as the tight hair curls surmounted by a pointed flame. Most works from Laos here are 18th- and 19th-century.

First floor

China: The department contains some 20,000 exhibits covering seven millennia from the Neolithic period (c. 5000 BC) to the 18th century. Ancient China and Central Asia including Buddhist China are here on the first floor; Classical China, including Painting and Decorative Arts, are on the second floor; China of the Qing is on the third floor; and the Lacquer Rotunda on the fourth floor.

Ancient China: Archaeological evidence has identified three outstanding separate but concurrent Neolithic cultures: the painted pottery culture of Yangshao, northwest China, is represented by the slender *Jandipin Amphora* (4800–4000 BC) from Shaanxi, for carrying liquids; the Hong Shan culture, in the east, produced pottery and carved hard green nephrite or jade to represent a magic creature, the *zhulong* or Dragon-Pig; the Liangzhu in the lower Yangzi used jade or bone, to produce the *cong* or tube, which carried a mystical and authoritative significance. Cult objects in jade include pierced *bi* discs, representing heaven and earth, which were placed on corpses. Terracotta pottery of this era shows sophisticated form and decoration

The Shang dynasty in the 16th century BC learned to cast bronze earlier than western cultures. A typical bronze production is the *liding*, a sacrificial vessel used in ancestor worship and libation vessels such as the *Camondo tsun*, from Southern China, in the shape of an elephant. The lacquered *Doe* (481–221 BC, Warring States period) supported a drum.

The Empire under the Qin dynasty was founded in 221 BC by Emperor Huangdi (260–210 BC) who began the Great Wall and amassed a terracotta army of 6,000 figures.

The Han dynasties (206 BC–220 AD), which followed, produced a wide repertoire of *mingqi* (funerary statuettes) including musicians, servants and spirited horses. The Northern Wei dynasty (386–589) continued the production of graceful terracottas, but the most outstanding figures are from the Tang dynasty (618–907). The Tang ruled over a vast Empire crossed by trade routes, with their capital at Ch'ang, and fostered a period of artistic exuberance. The production of superbly modelled *sancai* figurines for tombs includes graceful dancers and courtiers. The *Bactriane camel with Rider and Load* (2nd half 7th century) is a superb example of a popular motif during the Wei and Tang periods.

The introduction of Buddhism along the Silk Road is explicit in a 9th-century painting on silk of a monk carrying books, surrounded by all his attributes. The painting came from the

cave at Dunhuang where some 500
manuscripts were discovered.
Mediterranean influence contributed to
the increasing naturalism found in
Bodhisattva Sitting in Royal Relaxation (6th
century), from the Longmen caves,
Henan province, and *Head Crowned with
Feathered Tiara* (6th–7th centuries) from
Xingjiang province. Central Asia, also
called Serindia, developed a brilliant
culture in the 2nd–11th centuries.

Pakistan and Afghanistan: From the
1st–3rd centuries AD, the Kushans ruled
over a vast area of Northern India and
Afghanistan and Pakistan. Their culture
blended Graeco-Roman, Iranian and
Indian influences into the Gandhara
Style (*see box opposite*). Typical is the
expressive standing Bodhisattva carved
in green-grey schist. White and blue
blown glass, and other luxury objects
come from Begram, north of Kabul. The
Art of Hadda, southeast Afghanistan,
combines Hellenistic and Indian
characteristics in 3rd–4th-century stuccos such as *The Spirit with Flowers*. Giant
Buddhas were sculpted in the cliffs during the occupation by Persian Sassanides
(c. 5th century). Typical of the last
Buddhist art is the heavily adorned

Bodhisattva from the Monastery of
Fondukistan (7th century).

Nepal and Tibet: Art of the Himalayas
shows both Tibetan Buddhist and
Nepalese Hindu influences. Nepalese art
is colourfully represented by several
painted book covers in wood (12th–14th
centuries), and the gilded, inlaid copper
Manjusri is a prime example of finely
wrought 13th–18th-century metal
sculpture. Paintings on fabric—linen,
cotton or silk—are called *thangka*,
literally 'rolled-up', and therefore
portable. A colourful *thangka, Vajrasattva
and his Consort* (1st half 13th century),
shows many characteristics of India
miniatures, such as geometric faces and
gentle modelling of forms. The *Mandala
of Vajramrita* (1st half 16th century) is a
prime example of a *thangka* which
borrows themes and colours from Nepal.

Riboud Gallery: Decorative Arts of
India (16th–19th centuries), includes
jewels, fabrics including saris, and jade
dagger handles, as well as pieces from
the Moghul dynasty. In the small circular space at the apex of the building is
Guimet's Library. Temporary exhibitions
of graphic art are displayed here.

Second floor

Classical China: Brush painting is
represented by 1,000 works ranging
from the Tang to the Qing dynasties
including a large group from the 13th
to the 18th centuries. There are
similarities in style across the centuries
although some, such as the 10th-century
Northern Song are more spiritual, and
the 12th-century *Southern Song* show a

lyrical quality. Chinese calligraphy and
painting is closely linked through their
spiritual and meditative qualities, and
also technically, as both are executed
with a brush and ink. The depiction of
bamboo holds an elevated position in
the established canons of Chinese
painting, falling somewhere between
calligraphy and tree painting. This is

GANDHARA SCULPTURE

Among the wide variety of treasures possessed by the Musée Guimet is the largest collection of Gandhara sculpture on public view in the West. These unusual pieces, mostly from the 2nd and 3rd centuries AD, are born of a remarkable union, in the valleys of the Hindu Kush, between Buddhism and Ancient Greek and Roman art. Gandhara refers to the area around Peshawar, including the Swat Valley and its ancient capital Taxila, near the border of modern-day Pakistan with Afghanistan. This is the area where Alexander the Great ended his eastward march in 325 BC: the legacy of that campaign was the settling of western colonists in the area. They flourished for many generations, well into late Roman times, on the wealth of the new trade routes between East and West, establishing in the process a school of provincial-style Roman art in the area. As Buddhism spread out from India, seeking to give visual form to its spiritual manifestations and to the image of the Buddha himself, it encountered fertile ground amongst these artistic descendants of the ancient western tradition. The classical idiom is perhaps most noticeable in the

form and sweep of the 'toga' on many of the Gandhara Buddhas—similar to Roman sculptures and Hellenistic terracotta figurines—but the facial profiles, poses and styles of hair, also often appear more Greek than local. The reduced simplicity of many of the forms contrasts radically with the intricacy of Hindu art, whose influence understandably dominated early Buddhist expression. A great deal of this extraordinary and beautiful art from Gandhara has been lost in the wars that have ravaged Afghanistan, making this collection both more valuable and more poignant.   N.McG.

Head of a Divinity (1st–3rd centuries AD) from Tapa-i-Kafariha in Afghanistan.

epitomised in the perfectly controlled use of numerous tones of black in the vertical, Yuan-period scroll *Bamboo* (1279–1368). In traditional Chinese painting the effect of perspective and depth is created by diminishing size and graduated colour.

The collection of ceramics under the Tan and the Song is a comprehensive panorama through around 10,000 pieces going back some 8,000 years to handcrafted earthenware. During the Neolithic period, stoneware was produced and the potter's wheel invented. The major contribution of Tang dynasty (AD 616–906) potters was their bold introduction of three-coloured ware, using yellow, green and white glazes, and the influence of Sassanide Persia. Tang pottery peaked in the 10th century with the development of pure porcelain from kaolin fired at very high temperatures to create vessels with a creamy white glaze. The success of ceramic production in the Song dynasty (960–1279) was based on monochromatic wares, the most spectacular of which was the Celadon, a type of transparent glaze. A beautiful example of early Song production is the globe-shaped celadon ewer (11th century) in porcelain-like stoneware, from Shaanxi, northern China, with a phoenix-head spout and extensive carved floral decoration under a blue-green glaze. The Liao dynasty (916–1125) from Mongolia, and established in northeast China, adopted many Chinese customs including ceramic techniques which they adapted to produce a unique repertoire of forms modelled on everyday objects. A very rare Yuan dynasty (1280–1368) ceramic is the porcelain

Meiping vase (mid-14th century) which uses a strong cobalt blue glaze with a white slip dragon motif. The Yuan capital, Tatu, on the site of Peking (Beijing), was rebuilt by the Ming dynasty (1468–1644) and raised to the rank of Imperial city. Porcelain was produced in great quantity, the most important centre being Jingdezhen. A flourishing export business developed, and blue and white ware was adjusted to the taste of European customers.

Korea: This department has some 1,000 objects, covering the main periods of Korean art. Susceptible to Chinese influences, the phases of Korean art waxed and waned, but throughout is endowed with a sense of discretion and reserve, frequently with a sense of ironic humour. Buddhism and writing were introduced from Han China early in this era, and a particular style of Buddhist art emerged from the 4th century. The three kingdoms are represented here by their art. From the Paekche Kingdom in the southwest is a small, cross-legged Bodhisattva meditating (6th century); from Silla Kingdom, the last to convert to Buddhism, comes a remarkable gilded bronze crown (5th–6th centuries), influenced by Siberian Shamanist art. The Koryo dynasty which unified the Kingdom of Korea in 918 produced large serene Buddha sculptures, such as the meditative *Teaching Buddha* (11th–12th centuries) in gilded wood. Very high-quality celadon or *maebyong*, developed characteristics specific to Korea and brought renown to its ceramicists. With the Choson dynasty (1392–1592), the capital was established in Seoul and Confucianism became the official religion. The near-caricatures of *Three Sitting Monks* (14th–15th centuries), carved in stone, were not unusual. The production of ceramics was revived; green Punch'ong replaced Celadon, and white porcelain was developed. For most of the 17th century, Korea, under the domination of the Manchus who founded the Qing dynasty, was described as the Hermit Kingdom, and only in the 18th century was there a revival in art.

Japan: The Japanese department is extremely rich, with around 11,000 works from its origins (3rd–2nd millennia BC) to the beginning of the Meiji era (1868). The production of ceramics, from c. 10,500 BC to c. 300 BC, the Jomon period identified by the rope-cord pattern on terracotta pots and fig-urines. The succeeding culture, Yayoi, when rice was introduced, made undec-orated ceramics, and bronze and iron objects. The Kofun Period (AD 300–538), was named after the large tombs (*kofun*) built for the political leaders of that era, during which time (c. 400 AD) the country was united as Yamato Japan. Remarkable clay figures or *Haniwa* (meaning clay cylinders) devel-oped in conjunction with funerary ritu-als. During the Nara period (710–749) Japanese Buddhist art followed in the wake of Chinese paradigms. From the mid-8th century, works of the Heian period showed greater independence and the country was indeed liberated from China in 894.

Under the Fujiwara (until 1185), and the shogun warriors of Kamakura (until 1333), Zen Buddhism appeared. The art of Zen emphasised portraits, austere ink paintings, calligraphy and direct aids to meditation, including gardens, tea rituals, and Noh theatre. The *Kannon Bodhisattva* which portrays the Great Being of Compassion, placed on a lotus-flower pedestal, symbol of purity, is typical of the Fujiwara period.

Ceramics were the ultimate manifes-tation of the art of the Momoyana peri-od (1558–1637) epitomised in the *Raku Tea Bowl. Raku*, meaning enjoyment or ease, is a form of pottery fired at low temperatures using lead glazes and removed from the kiln while glowing hot. It is the traditional hand-made manufacture of bowls for the Japanese tea ceremony, ensuring each bowl is unique. Western influences arrived with the Portuguese in 1543 and a direct result is the Edo period painting *The Portuguese* (17th century) interpreted on the *Folding Screen of Namban Byobu*. In 1603, *Edo* (modern Tokyo) was estab-lished as the military and administrative centre, while Kyoto remained the artis-tic centre. Subsequently *Edo* overtook Kyoto artistically and became famous for wood-block prints in colour, known as *ukiyo-e* (pictures of the fleeting or floating world). Leading artists were Utamaro Kitagawa (1753–1806), Hokusai Katsushika (1760–1849) and Hiroshige Utagawa (1797–1858). The iconography includes genre pleasure scenes, portraits and landscapes; the Guimet contains almost 3,000 prints. Their fame spread world-wide, to influ-ence many western painters such as Degas and Whistler. In 19th-century France, the portrait prints of elegant and beautiful women by Utamaro Kitagawa were popular and widespread, but very few were authentic originals.

Third and fourth floors

Qing China: China was ruled by foreigners for a second time under the Manchu, who founded the Qing dynasty (1644–1911). The arts flourished again under Emperor Kangxi (1662–1722) when skills in porcelain, enamel, inlay and lacquer techniques were perfected. The colour-palette of enamels expanded: to green (*famille verte*) was added pink (*famille rose*); later in the 18th century, still more colours and the *cloisonné* technique became sought after. The *Vase of a Thousand Flowers* (1736–95, Qianlong period) is a spectacular example.

Lacquer Rotunda: This top room contains beautiful examples of Coromandel folding screens in lacquered wood.

No. 19 Avenue d'Iena

In the adjacent building is the **Buddhist Pantheon** consisting of some 150 Japanese and 30 Chinese Buddhist works. In 2001 a Japanese tea house was created in the Japanese garden here where tea ceremonies can be attended by reservation.

MUSEE DE CRISTALLERIES DE BACCARAT
Map p. 484, A4

Open Mon, Wed–Sat 10–7; closed Tues, Sun and holidays; T: 01 40 22 11 00, www.baccarat.fr
North of the Guimet, the prestigious manufacturer of crystal ware, Baccarat, has a gallery and museum at no. 11 Place des États Unis. It is housed in the very fine former private mansion of Marie-Laure de Noailles. Witty details include a crystal chair and crystal beads edging the stair carpet. The museum has beautiful and novel pieces, from an *Elephant Vase* (1880) to an elegant transparent table setting (1946). Tableware as well as jewellery is on sale and there is also a smart restaurant (*see p. 435*).

MUSEE D'ART MODERNE DE LA VILLE DE PARIS
Map p. 473, E1

Open Tues–Sun 10–5.30; Wed during temporary exhibitions 10–10; closed Mon and holidays; T: 01 53 67 40 00.
The Palais de Tokyo, at no. 11 Av. du Président-Wilson, was constructed for the Universal Exhibition of 1937 on a site where once stood the old *savonnerie* or soap factory which later became a carpet workshop (*see p. 100*). The building is in two parts, divided by a terrace. On the façade and the terrace walls are reliefs by Alfred-Auguste Janniot (1889–1969) and statues by Bourdelle including the bronze *La France*, installed in 1948. The museum was inaugurated in 1961 to house the municipal collection of 20th-century works built up from donations since the 1930s, plus acquisitions. It reopened in February 2006 after a two-year refurbishment.

The Historic collections

The permanent collections are divided between Historic and Contemporary and are likely to be rotated, often forming the basis for temporary exhibitions. The Historic section focuses on Fauvism, Cubism and Post-Cubism, and Orphism, the School of Paris artists, and Jean Fautrier.

Salle Matisse: The large decorative scheme in this room contains two large triptychs by Henri Matisse. These began with a commission in 1930 for the Barnes Foundation, in the USA, for which Matisse returned to a favourite theme, the dance. *La Danse Inachevée* (1931) was sketched on scaled-up paper using charcoal fixed to a bamboo stick, and painted in grey oils on a blue ground. It contains eight figures, two partly obscured, intended to create a continuous chain as in *La Danse* of 1909–10 for Shchukin. In 1931 Matisse, exhausted, abandoned it. He began a new version using cut-outs of coloured paper, which was discarded in 1932 because of an error in the dimensions. The Merion mural was finally completed in 1933. Matisse then returned to the 1932 version which became known as *La Danse de Paris* (1931–33). Against orthogonal pink, black and blue bands are energetic, muscular dancers, setting up a vibrant surface pattern. This work revolutionised architectural decoration and Matisse's work from then on. It was bought by the Ville de Paris in 1937 to decorate a specially designed room in the museum; *Danse Inachevée* was acquired in 1993. In the same room is a Matisse bronze, *The Back*, as well as *Mur des Peintures* (1995) by Daniel Buren (b. 1937), a wall of 20 coloured stripes—black, red, blue, grey, orange—in varying sizes, vertical on different canvases.

Fauvism: Colourful paintings from the pioneers of the Fauve movement (1905–06) include *L'Olivier près d'Estaque* (1906) by the masterful Georges Braque. The Dutch cycling enthusiast Vlaminck worked closely with Derain at this period, and the cross-fertilisation of colour and energy is evident in *Berges de la Seine à Chatou* (c. 1905), and *La Rivière* (1905) respectively. The museum is rich in mainly pre-1918 works by Georges Rouault, including his entire production of copper engravings. He painted recurring themes in a singular graphic, expressionistic style including *A Tabarin—Le Chahut* (1905) depicting the popular dance hall; later he became a well-known religious painter, in biblical landscapes such as *Crépuscule* (1938–39).

Cubism: A rare, early, pre-Cubist work by Picasso, *Evocation* (c. 1901), was a tribute to his good friend Casagemas who committed suicide in a café in 1901. From his Analytical Cubist phase is *Le Pigeon aux Petits Pois* (1911) whereas Braque's *Nature Morte à la Pipe* (1914), using sand and other media, belongs to Synthetic Cubism. Also represented in the Cubist collections are Gris, and the sculptor Henri Laurens (1885–1954) who uses multiple viewing angles in *Danseuse Espagnole* (1915). Albert Gleizes and Jean Metzinger (1883–1957), who published a theoretical pamphlet *Du Cubisme* (1912), introduced a diluted form of Cubism, as

Fernand Léger: *The Discs* (1918), in the Musée d'Art Moderne de la Ville de Paris.

did André Lhote (1885–1962). Derain's *Baigneuses* (c. 1908) shows the influence of both Cézanne and Cubism.

Robert Delaunay (1885–1941) and Fernand Léger (1881–1955) play an important part in the collections. Both celebrated the technical age, and their styles crossed for a time. Delaunay's main concerns were with the primacy of colour over form. He was closely associated with a movement dubbed Orphic Cubism by Apollinaire, a 'purer' form of Cubism, detached from anything that came before. His interest in light and colour led to the first abstract works by a French painter. *The Cardiff Team* (1912–13) is a colourful variation of a Cubist collage, and in the watercolour *Homage to Bleriot* (1913–14) he introduces the law of simultaneous contrasts described by Chevreul (*see p. 352*). There are also works in the collection by his wife Sonia Delaunay including a large mural, *Rhythm* (1938). *Large Still Life* (1926) by Amédée Ozenfant (1886–1966) is a Purist form of Cubism in a rigorous architectural setting.

Léger's early style went through various phases. Part of the avant-garde group around 1908, like Delaunay, he was interested in the Bergsonian concepts of simultaneity and dynamism, duration and time. The dynamic shapes of mechanized cones, cylinders, wheels and pistons are colourfully introduced in *The Discs* (1918). A passionate humanist and moralist, he was deeply moved by the *poilu* (the enlisted men), next to whom he fought in the trenches during the First World War. From then he abandoned abstraction and sought to create an art accessible to ordinary people based on the human figure

although *L'Homme à Pipe* (1920) features a robotic, mechanical man.

Abstraction: Abstraction between the Wars varies from the rigorous *Planes Diagonaux* (1925) by Franz Kupka (1881–1957) to the hard-edged painted wood relief *Polychrome Relief* (1920) by Auguste Herbin (1882–1960), and the biomorphic shapes in *Constellation aux Cinq Formes Blanches et Deux Formes Noire* (1932) by Jean Arp (1887–1966).

Dada and Surrealism: Collages by Dada artists include Kurt Schwitters (1887–1948), *Miroir Collage* (1920–22), made of rubbish and framed by Tristan Tzara who donated it to the museum; *Vase de Fleurs* (1924–26) by Francis Picabia (1879–1953), elegantly 'drawn' in wire and straw; and Jean Crotti's (1878–1958) *Le Clown* (1916), on glass. De Chirico (1888–1978), an inspiration to the Surrealists, is represented by *Mélancolie Hermétique* (1919). There is a host of Surrealist memorabilia, including the 1938 International Surrealist Exhibition catalogue, works by André Masson (1896–1987), Picabia, and Max Ernst's *Fleurs* (c. 1928–29) using the technique of *frottage*, as well as examples of the *Cadavre Esquis* (1927–31), a game of folded paper where each member of a group adds a drawing. The large collection of works by Victor Brauner (1903–66), includes a portrait of André Breton.

School of Paris: Examples of diverse interpretations of the human figure by School of Paris artists include *Woman with a Fan* (1919) one of many portraits of Lunia Czechowska, a typically stylised and flat painting by Modigliani, and the enigmatic portrait of a society beauty, *The Sphinx* (c. 1925) by Kees Van Dongen (1877–1968). *The Dream* (1927) by Chagall is a colourful painting inspired by the circus and open to deeper interpretation. Ossip Zadkine (1890–1967) was an inspired woodcarver who combined Cubism and Classicism in *Orpheus* (1928–30). There are also Expressionist portraits by Chaime Soutine (1894–1943), deformed and almost caricatural; paintings and sculptures by the Bulgarian dandy Jules Pascin (1885–1930); and an elegant nude by Foujita (1899–1968), *Femme Couché à la toile de Jouy* (1922). Marcel Gromaire evokes the conditions of toil and resignation in his monumentally composed works such as *Le Faucheur Flamand* (1924).

French painting: The museum owns 104 works by Raoul Dufy (1877–1953), covering his career from his brief brush with Fauvism to a more graphic and distinctive pre-war style, in works such as the *Abandonned Garden* (1913), a style that softened in the 1930s into a technique reminiscent of watercolour, such as *Thirty years or La Vie en Rose* (1931) where line and colour separated. By the 1940s he was producing tonal paintings of hedonistic scenes and throughout much of his career he was a well-known fabric designer.

Edouard Vuillard painted portraits of his fellow artists, including Pierre Bonnard (*see box opposite*). Bonnard's paintings in the museum reflect his production in the South of France after 1925, such as *Luncheon* (c. 1932) and *Nude in the Bath* (1936).

The work of Jean Fautrier shows a desire to create a living reality, and was first received with incomprehension. He remained a solitary figure who donated 14 works to the museum. An ironic early work is *Sunday Walk* (1921–22), of doll-like figures during the inter-year wars in Tyrol. From his black period is *The Great Black Boar* (1926). *The Jewess* (1943), in thick impasto layers, was painted during executions which took place near the painter's home, and is linked to his important *Hostage Series* (1945; *see p. 270*). From his series *Objects* comes *The Ink Well* (1948), which uses plaster impasto with a sprinkling of pigment or diluted oil paint. His work is seen as the forerunner of Art Informel, spontaneous abstract painting which dominated the 1950s.

Jeunes Peintres de Tradition Française was the name of a group of French and foreign artists who aimed to continue, in a modern, predominantly non-figurative way, the French artistic heritage. Among them were Jean Bazaine (1904–2000), inspired by Cubism and medieval stained glass; Alfred Manessier (1911–93); and Joseph Sima (1891–1971).

Gaston Chaissac (1910–64) who exhibited in the Art Brut exhibition in 1949, is represented by *Totem* (1963–64), a humorous and roughly hewn painted object. Jean Dubuffet (1901–85) who coined the term Art Brut, is represented by *Chaussée Boiseuse* (1959), made from plant material, part of a series *Elements botaniques*.

Lyrical Abstraction: Post-1960s Lyrical Abstraction, which owes a debt to Japanese calligraphic painting and experimented with single colours, is the

Pierre Bonnard (1867–1947)
Bonnard is renowned for his emotionally charged canvases, luminous with colour. Initially using decorative pattern in contrast to areas of flat colour, in later works paint texture and colour become as important as the subject. The painter would take a daily walk, noting down compositions on tiny scraps of paper or in his pocket diary, with a blunt pencil. These drawings were his emotional response to the walk, what he called his 'sensations'. For Bonnard, colour was 'reasoning', and many of his paintings took him years to complete as he agonised over colour balances, trying to find equivalents in paint for his pencil notations. There are stories of Bonnard revisiting his pictures, even in museums, and secretly touching up small areas that did not satisfy him. One of his main sources of inspiration was his life-long partner Marthe who is seen frequently in the bathroom. She was a reclusive figure, apparently suffering from a nervous condition—hydrotherapy was then a popular medical treatment—but the bathroom itself gave Bonnard the chance to understand the problems of painting white. In many of his paintings the walls and floor of the bathroom blaze with colour while Marthe's ageless figure glows in the tub. Bonnard's pictures are unusual in that it takes us some time to understand the viewpoint. Bonnard said that his paintings should give you the sensation of walking into a room where you see 'everything and nothing at the same time'. They are very carefully composed but loosely painted. 'To tell you the truth I have trouble with painting', he said, but it is through his struggle with colour that he gives us back the emotion that he first felt on his morning walk.

Pierre Bonnard: *Nude in the Bath* (1936).

IMPRESSIONISM

The style that became known in 1874 as Impressionism changed the art world for good. It revolutionised painting techniques, altered the way colour was used, and threw open the choice of subject. It represented a new approach to capturing nature on canvas and the fleeting effect of light on different objects through the analysis of tone and colour with a heightened palette. It was a rupture with the accepted norm of a laboriously outlined image. To a confused and unprepared public, it appeared unfinished and blurred, yet this revolution had been underway since the 1860s. When Monet's *Impression Sunrise* (1872) of the dawn over the port of Le Havre (*pictured on p. 354*) was exhibited in 1874, the journalist Louis Leroy wrote a derisory article, calling it *L'Exposition des Impressionistes*. The name stuck and the event became known as the First Impressionist Exhibition. As well as Monet, another 38 artists contributed over 165 works, including Degas, Renoir, Sisley, Pissarro, Cézanne, Guillaumin, Boudin and Berthe Morisot. The exhibition ran for a month from 15th April in studios formerly used by the photographer, Nadar, on Blvd des Capucines (*see p. 244*). Despite the ridicule, this was a major turning point for the *plein-air* painters, several of whom had been turned down by the Salon. The group had established its solidarity and identity. Eight more Impressionist exhibitions were held, the last in 1886.

The threads that were drawn together can be found in philosophy, the work of earlier painters, social and demographic changes, and scientific developments. In the early part of the 19th century, the philosopher Jean-Jacques Rousseau and the novelist George Sand drew attention to the healing properties of country life and solitude. Life was changing for the general public during the Second Republic, with the creation of public parks and gardens, the vogue for sea bathing and boating, and the *guingettes* or *bals*, open-air dances. In the first half of the 19th century colour theory was also a hot topic, based on the research work of chemist Michel Eugène Chevreul (1786–1889) whose colour wheel for the Gobelins tapestry house illustrated how colours influence each other. In 1839 he published his law on simultaneous contrasts, demonstrating that the eye demands that opposite colours or contrasts be generated, and on optical mixing, the way that the eye fuses colours. He codified something that painters probably already knew instinctively, such as the complementary colour of a shadow. The Director of Fine Arts, Charles Blanc (1830–82), expanded on Chevreul's work in 1865, and these ideas were further explored by American physicist N.O. Rood (1855–1902) and the French scientist philosopher Charles Henry (1849–1926).

Impressionist artists are described as painters of modern life. Their aim was to record life as it was experienced, in opposition to the studied and overworked academic classics of history, religion or artificially picturesque landscapes. The young painters came from all walks of life, and were generally apolitical, making little comment on social hardships even though some suffered considerable deprivation themselves. They captured the spontaneity of regattas, celebrations, boating parties and picnics, in beautiful settings; also city streets, railway stations, factory chimneys, foggy London and frozen landscapes, to record an effect. Their subject matter also proved to be more accessible to the public. The use of bright prismatic colours applied in small patches produced a flickering effect and a vivacity never previously found in finished paintings.

In the 18th century painters made oil-studies out of doors, and landscape as a subject had begun to be appreciated seriously in the wake of English and Dutch landscape painters and in France through Corot, Boudin and Jongkind. Changes in technique were encouraged by the freer brush-strokes and more innovative use of colour that had been pioneered by Delacroix and Courbet. The most direct influence on the future Impressionists was the Barbizon group, who experimented in *plein-air* painting in Fontainebleau Forest. The capture of the moment out-of-doors, however, and the application of new colour theories, could never have been fully explored without the more affordable synthetic pigments developed in the 19th century. They offered a greater choice of hues, and provided the saturated colours necessary to the new movement. Ready-mixed with a support such as oil or gum Arabic, and after 1841 available in collapsible metal tubes, they greatly enhanced the possibilities of painting *en plein air*. Alongside were improvements in the type of brushes available and outdoor painting kits with lightweight easels.

Photography was also challenging the reasons for painting, and providing a new way of seeing. In 1826 Nicéphore Niepce took the first steps in France on the road to photography, and by 1850–60 the medium had made great strides. Early photographs on glass plates were blurred or showed the effect of strong sunlight eating into solid objects destroying the clarity of contour. The work of photographers in Fontainebleau Forest was secretly admired by the Barbizon painters. The influence of Japanese art also opened up new possibilities— unconventional viewpoints, seemingly arbitrary cut-off points, rejection of traditional perspective, patches of flat colour, or the omission of detail.

By the 1880s Impressionism was going through a crisis, triggered by disunity, attacks by critics, and new trends such as Symbolism. Many who were connected with Impressionism for a time, such as Cézanne, Manet, Renoir, van Gogh, Gauguin and Seurat, developed in different directions. Speed and spontaneity began to be shunned in favour of the monumental and timeless. Yet by the end of the century Impressionism had provided impetus and inspiration for many movements and artists, notably Post-Impressionism and Fauvism, Matisse and Léger. Pissarro and Sisley continued to embrace the Impressionist ethos, but it was Monet above all who pushed to the limit his quest for effects of light and colour to produce canvases as ephemeral as music. In the 20th century, Impressionism would come to be seen as decisive in preparing the way for Modernism.

Claude Monet: *Impression Sunrise* (1872).

interior of the cathedral in great detail, with animated and colourful figures. Distinctive for its curious iconography is *Nature's Lament to the Wandering Alchemist* by Jean Perreal, showing the alchemist in conversation with a winged figure, perhaps his spirit medium, his alchemical equipment in the background. Quite different in concept is the *Admiral of Graville Hunting the Wild Boar* (after 1493), an animated and vigorous French work with a decorative border featuring coats of arms. It comes from a manuscript called *The Terrier of Marcoussis* recording events in the life of a medieval aristocrat. The *Kiss of Judas* (late 15th century) from the *Great Hours of Anne of Brittany* by Jean Bourdichon, who was court painter and Fouquet's successor, evokes the intensity

of the episode with a crowded scene dramatically lit. Italian works include several beautiful examples by Lucchino Giovanni Belbello da Pavia (fl. 1430–62); and the remarkable Renaissance page of parchment *The Baptism of Constantine* by Giovanni dei Corradi, the intial 'P' made up of elements of Classical architecture.

Jules Marmottan Collection: From the original collection of Jules Marmottan, father of Paul, are Flemish, German and Italian works, including an elegant *Virgin and Child* (c. 1500) set in a charming medieval landscape with buildings, and *Descent from the Cross* by Hans Muelich. An outstanding 16th-century French tapestry illustrates the *Story of St Susanne*.

First Empire Collections: These collections are made up of decorative and fine arts. There is a considerable group of paintings associated with the Napoleonic Empire, notably of Italy, and of members of Napoleon's family, including a miniature portrait of the Viceroy of Italy, Eugène de Beauharnais as the Prince of Venice, by Giambattista Gigola, and a portrait of Désirée Clary (1910), the future Queen of Sweden, by Gérard. Landscapes include *Napoleon and Marie-Louise in a boat on the Carp Pond at Fontainebleau* by Xavier Bidault and Louis Boilly, and there are two paintings of the interiors of art studios. Furniture includes desks by George Jacob-Desmalter and Pierre-Antoine Bellangé; an extraordinary geographical clock, designed in 1813 but altered after the fall of the Empire, inlaid with painted Sèvres porcelain medallions representing time zones (it revolves at 4pm each day); and a *Surtout de table* by P.-P. Thomire, in gilded bronze.

Claude Monet Collection: The collection of works by Claude Monet in the Marmottan is the largest in the world. The works are displayed in the lower gallery and include the most notorious of all Impressionist works, *Impression Sunrise*. First exhibited in 1874, it gave its name to the most important artistic movement of the 19th century (*see pp. 352–353*). This priceless canvas, among others, was stolen from the Marmottan in 1985, but happily all were recovered five years later in Corsica. It shows a hazy blue dawn with indistinct outlines of boats, suggesting the chill of the early day, but a hint of colour from the rising sun reflects in the sky and in the water. The paint handling is very loose, and the sun's reflection is accomplished in vibrant impasto strokes.

The wealth of pictures here includes many drawings and sketches of his family and others. The *Beach at Trouville* was painted after his marriage in 1870 when the couple and their son Jean went to one of the seaside resorts that had become fashionable in the mid-19th century. Shortly after war was declared, and he left for London for some months.

Monet returned to live in Argenteuil, which became the subject of several works here, including *Walking near Argenteuil*, the *Railway Bridge* and *Argenteuil in the Snow*. Trains, stations and bridges were characteristic of his repertoire. *A Train in the Snow* (1875), similar to *Impression Sunrise*, is a symphony of greys with just the bright train lamps shining through the cold mist. He travelled from St-Lazare station to Argenteuil, and made many studies and paintings en route, including the great 19th-century bridge, *The Pont de l'Europe* outside the Gare St-Lazare.

His fascination with light reflected in water ran throughout his work. He captured different effects in *Vertheuil in the Mist* (1879), *The Beach at Pourville, Sunset* (1882), *The Etretat Cliff* (c 1885), and *London, Houses of Parliament* (1899) with a glinting Thames. *Rouen Cathedral, Effects of Sunlight–Sunset* (1892) is one of about 20 canvases over which he toiled to express variations created by light in different atmospheric conditions, rendering the cathedral an insubstantial shimmering object.

Most haunting perhaps are his views of the gardens at Giverny, where he went to live in 1883. He later bought the house, created the gardens, and from this time onward waterlilies, willows, wisteria, the Japanese Bridge and their reflections in the ponds, became his constant inspiration. From 1912 he suffered eye problems. After a cataract operation in 1916, his perception of colour remained irreversibly distorted. The beautiful soft blues and mauves of the earlier lily ponds, the soft oranges and yellows of the Hemerocalis and Iris, intensify into stronger tones with the Japanese Bridge in 1918. The views across the garden in the 1920s are crescendos of colour of barely decipherable form; despite his failing sight, they are extraordinary celebrations of colour.

Other Impressionists: The wealth of paintings in this small museum does not end with Monet. There is Corot's *The Lake at Ville-d'Avray seen Through Trees* (1871); *Monet Reading* (1872) by Renoir; the well-known *Paris Street in the Rain* (1877) which the painter Caillebotte gave to Monet; the glowing *Bowl of Tahitian Flowers* by Gauguin; several works by Berthe Morisot, including *Small Girl with a Basket*; and the magnificent *Portrait of Berthe Morisot* by Edouard Manet. Many other leading Impressionist painters are also represented in the museum, but may not necessarily be on show, among them Sisley, Jongkind and Pissarro.

FONDATION LE CORBUSIER
Map p. 472, A3

Open Mon 1.30–6, Tues–Thur 10–12.30 & 1.30–6, Fri 10–12.30 & 1.30–5, Sat 10–5, closed Sun and holidays; T: 01 42 88 41 53.

Villa Jeanneret and Villa La Roche are adjacent villas designed in 1923 by Le Corbusier (Charles-Edouard Jeanneret; 1887–1965). Situated at 8–10 Sq. Dr-Blanche, the former contains the library of the Le Corbusier Foundation which holds a large part of the Le Corbusier archives. Villa La Roche is a prime example of the spirit of Le Corbusier and an essential visit for anyone interested in the Modern Movement. The house, built for a Swiss banker, Raoul La Roche, is designed around a main hall leading to two different sections of the house—private and public—and contains paintings, sculpture and furniture. The overall impression is of light and carefully articulated space.

THE BOIS DE BOULOGNE
Map p. 472, A1

The Bois de Boulogne, at 845 hectares, is slightly smaller but better known than its counterpart on the other side of the city, the Bois de Vincennes (*see p. 315*). It encompasses gardens, lakes, the Longchamp and the Auteuil racecourses. The suburb of Boulogne-Billancourt lies to the south, and the Seine to the west, on the far side of which rise the hills of Mont Valérien, St-Cloud, Bellevue and Meudon. There are four main entrances to the Bois from central Paris, namely Porte Maillot (at its northeast corner); Porte Dauphine (at the western end of the Av. Foch); Porte de la Muette (at the south end of the Av. Victor-Hugo); and Porte d'Auteuil (at its southeast corner). Between the last two is the subsidiary Porte de Passy. The Bois is divided diagonally by the long Allée de Longchamp, leading southwest from Porte Maillot towards Carrefour de Longchamp, a popular equestrian rendezvous.

HISTORY OF THE BOIS DE BOULOGNE

The Bois de Boulogne is a tiny remnant of the Forest of Rouvray, part of the band of forest once surrounding ancient *Lutetia* which became a hunting ground for the kings of France. Although the châteaux of La Muette, Madrid and Bagatelle, and the Abbey of Longchamp were erected on its borders, the Bois was neglected until the middle of the last century. Quantities of timber went for firewood during the Revolution and a large part of the Allied army of occupation bivouacked here after Waterloo. It was the haunt of footpads and often the scene of suicides and duels. In 1852 it was handed over by the State to the City, tamed, landscaped and sub-divided into an extensive park, becoming a favourite promenade of the Parisians. The model was Hyde Park in London, which had so impressed Napoléon III. More trees were felled in 1870 to reduce protective cover for the Prussians. The equestrian scenes which were such a favourite subject of Constantin Guys often had the Bois in the background. Now the Blvd Périphérique tunnels below the eastern and southern edges of the Bois, which is bounded on the north by Neuilly.

PARC & CHATEAU DE BAGATELLE

Garden open May–Aug 9–8; Sept–April 9–7; Château open Sat, Sun and holidays, visits at 3 and 4.30; daily in summer during temporary exhibitions; T: 01 45 01 20 10.

Skirted by the Route de Sèvres at Neuilly, are the walls of the Parc de Bagatelle (24 hectares), a delightful and well-tended oasis, made up of several gardens in different styles, but most famous for its rose-garden, at its best in mid-June, when the annual International New Rose competition takes place in the Orangerie. Earlier in the year it is carpeted with spring flowers and later it has a display of asters. Concerts are also held here. Landscaped, with a wide selection of trees, as well as follies, streams, waterfalls and lakes, the planting shows the influence of the Impressionists' preference for massed blooms—J.-C.-N. Forestier, the Garden Conservator in 1905, was a friend of Monet.

History of the Château de Bagatelle

The small, elegant Château de Bagatelle, a *folie* or country residence, was built for a wager within 64 days by Bélanger for the Comte d'Artois, later Charles X, in 1779. The dome was added in 1852. Napoleon occupied it, and in 1815 it returned to the Comte d'Artois, before passing to the Duc de Berry. Purchased in 1835 by the eccentric Richard Seymour-Conway, 4th Marquess of Hertford (1800–70), on his death the house and its fine art collection became the property of his natural son Sir Richard Wallace (1818–90), as well as the apartments at no. 1 Rue Lafitte and no. 2 Rue Taitbout where Seymour-Conway also collected art treasures. Created baronet in 1871 and a Member of Parliament from 1873 to 1885, Wallace took up residence in London in 1873 taking with him much of his art collection. A great benefactor of Paris, he provided 50 drinking-water fountains (*see p. 36*) and also built the Anglican church of St-George (1887–88) in Rue Auguste-Vacquerie. In 1890 Lady Wallace (1818–97) inherited Sir Richard's property, and he was buried in Père Lachaise cemetery (*see p. 330*). She bequeathed the English collection to the Wallace Collection in London and the French property, including the contents of Bagatelle and Rue Lafitte, to her adviser, John Murray Scott (1847–1912). Bagatelle was acquired by the City of Paris in 1904. The contents of Rue Lafitte went via Lady Sackville of Knole to a Parisian dealer, dispersing the art collections throughout the world.

Elsewhere in the Bois de Boulogne

To the southwest is the Hippodrome de Longchamp, opened in 1857 and on the north, a windmill (restored), almost the only relic of the Abbey of Longchamp, founded in 1256 by St Isabel of France, sister of Louis IX. From the Carrefour de Longchamp (just east of the windmill), a road leads due east past the Grande Cascade (an artificial waterfall) to skirt the enclosure of the Pré-Catelan (according to legend, named after the troubadour Arnaud Catelan, murdered here c. 1300). The Jardin Shakespeare has specimens of plants and trees mentioned in Shakespeare's plays. Further east are buildings of the Racing Club de France, flanking the west bank of the Lac Inférieur, with two linked islands. Boats may be hired on the east bank. To the south is the Lac Supérieur, beyond the Carrefour des Cascades; in the southeast corner of the Bois is the Hippodrome d'Auteuil (steeplechasing).

NEUILLY-SUR-SEINE
Map p. 2, A1

From the Arc de Triomphe (*see p. 220*), Av. de la Grande Armée descends northwest to Porte Maillot, a great meeting of principal routes and the site of extensive blocks of buildings in recent years. Beyond Porte Maillot, the wide Av. Charles-de-Gaulle bisects Neuilly-sur-Seine, once the most fashionable suburb of Paris. Part of the district covers the former park of Louis-Philippe's château (built in 1740, burned down in 1848), which was developed as a colony of elegant villas, although later apartment blocks now temper the distinctive character of the neighbourhood. The southern part is adjacent to the Bois de Boulogne. In the old cemetery lie Anatole France and André Maurois and in the Cimetière de Lavallois-Perret, the suburb north of Neuilly, are the tombs of the revolutionary anarchist and *Communard* Louise Michel (1830–1905) and the composer Maurice Ravel (1875–1937).

OUTSKIRTS OF PARIS

Paris is in the middle of the Region of Ile de France, which includes six further *départements*: Hauts-de-Seine, Yvelines, Seine-Saint-Denis, Val-de-Marne, Essonne, Seine-et-Marne and Val-d'Oise. The sights described in this section fall outside the main ring road, the Boulevard Périphérique, but can easily be reached by Metro or RER. Those to the west are defined by the Seine which, after crossing Paris, makes a series of tight meanders before flowing away towards Le Havre and the English Channel. Hauts-de-Seine, which is defined by the first tight loop of the river, includes La Défense, Nanterre, Rueil-Malmaison, St-Cloud, Boulogne-Billancourt, Sèvres, Meudon and Sceaux. The former royal palaces of Versailles and St-Germain-en-Laye are further west, in the Département d'Yvelines, also on the banks of the Seine, as are Maisons-Laffitte and Poissy. La Villette is on the northern periphery of the city of Paris, whereas St-Denis is in the Departement de Seine-Saint-Denis and beyond (in Val d'Oise) is the Château d'Ecouen. Vincennes (although included in the Right Bank section, *see p. 137*) with a once-important royal château and large park, is also just beyond the confines of Paris in the Val-de-Marne.

LA DEFENSE

La Défense, the culmination of Parisian 20th-century bravado, is a distinctive and now familiar silhouette to the west of Paris beyond the Arc de Triomphe and the Seine, in the Département des Hauts-de-Seine (*on map p. 2, A1*). La Défense may not be everyone's idea of a great day out in Paris, but is fascinating for its modern art and architecture. It is at its best at midday during the working week, when this young and dynamic quarter comes to life, or during events such as fun-runs or the Fête de la Musique.

HISTORY OF LA DEFENSE

In 1958 a government project to set up a business centre in this area took shape and 750 hectares, belonging to the three adjacent communes of Courbevoie, Nanterre and Puteaux, on the edge of Paris, were earmarked. This is a revolutionary two-tier city, the upper level being car-free with all rail and road traffic networks hidden below ground including the RER, Metro and bus stations and car parks (26,000 spaces). The Blvd Circulaire which surrounds La Défense is, in fact, a nightmare to drive on. The vast expanse of main esplanade is the prolongation of the greatest of all Parisian perspectives, planned in the 17th century as a royal highway between Paris and St-Germaine-en-Laye (*see p. 395*). The project was never completed, but by 1863, Napoléon III had extended the Av. de la Grande Armée as far as Chantecoq Hill and placed a statue of Napoleon there. This statue was replaced by Barrias' *La Défense de Paris* (1883) to commemorate the defence of Paris against the Prussians in 1871, from which the area takes its name. EPAD, a public organisation, was set up to take overall responsibility for the development. The construction of the RER line in 1970 brought La Défense within rapid reach of central Paris. The first building of consequence was the CNIT Centre (1955–58), a triangular-shaped flat-domed exhibition hall designed by a group of young architects, including Jean Prouvé (1901–84), R.-E. Camelot, Jean de Mailly, B. L. Zehrfuss and Nicolas Esquillan, with the largest concrete vaulted roof in the world. It was renovated in 1980. The Grande Arche de La Défense was inaugurated in 1989 and another pioneering building was the 34-storey Tour Hoechst-Roussel, adjacent to Pont de Neuilly. The latest building is the CBX Tower (2005), described as *Une tour dans le vent*, by Kohn Pedersen Fox Associates, on the Blvd Circulaire. With 34 storeys and shaped like the hull of an ocean liner, it has a monumental entrance 18m high. La Défense is nearly 50 years old and is beginning to show considerable signs of wear and tear. A decision has been taken to launch a regeneration project, including the construction of new tower blocks, to be completed by 2013. EPAD will continue to oversee this project at least until 2010.

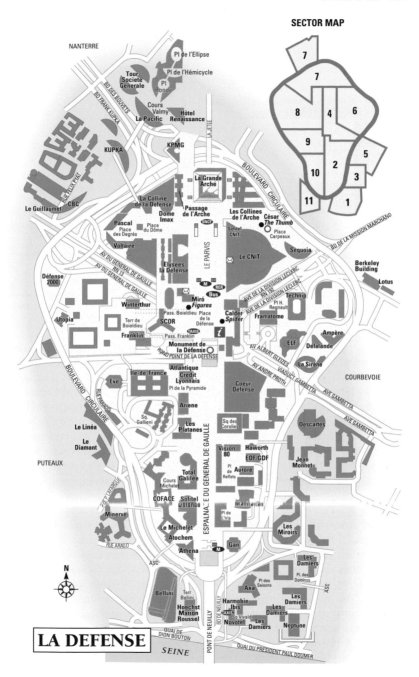

SECTOR MAP

LA DEFENSE

THE GRANDE ARCHE

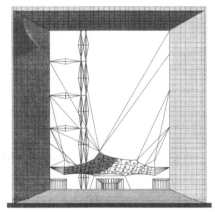

GRANDE ARCHE DE LA DEFENSE

ARC DE TRIOMPHE

Open April–Sept 10–8, Oct–March 10–7; T: 01 49 07 27 57; www.grandearche.com
This is an arch which dwarfs all others and dominates even the tallest *grattes-ciel*. A Danish architect, Johann Otto von Spreckelsen, chosen by Président Mitterrand from 424 projects, came up with the unusual design, which was completed in mid-1989. Although called an arch it might better be described as a colossal hollow cube, open on two sides. It sits on 12 huge piles sustaining a weight of 300,000 tonnes. The whole is pivoted very slightly from the main axis of La Défense. Suspended below the arch is a cloud-like awning. A series of exterior elevators rise to the summit from where there is an awesome view over the surrounding buildings and down the straight vista to the Arc de Triomphe, the Tuileries and finally the Louvre. On the 35th floor is a space for permanent exhibitions, Galerie 3D, and a room of models, also used for temporary exhibitions of contemporary art. There is also the gourmet restaurant Ô110 (*open 11.30am–2.30am; T: 01 49 07 27 32*), and a brasserie (*open 10–5*). Looking out from the Grande Arche, some of the most eye-catching buildings include, to the south, the angular Pascal Towers (1983), and to the northeast, the dark monolithic 46-storey Ariva Tower (1974), reflecting the prismatic Total Tower (1985) adjacent. The rectangular towers with rounded ends, east of the CNIT, are Coeur Défense (2001) and beyond that rises the Descartes Tower (1988). Due east at the end of the Esplanade stands the GAN Tower (1974) and opposite it is the triangular-shaped AXA Tower (1974). Facing the arch, on the other side of the main axis, is the sharp-angled AGF-Athena Tower (1984).

EXPLORING LA DEFENSE

In front of La Grande Arche is the Parvis de la Défense overlooked by the enormous CNIT building (National Centre for Industry and Technology), with hotels, shops, offices and event spaces, and on the opposite side Le Quatre Temps shopping mall (1981). Further east at 15 Pl. de la Défense is **Espace Info-Défense** (*open Mon–Fri 10–6: T: 01 47 74 84 24, www.epaladefense.fr*), an information bureau which also includes the Musée de la Défense where models, photographs and maps illustrate the key stages in the development of the area, and the projects that were never realised. From Pl. de la Défense is a view onto the 19th-century monument of La Défense on the Rond-Point below. Here also is Alexander Calder's large *Red Spider* stabile.

The Esplanade of La Défense is the largest pedestrian area in the Paris region. A kilometre long, it is bordered by green spaces and enlivened with a variety of sculptures, fountains and murals. There are some 60 contemporary works, witty and monumental, among them Agam's *The Esplanade Fountain*, with mosaics made in Venice, and a version of César's monument *Thumb*. Two colourful fantasy figures are typical of Joan Miró, and another water feature is Takis' *Pool and 17 Light Signals*. By Moretti, *Le Moretti*, is a 32m high ventilation shaft transformed by 672 fibre glass tubes in different colours, and Maurizio Toffoletti has carved giant white marble columns. Other works include Venet's *Indefinite Double Lines*, and installations by Calder and Anthony Caro. Curiosities include a piece of the Berlin Wall at the foot of the Aviva Tower.

An extensive development in Nanterre, just beyond the Grand Arche incorporates the 25ha **Parc André Malraux**, which is the largest park created in Paris since the beginning of the century, using soil extracted from the commercial district, and part of an ambitious scheme to improve the area. In Nanterre is the Université de Paris X, where student unrest began in 1968 (*see p. 54*).

Typical lunchtime scene on the steps of the Grande Arche de la Défense.

RUEIL-MALMAISON

Tourist information office: 160 Av. Paul-Doumer, 92500-Rueil-Malmaison, T: 01 47 32 35 75, www.rueil-tourisme.com; RER Line A (direction St-Germain-en-Laye) and Bus 258.
Rueil-Malmaison, on the banks of the Seine west of Paris, has close associations with the early Empire period through the Châteaux of Malmaison and Bois-Préau. The suffix Malmaison was added in 1928. This is an attractive town with walks along the Seine as well as Japanese and rose gardens near the tourist office. In the church of Rueil (1584, west façade of 1635 by Lemercier), is the tomb of the Empress Josephine (1825), and that of Hortense de Beauharnais is in the chapel erected in 1858 by her son, Napoléon III. He also donated the 15th-century Florentine organ-case by Baccio d'Agnolo. In the former *Mairie* is a Museum of Local History (*open Mon–Sat 2.30–6; closed Sun, Aug, and holidays*) ranging from the Neolithic period to the time when the Impressionists patronised the *guinguettes* on the banks and the islands of the Seine near Rueil.

MUSEE NATIONAL DU CHATEAU DE MALMAISON

Open April–Sept Mon, Wed–Fri 10–5.45, Sat, Sun 10–6.15; Oct–March Mon, Wed–Fri 10–12.30 & 1.30-5; Sat, Sun 10–12.30 & 1.30–5.45; closed Tues; T: 01 41 29 05 55.
Malmaison's collections concentrate on the earlier Napoleonic period, the Consulate and on Josephine and her two children by her first husband, Eugène (1781–1824) and Hortense (1783–1837). The annexe (*see p. 366*) is devoted to Napoleon in exile.

HISTORY OF THE CHATEAU DE MALMAISON

The château was built c. 1620 and became, from 1799, the country residence of Napoleon and Josephine, who chose it for the park, then covering 800 hectares, with the intention of rebuilding the house. Napoleon considered the best days of his life spent here, when all was going well, in the large country house which became an official residence. The work of transforming the interior was entrusted to Fontaine and Percier. Joséphine (Marie-Josèphe Rose) Tascher de la Pagerie (1763–1814), born in Martinique, the daughter of a nobleman, had married Alexandre, Vicomte de Beauharnais, in December 1779; he was guillotined in 1794. In 1796 she married Bonaparte, who crowned her Empress in 1804. Josephine retired here with her children, after her divorce in December 1809, and continued to develop her passion for botany and gardening. She died at Malmaison five years later of a chill caught while entertaining visiting allied sovereigns. Malmaison was later bought by María Cristina of Spain, and in 1861 was acquired by Napoléon III. Despoiled of most of its contents, it was sold in 1896 to the philanthropist Daniel Osiris (1828–1907), who refurnished it and presented the château to the State as a Napoleonic museum.

The collections

The Musée National du Château de Malmaison contains superb collections of furniture and fittings, carpets, porcelain, silver, clocks (all in working order) and a variety of objets d'art of the early Napoleonic period. Among the furniture are several pieces made specifically for the Consul and his wife by Jacob Frères and other *ébenistes*, and such personal pieces as Josephine's bed (designed by Jacob-Desmalter), dressing-table, dressing case and embroidery frame. Showcases display a large number of smaller souvenirs. All the rooms on the ground floor have been returned to their former state according to Fontaine and Percier's original drawings for the interior. Restoration work began in 1985 to recreate the original Neoclassical décor by the painstaking removal of up to eight layers of subsequent paint, followed by retouching where necessary. The antechamber of the Salon was restored in 2003. The next project is the first-floor apartments of the Empress.

Visiting the museum

The entrance is through an enclosed porch or vestibule in the form of a tent which was added in 1800. The **Main Hall**, on the ground floor, in Antique style, contains marble busts of the Bonaparte family; further busts are displayed throughout the building.

The paintwork in the **Billiard Room** has been stripped back to the original of 1812, and this room contains pieces by Jacob Desmalter from the great gallery and an Empire-style billiard table. In the **Drawing Room** (Salon Doré) are severe Egyptian-style furnishings by Jacob Frères including the chairs (c. 1800) in mahogany with Egyptian heads, upholstered in blue with gold trim. There are Romantic paintings by Gérard and by Girodet, both similar in style and both inspired by the poems of 'Ossian'. The poems of Ossian, published 1761–65, purported to be written by a mythical Gaelic bard, and inspired many 19th-century northern European painters and writers, but were in fact the work of the Scot's poet James Macpherson. The restoration of the delightful **Music Room** was completed in April 1999. It contains Josephine's harp and the pianoforte belonging to Hortense. In Josephine's day it was used as a gallery especially for pictures in the troubadour style, as depicted in the painting by Garnerey, and the chairs (1800) in red by Jacob Frères have been re-upholstered.

To the left of the Main Hall, the **Dining Room** has frescoes of dancers by Louis Lafitte inspired by Pompeii. The **Council Chamber**, the setting for the creation of the Legion of Honour, has been returned to its original design by Percier of a military tent and contains a portrait by Gérard, *Joséphine Seated* (1801), a signed version of the original in the Hermitage, St Petersburg. The adjoining **Library**, also by Percier and Fontaine, has books retrieved (about 500) from Napoleon's personal collection, originally some 4,500, a travelling chest for books used by him during his campaigns, and a desk from the Tuileries Palace. When the weather was fine, Napoleon worked outside.

At the foot of the stair is a *Head of Napoleon* by Canova. On the first floor were the apartments of Napoleon, of Hortense and Eugène, and of Josephine. The **Emperor's Apartments**, in part reconstructed, display various memorabilia, and his former bedroom replicates the original as closely as possible. It contains a copy of Gérard's painting of the *Emperor in Coronation Robes* (original at the Louvre), and the painting *Empress Joséphine* (c. 1809) by Gros shows the park of Malmaison. Here is one of Napoleon's grey coats, as worn at St-Helena, and his *nécessaire de toilette*.

Exhibition rooms are dedicated to Bonaparte as General and Consul, with objects such as one of his sabres, and the tricolour he carried in Egypt, as well as David's original painting of *Bonaparte crossing the St-Bernard Pass* (five replicas elsewhere), signed on the harness L. David, *l'an IX* (1800). It is a great propagandist work, showing the First Consul on a rearing white charger; Bonaparte in fact crossed the Alps on a mule. Bacler d'Albe's portrait, *General Bonaparte* (1796/7), can also be seen here. Other works include Isabey's drawing *Napoleon as First Consul at Malmaison* and *The First Consul after Marengo* by Gros. The pedestal table, known as the Austerlitz Table, in Sèvres porcelain and bronze, commemorates Napoleon's victory over Austria in 1805.

The rooms dedicated to Josephine in her role as Empress contain the portrait *Empress Joséphine* by Gérard and a bust by Joseph Chinard, as well as a display of luxury items, including porcelain such as the beautiful Egyptian tea set of Sèvres that was Napoleon's last present to Josephine before the divorce. Other items on display include a Louis XVI watch and chain which belonged to her, and her dressing table (c. 1800) from the Tuileries. A little painting of Malmaison c. 1805 was purchased by Josephine in 1799 while Bonaparte was occupied with Egypt. **Josephine's State Bedroom**, restored as it was after 1812 to an unusual but elegant red and gold tent-like oval, was shared by the couple until 1803, and is where she died. It contains the original bed. The **Empress's Ordinary Bedroom**, which she preferred, is brighter and lighter, and has hidden cupboards for her private papers and jewellery. On the second floor is space for temporary exhibitions.

Outside, only six hectares remain of the original 200 hectares of gardens. Beds are planted with those varieties of rose grown by Josephine with the help, until 1805, of her English gardener, Mr Howatson. The gardens were celebrated in their time and the blooms were later reproduced in coloured drawings by Pierre-Joseph Redouté. The famous cedar planted by Josephine to celebrate the victory of Marengo in June 1800 can be seen from the music room.

The coach house and park

To the left of the entrance lodge, on the way out, is the Coach House, with Napoleon's *landau en berline* used at Waterloo and taken by Blücher. Also here is the St-Helena hearse, presented by Queen Victoria. Behind is the Pavillon Osiris (closed for renovations until c. 2008) with collections of caricatures, medallions and snuffboxes propagating the Napoleonic legend, and a portrait of Tsar Alexander I by Gérard. Beyond the other side of the entrance drive is a summer house used as a study by Napoleon when First Consul.

From opposite the entrance, a few minutes' walk through the park will take you to the **Château de Bois-Préau**, dating from 1700, and acquired by Josephine in January 1810 as an annexe in which to accommodate her entourage and visitors, and to house part of her collections. It was later sold and in 1926 bequeathed to the State by its then American owner, the millionaire Edward Tuck (*see p. 216*). The château is closed for restoration for the foreseeable future.

The **Petite Malmaison** (*open by appointment Sun June–Sept; T: 01 47 32 02 02*), now privately owned, was constructed in 1805 for Josephine as a place to receive and entertain visitors when they visited the greenhouses, which were originally attached but no longer exist.

ILE DE CHATOU

Rueil 2000 is an attractive modern area on the banks of the Seine looking out towards the Ile de Chatou, also known as the Ile des Impressionnistes. On the island is the last remaining *guinguette* (an out-of-town café which also offers music and dancing), the **Maison Fournaise**, now a restaurant (*T: 01 30 71 41 91*) with a museum (*open Thur–Sun 12–6; T: 01 34 80 63 22*). As the setting of Renoir's *Le Déjeuner des Canotiers* (1881), this location has been revived as a tribute to the Impressionists who came to paint and eat here. An Impressionist Festival is held one Sunday in June. Just beyond Rueil, at Bougival, is the house where Georges Bizet died (1875) and also the datcha built by the Russian novelist Ivan Turgenev (*open Sun 10–6, T: 01 45 77 87 12*) where he died of cancer, urging his arch rival Tolstoy to 'return to literature', in 1883.

BOULOGNE-BILLANCOURT
Map p. 2, A4

Tourist information office: 28 Rue Le-Corbusier, Boulogne-Billancourt, T: 01 55 18 50 50, www.boulognebillancourt.com; Metro: Marcel-Sembat, Boulogne-J.-Jaurès

Boulogne-Billancourt, known as such since 1925, is celebrated as the town of the Modern Movement because of the remarkable concentration of buildings of the 1920s and 30s. It also has a 1930s' museum (*see below p. 368*). The automobile (Renault, in 1898) and aeronautical industries took root in the area, but in the 1920s it was still empty and inexpensive, and the Metro had just extended this far, an attractive prospect for artists and architects making their name, such as Juan Gris and Chagall, Landowski and Lipchitz, and Le Corbusier, Auguste Perret, Rob Mallet-Stevens and Tony Garnier; the film industry was represented by Abel Gance and Jean Renoir; art dealer Henri Kahnweiler lived here, as did André Malraux for 17 years. The Parcours des Années 30 is an architectural walk—or bike ride—past the best of the Modernist buildings (a booklet is available from Musées des Années 30). Around Rue Denfert-Rochereau are buildings by L.-R. Fischer, Le Corbusier and Robert Mallet-Stevens; at the angle of Rue des Arts and Allée des Pins are two *résidences-ateliers* of 1924, by Le Corbusier; and there are more examples of experimental architecture of the 1920s by Auguste Perret, and André Lurçat in Rue du Belvédère. In Rue Nungesser-et-Coli (near Parc des Princes) is an apartment block (1932) by Le Corbusier. The Musée-Jardin Paul-Landowski, 14 Rue Max-Blondat (*T: 01 46 05 82 69*) is included in the route.

MUSEE DES ANNEES 30

Open Tues–Sun 11–6, closed Mon, holidays and last two weeks of Aug; T: 01 55 18 46 42.
This is a small and very pleasant museum, installed at no. 28 Av. André-Morizet, Boulogne-Billacourt, in the old Hôtel des Postes (1938) by Charles Giroud (1871–1955). It has a rare collection of Neoclassical and avant-garde works of the inter-war period and reflects the artistic and industrial heritage of Boulogne-Billancourt which developed at the time. The Central European artists of the School of Paris are also well represented; the art dealer who supported them, Henry Kahnweiler, lived in the town at 12 Rue de l'Ancienne-Marie. There are some 800 paintings by artists such as Boutet de Monvel, who painted in a naïve style, and Lempicka who is best known for his angular portraits. There are also many landscapes by Henry de Waroquier, the result of his travels in Spain and Italy in the early 1920s, and sculpture is well represented with about 1,500 pieces by artists such as Belmondo, the monumental sculptor Paul Landowski, new classicist Joseph Bernard and the architect Alfred Janniot. The decorative arts include a glass screen by L. Barillet in the white glass that he pioneered, a chaise longue by Jean Prouvé, and chairs designed by Kahnweiler and Juan Gris.

MUSEE ALBERT KAHN

Open May–Sept Tues–Sun, 11–7, Oct–April Tues–Sun 11–6; closed Mon; T: 01 46 04 52 80; Metro: Porte de St-Cloud.
The Musée Albert Kahn, at no. 14 Rue du Port. is both a collection of early photographs and a garden. Albert Kahn (1860–1940), banker and humanist, lived here between the two wars. His vision was to create a utopia where all nations might coexist and communicate in perfect harmony through deeper knowledge and understanding. Such was his fortune that he was able to finance photographic and film records of the customs and environment of about 50 countries between 1900 and 1931 for his Archives of the Planet. These amount to 72,000 autochrome images—the earliest colour photography—on glass plates, 4,000 black and white images, and around 183,000m of filmed sequences in black and white. They form a remarkable and precious record, as well as being often beautiful images in themselves, of countries such as China in 1905, Ireland in 1913, or Patagonia in the early 20th century. Annual exhibitions draw on the collections, which can also be viewed on interactive terminals. Kahn was ruined by the stock market crash in 1929. His garden, the Jardin du Monde, covers 3.9 hectares, landscaped between 1895 and 1920, and continues the theme of bringing nations together. The informal English garden is jux-taposed with the formal French one, a Palmarium and a rose and fruit garden. Beyond are wooded landscapes representing the Vosges and the North American Blue Forest divided by the Prairie and the Swamp. Close to the gallery are his original Japanese Village, and a modern Japanese Garden (1990) which evokes Mount Fuji and symbolically represents the life of Albert Kahn.

DOMAINE NATIONAL DE SAINT-CLOUD

Map p. 2, A4

Open daily May–Aug 7.30–10; Mar–April, Sept–Oct 7.30–9; Nov–Feb 7.30–8; museum open Wed, Sat and Sun 2–6; T: 01 41 12 02 90. Metro: Pont de Sèvres/Boulogne-Pont de St-Cloud.
The great park of St-Cloud (Domaine National; 460 hectares) lies on a ridge overlooking Paris, with grand perspectives, views and sophisticated cascades and fountains. Philippe d'Orléans (Monsieur), younger brother of Louis XIV, employed Le Pautre and Hardouin-Mansart to design a palace and fountains, and Le Nôtre to create the gardens. St-Cloud's porcelain factory (1695–1773) and palace both burned down, the latter during Prussian occupation (1870–71), and the ruins were cleared away in 1891. From the main entrance you pass the former outbuildings of the château, one of which contains a very modest museum. On the terrace, the site of the château is marked out with flowerbeds and yews. To the north is the English-style Jardin de Trocadéro with a small lake, created at the time of Louis XVIII and in the opposite direction is the Bassin du Fer à Cheval extended by an alley to a green amphitheatre created in the 18th century. Below the château terrace is a large pond that serves as reservoir for the **Grande Cascade**. This magnificent example of hydraulic magic, using only gravity, is brought to life on Sundays in June. The upper part of the cascade, all of which is decorated with sculptures of figures, sea monsters, masks and *rocailles*, was the work of Le Pautre in 1660–65 and the lower part was by Hardouin-Mansart in 1698–99. Not far from here is the **Grand Jet**, which dates back to the 16th century, and a fountain with six nymphs. To the west, beyond the terrace, is the fountain with 24 water jets, long perspectives, alleys, more basins, fountains and woodland. During the gales of Christmas 1999, some 17,500 trees were lost but have since been replaced.

SEVRES

Tourist information office: Hotel de Ville, 54 Grande Rue; open Mon–Fri 8.30–12.30 & 1.30–5.40, Sat 8.30–12; T: 01 41 14 10 10; www.ville-sevres.fr
Sèvres is a pleasant town which has retained something of a village atmosphere. Illustrious residents have included Sisley, Balzac, Eiffel and Gambetta. It was once an important port on the Seine, but is most closely associated with the Royal Factories of glass and porcelain.

MUSEE NATIONAL DE CERAMIQUE DE SEVRES

Open Wed–Mon 10–5, closed Tues; T: 01 41 14 04 20; www.musee-ceramique-sevres.fr Metro: Pont de Sèvres; Tramway T2.
On the edge of the park of St-Cloud at Pl. de la Manufacture is the Musée National de Céramique de Sèvres established here by Alexandre Brongniart, director of the factory 1800–47 and son of the great architect, at the beginning of the 19th century,

in a magnificent building. Porcelain is still produced here: a boutique sells replicas and modern pieces. The porcelain factory founded in 1738 was moved here from Vincennes in 1756 at the request of Mme de Pompadour, and since 1760 has been state-controlled. Among designers of Sèvres porcelain were E.-M. Falconet and J.-B. Pigalle.

The collection

This is an immense collection of some 5,000 ceramic pieces from France and other countries, dating from Antiquity to the present. It is laid out geographically and thematically, arranged by country and by technique or type, over two floors. The collections include Greek and Roman pottery, European glazed pottery from the 12th to the 18th centuries such as a Byzantine plate and a piece by Bernard Palissy; Chinese and Islamic ceramics from antiquity to the 14th century; Ottoman and Safavid siliceous ware (15th–18th centuries); 14th- to 18th-century Italian majolica and Hispano-Moresque faience, and South American pre-Columbian pottery. Sèvres porcelain is, of course, given pride of place, with displays devoted to the history of the factory, the history of porcelain, and examples of Sèvres porcelain from 1740 to the present day up to the 20th century. Seventeenth and 18th-century European porcelain is represented by faience from Nevers, Moustiers, Rouen, Strasbourg, Marseille and Sceaux and others.

MAISON DES JARDIES & VILLE D'AVRAY

Open Thurs–Sun 2.30–6.30; otherwise by appointment; T: 01 44 61 21 69.
In Sèvres (off the N10 towards Ville d'Avray), the Maison des Jardies, at no. 14 Av. Gambetta, was the occasional country retreat of Balzac in 1837–41. More importantly, it is now preserved as it was when inhabited by Léon Gambetta (1838–82), a proclaimer of the Republic in 1870, while president of the Chamber from 1879 to 1882.

The 18th-century church of St-Marc-St-Nicolas in Ville d'Avray (mainline station), contains frescoes by Corot, who often painted the lakes in the Bois de Fausses Reposes, further southwest.

MEUDON-SUR-SEINE

Meudon, whose benefice Rabelais enjoyed in 1551–52 and where Wagner wrote *The Flying Dutchman* in 1841, is southwest of Paris, and was home to August Rodin.

MUSEE-ATELIER DE RODIN

Open April–Sept Fri–Sun 1.30–6; T: 01 41 14 35 00. RER Line C to Meudon Val Fleury then bus 169, or Metro 12 to Mairie d'Issy then bus 190.
Rodin lived at the modest Villa des Brillants with Rose Beuret, from 1895 until his death in 1917. The Rodin Museum (*see p. 116*) in Paris was never the sculptor's home. The house is set in a large garden above the Seine, and behind is his large, glazed *atelier*. A

few rooms of the house can be visited, including the dining room which contains his academic gown from Oxford. In the *atelier* are numerous plasters, large and small, which demonstrate the inventive re-use and reassemblage he made of existing parts, and casts of his major works. In the garden is part of the sculptor's collection of antiquities.

CHATEAU DE SCEAUX

Open April–Sept Wed–Mon 10–6; Oct–March 10–5, closed Tues; T: 01 46 61 06 71. RER Line B to Bourg-la-Reine/Sceaux/Parc de Sceaux
The long, broad Allée d'Honneur leads across a stone bridge over the dry moat to the entrance of the Château de Sceaux whose great park takes up a large part of the town of Sceaux and is a popular place on a summer's day. The entrance to the château is grand enough, announced by gates, with crowns and monogrammed NT (Napoléon-Trévise), between two sentry posts (1670–73) with sculptures of a unicorn overcoming a dragon and a dog overpowering a wolf, symbolising probity and fidelity respectively. Just before the entrance on the right is an early 18th-century drinking trough. Beyond is the domed Pavillon de l'Aurore (*open April–Sept Sat, Sun, 4–6; Oct–March Sat, Sun 3–5*), which faces east and was designed by Claude Perrault in 1670–72. The interior of the cupola is decorated inside with an allegory of Aurore, Roman goddess of the dawn, by Charles le Brun. Very few of these garden pavilions, an Italian fashion, have survived in France. Inside the gates, to the right, is the *Intendance* (the steward's house) dating from the end of the 18th century.

HISTORY OF THE CHATEAU DE SCEAUX

The château itself is somewhat disappointingly a 19th-century pastiche of a Louis XIII mansion which replaced the sumptuous 17th-century château built here for Jean-Baptist Colbert (1619–83), who rose to be Secretary of State to Louis XIV. Colbert and his son, the Marquis de Seignelay (1651–90), created the magnificent park and gardens. Jules Hardouin-Mansart was appointed by the Marquis de Seignelay to build a new orangery in 1686, about 88m long. It was damaged in 1870, and reduced by about a third. Restored, it is now used for exhibitions and conferences. In 1699 the estate passed to the Duc du Maine, son of Louis XIV and Madame de Montespan. The duke spent his time translating Latin works, while the ambitious duchess (1676–1753) created a literary and artistic court. Voltaire wrote *Zadig* here; and works by Racine, Molière and Lully were performed in the Orangerie. Sold during the Directoire, the house was razed and the gardens levelled and in 1856, the Duc de Trévise had the present house built (1856–62) by Joseph-Michel le Soujaché. The interior is decorated in the Louis XIV and Louis XV styles, fashionable during the Second Empire.

Musée de l'Ile de France

Since 1937 the Château de Sceaux has contained the Musée de l'Ile de France. It includes displays on the history of the property and its main owners, with original plans and drawings from the time of Colbert and the Marquis de Seignelay up to the 19th-century château, portraits of Colbert attributed to Lefebvre, and of the Duchess of Maine by De Troy. The **Royal Residences Room** displays paintings, engravings and furniture evoking the châteaux of Marly, St-Germain-en-Laye or Choisy, as they once were. There is a collection of predominantly 18th-century ceramics and porcelain from the Paris area and a series of views of the Ile de France, several by Paul Huet. Donations from artists, such as the watercolours and engravings by Dunoyer de Segonzac, and sculptural and painted versions of Jean Fautrier's series *Hostages* (*see p. 270*), are also included in the museum.

The park and environs of the Château de Sceaux

The majestic park with its pleached limes and great perspectives, was laid out by Le Nôtre, and is a miniature of Versailles'. South of the château is a series of cascades leading to the Octagon. Parallel to the west is the Grand Canal. From here you have a view of the Pavillon de Hanovre, moved here in 1934 from the Blvd des Capucines. After the Revolution many of the statues which embellished the park were taken to the Louvre and the Jardins de Luxembourg. Close to the chateau are 19th-century copies from the antique; near the cascades are bronze *mascarons* by Rodin, and around the Octagon are 17th-century copies from the antique. At the end of the Tapis Vert west of the chateau are four statues, two 17th- and two 19th-century.

A short distance northwest of the château, across the park, is the old churchyard of Sceaux, where the fabulist Florian (1755–94) is buried. The simple tombs of Pierre (1859–1906) and Marie Curie (née Sklodowska; 1867–1934), the discoverers of radium, are in the local cemetery (though their remains have been translated to the Panthéon; *see p. 48*). Some 2.5km west, in the Parc de la Vallée aux Loups, is the residence of Chateaubriand (1768–1848), restored in 1807–18 (*open April-Sept Tues–Sun 10–12 & 2–6; Oct–March 10–12 & 2–5; T: 01 43 50 42 48*).

North of Sceaux, the double Aqueduct de Arceuil crosses the valley of the Bièvre (*see p. 101*) 2km south of the Blvd Périphérique. The lower part was built in 1613–23 by Marie de Médicis to supply the Luxembourg fountains; it was preceded by a Roman aqueduct, built in the 4th century to bring water to the Palais des Thermes. Both the composer Erik Satie and the artist Victor Vasarely lived in the suburb of Arceuil.

VERSAILLES

The town of Versailles is dignified and affluent, as befits its regal history, with imposing avenues that converge on the château and park, and regularly laid out streets. With a population of some 90,000, it lies on a low sandy plain between two lines of wooded hills and is the Préfecture of the Département of Yvelines. The town is well worth exploring and makes a very pleasant alternative base to Paris. It has many elegant 17th- and 18th-century buildings, a lively market area, and hotels and restaurants of all categories. Pl. d'Armes and Av. de Paris divide the centre into two distinct *quartiers* around its two main churches, the cathedral of St-Louis and the church of Notre-Dame (*see p. 393*). Versailles can easily be reached from Paris on RER line C5 to Versailles-Rive Gauche (the nearest station to the château); and on mainline trains from Gare St-Lazare to Versailles-Rive Droit or from Gare Montparnasse to Versailles-Chantiers.

CHATEAU DE VERSAILLES

Versailles is the most famous palace in the world. Begun by Louis XIV in the 17th century, from the start it was the model that royalty all over Europe wished to emulate. Adapted and amended by his successors, Louis XV and Louis XVI, the combination of palace, museum and gardens is almost overwhelming, both in splendour and size; to appreciate thoroughly it would ideally require two days. Over one hundred rooms of the former royal palace can be visited and another hundred contain the Musée de l'Histoire de France. The 815 hectares of grounds encompass two smaller palaces, the Grand Trianon and the Petit Trianon on Queen Marie-Antoinette's estate, the Baroque garden designed by Le Nôtre, and the wooded park along the Grand Canal.

Opening times
April–Oct Tues–Sun 9–6.30; Nov–March 9–5.30; last admission is 30 minutes before closing Closed on Mondays, some public holidays and during official ceremonies.

Information
Recorded information T: 01 30 83 77 77; general information T: 01 30 83 78 00; information on guided tours and other activities T: 01 30 83 77 88; www.chateauversailles.fr

Types of visit
The château and gardens may be visited independently; guided tours (tickets sold on the day from 9 am) include parts of the château not open to independent visitors. Themed visits, Sept–June, in French, are described in the brochure 'Découvrir Versailles'; advance telephone reservation is essential on T: 01 30 83 77 89.

One Day Pass (*Entrance* **E** : *see plan on p. 378*): *Includes priority access, with audiogu-ide, all year round to all non-guided visits of the State Apartments, Chapel and Opera House, History of France Galleries, the Dauphin's Apartments and King's Bedchamber, plus at week-ends the Grand Trianon. In high season (April–Oct) also included are Marie-Antoinette's Estate, plus the Coach Museum and Grandes Eaux Musicales at weekends and on holidays.*
Palace Ticket: *Includes State Apartments, Chapel and Opera House, History of France Galleries, Dauphin's Apartments and King's bedchamber, and at weekends the Mesdames' Apartments, and high-season weekends also the Coach Museum.*
On-Line Ticket Sales: *In development at time of writing; www.chateauversailles.fr*
Horse-drawn carriages: *Rides through the gardens depart from the north terrace, T: 01 30 97 04 40, www.caleches-versailles.com*
Shuttle Service: *By tourist train, return journeys from the North Terrace to to Marie-Antoinette's Estate and Trianon Estate, and La Petite Venise; T: 01 39 54 22 00, www.train-versailles.com*

Bookshops, cafés and restaurants

The Ancienne Comédie bookshop specialises in 17th- and 18th-century works, in Cour des Princes, T: 01 30 83 76 90. Cafés and restaurants include the Cafeteria, in Cour de la Chapelle, T: 01 39 50 58 62; and in the grounds La Flottille Restaurant, T: 01 39 51 41 58; and La Petite Venise Restaurant, T: 01 39 51 41 58.

HISTORY OF THE CHATEAU

Versailles emerged from obscurity in 1624, when Louis XIII built a hunting lodge on this site, which was extended into a small château, with a garden laid out in 1639. The royal estate once covered an area of 8,000 hectares, surrounded by a 43km-long wall and entered by 22 gates. It was reduced to 815 hectares after the Revolution. The château was the birthplace of Louis XV (1710–74), Louis XVI (1754–93), Louis XVIII (1755–1824) and Charles X (1757–1836). The real creator of Versailles was the Sun King, Louis XIV, who after his marriage to Marie-Thérèse in 1660 conceived the building as a lasting monument to his reign. Louis le Vau (*see p. 38*) was entrusted with the renovation and embellishment of the old building around the Cour de Marbre, while Le Nôtre laid out the park (1660–70). After Le Vau's death in 1670 the work was continued by his pupil François d'Orbay, and the interior decoration was supervised by Charles le Brun. Jules Hardouin-Mansart, appointed chief architect in 1678, radically remodelled the main body of the château, replacing Le Vau's terrace with the Hall of Mirrors (*see p. 380*). The South Wing and then the North Wing followed, resulting in the immense façade of 580m with 375 windows. On 6th May, 1682, Louis XIV announced his intention to make Versailles the seat of government. The workforce employed on the building and in draining and laying-out the grounds in 1684 amounted to 22,000 men and 6,000 horses, which emptied the coffers of France. Yet the Trianon was built 1687–88. Louis XIV lived on a construction site for the whole of his reign. Life at Court was a superficially scintillating scene that disguised monotonous

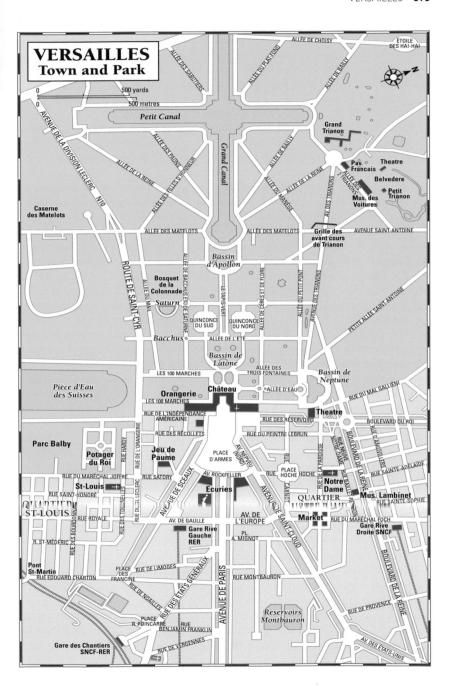

VERSAILLES
Town and Park

0 | 500 yards
0 | 500 metres

ALLÉE DE CHOISY

ÉTOILE DES HAI-HAI

ALLÉE DES SABOTIERS

ALLÉE DU PLAFOND

ALLÉE DE BAILLY

Petit Canal

ALLÉE DES PAONS

ALLÉE DE LA REINE

ALLÉE DE BAILLY

Grand Canal

ALLÉE DES FILLES D'HONNEUR

ALLÉE DE LA REINE

ALLÉE DE LA REINE

ALLÉE DU MANÈGE

AVENUE DE LA DIVISION LECLERC N10

Grand Trianon

Pav. Francais

Theatre

Belvedere

AV. DES TRIANONS

ALLÉE DES 2 TRIANONS

Petit Trianon

Mus. des Voitures

Caserne des Matelots

ALLÉE DES MATELOTS

ALLÉE DES MATELOTS

Grille des avant cours de Trianon

AVENUE SAINT-ANTOINE

Bassin d'Apollon

ROUTE DE SAINT-CYR

Bosquet de la Colonnade

ALLÉE DU MAL

ALLÉE DE BACCHUS ET DE SATURNE

Saturn

LE TAPIS VERT

ALLÉE DU PETIT PONT

AVENUE DES TRIANONS

PETITE ALLÉE SAINT-ANTOINE

QUINCONCE DU SUD

QUINCONCE DU NORD

ALLÉE DE CÉRÈS ET DE FLORE

Bacchus

ALLÉE DE L'ÉTÉ

Bassin de Latone

ALLÉE DES TROIS FONTAINES

Bassin de Neptune

LES 100 MARCHES

Pièce d'Eau des Suisses

Orangerie

Château

ALLÉE D'EAU

RUE DU MAL GALLIÉNI

LES 100 MARCHES

ALLÉE D'EAU

Theatre

BOULEVARD DU ROI

RUE DE L'INDÉPENDANCE AMÉRICAINE

RUE DES RÉSERVOIRS

RUE DES RÉCOLLETS

RUE DU PEINTRE LEBRUN

RUE D'ANGIVILLERS

Parc Balby

RUE HARDY

RUE DE L'ORANGERIE

Jeu de Paume

PLACE D'ARMES

AV. NEPVEU (NORD)

RUE DE LA PAROISSE

RUE NEUVE NOTRE-DAME

BOULEVARD DE LA REINE

RUE SAINTE-ADÉLAIDE

Potager du Roi

RUE SATORY

AV. ROCKFELLER

PLACE HOCHE

HOCHE

RUE BAILLE ROBINE

Notre Dame

RUE DU MARÉCHAL JOFFRE

RUE DE SCEAUX

RUE

CARNOT

Mus. Lambinet

St-Louis

RUE SAINT-HONORÉ

RUE DE TOURNELLES

Ecuries

AVENUE DE SAINT-CLOUD

QUARTIER NOTRE-DAME

RUE SAINTE-SOPHIE

QUARTIER ST-LOUIS

RUE DE LECLERC

AV. DE GAULLE

AV. DE L'EUROPE

Market

RUE DU MARÉCHAL FOCH

RUE ROYALE

Gare Rive Gauche RER

PL. A. MIGNOT

Gare Rive Droite SNCF

R. ST-MÉDÉRIC

RUE DES BOURBONNONS

Pont St-Martin

PLACE DES FRANCINE

RUE DE LIMOGES

AVENUE DE PARIS

RUE MONTBAURON

BOULEVARD DE LA REINE

RUE EDOUARD CHARTON

RUE DE NOAILLES

RUE DES ÉTATS GÉNÉRAUX

Reservoirs Montbauron

RUE DE PROVENCE

PLACE R. POINCARÉ

RUE BENJAMIN FRANKLIN

RUE DE VERGENNES

Gare des Chantiers SNCF-RER

AV. DES ÉTATS-UNIS

routine, rigid protocol and ceremonious etiquette. Members of the Court fluttered in the orbit of the king during the daily drama of Versailles which was rife with intrigue and hypocrisy, all superbly described by the Duc de Saint-Simon in his *Memoires*. The king, absolute monarch by divine right, kept the nobility close to him to avoid plotting, reinforced by a network of spies. The main wings of the château were divided up into numerous diminutive suites to house individual courtiers and their families.

After Louis XIV's death in 1715, the château was abandoned until Louis XV attained his majority in 1722, when the Court returned, and remained until the Revolution. During his reign the building was further modified and transformed to the current style. The Salon of Hercules, one of the colonnaded pavilions in the entrance court, the interior of the Opera and the Petit Trianon were all built around this time by Jacques-Ange Gabriel. Louis XVI redecorated a suite of apartments for Marie-Antoinette and completed the rustic village or Hameau in 1783.

The independence of the United States was formally recognised by Britain, France and Spain in the Treaty of Versailles, signed in 1783. The meeting of the Assembly of the Estates-General was held in Versailles in 1789, where on 20th June the deputies of the Third Estate formed themselves into the National Assembly. On 6th October an angry mob, some 7,000 strong, led by the women of Les Halles, marched to Versailles and forced the royal family to return with them to Paris, where they were confined to the Tuileries. The Ancien Régime had amassed an incomparable collection of works of art, which was then split up. The furniture was publicly auctioned, paintings, antiques and gems went to the Louvre, and books and medals to the Bibilothèque Nationale.

The château was preserved by the Republic, but the Grand Canal had run dry. The palace hosted a museum, a school and a library. With the proclamation of Empire, Versailles became Napoleon's residence and he commenced refurbishment. During the Restoration, the second colonnaded pavilion was completed, but it was not occupied by royalty. Louis-Philippe (1830–48) rescued the palace from destruction, yet did irreparable damage to the apartments in order to house his Glories of France museum, inaugurated in 1837. During the Franco-Prussian War (1870–71), Versailles was used as a hospital and became the headquarters of the German armies. On 18th January 1871, King Wilhelm I of Prussia was crowned German Emperor in the Hall of Mirrors and on 26th January the peace preliminaries were signed at Bismarck's quarters at 20 Rue de Provence. The French Government took refuge here from 1871–75 and the National Assembly proclaimed the Third Republic from the opera-house, on 25th February, 1875. The general restoration of the complex began after the appointment of Pierre de Nolhac as curator in 1887.

During the First World War, Versailles was the seat of the Allied War Council. The Peace Treaty with Germany was signed in the Hall of Mirrors on 28th June 1919. Further extensive restorations were made in 1928–32, thanks largely to the Rockefeller Foundation, and continued after the Second World War under the curatorship of Gerald van der Kemp. During that war, the Allied GHQ was at Versailles from September 1944 until the following May, and many buildings were requisitioned by the military.

VISITING THE CHATEAU

Everything at the Château de Versailles is designed to impress, in dimensions and in beauty. There are scarcely superlatives sufficient to describe the whole ensemble of palace, gardens, park, water-features and Trianon palaces. The first view of it is designed to resemble a great Baroque theatrical set. Three wide Avenues (St-Cloud, de Paris and de Sceaux; *see plan on p. 375*) converge on Place d'Armes east of the château, which is separated from the courtyards by a monumental curtain of railings. Opposite the château entrance, between the avenues, are the Grandes Ecuries (housing the Carriage Museum; *see p. 386*) and Petites Ecuries, the royal stables in grand buildings of equal size. The main gate leads to the wide forecourt (Cour des Ministres) of the château which is flanked by detached buildings, once assigned to Ministers of State. At time of writing there is work on-going to reinstate Hardouin-Mansart's original wrought-iron railings and new walkways are being created. The long-term programme to restore the gardens to their original state, with the help of the archives, was accelerated after the storm of 1999, and improvements to the forecourt will be on-going until 2008.

Adding to the splendour of the forecourt are two groups of sculptures which symbolise *Victories over the Empire* by Gaspard Marsy, and *Victories over Spain* by Girardon. In contrast are *Peace* by Tuby and *Abundance* by Coysevox, themes repeated in the Hall of Mirrors and in the gardens. Beyond, between two colonnaded pavilions dating from 1772 (right) and 1829, is the Cour Royale. The equestrian statue of Louis XIV (erected 1836) which stands here, is being restored. At the time of Louis XIV, only those who possessed the 'honours of the Louvres'—called *cousin* by the king—had the right to enter by this route and to bring their carriage and liveried servants into the great courtyard. The charming little **Marble Courtyard** (Cour de Marbre), at the end of the Cour Royale, indicates the position of Louis XIII's château which was enveloped in later extensions by Le Vau and Hardouin-Mansart.

The State Apartments of the King

Entrance **A** *: this is the most frequented part of the palace, usually less crowded during mid-afternoon.*

The State Apartments (Grands Appartements du Roi) have conserved their original decoration, inspired by Italian palaces, including marble inlay, sculptured and gilded bronzes, carved doors and painted ceilings, carried out under the supervision of Charles le Brun for Louis XIV. They were intended as his Majesty's living quarters but from 1684 he had apartments prepared in the older part of the palace, where he and his successors resided. The original suite of rooms was then used for entertainment. Designed for the glorification of the Sun King, it derived its planetary theme (Abundance, Venus, Diana, Mars, Mercury and Apollo) from the Pitti Palace in Florence, and related to the king's actions, but in 1710 the theme was interrupted with a new room dedicated to the mythological hero, Hercules. The original furniture was sold after the Revolution.

CHATEAU DE VERSAILLES

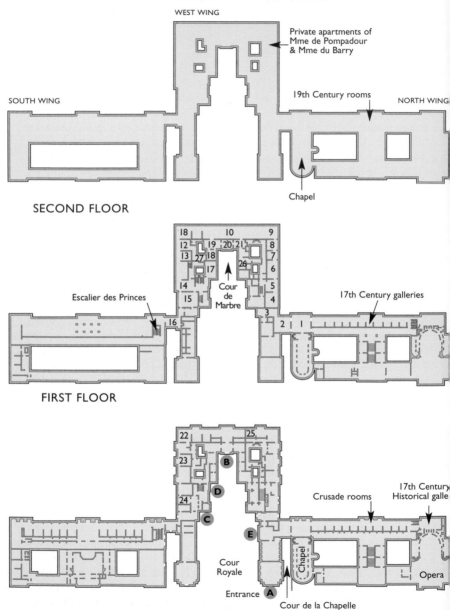

WEST WING

Private apartments of
Mme de Pompadour
& Mme du Barry

SOUTH WING

19th Century rooms

NORTH WING

Chapel

SECOND FLOOR

Escalier des Princes

Cour
de
Marbre

17th Century galleries

FIRST FLOOR

Crusade rooms

17th Century
Historical galle

Cour
Royale

Chapel

Entrance

Cour de la Chapelle

Opera

GROUND FLOOR

From the **Vestibule de la Chapelle** (1) on the first floor is a striking view of the Chapel, dedicated to St Louis (Louis IX). This is the level of the royal apartments and of the Royal Gallery where the king attended mass daily at 10am for about 30 minutes, descending to the nave only for major ceremonies. Mass was accompanied by music.

The **Salon d'Hercule** (2) one of the most impressive in the château, was fitted up by Louis XV in the Louis XIV style and inaugurated in 1739. It replaced a chapel demolished in 1710. The marbles and bronzes are of exceptional quality and announce the decoration of the Hall of Mirrors. The room is dominated by the great work by Paolo Veronese *Dinner in the House of Simon* (1570) given to Louis XIV in 1664 by the Republic of Venice, and has a grand frame moulded by Jacques Verberckt. The painting was installed only in 1730, at the time of Louis XV, and inspired the décor and colours of the room, including, on the ceiling, the vast *Apotheosis of Hercules* painted by François Lemoyne in 1733–36.

The **Salon de l'Abondance** (1680; 3) was a small reception room that Louis XV used for rare paintings and objets d'art, and it was also used for refreshments during major receptions. It has royal portraits by Rigaud and by J.-B. van Loo.

The **Salon de Vénus** (4) the main entrance to the State Apartments, named after its painted ceiling, has marble decorations in early Louis XIV style and original *trompe l'oeil* perspectives by Jacques Rousseau. In the central alcove is a statue *Louis XIV in Antique Costume*.

The former billiard room, the **Salon de Diane** (5) features the goddess of the hunt on the ceiling and a Bust of Louis XIV aged 27 (1665) by Bernini.

The **Salon de Mars** (6) had various uses, as gaming-room, concert hall and ball-room, and has paintings of Louis XV and Queen Marie Leszczynska by Carle van Loo.

Mercury on his Chariot on the ceiling of the **Salon de Mercure** (7), is by J.-B. Champaigne. The room has an 18th-century look with red-damask walls, a clock by Antoine Morand (1706), with automata, originally here, and two ornate tables with drawers by André-Charles Boulle made for the Trianon. This was the King's Bedchamber for a time, and Louis XIV lay in state for eight days here.

The most sumptuous room, the **Salon d'Apollon** (8) housed the nearly three-metre high silver throne, but was also used for dancing. In the centre of the ceiling is Charles de la Fosse's masterpiece, depicting Louis XIV (the *Roi Soleil*) as *Apollo in a Chariot Escorted by the Seasons*. The portrait of the king is a version by Rigaud of the original in the Louvre (*see p. 149*).

The **Hall of Mirrors** (10), together with its antechambers at either end, the **Salon de la Guerre** (9) and **Salon de la Paix** (11)—the War and Peace Rooms—form a brilliant ensemble occupying the west front of the building.

The **Salon de la Guerre**, completed in 1678, still has three of the six busts of Roman emperors, bequeathed by Mazarin and a stucco medallion of *Louis XIV on Horseback* by Antoine Coysevox. The ceiling painting, the first of a series designed by Le Brun, represents *France Victorious, Bearing on her Shield the Portrait of Louis XIV*.

The 73m-long **Hall of Mirrors** (Galerie des Glaces) is the best-known of all the rooms at Versailles and represents the apotheosis of the Sun King's palace. A scintillating masterpiece, it was begun by Jules Hardouin-Mansart in 1678 and its decoration, by Le Brun, was completed in 1684. Seventeen windows overlook the park, and opposite each is a bevelled mirror of equal size, made by the Manufacture Royale de St-Gobain, altogether an excessively lavish installation in the 17th century. Arches, surmounted by Apollo and the Nemean lion, are separated by red marble pilasters with bronze capitals featuring *fleurs-de-lys* and Gallic cocks. The gilded stucco cornice is adorned with crowns and the orders of chivalry. There are marble copies from the Antique of Venus, Paris, Mercury and Minerva. It is easy here to imagine the scene at the time of Louis XIV, with candlelight from 20 silvered bronze Bohemian glass chandeliers reflecting in the mirrors and falling on lavish furnishings and fabrics. Le Brun used his creative genius to the full in the decoration of the vaults, including paintings which illustrate the civil and military achievements of Louis XIV over the course of some 20 years. The central ceiling-painting, by Charles Le Brun, is *Louis XIV Omnipotent*. Heads of State are still entertained here during official visits.

The Apartments of the Queen

The Appartements de la Reine were occupied by Marie-Antoinette when she became Queen of France. Here she had to submit to all the formal public rituals against which she rebelled. The **Salon de la Paix** (11), was the queen's card-room. The ceiling completes Le Brun's scheme, depicting *France Bringing the Benefits of Peace to Europe*.

The **Chambre de la Reine** (Queen's Bedchamber; 12), has been lavishly restored to its appearance when Marie-Antoinette fled on 6th October, 1789. The chimney-piece comes from the Trianon and the ceiling painting by François Boucher was commissioned by Louis XV, c. 1730. Marie-Antoinette up-dated the décor with new silk hangings supplied by Lyon in 1787, and these were copied at Lyon in 1976 from pieces of original fabric. Her jewellery cabinet is by Schwerdfeger (1787) and bust by Félix Lecomte. The confinements of the queens of France took place in this room, and both Marie-Thérèse and Marie Leszczynska died here (in 1683 and 1768 respectively). The **Salon des Nobles** (13) was the queen's presence chamber.

Salle de Garde de la Reine (14) still has the marble décor of Louis XIV's time and original ceiling by Noël Coypel. It was here at the time of Louis XVI and Marie-Antoinette that the revolutionary mob, having mounted the staircase, burst in. Three of the Swiss Guards died in the queen's defence.

The **Salle du Sacre** (Coronation Room; 15) was restored following alterations by Louis-Philippe. Among the 19th-century paintings here, those above the door are by Gérard and on the walls are huge scenes by David, with titles which match the ostentation of the Ancien Régime, such as *Napoléon Presenting Eagles in the Champ-de-Mars* (1804), and the *Crowning of the Empress Josephine at Notre-Dame* (a copy of the Louvre original) as well as *Murat at the Battle of Aboukir* (1799) by Gros.

A small room leads to the **Salle of 1792** (16) with military portraits, which was originally the Salle des Marchands where vendors sold their wares to palace residents.

The **Escalier des Princes** gave access to the south wing, once reserved for the princes of the blood.

The Hall of Mirrors.

The King's Bedchamber

Reached via Entrance **C**, this is part of the main tour, but includes the Apartment of Louis XIV, the Hall of Mirrors, and the Apartments of the Dauphin and Dauphine. It is usually less crowded than the State Apartments. Initially these apartments were reserved for the Queen, but by 1683, Louis XIV had them adapted and preferred to live here rather than in the public State Apartments.

The Queen's Staircase leads to the first floor. Everyone passed through the **Salle de Garde du Roi** (17). The **Première Antichambre** (18) is where the king dined in public at 10 o'clock, with his back to the fireplace, an ancient royal ritual. The *grand couvert* was part of daily protocol, when Louis XIV was accompanied by the queen, his children and grand-children; at the *petit couvert* the king dined alone. The custom was less frequently observed during Louis XV's monarchy; on 1st January, 1764, Mozart (barely 8 years old) was invited with his father to attend the *grand couvert*. By the time of Louis XVI, the *grand couvert* occurred only on Sundays and holidays, an exercise that Marie-Antoinette found particularly tedious. The portrait of Marie-Antoinette in 1779 is by Elisabeth Vigée-Lebrun, who also painted the queen with her children (1787). Other portraits are of Louis XIV's aunts.

The Seconde Antichambre, known since 1701 as the **Salon de l'Oeil-de-Boeuf** (19) after the oval bull's-eye window, was the room where courtiers waited for admission to the king's *lever* (rising). The decorations are original, including the stucco frieze showing children frolicking on a gold background and busts of Louis XIV by Coysevox, Louis XV by Gois, and Louis XVI by Houdon.

The lavishly restored **Chambre du Roi** (20) became Louis XIV's bedchamber at the centre of the chateau in 1701 overlooking the Cour de Marbre. Here the ceremonious *lever* and *coucher* (retiring) of the king took place. Up to 100 members of the Court might attend the king as he prepared for the day. He would lunch daily at a little table placed before the middle window, and it was here that he died on 1st September 1715. The decorations of carved wood including the balustrade separating the (reconstructed) bed from the rest of the room have been regilded, but are in part original. Most of the rich brocades and other fabrics are modern remakes, scrupulously copied at Lyon from original samples. The sculpture of gilded stucco above is by Nicolas Coustou and the chimneypieces (1761) have bronzes by Caffieri. There is a *Bust of Louis XIV* by Coysevox and a *Self-portrait* by Van Dyck. On 6th October, 1789, it was from the balcony of this room that Marie-Antoinette and Louis XVI, at La Fayette's suggestion, showed themselves to the mob.

The adjacent large **Cabinet du Conseil** (21), a more sober room, dates in its present form from 1755, with *boiseries* by Antoine Rousseau. It contains the table on which the Treaty of Versailles recognising American Independence was signed in 1783. The route takes you through part of the Galerie des Glaces back to the Oeil-de-Boeuf room.

Apartments of the Dauphin and Dauphine

Also accessed via entrance **C**, the Apartments of the Dauphin and Dauphine are on the ground floor, overlooking the gardens, and were successively occupied by eight *dauphins* and their wives. The apartments have been repeatedly altered and much of the original decoration was spoiled or even destroyed by Louis-Philippe.

The Antichambre gives access to the Dauphin's **Seconde Antichambre** which contains some of Nattier's masterpieces including *Marie Leszczynska in a Houserobe*. The room with green decoration was the bedroom of Monseigneur (1661–1711), son of Louis XIV. It contains portraits of Spanish nobility. This room and the next, the **Grand Cabinet** (Dauphin's Study; 22), are graced with furnishings by the great 18th-century cabinetmaker, Bernard van Rysenburgh, who made the red lacquer Chinese style *cabinet* or library, and the flat-topped desk (1745) in the Grand Cabinet which belonged to the Dauphin. In this room, on the corner of the building and benefiting from garden views, are also chairs by Georges Jacob (*see p. 185*) which came from Louis XVI's Gamesroom at the Château de St-Cloud (*see p. 369*). A terrestrial and celestial globe enclosing a second one, on which are reliefs of the sea floor, was made by Mancelle in 1781 for Louis XVI who intended it for his son's education.

The **Cabinet de la Dauphine Marie** (23; a *cabinet* being an inner room) retains its original woodwork decoration. Above the door are *The Four Seasons* painted by Oudry, while the room has a *lit à la polonaise* (with four columns and an ornate canopy), the style introduced by Louis XV's wife Marie Leszczynska, daughter of Stanislas, deposed King of Poland. Louis XVI, Louis XVIII and Charles X were born in this room, which was also the bedroom of Marie-Antoinette on her arrival in France from Vienna in May 1770.

The **Première Antichambre** (24) of the Dauphin was originally a chapel, and is now devoted to the early years of Louis XV. Among many paintings are two portraits of the young Louis: *Louis XV as a Child* by Rigaud which shows him in 1716 at the age of five, after his accession to the throne; the other is by Simon Belle, *Louis XV In Coronation Robes* painted when he was 15. The young king succeeded his grandfather Louis XIV in 1715, and spent several years at Vincennes (*see p. 312*) before returning to Versailles.

Museum of the History of France

Entrance Ⓐ · *The galleries are not continuously open; 19th–century rooms by guided tour only; information T: 01 30 03 77 88/01 30 84 76 20.*

The huge collection, which covers 18,000 square meters, is dedicated to 'All the Glories of France' in paintings and sculpture. It was founded in 1837 by King Louis-Philippe, who commissioned 3,000 paintings and created the galleries. The glories—there are no defeats here—begin with the Crusades (Salle des Croisades, ground floor), and continue in the 17th-century rooms (ground and first floors), with an impressive collection of portraits and historical paintings from the accession of the Bourbons to the throne of France to the death of Louis XIV. Among the multitude of works is *Louis XIV at the Time of his Accession to the Throne* (1643), *Jacques Lemercier* by Philippe de Champaigne, and *The Carrousel* (tournament) by Henri de Gissey, which took place in front of the Tuileries Palace (*see p. 193*) in 1662. The 19th-century rooms (second floor) including the Battle Gallery, have few works concerning the Revolution, but many of the Directory, Consulate and Empire periods. Several rooms contain views of the many battles fought in the Revolutionary and Napoleonic wars such as *The Battle of Taillebourg* by Delacroix and portraits of the imperial family including Gérard's *Napoléon as Emperor of the French*. The collections include the Carriage Museum (*see p. 386*) and the Jeu de Paume.

The Chapel and Opera

Entrance **A**: *Mass is held in the chapel once a month in winter. Baroque Music Centre, Musical Thursdays, Royal Chapel Nov–June, T: 01 39 20 78 00.*

The chapel, with its colonnade of Corinthian columns, was begun by Jules Hardouin-Mansart in 1699 and completed in 1710 by Robert de Cotte. The high altar is of marble and bronze with sculptures by Van Clève. François Couperin was one of the great organists who played here. The central ceiling-painting is by Antoine Coypel, and above the royal pew is a *Descent of the Holy Ghost* by Jouvenet.

The Opera, or Salle de Spectacles, at the far end of the North Wing, is reached via two galleries. The Foyer retains its 18th-century decoration by Pajou. Although planned in the 1680s, the Opera was built for Louis XV by Gabriel in 1770 and was first used on the occasion of the marriage of the Dauphin (Louis XVI) and Marie-Antoinette, when Lully's *Perseus* was performed. It was repainted under Louis-Philippe, and in 1855 was the scene of a banquet given in honour of Queen Victoria. Modelled on the King of Sardinia's theatre in Turin, it is a perfect example of Louis XV decoration, having been skilfully restored (1955–57) by Japy, even the upholstery being copied from the original specifications.

Apartments of Mesdames, the Daughters of Louis XV

Entrance **B** : *Open to holders of One-Day Pass, and of Palace Ticket at weekends.*

The 18th-century rooms of Mesdames Victoire and Adélaïde are on the ground floor adjacent to the Royal Apartments, and include the Hall of the States General.

The **Première Salle** (25), once part of the former Bathing Apartment (a suite of bathrooms), was later occupied by Mme Victoire, an accomplished musician to whom Mozart dedicated his first six harpsichord sonatas in 1784. Paintings include *The English Tea-Party*, with Mozart at the harpsichord, by Barthémy Olivier. Over most doors are paintings by Oudry from *The Fables* of La Fontaine, or by J.-B. Restout of *The Seasons*, and portraits of Mesdames. There are also a harpsichord by Blanchet and a Gagliano violin which belonged to Mme Adélaïde. The first room of Mme Adélaïde's Apartments was the scene of Madame de Pompadour's unhappy death aged 42.

Private Apartments of Louis XV and Louis XVI

Guided visits only. Entrance **D** : *Reservation required at information desk on arrival. Information T: 01 30 83 77 89 /01 30 83 76 20.*

The Petits Appartements de Louis XV et de Louis XVI were known as the Cabinets du Roi in Louis XIV's day, where the king kept his most precious art treasures. This series of rooms was transformed by Louis XV in 1735 to provide a retreat from the tedious etiquette of his court. The rooms include the panelled bedroom in which Louis XV died of smallpox on 10th May, 1774; and the Cabinet de la Pendule named after a clock, by Dauthiau and Caffieri, placed here in 1754, surmounted by a crystal globe marking the phases of the sun, moon and planets. The sport of kings is illustrated by a frieze of hunting scenes in the Cabinet des Chiens, which was occupied by lackeys and the king's favourite hounds. Next door is the Dining Room des Retours de Chasse (after the hunt) overlooking the Cour des Cerfs. The **Cabinet Intérieur du Roi** (26), in the angle, is the grandest room in the apartment, with panelling and mirror frames considered the finest made by Verberckt, with original furniture of the time of Louis XV still in place, including a famous rolltop desk by Oeben and Riesener (1760–68). The Arrière Cabinet or Private Study, where Louis XV met his secret agents, led into the apartments of Madame Adélaïde.

The Cabinet de Musique de Mme Adélaïde, also with fine gilded boiseries by Verberckt, is where, in December 1763, Mozart played the harpsichord before Mme Adélaïde (1732–1800, 4th daughter of Louis XV) and other members of the family. The Bibliothèque de Louis XVI has Louis-XV furniture. The Salle à Manger of 1769 is sometimes known as the Porcelain Room, as an exhibition of Sèvres was held here each Christmas in Louis XVI's time. The Salle de Billiard and Salon des Jeux, where Louis XIV's collections of paintings and gems were displayed, became part of Mme Adélaïde's suite.

Private Apartments of Marie-Antoinette

Guided visits only. Entrance **D** : *Reservation required T: 01 30 83 77 89 /01 30 83 76 20.* The small and very secluded suite of Marie-Antoinette, situated between the state rooms and courtyards (27), offers a fascinating insight into the private life of the Court. The rooms retain their superb original decoration although fabrics have been remade. Among them are the Salle de Bains and the Nouvelle Bibliothèque used by the ladies-in-waiting. In the Salon de la Reine she received her intimate friends, and her musicians, Gluck and Grétry, and sat to Mme Vigée-Lebrun for her portraits. The Bibliothèque has imitation bookshelves over the doors and adjustable shelving. The Méridienne or Sofa Room, is an octagonal room redesigned by Mique in 1781, with the queen's day bed, the original pedestal table and two armchairs by Georges Jacob. Exquisite rooms used by the Queen for informal entertaining include the Salle à Manger and a bijou withdrawing room, which can hold a maximum of 10 people. There was a discreet route between the king's and queen's bedroom along back corridors.

The tour continues on the ground floor to the part of a three-room apartment adapted in 1784 for Marie-Antoinette with a charming blue and white Salle de Bains, a Louis XVI bed, and a Bibliothèque, its décor lost in the 19th century. The Galerie Basse, below the Galerie des Glaces, has been totally altered since Le Vau designed it in 1669. The steps between the two parts of the gallery compensate for the difference in level between the old and new châteaux. Molière put on several of his plays here, including the first performance of *Tartuffe* (1664). A bedroom, in pale green, with Georges Jacob bed and chairs and a dressing table by Riesener, contains the last state portrait of Marie-Antoinette (1788) by Vigée-Lebrun.

The four rooms—the Grand Cabinet, Inner Cabinet, Antichambre and Chambre—which make up the Appartements du Capitaine des Gardes, contain a painting of

Marie-Antoinette, aged ten, dancing at Schönbrunn. Also displayed is a copy of the famous diamond necklace which was the subject of a scandal in 1785. A scheming woman, calling herself Countess de la Motte-Valois, persuaded Cardinal de Rohan to buy the necklace to give to Queen Marie-Antoinette. When the necklace subsequently disappeared the Cardinal was arrested at Versailles. The scandal which ensued brought discredit on the queen despite the fact that she was not at all implicated in the affair.

Private apartments of Mme de Pompadour and Mme du Barry

Guided visits in French on certain days only. Information T: 01 30 83 77 89
On the attic floor of the North Wing, a diminutive suite was occupied by Mme de Pompadour (1721–64) from 1745–50 after which, no longer the king's mistress but still his confidante, she moved to the ground floor. Mme du Barry (1743–93) lived in these apartments from 1769–74. The beautiful *boiseries* have been restored.

Musée des Carosses

Open April–Oct Sat, Sun 9–6.30; T: 01 30 83 77 88.
The Carriage Museum is housed in the Grandes Ecuries (Great Stables), the domain of the Grand Equerry who was in charge of riding horses, built by Hardouin-Mansart in 1679–85 to accommodate 200 carriages and 2,400 horses. The collection was part of Louis-Philippe's History Museum (*see p. 383*), with vehicles dating mainly from the 19th century. Only six sleighs, sedan chairs and the Dauphin's berlin (future Louis XVII, d. 1789) are from the Ancien Régime. There are berlins used during the marriage of Napoleon, vehicles from the Imperial Court, and Charles X's coronation coach.

Jeu du Paume

Open April–Oct Sat, Sun 12.30–6.30; T: 01 30 83 77 88.
The Royal Tennis Court (1686) became famous on 20th June, 1789, when the deputies of the Third Estate, finding themselves locked out of the States-General, adjourned here. With the astronomer Jean-Sylvain Bailly (1736–93) as their president, they swore not to separate until they had given France a proper constitution. This is known as the Oath of the Tennis Court.

THE PARK & GARDENS

The Gardens and Groves are open daily, except during official ceremonies, and there is an admission charge on weekends from April–Oct 9–6.30. No charge after 6.30 and Nov–March. The park is open from 7 on summer mornings, from 8 in winter, and closes at dusk. Picnics are not allowed. Cycle hire is available. Grandes Eaux Musicales take place between 11 and 5.30 at weekends April–Oct; Grandes Eaux Nocturnes take place at 9 in July; Fêtes de Nuit take place at 9.30 on certain evenings Aug–Sept, for information T: 01 30 83 78 88.
The Gardens of Versailles are a *tour de force* of geometric perspectives creating a link between the architecture of the château and its surroundings. They divide into three

main sections: the formal ornamental gardens or *parterres* immediately surrounding the château; the forest in the distance, crossed by broad radiating alleys; and the area of the *bosquets* or groves, which provide the transition between the two. Louis XIV was as much involved in the gardens as in the palace and the whole project combines many devices to enhance the vistas and sense of drama, such as artificial lakes and ponds, rigorous alleys of trees, formal *parterres* designed to be viewed from above, statues and vases of marble and bronze, and the ultimate embellishment, the spectacular fountains.

HISTORY OF THE GARDENS

Louis XIV commissioned the celebrated landscape-gardener André le Nôtre to design the gardens, which were first laid out in 1661–68. The land was unpromising, with a sharp escarpment and marshes, entailing prodigious preliminary work of levelling and draining, and the importation of thousands of trees. Inspired by Italian originals, but interpreted on an unprecedented scale, Versailles represents the pinnacle of formal 17th-century French garden design. In their general lines and their Classical sculptural decoration, the gardens remain as planned, but it was not until the 18th century, at the time of Louis XV, that trees were planted to the present extent. Le Nôtre was aided by Jean-Baptiste Colbert (1619–83) who managed the overall project, and Le Brun for sculptural decoration and designs for the fountains. The supply of water to the fountains was, and still is, a subject of concern. Louis XIV's engineers devised a remarkable hydraulic system to bring water from the Seine via Marly (*see p. 402*). There are around 400 sculptures, the majority of them in place for some 300 years (the more fragile are replaced by plaster copies). Later, Jules Hardouin-Mansart introduced more sober décors, and doubled the size of Le Vau's Orangery. Each of the kings incorporated their own ideas, including areas inspired by the paintings of Hubert Robert at the time of Louis XVI. During the 19th century much was lost or altered. A 20-year programme of replanting to recreate the contrasting styles of Le Nôtre and Hubert Robert was provoked by the gales of 1990, but it was violently interrupted by the devastating storm of Christmas 1999, when some 10,000 trees were blown down. Among the 80 per cent of rare species and historic trees lost were two junipers planted by Marie Antoinette, the Virginian Tulip tree, and the Cedar planted in 1772 near the Hameau. The huge task of replanting began in March 2000. The initial stage was replanting the central area of the Petit Parc from the Allée du Tapis Vert and the six groves surrounding it. This was completed with the reconstruction of the two oldest groves, the Dauphin and the Girandole. The Trianon walk was regenerated in 2000–2001 and work is progressing, notably in the Trianon area which was especially badly damaged.

The parterres

West of the château, a large terrace was built above the surrounding land, and from here the eye is led the full length of the central axis past ponds and formal flowerbeds, along a straight lawn and the canal lined with serried ranks of trees, to the woodland beyond. The terrace was designed to be viewed from the first floor and is adorned with bronze statues and marble vases including *War* by Antoine Coysevox, and *Peace* by Tuby. Corresponding to the centre of the château façade, below the Hall of Mirrors, is the Parterre d'Eau (Water Garden), laid out in 1683 with two large ornamental basins which mirror the building, decorated with bronzes (1690) of reclining figures of water nymphs and the Kingdom of France represented by allegorical figures of the four great rivers and their main tributaries.

From the top of the Marches (steps) de Latone are the magnificent perspectives of the gardens. In the opposite direction, the whole façade of the château comes into focus with the centrally placed statues of Apollo and Diana, central to the theme and symbolic layout of the Gardens, based on the myth of Apollo and Diana, sun god and moon goddess. The sculpted group at the foot of the steps, *Latona with her Children Apollo and Diana*, depicts Latona, or Leto, insulted by Lycian peasants who as a result are turned into frogs by Zeus at her request.

To the south steps lead to the Parterre du Sud which has box trimmed into an elaborate design combined with flowers and 17th-century sculptures of children mounted on sphinxes. The Cent Marches (Hundred Steps) descend from here, to the Parterre

Apollo's Chariot Rising from the Waves to start its Course Across the Firmament (1671) by Jean-Baptiste Tuby, in the Bassin d'Apollon in the gardens of Versailles.

de l'Orangerie, a formal garden which has recently been returned, based on archival evidence, to Le Nôtre's original design, with clipped yews and cypresses arranged in harmonious shapes. The Orangery (1681–88), one of the largest in the world, with three naves—two of 110m beneath the steps, and the third running south for 156m— was designed by Le Vau. It has 5m-thick walls and double-glazing to withstand the cold. Over 1,000 trees in containers, including orange and lemon trees over 200 years old, are over-wintered here and returned to the Parterre de l'Orangerie from spring to autumn. The Communards were herded into the Orangery in 1871 prior to their imprisonment. Further south, beyond the St-Cyr road, you see Pièce d'Eau des Suisses (Swiss Lake) 682m long by 134m wide, excavated in 1678–82 by the Swiss Guards, many of whom are said to have died of malaria during the operation.

The Parterre du Nord (North Garden), with box hedges and grass, leads through numerous statues to the elegant Pyramid Fountain and the Bath of Diana's Nymphs (both by François Girardon , 1679) and either side the Bosquet de l'Arc de Triomphe with *France Triumphant* (Coysevox and Tuby) and the Bosquet des Trois Fontaines. The Allée d'Eau (Water Avenue), designed by Perrault and Le Brun (1676–88), leads directly to the amphitheatre Bassin de Neptune (1740), the largest fountain-basin in the gardens. Formerly, the Apollo cycle (which begins with the Apollo Basin) ended in Thetis's Grotto, which was destroyed when the north wing of the château was built. (From the Bassin de Neptune is the most direct route to the Trianon.)

Beyond the oval Bassin de Latone extends the Tapis Vert (Green Carpet), or Allée Royale, a lawn 330m long and 36m wide, lined with marble vases and statues, many of them copies from the Antique. The Tapis Vert leads to the Bassin d'Apollon, where the sun god setting out on his daily journey is represented by *Apollo's Chariot Rising from the Waves to start its Course Across the Firmament* (Tuby; 1671; *pictured opposite*). To the right is Petite Venise (Little Venice) where Louis XIV's Venetian gondoliers were housed. Beyond the Bassin d'Apollon, and separated from the gardens by railings is the Petit Parc, divided by the Grand Canal, 1650m long and 62m wide, the scene of Louis XIV's boating parties. Almost at its central point it is crossed by a transverse arm (c. 1070m), extending from the Grand Trianon, to the north, to the few remaining buildings of the former royal menagerie.

The bosquets

The *bosquets*, carefully planned and furnished al fresco 'rooms' within walls of greenery, were regularly used for amusement and entertainment at the time of Louis XIV. Secreted among the alleys, of the original 14, just six have been preserved although some of the sculptures have been lost. They include the **Salle de Bal** (Ballroom) south of the Bassin de Latone and further west is the **Bosquet de la Colonnade**, a circle of marble arches (Hardouin-Mansart, 1885–88), which has lost its central sculpture of the *Rape of Prosperine* by Girardon. North of the Tapis Vert, is the **Bosquet des Dômes**, with several statues including *Acis and Galatea* (Tuby), and the **Bosquet de l'Encelade**, which needed major restoration to return it to its original state. Taken from the myth of the Earth-born giants who attempted to overthrow

Jupiter, the giant Enceladus, in a work by Marsy, is about to throw a last rock and utter a final curse, symbolised by a jet of water, against Jupiter. In a Romantic spirit, very different from Le Nôtre's formal symmetry, is **Bosquet des Bains d'Apollon** within a grove laid out by Hubert Robert for Louis XVI. *Apollo served by Thetis's Nymphs* (Giradon and Renaudin, 1672) is the survival from the Grotto of Thetis. The **Bosquet des Trois Fontaines** has been recently restored. Always a delightful discovery, the Bosquets are at their most enchanting during the Grandes Eaux Musicales. Other parts of the Bosquet area to explore are the Salle des Marronniers, a chestnut grove behind the Colonnade, the Bassin de Saturne or Winter Basin, the Bassin du Miroir, and the Bassin de Bacchus or Autumn Basin, with sculptures by Girardon and Marsy and the glade known as the Bosquet de la Reine.

MARIE-ANTOINETTE'S ESTATE

Open daily April–Oct 12–6.30 including Grand Trianon, Petit Trianon, Chapel, Queen's Hamlet, Queen's Theatre, Belvedere, Temple of Love, Grotto, Landscaped Garden, Refreshments Dairy, and French Pavilion; and open Nov–March 12–5.30 including Grand Trianon and Petit Trianon Gardens.

THE GRAND TRIANON

The Grand Trianon was a miniature palace designed by Hardouin-Mansart and Robert de Cotte for Louis XIV in 1687. It replaced a modest summer house for picnics, tiled inside with blue and white Delftware, and known as the Porcelain Trianon, erected on the site of the village of Trianon, which had been razed in 1663. The Grand Trianon served as Louis XIV's retreat from court life where he could commune with nature. The U-shaped low building with an Italian-style roof, also known as the Palais Rose because of the profusion of pink marble from French quarries, has extensive wings to the north which are not immediately obvious. Baroque rhythms and play of light are set up by the flat pilasters and round-headed windows of the wings accelerated by the colonnade or loggia. The loggia, huge French windows, and mirrors were part of the plan to bring the outside inside, creating a 'palace of flora' for Louis XIV. The botanical aspect of the Trianon also permeated the interior decorations, including the woodwork and the paintings which were based on nature and mythological themes such as Europa and Narcissus, in contrast to the mighty Apollo myth of the château. During the reign of Louis XIV, apartments were occupied by members of the royal family, including the king's sister-in-law, the Princess Palatine, and the Duchesse de Bourgogne. The duchess, of whom the king was very fond, was his grandson's wife, and mother of Louis XV. Czar Peter the Great also stayed here in 1717. Louis XV rarely used it and Louis XVI gave the estate to Marie-Antoinette who invited only personal friends here and adopted a less formal way of life. Napoleon, after his divorce from Josephine in 1809, often stayed here with Marie-Louise, his second wife. Napoleonic souvenirs and Empire furniture have remained. Louis-Philippe installed his younger son here and introduced 19th century Romantic furnishings. At the time of President de Gaulle, one entire wing was restored to receive Heads of State on official visits and this custom continues, with visits from President Chirac at certain times.

The interior

The apartments opposite the gardens have white wood panels, easier to maintain and for insulation. During the time of Louis XIV there were apartments for him, the queen, his favourite Madame de Maintenon, his granddaughter, Duchesse de Bourgogne, and a Salle de Theatre. The king often changed apartments. The visit includes rooms on both sides of the courtyard, and while the decoration is largely Louis XIV, the rooms are richly furnished, mainly in 19th-century pieces.

Empress Josephine's Boudoir contains a gondola-shaped sofa, and next to it is the mirrored Salon des Glaces. The Salon des Colonnes is one of the most beautiful rooms in the Trianon, and contains Napoleon's bed (1809) from the Tuileries. The Antichambre de la Chapelle was transformed in 1691, but still contains a small sanctuary. Beyond the peristyle in the north wing, the Salon Rond contains paintings entitled *Flowers and Fruit of America* by Desportes. At the time of Louis XIV, this served as a vestibule opening onto a theatre which stood here until 1703, and the apartment was further transformed in the 18th and 19th centuries. The Salon de Musique and Grand Salon precede the Salon des Malachite, with a malachite bowl given by Alexander I of Russia after the Treaty of Tilsit in 1807. The Salon Frais was built to protect fragile blooms in the upper garden, and has four *Views of Versailles*, by J.-B. Martin. The *Gardens of Versailles and Trianon at the time of Louis XIV*, most by Jean Cotelle (1645–1708) and his brother, in the adjoining gallery, were valuable documents for the restoration of the *bosquets*. The Salon des Jardins faces the Grand Canal and the Salon des Sources has *Views of Versailles* by P.-D. Martin (1663–1742) and Charles Chastelain (1672–1740). The Appartement de l'Empereur (guided visit only) at the time of Louis XIV was used by Mme de Maintenon, and in 1741 by Stanislas Leszczynski, and subsequently by Mme de Pompadour, and Napoleon with Marie-Louise.

The gardens

The gardens, laid out by Mansart, reflect the traditional garden design of Le Nôtre with pools, perspectives and borders of colour. The *parterres* are on two levels, the Upper Garden with two basins and statues by Giradon, and the Lower Garden, with one basin. The central axis leads to the Plat Fond (flat-bottom basin) decorated with dragons. To the west is the secondary branch of the Grand Canal. The large Water Buffet (the main fountain) of 1703, designed by Mansart, has the only mythological theme, *Neptune and Amphitrite*. Louis XIV collected scented plants, which were kept in pots and could be rearranged and replaced. It took around a million to fill the garden. A bridge leads from the Jardin du Roi, behind the palace, to the gardens of the Petit Trianon.

THE PETIT TRIANON

The Petit Trianon (1762–68), with two floors and an attic storey, is a charming pavilion built by Ange-Jacques Gabriel for Louis XV as a country retreat for himself and Mme de Pompadour, who did not live to see it completed. Mme du Barry then occupied it and it was here in 1774 that Louis XV was taken fatally ill and then moved to the château to die. It became a favourite residence of Marie-Antoinette, who at first came only during the day, but as time passed, also slept here. It was subsequently occupied by Pauline Borghese, Napoleon's sister. To the left of the courtyard is the chapel.

The interior
Many of the rooms in the Petit Trianon retain their original woodwork, including chimneypieces by Guibert in the dining room and *grand salon*, and sliding panels to obscure the windows to provide screens from prying eyes. In the dining room, traces of a trap-door, through which tables would appear ready-laid, are still visible in the floor, but Marie-Antoinette did away with the device. The entrance is in the former billiard room and the first floor is open to the public for a non-guided visit of ten rooms all containing paintings and furnishings of high quality. (*Guided visits only to the attic storey.*)

The gardens
The gardens of the Petit Trianon were originally a *ménagerie* and botanical garden laid out by Bernard de Jussieu for Louis XV, a passionate botanist, who cultivated rare plants in large hothouses (now gone). The French Garden Pavilion, in Rococo style was built in 1750 by Gabriel and was used by the king to pause during visits to his gardens. Marie-Antoinette had the gardens altered in the English style (1774–86) and Louis XVI liked to gather his own herbs here. The queen loved music—Gluck was a regular guest—to dance and to play cards, and to act. To satisfy her enthusiasms, in 1776–83, Richard Mique (1728–94) the last of the royal architects at Versailles, built a circular Temple of Love, a Grotto and the Belvedere, on rocky outcrops, and a stream running between small artificial islands. Mique also built a theatre where the queen made her acting début, not always meeting with approval, and a mechanised Chinese Tilt Ring. Among the varied entertainments arranged by Marie-Antoinette were country balls to which ordinary people were invited, but rather than endearing her to them, they found her un-queenly behaviour disturbing.

HAMEAU DE LA REINE

Some few minutes' walk to the northeast is Marie-Antoinette's *hameau* (hamlet), also built by Mique in 1783, with several rustic buildings picturesquely arranged around a lake. Here the queen could indulge her taste for nature, as popularised by Jean-Jacques Rousseau and Diderot, but this flight of fancy was more authentic than most *hameaux* built for the aristocracy at that time. It was a working concern with a farmer and his wife, where the queen could introduce her children to milking and other delights of rural life. The produce was used in the château, but in the nearby village of St-Antoine farmers were dying of hunger. The main building is the Queen's House with several rooms, decorated with blue earthenware pots carrying her initials. Other buildings include the Boudoir (where she rested), dairies, the Tour de Marlborough, the remains of a barn, and a dovecote.

THE TOWN OF VERSAILLES

Tourist information: 2bis Avenue de Paris, T: 01 39 24 88 88; www.versailles-tourisme.fr
The Quartier St-Louis or Old Versailles, south of Pl. d'Armes, was begun at the time of Louis XIV. Where Av. de Paris meets Place d'Armes are the old stables (*see p. 377*). Since 2003 the stables have been occupied by the Academy of Equestrian Arts which offers a programme of equestrian performances and visits (*Feb–Dec; T: 01 39 02 07 14; www.acadequestre.fr*). The Hôtel de Ville (1899) is at no. 11–13 Av. de Paris, and at no. 22 is the Hôtel des Menus Plaisirs, the warehouse built for Louis XV where theatrical scenery and props, and other playthings were stored. The Hôtel de Mme du Barry (1751, private), is at no. 21, with a monumental portal by Claude-Nicolas Ledoux (*see p. 318*). Comte Robert de Montesquiou (1855–1921), on whom Proust based his Baron Charlus and Huysmans his Jean des Esseintes in *A Rebours*, lived at no. 53. Immediately south of the château is the Grand-Commun, built by J. Hardouin-Mansart in 1684 to accommodate court functionaries. Adjacent is the former Hôtel de la Guerre (1759) and Hôtel des Affaires Etrangères et de la Marine (1761), now the municipal library, with Louis XV decoration. The Jeu de Paume (*see p. 386*) is south of Pl. D'Armes. Rue de Satory has a choice of restaurants. The church of St-Louis (1742–54) by Jacques Hardouin-Mansart de Sagonne, is a rare example of a church of the period of Louis XV. A restrained version of Baroque, it was designated a cathedral in 1802. Square St-Louis is a pretty place with 18th–century houses. Nearby, at no. 10 Rue du Maréchal Joffre, is the **Potager du Roi** (*open April–Oct 10–6; guided visits Sat, Sun, and holidays at 10.30, 11.30, 1.30, 2.30, 3.30 & 4.30; T: 01 39 24 62 62.*) formerly Louis XIV's kitchen-garden created by La Quintinie in 1678 to provide for the Court. It covers nine hectares and has retained its original 16 divisions, which contain serried ranks of fruit and vegetables, around a small lake. It incorporates Parc Balbi, a small 18th-century Anglo-Chinese style landscaped garden. The Potager is also a horticultural college, and the produce is sold.

The New Town
The Quartier Notre-Dame, or 'New Town' is northeast of Place des Arms (in front of the château). At the heart of this busy district is the Church of Notre-Dame (1684–86), by Jules Hardouin-Mansart, the covered market and antiques area around the old Court House of 1724 and dungeons. This is a good place to eat. West of this quartier, the Hôtel des Réservoirs, originally built by Lassurance for Mme de Pompadour, still bears the marquise's arms. Proust isolated himself here for almost

five months in the latter half of 1906. At no. 13 Rue des Réservoirs is the elegant Théâtre Montansier (*box office open Tues, Fri, Sat 4–7; T: 01 39 20 16 16*), founded by the actress Mlle Montansier, was built by Heurtier and Boulet in 1777. Northeast, at 54 Blvd de la Reine is the Musée Lambinet, housed in a mid-18th-century mansion. In the collection are sculptures by Houdon and early prints with interesting views of Versailles.

Trianon Palace Hotel

1 Blvd de la Reine, T: 01 30 84 50 00, www.starwoodhotels.com
At the extreme west of Blvd de la Reine, next to the park, is the Trianon Palace Hotel, a luxury hotel built by René Sergent, the architect of the Plaza Athénée in Paris, in 1910. It has two restaurants, the Brasserie la Fontaine, in the annexe, and in the main building the gourmet Les Trois Marches under chef Gérard Vié, although at time of writing the British TV chef Gordon Ramsay was set to take over the kitchens. During the First World War the Trianon Palace was a hospital for British troops and in April 1917 the Allied Military Committee installed its permanent War Council here. It was chosen by Allied politicians for meetings preceding the signing of the Treaty of Versailles in the château. In the conference room is a plaque recording the handing of the conditions for peace by Georges Clemenceau to the German High Command on 7th May, 1919. The building was requisitioned by the Royal Air Force in 1939, by the Luftwaffe in 1940 and by the Americans in 1944 when it was again the meeting place for decisions that settled the peace. Since then the Trianon Palace Hotel's original architectural splendours have been lavishly restored.

SAINT-GERMAIN-EN-LAYE

St-Germain-en-Laye, within easy reach of Paris, is on the edge of the Forest of St-Germain. The suffix 'Laye' is thought to derive from a Celtic word connected with the forest. It is an interesting, attractive town with royal connections and in the middle are well-kept 17th- and 18th-century mansions and elegant shops. From Paris the RER Line A1 from Charles de Gaulle-Etoile runs to St-Germain-en-Laye, arriving opposite the château that is home to the Musée d'Archéologie Nationale, standing in a park with panoramic views of Paris. This museum and also that devoted to the painter Maurice Denis make a visit to St-Germain well worthwhile. In addition, the birthplace of Claude Debussy (1862–1918) is now the tourist information centre (*38 Rue au Pain, T: 01 34 51 05 12, www.tourisme.saintgermainenlaye.fr*).

CHATEAU DE SAINT-GERMAIN-EN-LAYE

The Château de St-Germain-en-Laye is strategically placed on an escarpment dominating a bend in the Seine. It was one of the principal seats of the French Court until abandoned by Louis XIV. The Renaissance château was restored and adapted in the 19th century to house the collections of French archaeology, an interesting visit on both counts.

History of the Château de St-Germain-en-Laye

The first château, erected in the 12th century by Louis VI, was enlarged by St-Louis (Louis IX), who built the free-standing chapel in 1230–38. During the Hundred Years War, the castle was destroyed by the Black Prince in 1346, except for the keep and chapel. The chapel (1230–38) is attributed to Pierre de Montreuil, hence slightly predates the Sainte-Chapelle in Paris (*see p. 32*). François I and his first wife, Claude de France (1499–1524; daughter of Louis XII), Louis XIV and his son, the Grand Dauphin, were all baptised here. It has lost most of its furnishings over the years and contains copies only of tombs from the Alyscamps at Arles and a modern maquette of the new and old châteaux. Later in the 14th century, Charles V rebuilt the château within the earlier walls, linking the chapel and keep. François I began rebuilding in brick in 1539, under the direction of Pierre Chambiges, who followed the uneven pentagon of the earlier building. The project was completed at the time of Henri II in 1557, and he began the Château-Neuf below the original castle, a vast structure which was completed by Henri IV. The infant Mary Stuart lived here from October 1548 until her marriage to François II in April 1558 and it also afforded refuge to Henrietta Maria of England (1644–48), sister of Louis XIII. Louis XIV was born in the Château-Neuf, and spent part of his childhood here and lived here as king from 1660. Major improvements were carried out in 1664–80 and Le Nôtre designed the terrace c. 1660, but in 1682 the Court moved to Versailles (*see p. 373*). After 1688 it became the residence and Court in

Exile of James II of England (1633–1701) who died here, as did his wife, Mary of Modena (1658–1710) who helped the impoverished English who filled St-Germain. The Château-Neuf was demolished in 1776, except for the Pavillon Henri IV (*see p. 398*). Degraded after the Revolution, the castle was due for demolition but Queen Victoria, following a visit in 1855, persuaded Napoléon III to save it. Restoration began in 1863 and then the installation of the Museum of Celtic and Gallo-Roman Antiquities.

MUSEE D'ARCHEOLOGIE NATIONALE

Open Mon, Wed–Sun 9–5.15; May–Sept Sat, Sun 10–6.15; closed Tues; admission free for under 18s, on first Sunday of the month, and to chapel and courtyard; T: 01 39 10 13 00; www.musee-antiquitesnationales.fr

Following a lengthy reorganisation, the Museum of National Archaeology has emerged as a beautifully presented and accessible journey which traces the existence of man in France from his origins to the Middle Ages (500,000 BC to the 8th century AD). Among the some 29,000 objects on display, is one of the world's most remarkable collections of portable decorated pieces from the Paleolithic period.

Mezzanine floor

Rooms 1–9: Rooms on the mezzanine floor span the Palaeolithic and Neolithic periods through to the Bronze and Iron Ages to Celtic Gaul. The Palaeolithic Period subdivides into Lower, Middle and Upper. Man's evolution is followed through a judicious choice of flint tools used by early hunter-gatherers, and examples of the techniques used to produce them. The first humans to emerge in France some 500,000 years ago, Tautavel man, made rudimentary tools from pebbles. Neanderthal man produced more sophisticated implements and was the first to bury his dead accompanied by offerings. Cro-Magnon man, *Homo Sapiens Sapiens*, present-day man's direct ancestor, appeared around 35,000 years ago, and developed a greater diversity of tools for precise applications such as scraping, cutting, piercing and so forth, which reached perfection with the 'laurel leaf' shape. Needles and harpoons were made from bone and horn, and assegais for throwing. Animal teeth and horn, as well as shells from afar, were used for adornment. From c. 25,000 BC, prehistoric art in France developed to a remarkably sophisticated level. Images tended to be restricted to animals, including mammoths, reindeer, horses and bovines. Among examples are a limestone relief of antelopes facing each other (c. 18,000 BC), from the Charente, a reindeer horn engraving from La Madeleine, in Dordogne, of a bison licking itself (c. 13,000 BC), and of the same period, the *Horse from Lourdes* (Hautes-Pyrenees), carved in the round from mammoth ivory. Human figures, rarer than animals and normally associated with female fertility, are described as *Venuses*. One of the oldest and most remarkable is here: the *Lady with the Hood* (c. 21,000 BC), from Brassempouy (Landes), also of mammoth ivory.

During the Neolithic period (or New Stone Age) c. 5800 BC, farming and more organised societies demanded new types of polished stone tool for cultivation and working with wood. A find of polished axe heads from Brittany demonstrates the high-quality finish given to these tools. Most Neolithic period objects were found in cairns or tumuli, stone burial chambers originally covered with earth and bearing witness to the skills acquired during this period, such as weaving and pottery. A unique production, however, was the statue-menhir or standing stone, found outside tombs and exclusive to a part of Southwest France where around 50 have been identified. An example from the Aveyron, which is engraved on all four faces, represents a standing female figure.

During the last period of prehistory, the Bronze Age (c. 2000–750 BC) hierarchies developed and competition for metal deposits led to an increasingly combative society. Skills developed and pottery acquired a variety of shapes, while gold objects were more frequent. Most pieces in the collection were associated with votive cults or sacrifice. An unusual juxtaposition of gold goblets and adornments (1600–1300 BC) was found in the Marne and a group of seven bronze breast plates (9th–8th centuries BC) from Haute-Marne is thought to be a votive offering linked to a spring. A deposit of 65 pieces from the Franco-German border highlights the importance of the military hierarchy. Here pieces of jewellery, a harness, and chariot attachments including a tintinnabulum for parades, were found in a pile with a sword on top.

The First Iron Age (850–450 BC), also known as the Hallstatt period, was a time of demographic change, increasing disparity in levels of society, and a growing dependence on Etruscan then Greek economic and cultural models. Tombs and their contents are proof of social transformations over the period. From the 9th–6th centuries most men were buried individually, but in time individual burials were accorded to only the most important members of the society, mainly men, but occasionally high-ranking women. These were known as chariot tombs, where the deceased was placed on the chassis of a chariot, with the wheels and valuable objects placed alongside. Finds include drinking vessels, bronze swords, harnesses, fine ceramics, and gold jewellery, and a remarkable 3rd-century BC helmet in bronze, gold and enamel. Even more precious are fragments of fabric which enveloped the objects. Also illustrated is the technique of casting bronze fibulae in a mould.

The Second Iron Age (450 BC to the start of the present era), also called La Tène period, coincides with the existence of populations called Gaul by the Romans, during which time there was rapid economic and cultural development, and fortified centres or *oppida* appeared. Chariot tombs in cemeteries in the Aisne-Marne region have astonishing deposits of precious objects in gold, which point to the existence of cult sacrifices. But the most exciting finds are the mass of Celtic and Roman weapons from the battlefield of Alésia, and the discovery of ancient *Bibracte*, capital of the Eduens, where Caesar withdrew to write his commentaries on the Gallic War.

First floor

Rooms 10–16: Roman Gaul from the 1st century BC to the 5th century AD is covered here, arranged thematically to conjure up life in the Gallo-Roman period with a cross-fertilisation of divinities and of artistic styles. The curious Gallic Divinity from Essonne (end 1st or beginning 2nd centuries) with glass eyes and a neck torque, shows little Roman influence except in the hair, whereas the statuette of Mercury from the Lyon area (1st–3rd centuries AD) has all the classical attributes. Small sculptured objects include the charming and unusual terracotta from Bordeaux, called *Les Amants de Bordeaux*, of an embracing couple in a bed with a dog at their feet. Unusually, a collection of military equipment and coins was found in the sepulchre of a Roman soldier. A large 3rd-century mosaic pavement from St-Romain-en-Gal (on the Rhône) depicts a rustic calendar of the seasons. A variety of domestic objects includes bowls, plates and sigillated pottery and spoons in glass, wood, and silver; new skills are demonstrated in blown and moulded glass. Fashions were also important, one of the main sources of evidence being coins.

Rooms 17–18: These two rooms are dedicated to Merovingian Gaul (481–751). Metalworking embraced *cloisonné* and damascene techniques. Christianity took root. Dagobert I was the first to be buried at St-Denis (*see p. 407*), in 638, but the pagan custom of burying possessions with the deceased continued. Men, such as the Chef de Lavoye (319), possibly a close companion of the king, Clovis, were buried with exceptional collections of arms, and women with their finery, as revealed by ornate fibulae and jewellery from a sepulchre from Val d'Oise (mid-6th century). From St-Denis are two fibulae and a gold cross buried in a tomb in the late-5th century, and a late 6th-century bronze belt buckle is engraved with a relief of *Daniel in the Lions' Den*.

Room 19: Comparative Archaeology occupies Henri II's ballroom, famous at the time as one of the largest in the kingdom where specially created pieces by Luly and Molière were performed. The gallery contains objects from five continents which relate to the same period as the French collections.

The park

To the north of the château is the Grand Parterre, originally part of a scheme by Le Nôtre laid out between 1662–74, which once included the Jardin de la Dauphine to the east, now planted with rows of elms, and the Grande Terrasse. The Jardin Anglais was created in the 19th century. At its southeast corner is the Pavillon Henri-IV, all that remains of the Château Neuf, which has been a hotel (*see p. 433*) since 1836. Here Alexandre Dumas (1802–70) wrote *The Three Musketeers* and *The Count of Monte Cristo*. The 1.95km of the Grande Terrasse of St-Germain extends northeast across the park of St-Germain-en-Laye, commanding a splendid view of Paris—particularly of La Défense: Notre-Dame is approximately 21km to the east. At the far end is the Grille Royale, the entrance to the Forêt de St-Germain-en-Laye, a former royal hunting preserve.

TOWN OF SAINT-GERMAIN-EN-LAYE

The church of St-Louis (opposite the château), the third version, is a Neoclassical building designed c. 1765 by N.-M. Potain, but not completed until the early 19th century. It was re-orientated to face the château, and the entrance is on the north. It contains the tomb of James II of England, erected at the request of George IV, and in which his partial remains were re-interred in 1824. His skull was translated to the Collège des Ecossais in the Latin Quarter.

MUSEE CLAUDE DEBUSSY

Open Tues–Fri 2–6, Sat 10–12.30 & 2–6; closed Sun, Mon; T: 01 34 51 05 12.
The composer Claude Debussy (1862–1918) was born here at no. 38 Rue au Pain on 22 August 1862. He spent his childhood in this fine 17th–18th-century house built around a courtyard, where his parents owned a small shop. The museum contains a collection of memorabilia presented by Madame de Tinan, the composer's daughter-in-law, arranged to follow the development of the his career. On the second floor is a Salon de Musique with a Bechstein of c. 1915 for faithful recitals of Debussy's *oeuvre*. The Patisserie Grandain makes a Gâteau Debussy and other St-Germain specialities.

MUSEE MAURICE DENIS

Open Tues–Fri 10–5.30; Sat, Sun, and holidays 10–6.30; closed Mon; T: 01 39 73 77 87.
At no. 2bis Rue Maurice-Denis (a short walk along the continuations of Rue au Pain Rues A. Bonnefant and de Mareil), the museum occupies a former royal hospital founded by Mme de Montespan in 1678. Maurice Denis (1870–1943) rented a studio here in 1905. He bought the property in 1914 and, with the help of Auguste Perret, built a workshop and restored the ruined chapel before moving in with his large family. He called the house the Priory and lived here until his death. The late 17th-century building, which was never completed, is in a garden setting, and has a vaulted entrance and a double-helix staircase. The museum, inaugurated in 1980, throws an interesting light on the development of Modern Art. The bequest by the artist's family and works by his contemporaries has been increased by acquisition over 15 years. As well as paintings, the collection includes sculptures, decorative arts, engravings, manuscripts and pastels. The museum covers eight rooms and the chapel, over two floors.

The museum
The museum contains works from the whole career of Maurice Denis, including decorative commissions and designs for furniture, wall-papers, ceramics and stained glass. Denis was also a prolific writer on art, and his famous dictum was that before anything else, a painting is a flat surface with colour assembled on it in a certain order. Among Denis' early experimental Symbolist works is the small *Le Chemin dans les*

Arbres (c. 1891), a spectral scene with figures dwarfed by tall straight trees. The road disappearing into the distance was to become a recurrent theme in his work. *Madame Ranson and her Cat* (1892) combines the Nabis principles of flat pattern and colour, no attempt at depth, and a decorative quality heavily influenced by Japanese prints. Similarly, *Ladder in Foliage* (1892), intended as a ceiling decoration for music editor Henri Lerolle, shows variations on a theme of the same woman, *échelle* (ladder) also meaning a musical scale in French. *Pilgrims at Emmaus* (1895) is a modern version of a religious theme. In contrast are works inspired by Brittany, such as the colourful *Regatta at Perros Guirec* (1897), with a disturbing use of perspective which animates the painting. Breton subjects by other painters include Sérusier's sombre *The Old Breton Woman* (c. 1898) holding a digitalis in her large hand and wearing clogs, and *Landscape with Wrack* (seaweed) painted in 1888 by Emile Bernard (1868–1941). From 1906 there was a marked increase in colour in Nabis painting, influenced by Cézanne, whom Denis met in Provence that year. *The Beach and a Red Bonnet* (1909) introduces a new luminosity, more tonal modelling and the nude in a seascape.

Denis was married twice; his first wife Marthe died in 1919, and he married Elisabeth Graterolle in 1922. In *Self Portrait*, which uses a more varied style, the painter is shown at his easel in the garden of the Priory with both his wives and his children in the background. Edouard Vuillard's (1868–1940) *Garden at l'Etang-la-Ville* is based on a photograph of his friend Roussel's garden. Paul Gauguin (1848–1903) is also represented here by *The Patron's Daughter* (1886), in a more Impressionist than Symbolist style, using small brushstrokes that create no depth but do enhance the colours.

Among Maurice Denis' many commissions was the decoration of a narrow room for Baron Denys Cochin, intellectual and huntsman, at his property in Melun. The Baron chose the theme of the Legend of St Hubert and of Beau Pécopin as told by Victor Hugo in *Le Rhin*. The painter made lengthy preparations, including visits to Fontainebleau Forest, before painting the seven panels in 1896–97. This project brings together all the Nabis precepts of harmony, decoration, symbolism and colour. Denis was also influenced by the Florentine, Lorenzo di Credi (c. 1458–1537). The rhythms change from panel to panel, and it introduces members of the Cochin family as well as Victor Hugo. Ten panels that Denis painted for Gabrielle Thomas's villa in Meudon, *Eternal Spring* (1908), using white and pastel colours, are presented with a reconstruction of her dining room.

In 1919 Denis, a devout Catholic, established the Ateliers d'Art Sacré, with a view to bringing sacred art up-to-date. With the architect Auguste Perret, he brought about the restoration of the badly neglected Chapel, which was reconsecrated in 1922. Modest materials were used, and Perret designed the woodwork while Denis took care of the decorative scheme with blue frescoes and Stations of the Cross, including the designs for the stained-glass, with the exception of the round *Visitation* by Marcel Poncet. Colleagues helped with the murals and Denis enlisted his family and friends to model for paintings such as the *Life of Christ* and the *Last Supper*. The painting of St Louis introduces an element of patriotism, and the geometric *Crucifixion* refers to the horrors of the First World War. Among decorative arts of the period are objects designed by Denis, together with glass which demonstrates the skill of the Daum brothers, glassmakers of Nancy, as well as furniture, ceramic tiles, and stained glass.

In the gardens are bronzes by Bourdelle and the workshop (closed at time of writing but scheduled to re-open) built by Auguste Perret in 1912 when Denis began working on large decorations for the Théâtre des Champs-Elysées. Both Perret and Bourdelle were associated with the design and décor of the theatre. The terraced gardens have been adapted for public use, and there is an attempt being made to return them to something like the form of Maurice Denis' day.

THE NABIS

Maurice Denis was co-founder and principal theorist of the Nabis, a group named by the poet Cazalis with the Hebrew word for prophet, who were searching for a new impetus to painting. Maurice Denis (*le Nabi aux belles icônes*), Pierre Bonnard (1867–1947; *le Nabi très japonard*), and Paul Ranson (1864–1909) studied at Académie Julien, and were inspired by a painting made on the bottom of a cigar-box by fellow student Paul Sérusier (1864–1927). It became known as *Le Talisman* (Musée d'Orsay collection) as it was crucial in disseminating new ideas learned from Gauguin in 1888 at Pont Aven in Brittany. The group was swelled by Edouard Vuillard (1868–1940) and Ker-Xavier Roussel (1867–1944), Felix Vallotton (1865–1925) and the sculptor Aristide Maillol (*see p. 122*). All these artists adapted the Nabis principles to their personal approach and application, some sooner, others later, and are represented in the museum. A leading Nabis, Emile Bernard (1868–1941), painted the *Portrait of Dom Verkade*, of a Dutch painter who adapted Nabis ideas to mural painting in Germany.

LA ROSERAIE

Open on the fourth Sat and Sun of each month and some holidays: T: 01 30 74 70 04. RER line A from Paris to St-Germain-en-Laye and then bus BC; or RER Line A Paris-Poissy and then bus 8.

At no. 64 Grande Rue, Chambourcy, La Roseraie was the 18th-century home of André Derain (1880–1954) from 1935, where his studio is still intact and can be visited.

VILLA SAVOYE

Open Wed–Sun May–Aug 10–6; March–April, Sept–Oct 10–5; Nov–Feb 10–1 & 2–5; closed Tues; T: 01 39 65 01 06. RER Line A Paris-Poissy, and then bus 50 to Les Œillets.

At no. 82 Rue Villiers, in Poissy, is Le Corbusier's Villa Savoye (1929), one of the architect's virtuoso designs. It was built in 1919–31 for Pierre and Eugenie Savoye who lived here until 1940. The Villa was damaged when expropriated during the Second World War but a long and careful restoration (ending in 1997) has returned it as near as possible to its original state. Known as *les Heures Claires*, the house was designed to take advantage of the site which then commanded views towards Paris (now obscured). A seemingly simple design, it incorporates the architect's basic tenets of modernism. From the exterior it presents a white box on pilotis or stilts, with a flat roof and horizontal rhythm. The interior reveals a more complex articulation of space and light, combining large windows and a roof terrace with practical living spaces.

MAISON D'EMILE ZOLA

Open Sat, Sun and holidays 2–6.30; T: 01 39 75 35 65. RER Line A, Paris-Poissy, then SNCF train to Poissy-Villennes.
In Médan, near Poissy, is Emile Zola's home from 1878–1902, and where he wrote *Nana*, *Germinal* and *La Bête Humaine*. Something of a time capsule, many of the writer's belongings are still in place, with a collection of original manuscripts and photographs taken by him.

MARLY-LE-ROI

Tourist information: 2 Av. Des Combattants, Marly-le-Roie; T: 01 30 61 61 35; RER Line A from Paris to St-Germain-en-Laye and then bus 10; SNCF Gare-St-Lazare–Marly-le-Roi.
The royal Château de Marly, built in 1679–86 by Jules Hardouin-Mansart for Louis XIV, was a favourite retreat from the formality of Versailles. Its name is preserved in the town of Marly-le-Roi. Unlike other royal residences, Marly was planned as a group of 12 guest-houses around the central royal pavilion, based on the signs of the zodiac, and dedicated to carefree conviviality. The buildings and the parkland setting were fully integrated and much use was made of *trompe l'oeil* and water. The famous Marly horses, by Coysevox and Coustou, which adorned the pools, were gradually transferred to the Tuileries between 1719 and 1794 (*see p. 212*). Sold at the Revolution, the château was used as a factory until 1809. Then plundered for its stone, it was finally demolished in 1816.

Vestiges remain of the park, where the famous hydraulic Machine de Marly stood. The machine was originally constructed in 1681 to raise water from the Seine to the Marly aqueduct, which in turn carried it to Versailles. New machinery was installed in 1855–59, taking its water from an underground source, but the whole thing was dismantled in 1967.

The Museum (*open Thur–Sun 2–6; closed Mon–Wed and holidays; T: 01 30 69 06 26.*) in the Park of Marly evokes the great days of the château, and has a room dedicated to the Machine de Marly. The church of Marly-le-Roi was also built by Hardouin-Mansart (1689) and contains some works originally in Versailles.

Château de Monte-Cristo

Open April–Nov Tues–Fri 10–12.30 & 2–6; Sat, Sun 10–6; closed Mon. Nov–March, Sun 2–5, closed Mon–Sat; T: 01 39 16 49 49. Port-Marly; RER line A Paris-St-Germain-en-Laye and then bus 10.

At Port-Marly is the Renaissance-style château that Alexandre Dumas built as a haven in which to live and work and that bankrupted him a year after completion in 1847. It is surrounded by English gardens, and inside is a Moorish-style living room.

CHATEAU DE MAISONS-LAFFITTE

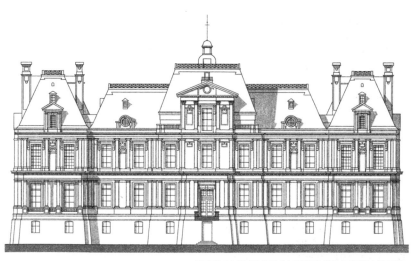

CHATEAU DE MAISONS-LAFFITTE: THE GARDEN FRONT

Open May–Sept Wed–Sun 10–12.30 & 2–6; Oct–April 10–12.30 & 2–5; closed Tues; T: 01 39 62 01 49. RER Line A Paris–Maisons-Laffitte

The Château de Maisons-Laffitte, in the pleasant residential town of Maisons-Laffitte, is the most complete surviving work by François Mansart (1642–51), representing better than any other building his genius. It is also the only building by Mansart in which his interior decoration survives.

History of Maisons-Laffitte

The very fine Château de Maisons was built 1634–46 for René de Longueil (1596–1677), first Marquis de Maisons, Président of the *Parlement* and Governor of the Châteaux of Versailles and St-Germain. The property was bought in 1777 by the Comte d'Artois (brother of Louis XVI, later Charles X) and partly redecorated by

Bellanger. Abandoned at the Revolution and its contents dispersed, in 1804 it was acquired by Marshal Lannes, Duc de Montebello. Sold in 1818 to Jacques Laffitte (1767–1844), head of the Banque de France, in 1833 he demolished the stables and sold off the estate. Further fragmented by a subsequent owner, the shell of the château was saved from demolition in 1905 when it was acquired by the State.

Visiting the château

Entrance is via the **chapel**. The Baroque proportions of the interior are on a human scale, but the décor has been subjected to three centuries of alterations. The **Salon des Captifs** has a fireplace carved by Gilles Guérin with captives representing four provinces won by the Crown, a tribute to the power of Louis XIII. The magnificent **Entrance Vestibule** is richly restrained, without gilt or colour. Decorated in the Doric order, with allegorical reliefs and the eagles of the Longeuil on the entablature, it spans the width of the château. The two sets of wrought iron doors leading to the exterior (1650) were transferred to the Louvre in 1797. The gardens stretched via a parterre to the Seine, and across to an island with a double avenue. The splendid staircase around an open square, embellished with putti by Philippe de Buyster, has a particularly fine balustrade.

The **King's Apartment** on the first floor comprises the Ball Room in grey and gilt paint, possibly original, 18th-century Gobelins tapestries of the *Hunts of Maximilian* and a musicians gallery; the King's Bedroom with a replica 17th-century bed, velvet walls and a bust of Louis XIII; and the domed Cabinet aux Miroirs with marquetry floor. The south wing, formerly the Queen's suite, was transformed by Lannes and is furnished in Empire style and has a painting of the *Remains of Napoleon I Returning to Paris*. Voltaire wrote *Marianne* when a guest here in 1720. The corner room on the ground floor was the summer dining room of the Comte d'Artois. The basement kitchens are used for temporary exhibitions.

The town of Maisons-Laffitte

Tourist information T: 01 39 62 63 64; www.tourisme-maisonslaffitte.fr
The land adjacent to the château sold by Laffitte was developed in the 19th century with attractive villas for Parisians. Although the railway station was known as Maisons-Laffitte as early as 1843, the town adopted the name officially only in 1882. It is now also well known as a horse racing centre, with training-stables and a racehorse museum (*see p. 419*). The town was the birthplace of poet-novelist Jean Cocteau (1889–1963).

LA VILLETTE, SAINT-DENIS & ECOUEN

La Villette is the largest green urban space in Paris. The site of the 19th-century cattle-market and abattoirs, on the edge of the 19th arrondissement and the Département de Seine-Saint-Denis north of Paris, it was transformed between 1980–96 into a multi-cultural public park covering 55 hectares and extending to both sides of the Canal de l'Ourcq. The wide programme of activities on offer embraces music, theatre, film, popular arts (circus, cabaret, puppets), new forms of expression (hip-hop, rap, new music and dance) as well as current affairs (with exhibitions and debates on topical issues). At St-Denis are the Royal Basilica and the Stade de France, while the Château d'Ecouen houses the Musée National de la Renaissance, the 'sequel' to the Musée National du Moyen Age in the Latin Quarter.

PARC DE LA VILLETTE

Open daily from 6am–1am; general information T: 01 40 03 75 75, www.villette.com Information in the park: Folie Information, open daily 9.30–6.30, at exit of Metro Porte de Pantin. Guided tours of the park available. Access from central Paris: Metro Porte de Pantin for south entrance; Porte de la Villette for the north entrance. Canal trips from the Bassin de la Villette T: 01 42 39 15 00, www.canauxrama.com

The Parc de la Villette was designed by Bernard Tschumi around three main constructs: providing focal points are 26 bright red enamelled metal follies, each in a framework of 120m x 120m and with a unique form and function; secondly, three kilometres of walk-ways unroll across the park, the main axes linking the Porte de Pantin and the Porte de la Villette characterised by an undulating roof, and the east-west Gallery de l'Ourcq, alongside the canal; and thirdly, surface textures are provided by seven hectares of meadows, dubbed the Circle and the Triangle. In addition, Philippe Starck designed the park furniture (chairs, bins, lamp posts and so forth). The themed gardens are designed to be informative and fun, especially for children. Among them are a trellised garden with vines and fountains, a bamboo forest, a mirror garden, another that evokes the seaside, and one that enlists movement and balance; then there is a 'scary garden' and a 'dragon's garden'. The Maison de la Villette was the Rotonde des Vétérinaires in the 19th century, and now welcomes resident artists.

CITE DE LA MUSIQUE

Open Tues–Sat 12–6, Sun 10–6, closed Mon; T: 01 44 84 44 84; www.cite-musique.fr Metro: Porte de Pantin.

The Cité de la Musique, which opened in 1995, is dedicated to the world of music. Situated in the south of the Parc de la Villette, near the Conservatoire de Musique, its remarkable architecture is the work of Christian de Portzamparc. It provides access to music through concerts, a museum, exhibitions and educational activities. The new Médiathèque (Music Resource Centre) is open to all, offering a huge collection of documents to be consulted on site or on the web, covering all types of artistic trends.

Musée de la Musique

The Musée de la Musique is a reference resource in the world of music, with a collection of over 1,000 instruments, models and works of art as well as temporary exhibitions which broaden the field of knowledge and cover wide periods in history from antiquity to the most recent past. The collection, on several floors, is imaginatively displayed to illustrate the evolution of music and instruments, and the role of composers, musicians and patrons. Instruments, some exceptional and even unique, are presented so that they can be admired for both their sculptural and musical beauty. In the string collection are 17th-century Venetian archlutes and guitars by Voboam, an outstanding collection of French stringed instruments from the 18th and 19th centuries, and Cremona violins by Amati, Stradivarius and Guarnerius del Gesù. There are Flemish harpsichords by the celebrated Rucker dynasty, 18th-century French harpsichords, as well as pianofortes by Erard, including one played by Franz Liszt. There is an exceptional collection of brass instruments designed by Adolphe Sax (1814–94). Representing the 20th century are an electronic violin by Max Mathews, a MIDI saxophone, and Frank Zappa's E-Mu synthesizer. Recent acquisitions include guitars which belonged to Diango Reinhardt and a Hel violin owned by Stephan Grapelli. In addition there are instruments from around the world, such as a 17th-century Sàrangi from northern India and a 19th-century chest drum from Zaire.

CITE DES SCIENCES ET DE L'INDUSTRIE

Open Tues–Sat 10–6; Sun 10–7; closed Mon; T: 01 40 05 79 99; www.cite-sciences.fr Géode open Tues–Sat 10.30–9.30, Sun 10.30–7.30; T: 01 40 05 70 00.
The massive rectangular block forming the Cité des Sciences et de l'Industrie, covering over 3 hectares, opened in 1986. The auction-hall of a slaughter-house, begun on this site but abandoned incomplete in 1973, was imaginatively incorporated into the new structure by Adrien Fainsilber. The building also introduces the natural environment through the themes of water, light and vegetation. On the south side of the building are three glasshouses with plants establishing a point of transition between the building and the park; natural light floods in through two huge glazed cupolas; and the whole structure is surrounded by a moat. The main hall or nave is 100m long and 40m high and there are five levels to explore; transparent lifts glide within a stainless steel framework.

The exhibitions

The aim of the Cité is to demystify and popularise science, in a serious but entertaining enough way to attract visitors of all types and ages. To explain how scientific discoveries, innovative technology and revolutionary changes evolve hand-in-hand with industry and business, there are many and varied activities using models, multimedia displays and hands-on experience to encourage discovery and exploration. At the core of the Cité, covering 30,000 square metres is **Explora**, a series of permanent and temporary exhibitions covering science, technology and industry using models and audiovisual and interactive presentations. Among several scale models are the submarine *Nautilus*, a model of the *Ariane 5* rocket, 1:5 scale, 13m high; and a Mirage IV jet. The *Argonaute* is a full-scale submarine, launched in 1957. There is also a Planetarium. Further interactive and entertaining presentations involve the sensory, conceptual and technical capabilities of human mechanics in five exhibitions including Computer Science, Expression and Behaviour, Sound, and Mathematics. There are also exhibitions illustrating fundamental questions about ourselves and the environment. The **Cité des Enfants**, is designed specifically for children with a variety of activities for different age groups, following itineraries through the science village. There is also an aquarium, a cinema and a *médiathèque* (multi-media library).

Immediately to the south, reached from the main hall but outside the main building, are further entertainments. The **Géode** is an Omnimax cinema of 36m diameter. The exterior of the spherical dome is clad in 6,433 triangular plates of polished steel and inside are some 395 tiered seats facing a huge hemispheric cinema screen of 1000 square metres, 26m in diameter. Specially adapted films are projected at a vertiginous optical angle of 180°. **Cinaxe** is a 'total film experience'.

SAINT-DENIS

Tourist information: 1 Rue de la République, 93200 St-Denis, T: 01 55 87 08 70, www.saint-denis-tourisme.com. Metro: St-Denis-Basilique; RER Line D, Paris to St-Denis.
The modern, lively and cosmopolitan suburb of St-Denis is renowned for the vast modern sports stadium, the Stade de France, and the Royal Basilica of St-Denis, of vital historical significance as the burial place of the French kings. The town centre was transformed in the 1980s by imaginative redevelopment of commercial, domestic and educational buildings, which involved architects such as Roland Simounet and Oscar Niemeyer. The present market is the largest in the Ile de France (on Tuesday, Friday, and Sunday mornings). Basilica and stadium are linked by a Historic Trail, starting from the garden north of the basilica, which is indicated by 20 steel markers engraved with information on events and monuments associated with past and present St-Denis. The town also has a Museum of Art and History and a Museum of Silverware and holds an annual summer Music Festival.

History of St-Denis
According to a legend which developed in the 6th century, Dionysius, or Denis, of Paris, was the missionary apostle sent to *Lutetia* in 250. By the 9th century he was confused with two others also called Dionysius, and the tradition developed that after his execution at Montmartre c. 150 (*see p. 253*), he had carried his head to the spot

known as *Catolacus*, 11km north of Paris on the Paris–Beauvais route. At some point he was acclaimed as first bishop of Paris, and by the 12th century he was ousting St Martin of Tours as national saint. This suburb was already an important commercial centre in the Middle Ages: the Foire (fair) de St-Denis began in the 8th century, and the celebrated Foire du Lendit (held in the spring), established in 1050, received royal recognition from Louis VI until 1552. The 19th-century Grande Halle of the market and the 18th-century Maison des Arbalétriers (drying house) have been restored. When Paris was purged of heavy industry in the mid-19th century, much moved out to St-Denis, serviced by new canals. Those industries too have gradually disappeared.

THE ROYAL BASILICA OF ST-DENIS

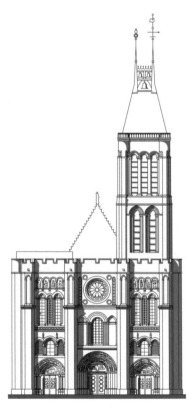

Open Apr–Sept 10–6.15, Sun 12–6.15; Oct–March 10–5.15, Sun 12–5.15; T: 01 48 09 83 54. A royal necropolis since the 7th century, the present basilica was begun in the 12th century. It shelters the tombs of the French kings, and is considered the birthplace of the Gothic style of architecture.

HISTORY OF THE ROYAL BASILICA OF ST-DENIS

The Gothic church of St-Denis stands over what is believed to be the burial place, c. 258, of St Denis and his companions Rusticus and Eleutherius (*see p. 253*). The abbey of St-Denis was founded c. 475, traditionally at the instance of St Geneviève (*see p. 42*), and enlarged in 630–38 by Dagobert, who also founded a Benedictine monastery. The first substantial church on the site was built by Abbot Fulrad in 750–75, and here in 754 Pope Stephen II annointed Pepin the Short, his wife and sons, thus establishing them securely on the throne that Pepin had recently usurped. Fulrad's church was replaced by another built by the powerful Abbot Suger (r. 1122–51), a momentous occasion in the history of architecture, for the new style adopted was the prototype of what would eventually become known as Gothic. The narthex (west porch, c. 1135–40), crypt and apse (1140–44) survive from this period. The rebuilding of the nave had barely begun before Abbot Suger's death, and the rest of the building, notably the nave and transepts, dates from 1231–81, following the designs of Pierre de Montreuil (d. 1267). The chapels on the north side of the nave were added c. 1375. The strong links between the Crown and the Abbey were reinforced at the time of Abbot Suger who, from 1127, was adviser to Louis VI and Louis VII, and Regent during the Second Crusade (1147–49). Dagobert had chosen to be buried close to the saintly relics of Denis and the Abbey Church finally became the sole royal mausoleum. With the exception of Philippe I, Louis XI, Louis-Philippe and Charles X, all the French kings since Hugh Capet were buried here. As well as being the last resting place of royalty, in 1120 Louis VI entrusted the abbey with the royal insignia, including the *oriflamme* (the military standard), and the coronation regalia. The association with royalty, and the fact that 13 bishops attended the dedication of the choir in 1144, assured the spread of its style of architecture throughout northern France. In 1422 the body of Henry V of England lay in state at St-Denis on its way from Vincennes to Westminster, and here Joan of Arc came seven years later to dedicate her armour. Henriette d'Angleterre, daughter of Charles I, was buried here in 1670 where her mother, Henrietta Maria, widow of Charles I, had been buried the previous year. At the Revolution the abbey was suppressed and its roof stripped of lead. During the Terror, the tombs were rifled, their contents dispersed and the corpses of the kings tossed into a common pit. The best of the monuments were saved from destruction by Alexandre Lenoir (1761–1839), who preserved them in his Musée des Petits-Augustins (Ecole des Beaux-Arts, *see p. 70*), from where they were later returned and quite drastically restored. Renovation of the fabric of the basilica was taken in hand in 1805, but in 1837 the north tower was struck by lightning. Debret undertook the rebuilding of the tower, which then collapsed in 1845 and was reconstructed by Viollet-le-Duc who, with Darcy, carried out the subsequent restoration.

The exterior

The west front, a development from the great Norman churches, notably St-Etienne in Caen, inspired generations of Gothic façades. Mighty buttresses divide the elevation vertically into three sections, corresponding to the internal structure of the church. An original element is the crenellated caesura between the façade and the set-back tower (originally twin towers). Three west portals, deep and finely profiled, animate the lower part of the façade. The central one is larger than the others and sets up a different rhythm in the central bay. The sculpture in the tympanums and voussoirs of all three portals has been terribly abused and was heavily reworked in the 19th century. The *Last Judgement* of the central tympanum has a few original elements—the images of God and Christ, and the Dove and the Lamb. The north door was possibly decorated with a mosaic in the first instance, representing for the first time on a tympanum a *Virgin in Majesty*. The present 19th-century carvings show the story of St Denis. The signs of the zodiac on the jambs are 12th-century. The south door tympanum is decorated with scenes from the Life of St Denis, mainly 12th-century but with 19th-century heads. The *Labours of the Month* on the jambs are 12th-century. The high relief statues of Old Testament kings in the jambs, which was a turning point in the integration of sculpture with architecture (coming before those at Chartres), were destroyed in 1771. Another innovative feature of the west façade is the large oculus (it is not known how it was originally subdivided) high in the central bay, the precursor of the rose window of Gothic architecture.

Abbot Suger undertook the enlargement of the east end to allow for the increasing number of pilgrims. The exterior of Suger's apse appears less innovatory than the west end, with Romanesque round-headed windows and relieving arches around the crypt, although the windows of the chapels are Gothic. The upper storeys with flying buttresses date from the 1230s. By Suger's death in 1151, the two ends of the church were still linked by the 8th-century construction. When the rebuilding of the nave and transept was undertaken during the mid-13th century, the upper level of Suger's choir was destroyed. The transeptal portals, each with a pioneering Rayonnant rose window, are mid-13th-century work. A small garden, Place Pierre de Montreuil, was created in 1998 on north side of the basilica, setting off the north door with its 12th–13th-century sculptures, and indicating on the ground the extent of the unfinished Valois rotunda with the monogram of Henri II and Catherine de Médicis in the centre (*see p. 412*).

The interior

Suger added to the west of the existing 8th-century church the large narthex supporting three chapels, an early medieval concept. The narthex, with incomplete towers, was consecrated in 1140. It is recognised as the first example of a Gothic façade flanked by towers, with an oculus designed to allow light into the low central chapel above the narthex. The reconstruction of the east end began immediately afterwards. Work consisted of enlarging both the crypt and, above it, the choir and the double ambulatory. The use of slender columnar supports in the ambulatory, rather than compound piers, looks back to Romanesque east ends and may have stemmed from a desire to harmonise the ambulatory with the 8th-century nave still in place. The shallow undulating chapels opening wide into the ambulatory are linked by ribbed vaulting (an ingenious combination of round and pointed ribs). In 1144, 20 new altars were consecrated. The rib vaults and the vast ratio of glazed to solid wall clinches St-Denis' reputation as the birthplace of Gothic. Also characteristic of Early Gothic are the ribs springing from strong piers enlivened by clusters of elongated shafts, and the tall openings between them. From Suger's records it is known that the central vessel was rib-vaulted. This elegant arrangement allows an uninterrupted view through to the large windows of the radiating chapels, two in each, fulfilling Suger's aim of flooding the church with 'wonderful and uninterrupted light'. The axial chapels of the crypt and ambulatory were both dedicated to the Virgin.

Work to rebuild the 8th-century nave began in earnest in 1231 and for part of the time (c. 1247) was under the direction of Pierre de Montreuil. The overall effect of the wide nave, slender shafts and exceedingly fine tracery, glazed triforium and vast expanses of glass in the clerestory, is elegant and lives up to its comparison with a lantern of light. The transepts are generous to allow for the royal tombs. They are pierced north and south with magnificent rose windows squared up to fill the whole of the bay and continuing behind the open triforium below, the first of their kind and emulated at Notre-Dame in 1258. The glass is 19th-century. The carved and inlaid high stalls of the ritual choir (1501–07) are from the chapel of Georges d'Amboise at the Château de Gaillon; the low stalls are 15th-century work from St-Lucien, near Beauvais. In the choir is a charming 12th-century *Virgin*, originally at the abbey of Longchamp.

The crypt, entered on either side of the choir, was constructed by Suger around the original Carolingian martyrium built by Abbot Fulrad, the site of the grave of St Denis and his companions. There are 12th-century capitals and traces of wall paintings, and excavations revealed Gallo-Roman Christian tombs and the tomb of Queen Aregonde, Clovis's daughter-in-law, and fragments of earlier churches.

The central chapel was the Bourbon burial vault until the Revolution, and contains the sarcophagi of Louis XVI and Marie-Antoinette *(see p. 225),* and those of Louis XVIII among other 18th- and 19th-century sovereigns. The ossuary on the north side contains the bones that were thrown into a pit when many tombs were rifled in 1793. On the south side is a 19th-century cenotaph in memory of the Bourbon kings, including Henri IV and Louis XIV. The stained glass in the Lady Chapel dates from the 12th century, placing it among the oldest in France, albeit restored in the 19th century. Among the 15 panels that have survived, mounted in modern glass in the east end, is a *Tree of Jesse,* in which Abbot Suger himself is represented. The baptistry window, designed by J. J. Gruber in 1932, is vividly different. On the south side of the ambulatory are a copy of the *Oriflamme* and statues of Louis XVI and Marie-Antoinette at prayer, commissioned by Louis XVIII.

The tombs

The tombs are a remarkable collection of funerary sculpture dating from the mid-12th to the mid-16th centuries. Among tombs in the south aisle, are those of Louis d'Orléans (d. 1407) and of Valentine de Milan (d. 1408), an Italian work of 1502–15, commissioned by Louis XII. This combines a figure in repose, in the French tradition, on an Italian-style sarcophagus where the 12 apostles replace the more usual *pleurants*. Opposite, against the southwest pillar of the crossing, is the heart-tomb of François II (d. 1560), by Germain Pilon and Ponce Jacquiau. Also in the south aisle, the urn (1549–55) by Pierre Bontemps, contains the heart of François I. In the south transept, the tomb of François I (d. 1547) and Claude de France (d. 1524), a masterpiece by Philibert de l'Orme, begun in 1547, is a classicised version of the tomb of Louis XII (*see p. 413*), in the form of a triumphal arch. Much use is made of coloured marbles skilfully worked by Bontemps. The royal pair appear kneeling, with their children, on the upper level, and again, recumbent, below. On the east side of the south transept are the tombs of Charles V (d. 1380), a remarkable likeness sculpted by André Beauneveu, commissioned before the king's death; the statue of his queen, Jeanne de Bourbon comes from the Célestins church in Paris. Bertrand du Guesclin (c. 1320-80), High Constable of France and hero of the Hundred Years War, is one of the few commoners buried here. The tomb of Charles VI (d. 1422) also resides in this transept.

At the west end of the choir is the tomb of Philippe III, le Hardi (d. 1285) by Jean d'Arras, using black and white marble, one of the first portrait statues. There is also a masterly effigy of his queen, Isabella of Aragón (d. 1271), and the tomb of Philippe IV, le Bel (d. 1314). At the left of the steps to the sanctuary is the 13th-century tomb of Dagobert (d. 638), with relief sculptures on three levels in a pinnacled niche, showing the torment and redemption of the king's soul, and a beautiful statue of Queen Nanthilde (13th century). The figures of Dagobert and his son are 19th-century restorations. Nearby is the tomb of Léon de Lusignan (d. 1393).

On the north side of the ambulatory are the tombs of Blanche and Jean (both d. 1243), children of Louis IX, a rare example of a tomb in metalwork and enamel. Transferred from St-Germain-des-Prés is a remarkable slab in cloisonné mosaic (11th century), of Frédégonde (d. 597), queen of Chilperic I; and Childebert I (d. 558), of the mid-12th century, the oldest funerary effigy in France. In the chapel at the top of the steps, are draped statues of Henri II (d. 1559) and Catherine de Médicis (d. 1589) by Germain Pilon (1583). In the sanctuary is the Altar of the Relics (by Viollet-le-Duc), on which are placed the reliquaries, given by Louis XVIII, of St Denis and fellow martyrs.

In the north transept is the temple-like tomb of Henri II, part of a grandiose scheme on the part of his queen, Catherine de Médicis, which included a huge rotunda in the Italian style on the north transept—never completed and demolished in the 18th century. Famous artists linked with its construction were Primaticcio, Lescot, Bullant, and A. du Cerceau and the tomb, designed by Primaticcio in 1560–73, was placed there by Henri IV. The monument, with recumbent and kneeling effigies of the king and queen, was sculpted by Germain Pilon and others. Here also are the tombs of Philippe V (d. 1322), Charles IV (d. 1328), Philippe VI (d. 1350) and Jean II (d. 1364), the last two by André Beauneveu. In the choir are tombs of Louis X (d. 1316) and his son Jean I (d. 1316).

The north aisle contains the tomb of Louis XII (d. 1515) and Anne de Bretagne (d. 1514), covered by a baldaquin, commissioned by François I and made by the Florentine Giovanni di Giusto, c. 1515–31. On the upper part, the royal pair is represented in life. Below, they are depicted after death in a remarkably sensitive manner (in contrast with the heavy allegorical figures surrounding them), and the chapel-like tomb enclosing the *transi* and the *transie* (the effigies of the dead pair) introduces a new element in funerary monuments. Bas-reliefs illustrate episodes in the king's career. Among other 13th–14th-century tombs, are that of Louis de France (d. 1260), the eldest son of Louis IX, with Henry III of England as one of the *pleurants* in the cortege around the base—an early example of this imagery.

The monastic dependencies

To the south of the basilica are restored monastic dependencies. Rebuilt in the 18th century by Robert de Cotte and Jacques V Gabriel, they were occupied after 1809 as a Maison d'Education de la Légion d'Honneur (*guided visits only; information from Tourist Office T: 01 55 870 870*), for the daughters of members of the Legion.

MUSEE D'ART & D'HISTOIRE

Open Wed, Fri, Mon 10–5.30, Thur 10–8, Sat, Sun 2–6.30, closed Tues and holidays; T: 01 42 43 05 10.

At no. 22 bis Rue Gabriel Péri, the museum of the town's history is installed in a Carmelite convent founded in 1625. The chapel by Mique, with an Ionic portico, has a fine compartmented cupola (1780), built while Louise de France was in residence (1770–87). St-Denis is one of the most researched towns in France, since revealing important finds during excavations for the Metro in 1972, and the museum was installed in the former convent in 1981. Three wings of the original cloister survived and the fourth has been replaced. Pious 18th-century mottos on the convent walls have been restored.

In the former chapter house is the reconstituted Pharmacy of the Hôtel-Dieu (demolished 1907) with other souvenirs of the former hospital. The refectory and kitchen of the Carmelite convent have been converted into an excellent archaeological and historical section explaining the role of the town since the time of ancient *Catolacus*—on the tin route across northern Europe, at the time of medieval St-Denis with its pilgrimage and fairs, in the evolution from monarchic to Communist associations, and in modern industries as varied as Pleyel pianos (until 1962), chemicals, Christofle glass, and gas—evoked in André Lhote's (1885–1962) painting *Usine à Gaz, St-Denis et Gennevilliers, 1937.*

The history of the Carmelites is recorded in the restored cells on the upper floor, one with memorabilia specific to Madame Louise, daughter of Louis XV. Works from the Besson Donation, notably by Albert André, friend of Renoir, are shown in adjacent rooms. On the second floor is a huge and fascinating collection devoted to the *Commune de Paris* (1870–71). The museum owns some 4,000 engravings and lithographs by Daumier (not necessarily on view). The recent modern wing of the cloister leads to the section devoted to the poet Paul Eluard (1895–1952), born in St-Denis. The exhibits include some of Eluard's manuscripts and works by Zadkine, Picasso, Max Ernst, Cocteau, Giacometti and Françoise Gilot, a *Portrait of Paul Eluard* (1952) by André Fougeron, as well as rare editions illustrated by his painter friends.

MUSEE CHRISTOFLE

Open Mon–Fri 9.30–5.30; closed Sat, Sun and holidays; T: 01 49 22 40 40. From Métro Porte de Paris, follow Blvd Anatole France southwest across the Canal St-Denis, and then turn right.

The Musée Christofle, at no. 112 Rue Ambroise Croizat, is the showpiece for the Société Christofle which was established in 1845. Its success was due to new industrial processes, not necessarily well received in the country at first, but by keeping abreast of trends and changes in demand, the company became the most important producer of silverware in France in the 20th century. The museum contains decorative silverware and tableware, with replicas of historical interest and original pieces of the art of the gold- and silversmith from tableware ordered by Napoléon III for the ministries, to creations for ocean liners and modern pieces.

STADE DE FRANCE

Guided visits every hour (except during events) from 10–5; in English in high season 10.30–2.30; T: 0892 700 900; www.stadefrance.com. Access from central Paris: Metro line 13 St-Denis-Port de Paris; RER lines B and D to Stade de France.

The regeneration of the area was boosted by the opening of the Stade de France in 1998 at Plaine-St-Denis. Designed mainly for football, rugby and athletics as well as large concerts, it was built in two years. A spectacularly well-organised complex, it seats up to 80,000 and the elliptical roof over the seating suspended from steel beams appears to hover like a flying saucer. The Panoramique Restaurant (*T: 01 55 93 04 40*), on the eighth floor of the stadium, serves gourmet food.

CHATEAU D'ECOUEN

From Paris Gare du Nord to Ecouen-Ezanville (suburban lines direction Luzarches or Persan-Beaumont par Montsoult); then bus 269 (direction Garges Sarcelles) to the Mairie d'Ecouen. Alternatively, a 20-minute walk from the station through the woods: a footpath leads to the château.

Ecouen is a small town in a rural setting, dominated by the magnificent Renaissance Château d'Ecouen which houses the Musée National de la Renaissance, inaugurated in 1977. It is the furthest museum from the centre of Paris in this book, but it is important because the collection follows on chronologically from the Museum of the

Middle Ages in Paris. There is little to see in the town except for the church of St-Acceul which has some notable stained-glass (1544) in the choir.

MUSEE NATIONAL DE LA RENAISSANCE

Open Wed–Sun 9.30–12.45 & 2-5.45, winter closing 5.15; closed Tues; park open daily summer 8–7, winter 8–6; T: 01 34 38 38 50, www.musee-renaissance.fr
This elegant, well-organised, and less well known museum, provides an overview of the decorative arts of the Renaissance in a château which itself is a prime example of Renaissance architecture.

HISTORY OF THE MUSEE NATIONAL DE LA RENAISSANCE

The construction of the château began c. 1538 for the Constable Anne de Montmorency. Among major artists employed were the sculptor Jean Goujon and the architect Jean Bullant. The building was put to a variety of uses during the Revolutionary period, and in 1805 became a school for girls. Many of its embellishments, including an altar by Goujon from the chapel, were removed during the Revolution, and reverted to the Duc d'Aumale, who chose to include them in his château at Chantilly. Built in two stages, beginning 1538 and 1547, the château is arranged around a courtyard, with square pavilions on the angles and moats on three sides. The elevations are simply articulated with pilasters and string courses, and ornamentation confined to the dormer windows, which show a progression in styles from the west to the north wings. After 1547, work began on the interior to provide luxurious apartments for the owners and King Henri II, and porticos were added. Those on both sides of the north wing have Henri II's insignia. The south portico, which uses the Colossal Order for the first time in France, is ascribed to Jean Bullant. It was intended as the setting for Michelangelo's *Slaves* (*see p. 191*) given to Montmorency by Henri II.

The museum

The entrance, through the east wing, is a replacement (1807) of the superimposed galleries. Above was an equestrian statue of the Constable, designed by Goujon or Bullant, destroyed in 1787 (a fragment of its decorative sculpture is in the museum).

Ground floor

The Armoury: The series of rooms on the ground floor begins with the Armoury which has a profusely decorated chimneypiece in the School of Fontainebleau style, the first of 12 depicting biblical themes which are a feature of Ecouen. The arms and armour include stirrups with the emblem of François I, and armour from the workshops of Maximilian I of Germany c. 1510–20.

The Kitchens: These contain a collection of fragments of stonework from Ecouen and carved wooden screens and other pieces from the Château of Gaillon (Normandy).

The Room of Roman Heroes: This room contains rare painted leather hangings from Normandy with Roman heroes and the chimneypiece shows *The Tribute to Caesar*. Small rooms are devoted to collections of magnificent alabaster, carved wooden plaques and panels and small sculptures. There are also pear-wood and box-wood statuettes, mainly German or Flemish. Outstanding bronze figurines include *Jupiter* by Alessandro Vittoria, *Virgin and Child* by Niccolò Roccatagliata, and *Fornicating Satyrs* by Riccio. There are also superb examples of damascened metalwork, cutlery and a collection of Renaissance door-furniture.

The Clock Room: Among the mathematical instruments and watches here are a celestial sphere in gilded copper and an exquisite automated timepiece masquerading as a miniature ship, by Hans Schlotlheim of Augsburg. An unusual object is the inlaid silversmith's workbench from Germany (1565), a full-scale working model made for a nobleman's pleasure rather than as a craftsman's tool.

Catherine de Médicis Chamber: This angle room has three tapestries showing the Battle of St-Denis (10th November, 1567) and a portable triptych with painted enamels.

The Queen's Room: Here is a monumental fireplace from a house in Rouen, and in the next room are sculpted and enamelled terracottas by Luca della Robbia as well as French sculptures including *The Three Fates*, in marble, by Germain Pilon, and *The Compassion of the Father* in terracotta. The museum owns a precious collection of portraits in wax in the form of medallions; it also has ten carved *mascarons* (heads) originally on corbels (c. 1600) of the Pont-Neuf in Paris, and two from the Palais du Louvre.

First floor

South Wing: The first floor has been arranged to evoke the owners' and the king's residence as it was after 1547. In the South Wing were the apartments of Anne de Montmorency and his wife, Madeleine. The décor incorporates reminders of his role as commander of the army—an unsheathed sword accompanying his coat of arms. The decorated chimneypiece in the Constable's Chamber has a scene of *Esau Hunting* and there are two School of Fontainebleau paintings. The reconstructed Constable's Library, above the chapel, is reached by a spiral staircase from these apartments. It has its original and unique décor of wooden panels inlaid with gilt arabesques and the monogram of Anne de Montmorency. The Apartments of Madeleine de

Savoie, are mainly a reconstruction. The antechamber contains an Italian spinet (1570) and the main rooms contain a 16th-century Venetian bureau inlaid with painted mother-of-pearl and notable carved doors (from elsewhere). Abigail's Pavilion takes its name from the painted decoration of the fireplace, which shows and episode from the legend of Abigail and David.

Psyche Gallery: The long Psyche Gallery originally had sumptuous decoration of stained glass and paving (remnants of which are exhibited elsewhere), and murals. The finely carved stone fireplaces are from Châlons-en-Champagne (1562), with reliefs of *Christ and the Samarian Woman*, and *Actaeon Surprising Diana in her Bath*. This room houses the raison d'être of the museum, the celebrated series of tapestries entitled *The Story of David and Bathsheba* (Brussels c. 1510). It is possible that Jan van Roome was involved in their creation.

Individualistic portrayal of the figures and architectural settings, typically Renaissance, is combined with a foreground reminiscent of medieval *millefleurs*. Stylised flowers form the border and the colours are still strong. The story, reading from left to right, begins with a scribe before an open book recording the episodes. Each of the ten tapestries contains several scenes. David, despised by his wife, brings the ark to Jerusalem, then departs for battle against the Ammonites at Rabbah, with Uriah, husband of Bathsheba. After seducing Bathsheba, David sends Uriah to his death and Bathsheba is received at David's court. The prophet Nathan

predicts the death of their child, while allegorical figures put Lust to flight. David and Bathsheba's child dies and David appeases God's anger by fasting and praying. He then resumes the battle and takes Rabbah. As the story ends the scribe closes the book.

West Wing: A small room in the west wing and the series of rooms that follow are the apartments of the king. Henri II's Chamber has a painted ceiling with the king's monogram and crescent, and a chimneypiece featuring *Saul in Anger Slaughtering Two of his Cattle*. Beyond a carved wooden staircase, from the Chambre des Comptes of the Palais de la Cité, is the Salle d'honneur, which has the only sculpted marble chimneypiece at Ecouen. Attributed to Jean Bullant, c. 1558, the coloured marble was a gift of Cardinal Farnese. The paved floor, originally in the Psyche Gallery, was made by Masséot Abaquesne (mid 16th century), who made his name at Ecouen. Displayed in this room are two tapestries of the *Fructus Belli* series (the other six dispersed elsewhere), woven in Brussels, 1546–48, by Jean Baudouyn from cartoons by Giulio Romano, which show the soldiers' payday and the general's dinner. In the next rooms are painted leather panels with scenes from Scipio and a chimneypiece with the *Judgement of Solomon* as well as secular stained glass from Ecouen with the emblems of Anne de Montmorency, Catherine de Médicis, François I and Henri II. The last room on this floor has embroideries made for Sully when he was Grand Master of the Artillery and occupied the Arsenal in Paris.

Second floor

The first room on the second floor is devoted to a remarkable group of Iznik Ceramics (ancient Nicaea, in northwest Turkey), dating largely from 1555–1700. French ceramics are represented by 16th-century tile panels, and ceramics by Masséot Abaquesne including a magnificent tiled floor of 1550 and pharmacy pots; also two rare pieces from the Saint-Porchaire workshops, c. 1560, and faience attributed to Bernard Palissy. There is a room dedicated to *cassoni*, painted panels from 15th-century Florentine marriage-chests, and Limoges enamel plaques; also collections of majolica, glass and among the jewellery, a swan pendant from Germany. Among fine examples of the gold- and silversmith's craft are notably a statuette of Daphne by Wenzel Jamnitzer, a goblet in the shape of a snail (Netherlands; c. 1700), and several magnificent examples from Nuremberg and Augsburg.

APPENDIX

The selected museums listed alphabetically below are not treated in the main body of the text. They are given here with brief details in order to assist in wider exploration of the enormous wealth and variety of the collections in Paris.

Aquarium du Trocadéro
Map p. 473, D1
Av. Albert-de-Mun. 16th. Open daily 10–10; T: 01 40 69 23 23.
Reopened after 21 years, the totally refurbished aquarium in the Trocadero Gardens contains 15,000 fish of 500 different species, including sharks, and sting rays divided among 43 pools containing 4 million litres of water. Access is by a tunnel which resembles an underwater walk and CinéAqua has 3 cinemas for underwater films. There is also a Japanese restaurant and bar.

Musée des Arts Forains
Map p. 3, E4
Les Pavillons de Bercy, 53 Avenue des Terroirs de France. 12th. Open by e-mail appointment Sat, Sun only; T: 01 43 40 16 22. www.pavillons-de-bercy.com
The magical Museum of Fairground Art, housed in former wine warehouses, includes fairground organs, carousels and other old-fashioned sideshows.

Musée de l'Assistance Publique
Map p. 475, F3
47 Quai de la Tournelle. 5th. Open Tues–Sun 10–6; closed Sun, Mon, holidays and Aug; T: 01 40 27 50 05.
The 9,000 objects and documents, and art works, including 260 paintings, give an overview of the history of Paris hospitals from the time of the foundation of the Hôtel Dieu in the 12th century up to the beginning of the 20th.

Musée Bouilhet-Christofle
Map p. 469, E4
9 Rue Royale, 1st. T: 01 49 33 43 00.
Some 2,000 pieces made by six generations of the same family are on display. They demonstrate the techniques used in the art of the silversmith, the evolution of the decorative arts over 170 years, and include 19th and 20th century table settings, as well as examples of unusual private commissions.

Musée du Cheval de Courses
Château de Maisons, Maisons-Laffitte. Open Sun–Mon April–Oct 10–12 & 2–6; Nov–March 10–12 & 2–5, closed Tues; T: 01 39 62 01 49.
A racehorse museum in the racing capital of Maisons-Laffitte, where the Comte d'Artois installed his English stable—80 race horses, a trainer, jockey and grooms—and introduced English-style racing in the 18th century, was refurbished and reopened in November 2006.

Palais de la Découverte
Map p. 468, C4
West extension of the Grand Palais, Av. Franklin-D.-Roosevelt, 8th. Open Tues–Sat 9.30–6, Sun and holidays 10–7, closed

in the gallery overlooking the Jardin de Luxembourg. Among exhibits are hundreds of meteorites, the most important of which is the Canyon Diablo Meteorite found in 1890 at the bottom of a ravine in Arizona.

Musée Pasteur
Map p. 473, F4
Institut Pasteur, 25 Rue du Docteur-Roux, 15th. Open Mon–Fri 2–5.30, closed Sat, Sun and August; T: 01 45 68 82 83.
The institute was founded by Louis Pasteur (1822–95) in 1887 and built by private subscription. Pasteur's apartment has become a museum, containing family memorabilia and the mausoleum with the chemist's tomb.

Bibliothèque Polonaise de Paris - Société Historique et Littéraire Polonaise
Map p. 475, F2
6 Quai d'Orléans. 4th. Open Thurs 2–6; T: 01 43 54 35 61.
This is a Polish library with souvenirs of the Romantic Polish poet, Adam Mickiewicz (1798–1855), political figure and friend of Victor Hugo. Also the Salon Chopin with memorabilia of the composer and the Musée Boleslas Biegas, Symbolist sculptor.

Musée de la Poupée
Map p. 476, A1
22 Rue Beaubourg, Impasse Berthaud. 3rd. Open Tues–Sun 10–6; closed Mon and holidays; T: 01 42 72 73 11.
Collection of dolls, from France and from around the world

Musée de la Préfecture de Police
Map p. 475, E3
5 Rue de la Montagne Ste-Geneviève. 5th. Open Mon–Fri 9–5, Sat 10–5, closed Sun and holidays; T: 01 44 45 52 50.
Exhibits associated with the history of the Prefecture of Police include a section devoted to the Resistance and the Liberation of Paris, records of important conspiracies, arrests, famous characters, archives, unique weapons and uniforms, and evidence from famous criminal cases.

Musée du Service de Santé des Armées
Map p. 475, D4
1 Pl. A.-Laveran, 5th. Open Tues, Wed 12–5, Sat–Sun 1.30–5; T: 01 40 51 51 92.
The collections of the Army Health Department are displayed in the historic building of Val de Grâce. These illustrate the history of French military medical service. The Salle Debat has a complete pharmacy, and a travelling pharmacy.

Tenniseum Roland Garros
Map p. 2, A3
2 Av. Gordon Bennett, 16th. Open Tues–Sun 10–6, closed Mon; T: 01 47 43 48 48. Metro Porte d'Auteil.
The first multimedia tennis museum, covering 2,200 square metres.

PRACTICAL INFORMATION

PLANNING YOUR TRIP

When to go

Parisian weather is temperate and variable, and while spring in Paris is most people's ideal, the autumn can also be glorious, when there are long periods of fine weather. Average temperatures from March to May range from 4° to 20°C, June to August 13° to 25°C, September to December 12° to 21°C, and January and February 1° to 7°C. The heaviest rainfall can be in August.

Websites on Paris

www.paris.fr	City of Paris
www.parisinfo.com	Paris Tourist Office and Convention
www.francetourisme.fr	French Tourist Office
www.pidf.com	Tourist Board of the Ile de France
www.franceguide.com	French Government Tourist Office, London
www.parismuseumpass.fr	Paris Museum Pass
www.monum.fr	Centre des Monuments Nationaux
www.raileurope.co.uk	European rail services: Information and bookings
www.disneylandparis.com	Eurodisney

Disabled travellers

Since 1978 French law has ensured that all new public amenities have disabled facilities and access. Considerable progress has also been made to overcome problems of access for the disabled to historic buildings, including hotels, museums, monuments and other leisure venues as well as restaurants. Disabilities are divided into four main categories: physical, mental, visual and hearing under the *Tourisme & Handicap* label and indicated by appropriate logos. A list of Parisian hotels and restaurants with this label is available on the Paris Tourist Office website, the Maison French Government Tourist Office, London, and at information offices in Paris. Certain bus routes and Metro line 14 and RER line A are partially accessible to people with limited mobility.

ARRIVAL

Eurostar

The most pleasant and efficient way to arrive in Paris from the UK is by Eurostar. At time of writing, trains depart from Waterloo International. From 14th November 2007, services are scheduled to depart from the new terminal at St Pancras. There are also departures from Ashford International Terminal, Kent. The journey time from

London is around 2hrs 40mins, and from Ashford around 2hrs, and will be reduced further when the new high-speed rail link is in use. Trains arrive at Gare-du-Nord in the centre of Paris. Information can be obtained and reservations made direct with Eurostar on T: 08705 186 186 (from outside UK +44 1233 617 575), or from most main line stations, or www.eurostar.com.

Airports

Roissy-Charles de Gaulle (CDG), has two separate terminals and is 23km northeast of the capital. Flight schedules T: 0 891 68 15 15, www.adp.fr; switchboard T: 01 48 62 22 80; customs T: 01 48 62 62 85; police T: 01 48 62 31 22. Air France Coaches (*T: 0 892 350 820, www.cars-airfrance.com*) leave every 15 mins between CDG-Porte Maillot-Etoile-CDG from 5.45am–11pm, taking 45–60mins. Trains run every 30 mins between CDG-Gare de Lyon-Gare Montparnasse-CDG from 7am-9pm. Roissybus (*T: 0 892 68 77 14*) leaves every 15 to 20 mins from CDG to Opéra-Rue Scribe from 6am–11pm, and from Opéra-Rue Scribe to CDG from 5.45am to 11pm. RER Line B (*T: 0 890 36 10 10*) every 8 mins, from CDG to Gare du Nord from 5.44am–0.11am, and from Gare du Nord to CDG from 4.56am–11.56pm.

Orly is 14km south of Paris. T: 0 892 68 15 15, www.adp.fr; switchboard T: 01 49 75 15 15; customs T: 01 49 75 78 51; police T: 01 49 75 43 04. Air France Coaches (*details as above*) leave every 15 mins from 6–11 between Orly-Gare Montparnasse, Gare des Invalides; between Gare des Invalides, Montparnasse, Orly from 5.45am-11pm. Orlybus (*T: 0 892 68 77 14*) leaves every 15 to 20 mins from Orly–Denfert-Rochereau from 6am–11.30pm; from Denfert-Rochereau–Orly from 5.35am–11pm. Orlyval shuttle train (T: 0 892 68 77 14), every 7 mins, connection with RER B at Antony from 6am–11pm. RER C (+ ADP shuttle bus): Every 15 mins, Paris–Orly 5.45am–11.15pm; Orly–Paris, 5.50am–10.50pm.

Beauvais is one hour from paris via the A16 motorway. T: 0 892 682 066 or 0 892 682 073, www.aeroportbeauvais.com. Shuttles from Port Maillot (Palais de Congres) 3 hours before flight departure. Train from Gare du Nord

Railway stations

The main stations of the SNCF are: Gare d'Austerlitz (*Map p. 476, B4*), Gare de l'Est (*Map p. 471, D3*), Gare de Lyon (*Map p. 476, C4*), Gare Montparnasse (*Map p. 474, B4*), Gare du Nord (*Map p. 471, D2*), and Gare St-Lazare (*Map p. 469, E3*). Most have left-luggage offices (*consignes*) or lockers, trolleys and information bureaux. Some, such as Gare d'Austerlitz and Gare du Nord, are also connected by regular bus services.

SNCF information and reservations: main line T: 08 36 35 35 35; in English: T: 08 36 35 35 39; Ile-de-France T: 01 53 90 20 20 (French only).

NB: French Railways do not have ticket control at platform barriers. Passengers travelling in France must validate (*composter*) their ticket in an orange-red machine (which punches and date-stamps it) at the platform entrance before boarding the train.

Paris Convention and Visitors Bureaux (Tourist Offices)

T: 0 892 68 3000, www.parisinfo.com
Main Centre: *25 Rue des Pyramides. Open June–Oct daily 9–7; Nov–May Mon–Sat 10–7, Sun and holidays 11–7. Metro: Pyramides/Tuileries/Opéra.*
Opéra–Grand Magasins: *11 Rue Scribe. Open Mon–Sat 9–6.30; closed Sun.*
Gare de Lyon: *20 Blvd Diderot. Open Mon–Sat 8–6; closed Sun and holidays.*
Gare du Nord: *18 Rue de Dunkerque. Open daily 8–6.*
Montmartre: *Syndicat d'Initiative, 21 Pl. du Tertre. Open daily 10–7; T: 01 42 62 21 21. Metro: Abbesses.*
Anvers: *72 Blvd Rochechouart. Open daily 10–6.*
Champs-Elysées-Clémenceau: *Av. Des Champs-Elysees/corner Av. Marigny. Open 3 April–15 Sept daily 9–7.*
Espace de Tourism d'Ile-de-France: *Carrousel du Louvre, Pl. de la Pyramide-Inversée, 99 Rue de Rivoli. Open daily 10–6; T: 0 826 166 666, www.pidf.com*

PUBLIC TRANSPORT

The Parisian public transport authority RATP, 54 Quai de la Râpée, operates the Métro, RER trains, and buses. This is an efficient system except for the lack of late-evening buses. Information for all three services (French) T: 0 892 68 77 14, (English) www.ratp.fr. Combined maps are available at Métro ticket offices.

Underground

The Métro (*Métropolitan*) runs between 5.30am and 0.30am and is frequent and efficient. There are 14 lines identifiable by their number and colour. The direction of the train is indicated by the terminal station. Interchanges are marked Correspondance. One ticket is valid for one Métro journey including interchanges.

RER

RER (suburban express railway) is a fast under- and overground service, Lines A, B, C, D and E. The Métro ticket is valid on these lines within central Paris but beyond Zone 2, RER fares are different.

Tram

The first modern tramway in central Paris, the T3 opened in 2006, with 17 stations open 5am to 12.30am. The five-mile route runs along a grassy track on the outer perimeter of the Left Bank (13th, 14th and 15th arrondissements).

Bus

Bus routes are numbered and mostly operate 6.30am–8.30pm. One ticket is needed for each bus journey (excluding interchanges) and should be date stamped (*composté*) in the machine near the driver. Routes and timetables are clearly displayed at individual bus stops which are all request stops (*arrêt facultatif*), and each is indicated by name on the stop, and on several lines stops are announced in advance. A few late-night buses run until 0.30am. Noctambus (night service) operates 18 bus routes seven days a week, between 1am and 5.35am. The Balabus stops at the main tourist sites between Bastille and La Défense between 12.30pm and 8pm, from April to September; stops are marked Balabus (Bb). The Monmatrobus is a round trip of Montmartre between the *Mairie du 18ème* and Pigalle. Paris l'Open Tour, (*T: 01 42 66 56 56, www.paris-opentour.com*) is a sightseeing/hop-on hop-off service.

Travel passes and tickets

The same tickets are used on Métro, RER and bus lines. They can be purchased at all RATP stations and some tobacconists. They are sold individually or in tens (*carnet*).

Paris-Visite: This is a travel pass valid for one, two, three or five consecutive days of unlimited travel by Métro, RER, bus, suburban SNCF trains and the Montmartre Funicular in zones 1–3 (excluding airports), and zones 1–5 (including airports and Chessy-Marne-la-Vallée for Disneyland) and zones 1–8. It offers reductions to numerous museums and monuments and L'Open Tour and can be purchased at all major tourist and transport interchanges. In England, it is on sale at Rail Europe, 178 Piccadilly, and in the Eurostar terminals.

Carte Orange: Valid for a week (*hebdomadaire*) or for a month (*mensuel*); a passport-size photograph is required for an SNCF identification card, which is used to buy further weekly or monthly tickets.

Mobilis: An unlimited stop-go travel ticket for a variety of transit zones, including SNCF suburban lines, Métro and bus. A one-day pass covering zones 1-2 up to 1-8 (excluding airports), is valid for that day (not 24 hours). It can be purchased at Metro, RER and SNCF stations and RATP shops. A photo is not required.

Bicycles, scooters, rollerblades and hiking

Bikes can be hired from: **Maison roue libre** *1 Passage Mondétour, Metro: Châtelet-les-Halles. Open 9–7; T: 0 810 44 15 34, www.ratp.fr*; **Paris Bike tour** *103 Rue de Villiers de l'Isle-Adam, Metro: Pelleport. T: 01 53 39 13 14, www.parisbiketour.com*
Bikes, motorbikes and scooters: **Motorail** *190 Rue de Bercy, Metro: Gare-de-Lyon. T: 01 43 07 08 09, www.motorail.fr*; **Sejem** *144 Blvd Voltaire. T: 01 44 93 04 03, www.sejem.com* There are two Rollerblade circuits, on Friday evenings for competent skaters and on Sunday afternoons for all. Parisians turn out in their thousands.

On water

Batobus *Port de la Bourdonnais, Metro: Bir-Hakeim. T: 01 44 11 33 99, www.batobus.com* is an original form of seasonal transport with eight stops on the Seine and runs most of the year; one-day or two-day tickets are available.

Cruise boats on the Seine leave from: Port de la Bourdonnais, **Bateaux Parisiens** *T: 01 44 11 33 44, www.bateauxparisiens.com*; Pont Bir-Hakeim: **Capitaine Fracasse/Le Grand Bleu** *T: 01 46 21 48 15, www.quai55.com*; Port de Solférino: **La Marina de Paris**

T: 01 43 43 40 30, www.marinadeparis.com; Square du Vert-Galant: **Vedettes de Pont-Neuf** *T: 01 46 33 98 38, www.pontneuf.net*; and Port de Suffren: **Vedettes de Paris** *T: 01 44 18 19 50*. On the Canal St-Martin: **Canauxrama**, *Bassin de la Villette, 13 Quai de la Loire, T: 01 42 39 15 00; www.canauxrama.com*; **Paris Canal**, *Bassin de la Villette, 19–21 Quai de la Loire, T: 01 42 40 96 97, www.pariscanal.com*

Taxis

Taxis have no particular distinctive form or colour, except for the white 'Taxi' sign on the roof (lit up when available). They can be found at train stations, airports, near major road junctions, at 470 taxi ranks, and can be hailed. At taxi ranks are telephones to call taxis. Standing pick-up charge, €2; minimum fare €5.20; for each passenger from the 4th onwards, €2.70; supplement charged for luggage from second piece placed in boot. No supplement can be requested from disabled using a wheelchair and/or animals accompanying them. It is advisable to request a receipt for each journey, in the event of dispute or lost property. In case of complaint, contact the **Préfecture de Police Service des Taxis** *36 Rue des Morillon; T: 0 821 00 25 25*. Average taxi fare from airports: between CDG and Paris €38 and €45; between Orly and Paris €46 and €54. Tipping is not strictly necessary.

HOTELS & ACCOMMODATION

Paris has something like 75,000 hotel rooms and over 2,000 hotels, with a huge range of styles, value and prices. Booking by internet or by phone assures a much better rate than the walk-in price. The more expensive the hotel the more likely are special offers, well worth searching for. There is a tourist tax of €0.20 to €1.20 per person per night, which may or may not be included in the quoted price; breakfasts are rarely included, unless on special offers. Prices are quoted per room per night. Hotels which are specially recommended are marked (■). Details of Blue Guide recommended hotels and restaurants are on www.blueguides.com

€€€	€300+
€€	€200–300
€	below €200

€€€ L'Hôtel. ■ *13 Rue des Beaux-Arts, 75006; T: 01 44 41 99 00, www.l-hotel.com Map p. 475, D2*. This is a very gorgeous boutique hotel in St-Germain-des-Prés in a building which carries lots of historic baggage yet remains resolutely up to the minute. Architecturally, its unique characteristic is a central six-storey circular balconied atrium supported by ancient stone cellars below which have been cunningly adapted to contain a hammam/*contre-courant* swimming pool. Owned now by Peter Frankopan and Jessica Sainsbury (who own Cowley Manor in Gloucestershire), this has been a hotel of distinction since the time of

Oscar Wilde who famously took his last breath here in 1900, and patronised by the glitterati in the 1970s/80s. Fashionable designer Jacques Garcia has carried out the latest transformation, bringing a different theme to each of the 30 bedrooms. Apart from the legendary Wilde bedroom, with English furniture, peacock mural and tiny balcony, others are the elegant 30s-style Mistinguette room, with objects from her home, the Cardinal room with a view of the belfry of St-Germain, or the Restoration style of the Roi de Naples room. The lounge, bar and restaurant (*see p. 439*) are intimate and comfortable, decked out in Garcia-Directoire style, and lead to a small courtyard with fountain. The staff is friendly, helpful and speak English. Tariffs range from €255–€740; breakfast €22.

€€€ **Hôtel Lutetia.** *46 Blvd Raspail, 75006, T: 01 49 54 46 46, 01 49 54 46 10, www.lutetia-paris.com Map p. 474, C3.* A seriously grand and traditional hotel built in 1910 at the instigation of the owner of Bon Marché department store, which is opposite. The Lutetia was built by Louis-Hippolyte Boileau (1878–1948). It has belonged to the Tattinger family since 1955, but now comes under the Concorde hotel umbrella. It has seen its fair share of celebrated guests such as Picasso, Matisse, Josephine Baker and General de Gaulle. The first Art Deco hotel in Paris, its authentic style has been retained inside and out. There is a huge lobby, a gastronomic restaurant 'Paris', a wonderfully authentic brasserie looking out to the street, which specialises in *fruits de mer*, and the glamorous Bar Lutece. The Ernest is a piano bar with jazz on certain evenings. All the 250 huge bedrooms

and suites (one suite contains works by the artist Arman) are beautifully appointed and have 1930s-style furnishings, using tones of gold and mahogany. Some of the suites (Literary and Eiffel) have spectacular views towards the Eiffel tower and the Suite Opéra, where the Director of Opera Garnier lived, is atmospheric in emerald green and light wood. Prices range from €280 up to €1450 for a suite; the Arman Suite, with a giant violin-shaped headboard and musical-score sheets, is €2500.

€€€ **Hôtel Pavillon de la Reine.** *28 Pl. des Vosges, 75004, T: 01 40 29 19 19, www.pavillon-de-la-reine.com Map p. 476, B2.* Opening from Pl. des Vosges, the beautiful square in the Marais in Henri IV style, completed in 1612, the hotel is entered across a pretty courtyard in the 17th-century house which has always been known as the Pavillon de la Reine. Lots of wooden beams, rustic and refined, and other picturesque features maintain the authentic atmosphere of this old building. The standard rooms are quite small but pleasant; there are duplexes under the roof which have more character and some suites have four-poster beds and beamed ceilings, while the Victor Hugo suite has a kitchen. Prices range from €350–€640.

€€ **Hôtel Bourg Tibourg.** *19 Rue du Bourg Tibourg, 75004, T: 01 42 78 47 39, www.hotelbourgtibourg.com Map p. 475, F2.* The fashionable designer Jacques Garcia is responsible for the Viollet-le-Duc look—incorporating neo-Gothic-Victorian with Oriental—in this luxurious hotel owned by the Frères Costes, and designed as a voyage in itself. No surface is ignored and no detail spared. Thirty or so smallish, warmly coloured rooms are luxuriously and beautifully appointed with superb touches such as fringed lampshades and Gothic-style gilded fretwork. Black granite and mosaic tiles feature in the bathrooms. There is also a tiny garden with just about room for two for breakfast. The whole effect is opulent, even somewhat over-egged, bordering on the look of a 19th-century upmarket bordello. Tariffs range from €160 to €350, breakfast €12.

€€ **Hôtel Buci.** *22 Rue Buci, 75006, T: 01 55 42 74 74, www.bucihotel.com Map p. 475, D2.* This is a very charming hotel which has got the balance just right. Beautifully situated on a little street deep in St-Germain, close to the traditional Buci street market, as well as to the galleries, antiques shops and boutiques of the quarter, it occupies a 16th-century building. The very attractive entrance lobby sets the standard for the subtle and thoughtful décor, with a very comfortable under-stated lounge. The breakfast room, which doubles up as a bar, is a small haven of tranquillity. The decoration of the bedrooms, some with exposed beams, is luxurious but not overwhelming. They are also a surprisingly good size and all have elegant marble bathrooms. The prices range from €170 for a simple double to €650 for a suite. Breakfast is around €15–20.

€€ **Hôtel Edouard VII.** ■ *39 Avenue de l'Opéra, Paris 75002, T: 01 42 61 56 90, www.edouard7hotel.com Map p. 470, A4.* This is a really good hotel, one of two (with the Aviatic) owned by the Corbel family where quality, efficiency and excellent service are apparent throughout. Built as a hotel in 1877, during the time of Entente Cordiale at the end of the 19th century, it was patronized by King Edward VII who enjoyed the view of the Opera House from the balconies on the angle between Av. de l'Opera and Rue Louis le Grand. The lobby is an open space with an eclectic choice of décor combining traditional marble, mahogany, Italian chandelier, and modern carvings by Nicolas Cesbron. Off the lobby is a very comfortable bar with the original stained-glass windows and modern furnishing. Meals, including the copious buffet breakfast, are served in the dining-room/restaurant, l'Angl'Opéra (*see p. 436*). The refurbished bedrooms have parquet floors and deep luxurious colour schemes and all the rest of the rooms are being renovated; bathrooms have granite floors, double basins, good lighting and bathrobes. Each room has a modem socket. Official rates from €390 to €1100, but be sure to check special offers on internet.

€€ **Hôtel du Jeu de Paume.** *54 Rue St-Louis-en-l'Île, 75004, T: 01 43 26 14 18, www.jeudepaumehotel.com Map p. 476, A3.* This is a very smartly converted 17th-century building where real tennis was once played. It is in the middle of the island, which is an idyllic setting in itself, and it has a small courtyard. The tennis court is converted into the lounge where there hangs a painting of a game in progress. The new features which assure a comfortable stay combine harmoniously with old beams and stone walls. Thirty elegant bedrooms use subtle but interesting colours teamed with carefully selected antiques and old pieces. There are also two very well appointed apartments for longer stays, on the first and second floors at the front of the building, one with three bedrooms, and both equipped with kitchen and bathrooms. The room prices are from €145 to €545, and the apartments are €450 to €900; breakfast is €18.

€ Hotel Arvor. ■ *8 Rue Laferrière, 75009, T: 01 48 78 60 92, www.arvor-hotel-paris.com Map p. 470, B2.* This may not be the most obvious area to stay, but it is a very interesting residential quarter, full of history and culture, just around the corner from the Pl. St-Georges, between Pigalle and Montmartre and the Grands Magazins. The hotel is in a tall building which has been modernised and the light entrance lobby opens onto a tiny courtyard-garden. There is a bar-lounge, and a library corner for guests providing guides and other books. The 31 bedrooms are fresh, light and very simple, with white paint and fabrics. Some are under the eaves, and one suite opens onto the courtyard. The higher rooms have windows that open onto some great views. There is an old staircase with attractive wrought iron balustrade as well as lift. The continental breakfast is good quality, part buffet, and served in the courtyard on fine days. Prices are around €115 to €165, and €9 for breakfast.

€ Hotel Aviatic. ■ *105 Rue de Vaugirard, 75006, T: 01 53 63 25 50, www.aviatic.fr Map p. 474, B3.* This is a very comfortable period piece in the Montparnasse district just off Rue de Vaugirard with the Tour Montparnasse nearby for a high cocktail (*see p. 442*). It is owned by the Corbel family (who also own the Edouard VII) and similar high standards prevail in this three-star establishment which occupies a historic site. In the 17th century this was the site of a house owned by the Marquise de Maintenon, where she brought up the illegitimate children of Louis XIV and Madame de Montespan. A hotel since 1856, this building became the principle residence of aviators based at the Issy-les-Moulineaux airfield during the First World War, and it also became a base for artists and writers. Bedrooms are ingeniously and individually decorated with restored furniture and artefacts, and beautiful Pierre Frey fabrics. The Millennium rooms are the deluxe version in warm tones and luxury bathrooms; family rooms with connecting doors are available. The entrance hall is typical of an old Parisian house, with a pretty staircase, and a small attractively decorated Empire-style lounge. The staff is very helpful, and the breakfast room has a café atmosphere (good teabags); buffet breakfast €13. Rates from €140–€295.

€ Hôtel de la Bretonnerie. *Rue Ste-Croix-de-la-Bretonnerie, 75004, T: 01 48 87 77 63, www.bretonnerie.com Map p. 475, F2.* This is a delightful, intimate hotel deep in the Marais with a pretty entrance hall and a fine 17th-century staircase. Although the old building does not allow for very spacious rooms, each of the 28 bedrooms (some are small suites), is individually decorated in lush warm colours or chintzes which contrast with exposed beams and stone walls. The bathrooms are nicely appointed. The breakfast room is created from the stone-vaulted undercroft and has red upholstered chairs which give it a rather medieval look. Room rates range from €116 to €205, and breakfast is €9.50.

€ Hôtel Brighton. *218 Rue de Rivoli, 75001, T: 01 47 03 61 61, www.esprit-de-france.com Map p. 469, E4.* The Brighton, like many others with English names, has been so-called since the cordial relations between England and France at the time of Queen Victoria. The interior has kept much of its original 1850s charm, including faux-marble and mosaics and it is in a marvellous position overlooking the Tuileries Gardens—an ideal base for visits to the Louvre or the newly re-opened Musée des Arts Decoratifs. The rooms are good quality and quite traditional, most being remarkably spacious with large bathrooms. Those at the back are quieter, but on the Rue de Rivoli side there is the advantage of the view, even better from the corner rooms and the higher rooms with balconies. Excellent value given the size of the rooms and the location. Rooms from €137 to €255, buffet breakfast €16.

€ **Hôtel Claret.** *44 Blvd. de Bercy, 75012, T: 01 46 28 41 31, www.hotel-claret.com Map p. 477, D4.* And now for somewhere different: the chance to stay in a former *relais-de-poste* of the old wine-trading area of Paris transformed into the Jardins de Bercy. Close to the Seine and the Bastille, this is one of the upcoming fashionable districts of Paris. Right on the doorstep in the Bercy gardens are the Cinemathèque and Museum of Cinema while across the gardens is Bercy Village with a multitude of shops, restaurants and wine-bars (*see p. 310*). It has 52 sound-proofed, functional and pleasant rooms in calm colours and three grades: standard, superior (overlooking the gardens), and mansart, the largest, under the sloping roof. The hotel restaurant is called the Bouchon et Bistrot, with outside dining in good weather. Room prices are reasonable, from €90 to €169; €10 for buffet-breakfast.

€ **Hôtel Ferrandi.** *92 Rue du Cherche-Midi, 75006, T: 01 42 22 97 40; hotel.ferrandi@wanadoo.fr Map p. 474, B3.* This pleasant hotel in a 19th-century building is in a very good position between the Luxembourg Gardens, St-Sulpice and St-Germain. The décor is a bit overloaded with antiques, *tromp l'oeil*, floral carpets and *toile de Jouy*. Nevertheless, the rooms are pleasant and a very good size with well-maintained bathrooms. Rates from €130 for a double, to €265 for a suite; breakfast €11.

€ **Hôtel Floride Etoile.** *14 Rue Didier, 75016, T: 01 47 27 23 36, www.floride-paris-hotel.com Map p. 468, A4.* Hidden away in the smart 16th arrondissement, close to the Champs-Elysées and the Trocadero, this small hotel with modern décor is very fresh and light and looks out on a patio garden. The rooms are decorated mainly in whites and creams with touches of colour. The lounge, breakfast room and bar are all restful and pleasing. Rooms range from €153 to €185; buffet breakfast €12.50–14.

€ **Grand Hôtel des Gobelins.** *57 Blvd St-Marcel, 75013, T: 01 43 31 79 89, www.hotel-des-gobelins.com Map p. 479, D1.* The 13th arrondissement is one of the newly fashionable parts of Paris on the Left Bank, close to Rue Mouffetard, to the Jardin des Plantes, and to the very popular Butte aux Cailles, in an area which takes its name from the Gobelins tapestry workshops. The hotel has lots of character, and is comfortable without putting on any airs and graces. It has an interesting lobby with public spaces on different levels and extremely friendly staff. None of the bedrooms is alike, though the standard ones are a trifle old-fashioned. All rooms have flat-screen TV. The bathrooms vary in size—some fairly large—with good showers, although storage space may be lacking. Prices are reasonable, from €90 to €150, and breakfast is €10.

€ **Hôtel Lenox.** *9 Rue de l'Université, 75007, T: 01 42 96 10 95, www.lenoxsaint-germain.com Map p. 474, C2.* The theme of this old literary hotel is Art Deco leather upholstery and polished wood. The Lenox Club bar features marquetry images of jazz musicians. A glass elevator takes you up to thoughtfully presented smallish and uncluttered bedrooms, with unusual duplexes under the eaves. The breakfast room is in the converted cellar. This is a great corner of St-Germain with its narrow streets. Rooms €125–€280.

€ **Hôtel Louvre-Opéra.** *4 rue des Moulins, 75001, T: 01 40 20 01 10, www.hotel-paris-louvre-opera.com Map p. 469, F4.* This Best Western hotel has been open for less than two years and occupies an old building, which has been totally renovated and refurbished, in a prestigious location on the Right Bank, as the name suggests, between Opéra and the Louvre. Nevertheless this is a quiet street. There are only 20 rooms, modern and uncluttered, for one to four people plus a junior suite; also a room for the disabled. All are fairly small, although the bathrooms are a reasonable size, careful use being made of the space. The prices vary enormously according to season and it is absolutely essential to book in advance to get the best rate, which may be as little as €129 for a room and up to €290.

€ **Hôtel de la Tulipe.** *33 Rue Malar, 75007, T: 01 45 51 67 21, www.hoteldelat-ulipe.com Map p. 473, B1.* This small, cheerful hotel, in the shadow of the Eiffel Tower and close to lively shopping streets, has a Provençal feel. Once a con-

vent, the building is arranged around a small interior courtyard where the breakfast tables are set out in the summer. Sunny yellow fabrics contrast with old beams and stone walls. The rooms are simple, but well equipped and reasonably priced. A single room on the street is €100 and prices go up to €260 for an apartment. Breakfast €9.

€ **Hôtel Le Clément.** ■ *6 Rue Clement, 75006, T: 01 43 26 53 60, www.hotel-clement.fr Map p. 475, D2.* This is a gem of an independent two-star hotel in a brilliant situation opposite the renovated Marché St-Germain, now a shopping mall. Discreet, quiet, cosy, utterly charming, with just 28 rooms. Everything is small (if you have a large suitcase it will probably have to travel alone in the lift) but perfectly presented. Bijou bedrooms have pretty prints on the walls and curtains, and cane furniture. They are all comfortable and well equipped. The brightest rooms overlook the street, the two-bed ones are especially good. Room 106 is the smallest and 107 the quietest, but looking over the courtyard wall. There are some family rooms. From the fourth floor is a rooftop view including the belfry of St-Sulpice. The reception area is comfortable and cosy, a bit like home, and there is a pretty breakfast room. It is close to great shops, within a stone's throw of St-Germain des Prés, and the Luxembourg Gardens. Prices per room between €117 and €150.

€ **La Villa des Artistes.** *9 Rue de la Grande-Chaumiere, 75006, T 01 43 26 60 86, www.villa-artistes.com Map p. 474, C4.* Not much to look at from outside, but close to the Luxembourg gardens and near Montparnasse, this hotel is in a quiet street. It has a patio-garden, and a pretty breakfast room—outside in summer—and agreeable salon-bar. The rooms are functional, and less attractive than the reception rooms, with modern furniture and coloured fabrics. Excellent bathrooms though. Rooms range from €149 to €179, breakfast €13.

€ **Hôtel de la Sorbonne.** *6 Rue Victor-Cousin, 75005, T 01 43 54 58 08, www.hotelsorbonne.com Map p. 475, E3.* This is one of the better two-star hotels in the capital, and the prices are fair. The ancient student quarter, close to the Panthéon, is a great area and the hotel is prettily turned out. There are 39 rooms which have nice decorative touches, very successfully using Designers Guild wallpapers and fabrics teamed with simple furniture. The shower-rooms are narrow, but there are some with bath. The Panthéon can be glimpsed from some rooms. Rooms with shower, €50–€110, rooms with bath, €70–€130.

€ **Hôtel de Nesle.** *7 Rue de Nesle, 75006, T: 01 43 54 62 41, www.hoteldenesleparis.com Map p. 475, D2.* Not for the faint hearted, this is a basic little hotel tucked away in the maze of the Latin Quarter, with a mini garden, between the Quai des Grands Augustins and Blvd St-Germain. The low prices reflect the minimal facilities, but if you like minimal décor, stay away. Fighting your way through the bibelots to the reception is just the beginning, and the rooms are decidedly quirky. Each has its own painted décor: Champollion is Egyptian, Antinéa has its own little hammam. They do not all have ensuite showers, some facilities are shared, nor do they offer breakfast but that's almost an advantage with all the cafes of the

quartier, including La Procope (*see p. 77*) round the corner. The hotel management particularly appreciate Anglo-Saxon clients. Reservations by phone only, rates €55 to €100.

Outskirts of Paris

€ **Pavillon Henri IV.** ■ *21 Rue Thiers, 78100 Saint-Germain-en-Laye, T: 01 39 10 15 15, www.pavillonhenri4.fr* To the west of Paris, St-Germain-en-Laye is an elegant town (*see p. 395*). The hotel was built in the 19th century on the site of the Château Neuf, where Louis XIV was born, but was abandoned in favour of Versailles and only the chapel and a small section of the old castle survived. It has a handsome entrance and lounge the length of the building with calm colours, wood floors, chandeliers and fireplaces, and an attractive restaurant serving excellent food which opens onto a large terrace, all of which benefit from the superb views. The bedrooms are huge, very comfortable, and with good bathrooms, making this four-star hotel remarkable value for money compared to the centre of Paris; rooms range from €125 to €550, breakfast €14.

€ **Péniche 'Oviri.** *Opp. 309 Quai de Stalingrad, 92130 Issy-les-Moulineaux, T: 01 46 44 88 50, www.boatforguest.net* An unusual way to stay in Paris, this early 20th-century Belgian-built barge offers an apartment for two on three levels, with kitchen, bedroom, salon and terrace. It is moored on the left bank of the Seine, on the edge of Paris. There is a link (5 min) by tram to La Défense and RER and Métro stations within easy reach. One night low season, single €50/double €80; high season single €70/double €110, breakfast included.

Per week, prices from €300 to €600.
€ Hôtel la Residence du Berry. *14 Rue d'Anjou, 75000 Versailles, T: 01 39 49 07 07, www.hotel-berry.com*. This is a small but beautifully turned out hotel, with 39 rooms in the centre of Versailles. Its most unusual feature is the 18th-century cellar where vintage wines are stored. To get the most out of Versailles, staying in this lovely little town is a pleasure in itself, and it provides an opportunity to enjoy all the special visits or activities at the château and park (*see p. 373*). In addition, it is easy to visit Paris for the day. A single room is €113, and the most expensive is the suite at €270, and breakfast is €12; they often have special weekend offers.

RESTAURANTS

In Paris there is every kind of restaurant at every price. After all, this is where the institution was invented and indeed was named, as in the case of the café, after the chief fare originally on offer: a *restaurant* or light *bouillon*. Listed below is a small selection of restaurants, mainly traditional or modern French. Blue Guide especially recommended restaurants are marked ■ Cafés and restaurants are also mentioned in the text, and especially in the walks. The least expensive way to eat a good meal is the *prix fixe* or *formule* menus at lunch, which most restaurants offer, including some of the top ones. To eat in a good restaurant is often barely more expensive than in a mediocre one. And it is also not true to say that you cannot eat badly in Paris. It is always advisable to telephone in advance to book and/or check opening times. The price ranges below are very approximate.

€€€€	€100+
€€€	€50–€100
€€	€30–€50
€	under €30

Right Bank

€€€€

Le Grand Véfour. *17 Rue de Beaujolais, 75001, T: 01 42 96 56 27. Closed Fri evening, Sat, Sun, Christmas, Easter and August. Map p. 475, D1.* This is one of the city's oldest great restaurants, under the arcades of the Palais Royal, and has been frequented by everyone from Napoleon Bonaparte to Jean Cocteau. It still attracts the great and the good who come to revel in the delights of chef Guy Martin's two-star Michelin cooking which continues to go from strength to strength. The choices range from classic to very adventurous haute cuisine. One of his most celebrated dishes is *raviolis de foie-gras à l'emulsion de crème truffée* and an unusual dessert is the *artichaut tourte*, a recipe from the chef's native Savoy. In addition to the setting, which is an 18th-century building with mirrors, painted panels and chandeliers, is the pleasure of impeccable but not intimidating service. The kitchens, the cellars and the cigar reserve may be visited. There is a lunch menu at €78, and a dinner tasting menu at €255; for *à la carte*, reckon €165–200 per person.

Crystal Room Restaurant, Maison Baccarat, *11 Pl. des Etats-Unis, 75016, T: 01 40 22 11 10. Closed Sun. Map p. 468, B4.* This has become an exclusive and sought-after place to dine, a truly glitzy affair: a restaurant combined with a gallery, boutique and museum. Designed by Philippe Starck, the Crystal Room is an eclectic setting for fine dining, with exposed brick walls, large mirrors, elaborate lighting, dainty chairs, pedestal tables, and pale-pink upholstery. The food is equally luxurious and the descriptions are detailed, for example: *Lièvre de la Beauce, La noisette comme une royale, compote de cuisses croustillante de foie gras, carbonara de buccatini et truffes noires d'automne.* The *Dégustation* of six dishes from the menu is €120. A meal without wine would cost around €80.

€€€

Café Costes. *Hôtel Costes, 239 Rue St-Honore, 75001, T: 01 42 44 50 00/01 42 44 50 25. Map p. 469, E4.* Close to Place Vendôme, in a very prestigious area, a long narrow entrance and dimly lit rooms gives the smart Hôtel Costes an air of mystery. The entrance gives onto a beautiful square patio open to the sky with terracotta walls, overlooked by a loggia and statues wreathed in ivy. Around the patio are small, intimate dining areas. Its reputation is as a place for the beautiful people, but they usually turn out to be the staff. The service can take a while to warm up, and the menu, in typical Costes' fashion, is quite limited but the food is excellent. It

ranges from Club Sandwich (€22), to lobster, and caviar at €175, and desserts including Trifle and Carpaccio of ginger.
Chez Jean. ■ *8 Rue St-Lazare, 75009, T: 01 48 78 62 73, www.restaurantjean.fr. Map p. 470, A3.* In 2006 this restaurant received its first Michelin rosette. In a lively part of Paris, near Rue des Martyrs (*see p. 253*), and the Musée Gustav Moreau, it has a cosy, pretty décor with *toile de Jouy* on the walls. The cooking, under the sure hands of Benoît Bordier, can be surprising and at times audacious. The dishes have quirky, fun Franglais names, such as Bugs Bunny, Duchesse de Windsor, Drôle d'Igloo, which give little idea of what they consist. Happily there are also explanations.
Macéo. ■ *15 Rue des Petits-Champs, 75001, T: 01 42 97 53 85, www.maceo-restaurant.com Map p. 470, B4.* A fashionable yet traditional address in a coolly beautiful setting, next to the Bibliothèque Richelieu (*see p. 241*), the staff handle all comers here with aplomb. Light and elegant, a period piece combined with some curious modern fittings, the space is divided into a bar area seating 20 serving light meals (€27 lunch menu); the main dining room, Salle Palais Royal, with large windows, and a tiny library corner with a couple of tables; upstairs is the beautiful Second-Empire Salle de Bal. The owner, Englishman Marc Williamson (of Willi's Wine Bar, *see p. 441*), takes care of the wine selection, and the reputation of chef Thierry Bourbonnais goes before him. The cooking is extremely fine and stylish but not overly elaborate. The choices change with the seasons and the market and there are a *Menu Vert* (vegetarian) for around €30,

and *Menu Découverte*, of 3 courses (with two choices on each) for €36. Butter is served with the bread. *A la carte* is around €50–60 for three courses.

Le Pharamond. *4 Rue de la Grande-Truanderie, 75001, T: 01 42 33 06 72, www.pharamondparis.com Closed Mon and Tues. Map p. 475, E1.* Some 40 years ago this restaurant could be described thus: 'Normandy food, old-fashioned, good for older people' and this is pretty much how it remains, although at that time Les Halles was still a working market, where the dawn air in summer was filled with the fragrance of strawberries and roses. Originally called A la Petite Normande, it became known by the name of the owner. Happily Le Pharamond's Belle Epoque décor of 1832, with its mirrors and *pâte de verre* panels, is protected, and the establishment has been revived by Jean-Michel and Josette Cornut. The brasserie fare is copious, good quality and affordable and waiters in white aprons are efficient. All-time classics include *escargots*, foie gras, *tripes maison*, *queue de boeuf* (ox tail) and game in season. There is also a terrace. It is *A la carte* only, about €50–70 per person.

€€

Angle'Opera. ■*39 Av. de l'Opéra, 75002, T: 01 42 61 86 25, www.anglopera.com Closed Sat and Sun. Map p. 470, A4.* This is an attractive and comfortable corner restaurant in the Edouard VII Hotel (*see p. 429*), close to Opéra, where the cuisine has been described as iconoclastic. The chef, Gille Choukroun, is famous for his interesting, even outrageous, combinations of ingredients and flavours—where scallops sprinkled with chocolate are really quite acceptable. The limited selection menu changes regularly, and it takes a while to tune into the descriptions which, conversely, guard the name of the key ingredient until the end, for example: *crème brulee*, green radish, soya sauce… and foie gras, or grilled grapefruit, green tea, spinach… and rumpsteak, or sorbet, szechwan pepper… and exotic fruit. The visual presentation is stunning. Meals are also served in the bar and on the terrace. Starters are €13, mains €22–€24, desserts €9 and lunch specials at €22.

L'Atelier de Joël Robuchon. *Rue de Montalembert, 75007, T: 01 42 22 56 65. Map p. 474, C2.* This is an informal bistrot where you sit on bar stools around an open kitchen. A revolutionary venture by one of the great French chefs, it offers small helpings with a Spanish influence of excellent quality. There are no reservations, and this is a long way from haughty haute cuisine. Turn up from around 6.30 and wait.

Au Bascou. *38 Rue Réaumur, 75003, T: 01 42 72 69 25. Closed Sat dinner and Sun. Map p. 471, D4.* Close to the Musée des Arts et Métiers, here you will find good authentic Basque cooking under the supervision of Basque chef Jean-Guy Loustau. The décor creates an image of the warm south, and so do the dishes, frequently flavoured with the red-hot *piments d'Espelettes* as well as sweet peppers. Basque seafood is a must-try, including squid in its ink (*chipirons a l'encre*), tuna, cod (*morue*), and scallops. Two-course lunch menu is €18, and average price of an *à la carte* meal, €33.

Café Marly. *93 Rue de Rivoli, 75001, T: 01 49 26 06 60. Map p. 475, D1.* This classic Frères Costes watering hole is in the Richelieu wing of the Louvre (*see p. 142*). From the outside terrace there is a view onto Cour Napoléon and the Pyramid, and from inside it looks onto the sculptures in Cour Marly inside the Louvre. Fun, fashionable and bustling, the setting and the décor largely account for its popularity and in fine weather the terrace under the arcades of the Richelieu Wing is much sought after. The reliable menu is fairly simple—a club sandwich or a main course—and doesn't offer a huge choice.

Le Café Moderne. *40 Rue Notre-Dame des Victoires, 75002, T: 01 53 40 84 10. Map p. 470, B4.* Just across from the Bourse (*see p. 249*) in a busy business quarter, professionals eat here at lunchtime. Light and cheerful, some thought has clearly gone into the décor and lighting, putting it quite a few rungs above the average bistrot. Service is professional, and in this less touristy area, English is limited. Its reputation rests on the three course €30 menu (lunch and dinner), which is good quality, traditional and very generous.

Le Soufflé. *36 Rue du Mont-Thabor, 75001, T: 01 42 60 27 19. Map p. 469, E4.* Tucked away in the corner of the street, close to the Tuileries and Pl. de la Concorde, this much-loved restaurant has been here for an eternity, and reassuringly has changed hardly at all. With just two smallish dining areas, it is the *soufflé* centre of Paris. *Soufflés* come in every flavour, and it is even possible to have one for each course, as starter, main and dessert. But there are alternatives, with meatier and crunchier dishes on offer. The *pièce de résistance* is *soufflé au Grand Marnier*, a retro dessert that evokes nostalgia for the 60s when it was *de rigueur* in all the best restaurants, but is now quite rare. Crisp on the outside,

slightly liquid in the middle, and *arosé* with the alcohol it is simply delicious.

Georgette. *29 Rue St-Georges, 75009, T: 01 42 80 39 13. Map p. 470, B3.* In the residential area between Rue La Fayette and Pl. St-Georges is this unpretentious restaurant with eclectic décor combining exposed beams with 60s formica. It opened in 2000 and the *patronne* (who is not called Georgette) is very much in charge. The food is traditional *cuisine de grandmère*, with interesting dishes such as *velouté de topinambours* (Jerusalem artichokes), *oreilles de cochon* (pig's ears), *andouillette* (pig's stomach sausage), and *cabillaud au sauce raifort* (cod with horseradish). Meals cost about €35.

€
La Boulangerie. ■ *15 Rue des Panoyaux, 75020, T: 01 43 58 45 45. Closed Sat lunch and Sun. Map p. 3, F2.* Near Métro Ménilmontant (*see p. 325*), a bit out of the way perhaps, but close to Parc de Belleville, and not far from Père Lachaise, this old bakers shop has been transformed into an unexpectedly good restaurant, with a calm and serious interior. The bread is very good, wine is served *au compteur* (by the amount you drink) and the food is excellent. Good, simple cooking is on offer here at very attractive prices: a three-course dinner menu is around €28, with five or so choices.

Le Fumoir. *6 Rue de l'Amiral Coligny, 75001, T: 01 42 92 00 24. Map p. 475, D1.* The slightly sombre interior here helps people take their relaxation seriously, combining bar, restaurant and library with comfortable chairs, appreciated by a young and confident crowd. It is right behind the Louvre, next to the church of St-Germain-l'Auxerrois (*see p. 209*),

therefore well positioned as an escape
for lunch, which is around €15 (drink
not included), or a *café glacé* (€2.80) in
the late afternoon.

Café de l'Homme. *Palais de Chaillot, 17
Pl. du Trocadero, 75016, T: 01 44 05 30 15
www.cafedelhomme.com. Meals served
lunch and supper. Map p. 473, D1.*
A brasserie-restaurant for hearty eaters
who want a 'proper' lunch, and those
include local business people. The décor
is 30s, in russet browns beneath the high,
star-spangled gold ceiling, with cascading
chandeliers, and large high windows
framing the Eiffel Tower. The set menu is
around €25 and might be something like
a salad with *coquilles St-Jacques*, *canard au
miel* followed by *tiramisu*.

Le Bistrot du Peintre. *116 Av. Ledru-
Rollin, 75011, T: 01 47 00 34 39. Map p.
476, C2.* Near Bastille, this Art Nouveau
brasserie (founded 1902) is a listed historic monument. A jolly place, with a
larger dining room upstairs, and round
tables, the cooking is good and the helpings generous: an onion soup or a large
salad are quite substantial. The main
courses change daily, although staples
such as *confit de canard* or *entrecôte de
salers* (beef from the Auvergne) are usually available. A meal costs around €25.

Le Petit Marché. *9 Rue de Béarn, 75003,
T: 01 42 72 06 67. Map p. 476, B2.* In a
quiet street in the Marais, this has fast
become a very popular place to eat.
Typical new-bistrot food and bistrot
ambience, small and a bit squashed, with
a tiny street terrace and speedy service.
Dishes include duck breast with ginger,
calves' liver and steak tartare. There is a
two-course set menu at lunch for €13,
and an average meal is around €30.

De La Ville Café. ■ *34 Blvd de Bonne-*

*Nouvelle, 75010, T: 01 48 24 48 09,
www.delavillecafe.com Map p. 470, C4.*
The 10th arrondissement, especially
around Republique, has become an up-
beat, party area. De La Ville Café is in a
19th-century building, which was initially a brasserie, then a *maison close* or bordello. Stylish yet low-key, a young, happening café by day and popular venue at
night, it has several rooms of strangely
contrasting décor inherited from previous occupants which include a butterfly
collection, the original elegant 19th-
century staircase and the lounge with
red, shiny, 60s banquettes, and stags
heads on the walls. The bar, with its
19th-century mosaic décor, is a quiet
place during the day, before the early
evening cocktail crowd arrives, and later
(Thur–Sat), there is a DJ. Outside is a
wide terrace. The cooking is good, the
helpings generous, and the choices range
from Zen Eat (sashimis of tuna and
salmon, crunchy vegetables), *Assiette
d'Antipasti*, *Tatare de boeuf*, or hamburger,
to a choice of several cheeses and crème
brulée (starters around €6.50, mains
€12–13, and desserts €7). The copious
Sunday brunch is €22.

Left Bank

€€€

Atelier Maître Albert. *La Rôtisserie, 1
Rue Maître Albert, 75005, T: 01 56 81 30
01, www.ateliermaitrealbert.com. Map p.
475, E3.* This very elegant and understat-
ed venue is in a small Left Bank street
perpendicular to the Seine opposite the
east end of Notre Dame. It became part
of Guy Savoy's empire in 2004, when he
took over a restaurant that had existed
here for some time. This is a fashionable

and expensive address, where traditional and modern marry successfully in the cuisine and the décor. Using neutral tones and incorporating some bare stone and a large fireplace, each table is in an individual pool of light giving diners a certain intimacy. Dishes are a blend of grandmother's cooking and modern chic, with seasonal choices such as *velouté de châtaignes* (€13; chestnut soup) for starters, grilled fish or meat (€19.50–27) for mains, and excellent puds (€10). A meal will cost around €70–80 with wine.
Le Bélier. ■ *13 Rue des Beaux-Arts, T: 01 44 41 99 00, www.l-hotel.com Closed Sun and Mon. Map p. 475, D2*. This discreet and elegant restaurant, in the L'Hôtel (*see p. 427*), is open to non-residents midday and evening and announced by the ram's head above the entrance to the hotel. Just as discreet and elegant is the food prepared by the charming young chef, Philippe Bélissent, and the excellent and friendly service (English spoken). The tiny but plush restaurant has seating for just 40 covers, and looks out onto the patio and its fountain. The food is excellent and not too quirky, expensive but not exorbitant; the fixed-price menu is €50 and there is also *à la carte* choice.
Le Télégraph. *41 Rue de Lille, 75007, T: 01 42 92 03 04. Closed Fri and Sat midday. Map p. 474, C1*. Behind the Musée d'Orsay, the old canteen for ladies working at the Télégraphs et Téléphones is a very elegant restaurant, in an original vaulted interior supported by columns, with large windows, a *Jardin interieur*, and excellent quality, traditional French cooking: several foie gras specialties, and delicious desserts such as a *triptyque des crèmes brûlées* (moka, vanilla and cocoa). It also does Kosher food.

€€
Montparnasse 1900. *59 Blvd de Montparnasse, 75006, T: 01 45 49 19 00. Map p. 474, B4*. This restaurant could easily be overlooked, but in fact it is very good value and in an attractive setting. Built as a brasserie in 1901, the décor dates from 1914—mirrors, mirrors everywhere, on walls, ceiling, and 'twixt the windows—with sinuous Art Nouveau frames, and pretty lamps down the middle of the dining room. It specialises in *fruit de mer* in winter, and roasts. The Belle Epoque set menu available all year at €32 includes an aperitif, three courses, half-bottle of wine and coffee; portions are generous.
Le Refuge du Passé. *32 Rue du Fer à Moulin, 75005, T: 01 47 07 29 91. Map p. 478, C1*. Tucked away near Rue Mouffetard, this place has a very friendly bistrot atmosphere and is open every day. It serves generous helpings of well-cooked traditional fare based on the cooking of Southwest France, hearty and reliable, including excellent steaks. The reasonably priced menus are: lunch €18 for one course and coffee; €26 for 2 courses; and €32 for the menu gourmet.
Mon Vieil Ami. ■ *69 Rue St-Louis en l'Ile St-Louis 75004, T: 01 40 46 01 35. Closed Mon and Tues. Map p. 476, A2*. A great place to eat on the beautiful Ile St-Louis, this small, chic restaurant under the aegis of Antoine Westermann, three-star chef of Buerehiesel in Strasbourg, is a minimalist and comfortable version of a bistrot. It has a 'communal' table down one side, and small intimate tables on the other. The excellent cooking is based on the cuisine of Alsace. A glass of Pinot blanc d'Alsace is the *apéro* on the house,

a great loaf of *pain de campagne* gets sliced during the evening, and the service is admirably professional. As for the food, everyone has their favourite: the pumpkin soup (in season) with sour cream perhaps, or *crème d'escargots*; for mains braised pork, or sweetbreads with noodles and wild mushrooms, crispy *Filet de lieu* (white fish) with celeriac mousse and leeks, and caramelised *choucroute*. The *Tarte au chocolat* is very popular. The price of the set menu including three courses is remarkably reasonable at €39; also à la carte, and affordable wine.

€

Le Bon Coin. *21 Rue de la Collegiale, 75005, T: 01 43 31 55 57. Map p. 478, C1.* This is a small, typically Parisian side-street bistro (near Les Gobelins Metro) with a limited but excellent menu with all the staples including delicious onion soup, plastic check tablecloths spilling out on to the street, busy, with very few tourists and a real dining experience.

Polidor. *Rue Monsieur le Prince, 75006. Map p. 475, D3.* A traditional setting a couple of steps from the Sorbonne. The clientele seems part academic, part American and European tourists, all enjoying traditional French cooking. Menu €12.50 for lunch.

Le Pré Verre. *Rue Thenard, 75005, T: 01 43 54 59 47. Closed Sun/Mon. Map p. 475, E3.* This is a popular Latin Quarter restaurant with daily delights listed on a blackboard, and a menu of around €24. Among specially good things are ravioli stuffed with snails and roast suckling pig.

Wadja. *10 Rue de la Grande-Chaumiere, 75006, T: 01 46 33 02 02. Closed Sun, Mon lunch. Map p. 474, C4.* A real

bistrot, tiny, run by *madame* with a menu at €14, for two courses, including the evening. Efficient and relaxed, although nothing special it is amusing and inexpensive and in a good position just off Blvd Montparnasse.

Cafés and bars: Right Bank

Angelina's. *226 Rue de Rivoli, 75001, T: 01 42 60 82 00. Map p. 494, E4.* A smart tea room to indulge in hot chocolate or a *mont blanc* made with *crème de marron*.
Drug-Store Champs Elysées. *133 Champs Elysees, 75008, T: 01 44 43 79 00. Map p. 468, B3.* A revamp of the 60s–70s establishment, using laminated glass, which combines café/restaurant, shopping, newsagents, groceries; until 2am.
Green Garden Courtyard. *Hôtel Regina, 2 Pl. des Pyramides, 75001, T: 01 42 60 31 10. Map p. 474, C1.* This open-air oasis offers a menu at €24 with choice of main course, starter or dessert and coffee. If not fine enough for the courtyard, the English bar in the Lounge Club serves the same menu.
Mariage Frères. *13 Rue des Grands-Augustins, 75006, T: 01 40 51 82 50, www.mariagefreres.com. Map p. 475, D2.* One of the city's more renowned *salons de thé*. Head upstairs for afternoon tea and patisserie Parisian style, or a light lunch.
Hôtel du Nord. *102 Quai de Jemmapes, 75010, T: 01 40 40 78 78. Map p. 471, E3.* Cocktails, music, internet wi-fi, excellent wine list, next to the Canal St-Martin. Film buffs will recognise the name.
L'Orée du Marais. *29 Rue des Francs-Bourgeois, 75004, T: 01 48 87 81 70. Map p. 476, B2.* Opposite the Carnavalet, a tiny café, slightly scruffy, which does home-made meals and tarts.
Le Pain Quotidien. *18 Rue des Archives,*

75004, T: 01 44 54 03 07. Map p. 476, A1. Part of a chain, this is the best address, in a former grocery store. Very good quality *tartines* and salads, and a different hot dish each day. Extremely popular for breakfast/brunch (€19.50) with large pots of honey or jam for your baguette.

Café de la Paix. *12 Blvd des Capucines, 75009, T: 01 40 07 36 36. Map p. 469, F4.* The revamped restaurant facing Place de l'Opéra is very grand. The terrace, facing Blvd des Capucines, is less so but is fun for a drink or a famous *millefeuille*.

Patisserie Viennoise. *Rue de l'Ecole de Medecine, 75005. Map p. 475, D3.* Very small and simple doing good food, especially cakes and desserts. About €8.

A Priori Thé. *35 Galerie Vivienne, 75002, Bourse, T: 01 42 97 48 75. Map p. 470, B4.* A popular salon de thé in a smart shopping arcade near the Bourse (*see p. 249*).

Chez Prune. *36 Beaurepaire, 75010, T: 01 42 41 30 47. Map p. 471, E3.* This is a good place for a drink or a snack, by the Canal St-Martin.

Café Puce. *68 Av. de la République (corner of Rue St-Maur), 75011, T: 01 47 00 64 64. Map p. 476, C1.* Genuinely friendly, laid-back café/bar/restaurant with deep leather armchairs, cocktails, good food, unhurried and relaxed. Sing-songs on the fourth Thursday of every month.

L'Atelier Renault. *53 Champs-Elysées, 75008, T: 01 49 53 70 70, Sun–Wed, 12–12; Thur–Sat 12noon–2am. Map p. 468, C4.* The Renault car showrooms with a restaurant on the Mezzanine.

Bar Saint-James. *6 Rue du 29 Juillet, 75001, T: 01 44 58 43 44, (Hotel Saint-James & Albany, 202 Rue de Rivoli). Map p. 474, C1.* In a smart shopping area, near Pl. de la Concord/Rue du Fbg. St-Honoré. A pleasant and restful oasis with a garden. Friendly service. Lunch only, 7 days a week; menu €18.50.

Viaduc Café. *43 Av. Daumesnil, 75012, T: 01 44 74 70 70. Open until 2am Tues–Sat, until 1am Sun and Mon. Map p. 476, C3.* Café under the arches of the Viaduc des Arts near Bastille (*see p. 307*) with a Sunday jazz brunch.

Vinea Café. *26-28 Cour St-Emilion, Bercy Village, 75012, T: 01 44 74 09 09, www.vinea-cafe.com Map p. 3, E4.* Café, bar, restaurant, serves brunch €23;

The White Bar. *15 Avenue Montaigne, 75008, T: 01 47 23 55 99. Map p. 468, C4.* In one of the most chic and fashionable avenues in town, off the Champs, this is the mezzanine bar of the Maison Blanche restaurant, Philippe Starck inspired, with luxurious white Italian sofas, black and white photos, and a phosphorescent bar which changes colour. The terrace is seven floors above the ground on the roof of the Théâtre des Champs-Elysées, in the shadow of the Eiffel Tower.

Willi's Wine Bar. *13 Rue des Petits-Champs, 75001, T: 01 42 61 05 09. Map p. 470, B4.* Opened by Englishman Mark Williamson in 1980, this was the first wine bar in Paris, and continues to be enormously successful, with around 250 wines on the list. In a 1930s building, the bar has a great ambience and a *dégustation* may be accompanied by a meal cooked by gifted chef, François Yon. The cooking has a Mediterranean slant, with excellent value daily specials and à la carte choices averaging for starters €12, mains €18, desserts €7.

Cafés and bars: Left Bank

Le Basile. *34 Rue de Grenelle, 75007, T: 01 42 22 59 46. Metro Rue du Bac. Map p. 474, C2.* A hangout popular with

politics students, an alternative to the famous brasseries, with music and snacks.
Chai 33. *33 Cour St-Fmilion, Bercy Village, 75012, T: 01 53 44 01 01, www.chai33.com Map p. 3, E4.* Interesting combination of wine boutique, wine tastings and restaurant, in an old wine warehouse (*see p. 312*).
Le Ciel de Paris. *Tour Maine Montparnasse, 33 Av. du Maine, 75006, T: 01 40 64 77 64. Map p. 474, B4.* A drink with a view, at the top of the Montparnasse Tower; also a restaurant.
La Closerie des Lilas. *171 Blvd du Montparnasse, 75006, T: 01 40 51 34 50. Map p. 475, D4.* Long-established, upmarket bar-brasserie, piano bar open to 1am. A popular place to eat, especially the terrace in summer, but fairly expensive.
Les Frigos. *Quai Panhard et Levassor, 75013, T: 01 44 24 96 96, www.les-frigos.com. Map p. 479, F2.* A sprawl of reclamation and the hub of emerging music venues, artists studios and more.
MK2. *128-162 Av. de France, 75013, T: 08 92 69 84 84, www.mk2.com Map p. 479, F2.* One of the best cafés to hang out in

this area is at the 14-screen multiplex MK2 Bibliothèque.
Le Rouge Gorge. *8 Rue St-Paul, 75004, T: 01 48 04 75 89. Map p. 476, B2.* Tiny wine bar and restaurant. Limited menu and even more limited space. Charming and authentic. Generous cooking on the spot (enormous *assiette de crudités* for €10).

Vegetarian restaurants

Aquarius. *40 Rue de Gergovie, 75014, T: 01 45 41 36 88. Closed Sun.*
Le Grenier de Notre Dame. *18 rue de la Bûcherie, 75005, T: 01 43 29 98 29. Map p. 475, E3.*
Lemoni Café. *5 Rue Hérold, 75001, T: 01 45 08 49 84. Map p. 475, D1.*
La Petite Légume. *36 Rue des Boulangers, 75005, T: 01 40 46 06 85. Closed Sun. Map p. 476, A3.*
Restaurant du Tibet Pema Thang. *13 Rue de la Montagne Sainte Geneviève, 75005, T: 01 43 54 34 34. Closed Sun, Mon lunch. Map p. 475, E3.*
La Victoire Supreme du Coeur. *41 Rue des Bourdonnais, 75001, T: 01 40 41 93 95. Closed Sun. Map p. 475, E1.*

MUSEUMS & GALLERIES

As a general rule, the national museums and monuments are closed on Tuesdays, and the municipal museums are closed on Mondays. The exception in Paris is the Musée d'Orsay, which closes on Mondays, thus giving visitors the opportunity to visit one major national museum on a Tuesday. Several museums have late openings one day a week. Details of admission times are given in the text. Some museums will not allow entry 45 minutes before closing time. The Tourist Offices (Paris Convention and Visitors Bureaux) have information on museums in Paris and the Ile de France with up-to-date admission times and charges.

The **Paris Museum Pass** (La Carte Musées et Monuments) gives reduced-price and unlimited access to over 60 museums and monuments in Paris and the surrounding region. It can be bought at participating museums and monuments, the Paris Convention and Visitors Bureau and the Espace de Tourism d'Ile-de-France

(Carrousel du Louvre), major Métro stations, and FNAC shops. It is available for two, four or six consecutive days and avoids the need to queue in the busier museums. It does not include temporary exhibitions or guided tours.

There is free access to the permanent collections of the 14 museums belonging to the Paris City Council (Ville de Paris). Admission to national museums is free on the first Sunday of each month. Certain museums offer free admission other days of the week.

Walking tours (in French) promoted by the *Caisse Nationale des Monuments Historiques et Sites* are listed in a quarterly brochure, *Visites Conférences* obtainable from the **Centre des Monuments Nationaux**, *7 Blvd Morland, 75004, directly or by mail, T: 01 44 54 19 30/01 44 54 19 35, www.monum.fr*

ENTERTAINMENT

Listings
For up-to-date information on theatres, cinemas, cabarets, night clubs, cultural events, sporting events, fairs, exhibitions and shows, consult the Paris Tourist Office (*Paris Convention and Visitors Bureau; T: 0 892 68 3000, www.parisinfo.com*). Weekly information can also be found in *Pariscope, l'Officiel des Spectacles* or *Zurban* on sale at newsagents.

SHOPPING

There are a great many different parts of Paris which are known for smart shopping. Designer boutiques are found in the 1st and 8th arrondissements, Rue St-Honoré and Place Vendôme, as well as Rue du Faubourg St-Honoré and Av. Montaigne, and Passy, in the 16th, is also very upmarket. The St-Germain district, on the edge of the 6th/7th arrondissements, around Rue du Four and Place St-Sulpice, has a younger edge.

Opening hours
Shops are usually open from between 9 and 10, until around 6 or 7. Fashion shops are generally closed on Sunday and some also on Monday morning. Food shops often open earlier and stay open until 7, and some open on Sunday morning.

Auctions
Auctions are held regularly at the rebuilt Salle Drouot, 6 Rue Rossini, 75009. There are numerous *brocanteurs* (second-hand dealers) in the 6th arrondissement.

Markets
There are markets all over Paris, which are listed on the Paris City website (www.paris.fr) by arrondissement. On Sundays the flowers of Pl. Louis-Lépine give way to a bird market, while opposite, on Quai de la Mégisserie, is a pet shop and market. The Viaduc des Arts (*see p. 310*), 9–129 Av. Daumesnil, near Bastille, is an arts

and crafts market. An open-air stamp market is held Thurs–Sun at Av. Matignon, Rond-Point des Champs-Elysées.

The Marché aux Puces (*open Sat–Mon*) is the most extensive and best-known flea market which might still produce a bargain among the bric-a-brac. It is a few minutes' walk north of the Porte de Clignancourt Métro; www.tourisme93.com

ADDITIONAL INFORMATION

Banking Services

Most banks are open Mon–Fri 9–4.30; closed on Sat, Sun, and holidays, although some open on Saturday mornings. Most shut at noon on the day before public holidays.

Crime and Personal Security

Emergency Services
Police   T: 17
Fire Brigade   T: 18
SAMU (Medical Aid)   T: 15

As in all large towns, pickpocketing can be a problem, especially on the Métro, in crowded tourist areas, and in some hostess bars. Theft or lost items should be reported immediately to the nearest police station in order to process insurance claims. It is always advisable to have photocopies of important documents. Visitors to Paris should carry identification. For the nearest police station, contact: Préfecture de Police, 9 Blvd du Palais, 75004, T: 01 53 71 53 71, www.prefecture-police-paris.interieur.gouv.fr

Pharmacies

Most pharmacies are open during normal working hours. Late-opening pharmacies are as follows:
Drugstore Champs-Elysées, 84 Av. des Champs-Elysées, 75008, daily 24hr, M: Charles-de-Gaulle Etoile.
des Arts, 106 Blvd du Montparnasse, 75014, Mon–Sat 9–midnight, M: Montparnasse.
Daumesnil, 6 Pl. Félix-Eboué, 75012, daily 24 hr, M: Daumesnil
Européenne, 6 Pl. Clichy, 75009, daily 24 hr, M: Pl. Clichy
Perreault, 14 Blvd de Sébastopol, 75004, daily 10–2am, M. Châtelet

Public Holidays

Almost everything closes on 1st January, 1st May, and 25th December. Post offices, banks, and some museums and shops are also likely to be closed on the following:
Easter Monday   15th August (Assumption)
8th May (VE Day)   1st November (All Souls)
Ascension Thursday (6th after Easter)   11th November (Armistice Day)
14th July (Bastille Day)

INDEX

Explanatory or more relevant references (where there are many) are given in bold. Dates are given for all artists and architects. Numbers in italics are picture references.

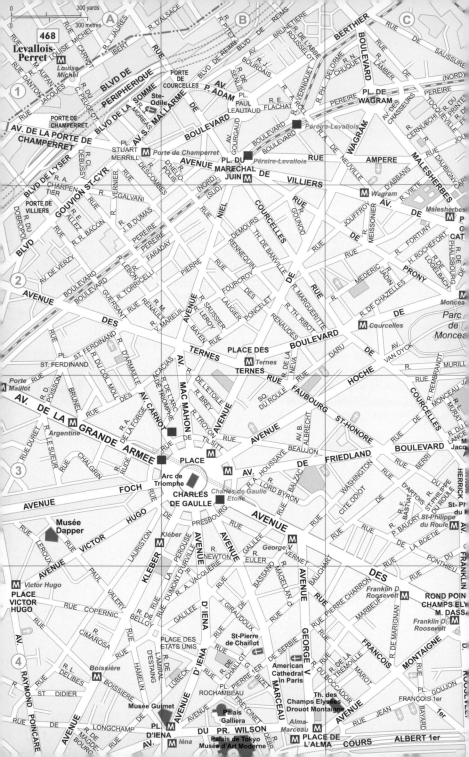

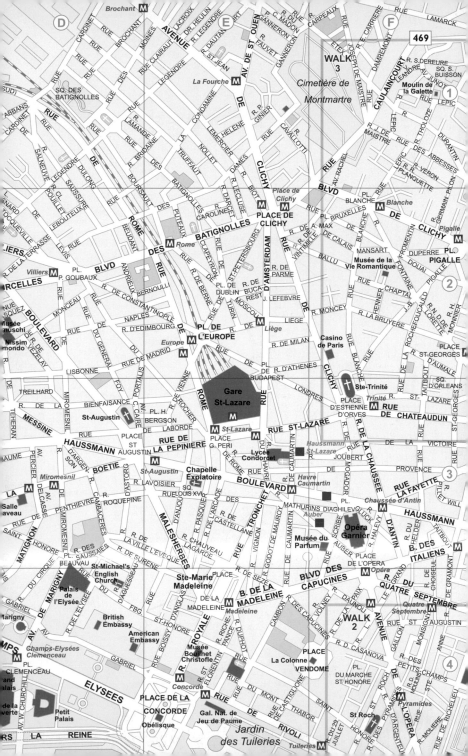

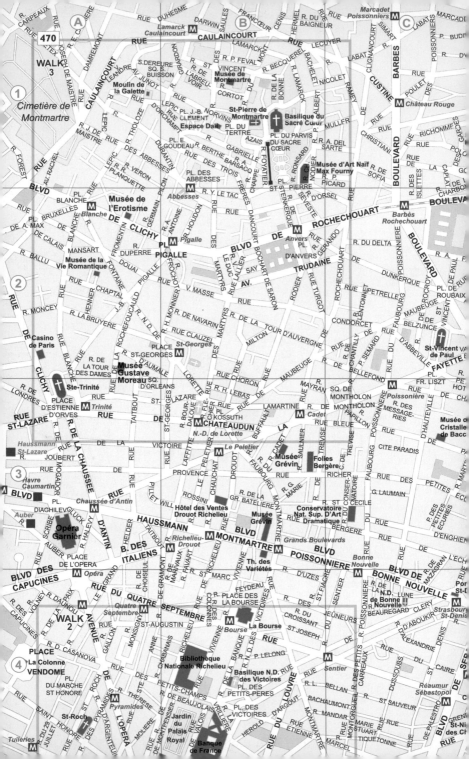

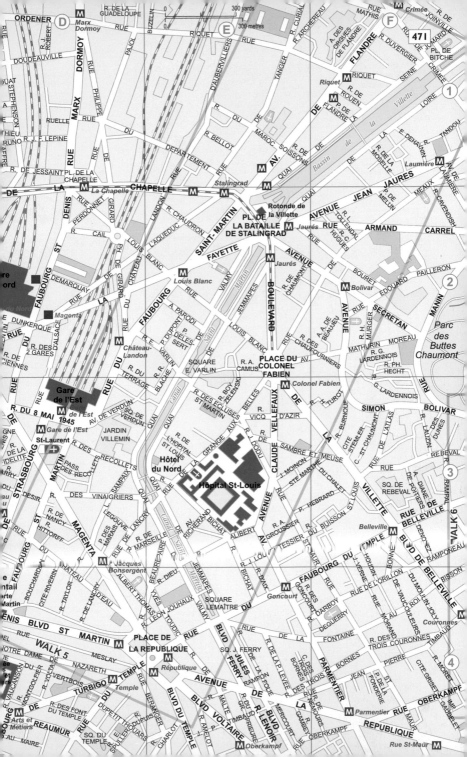

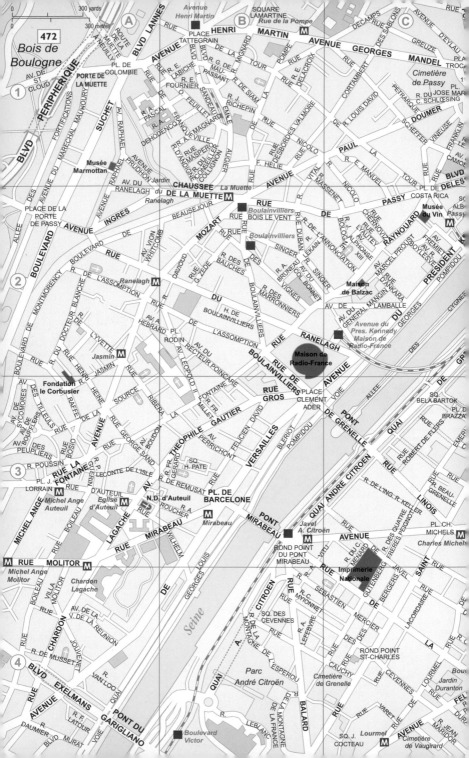

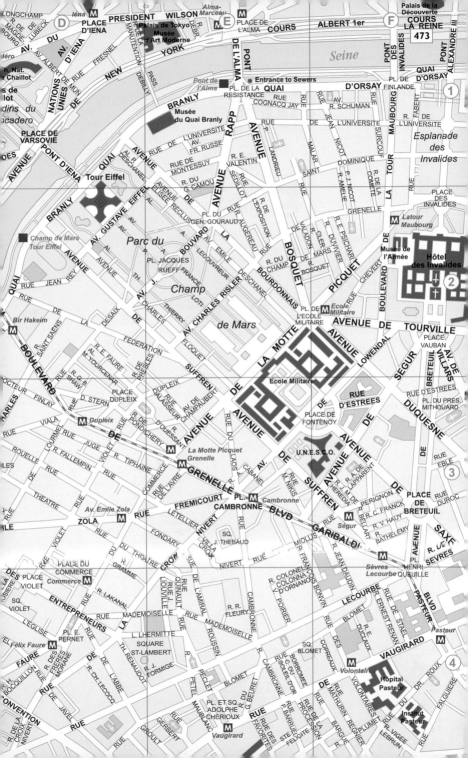

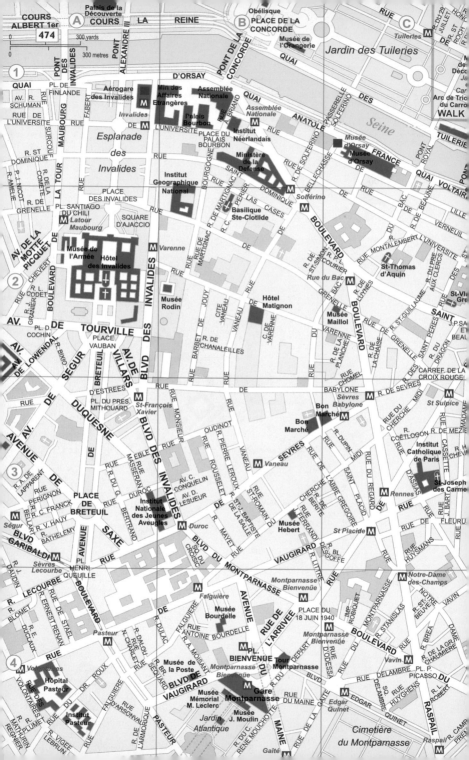

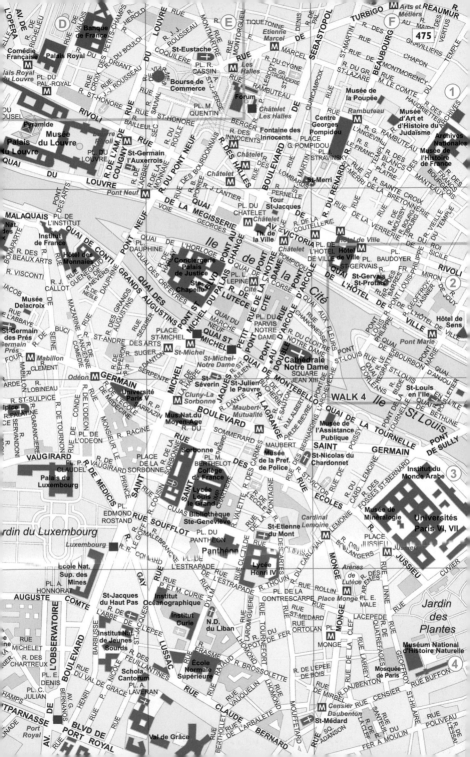

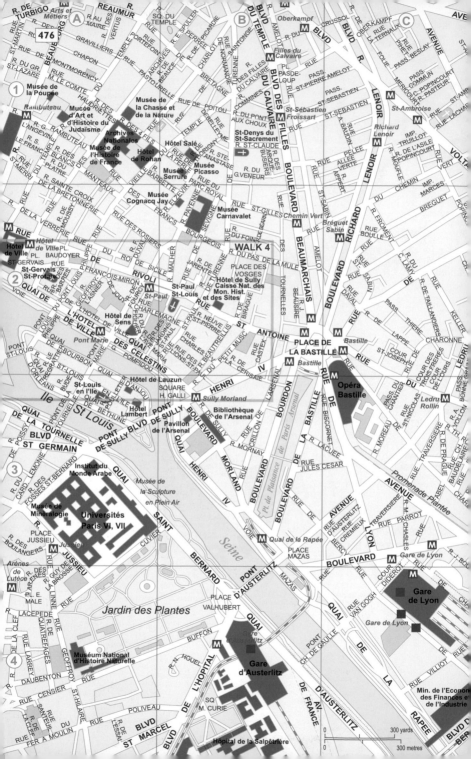

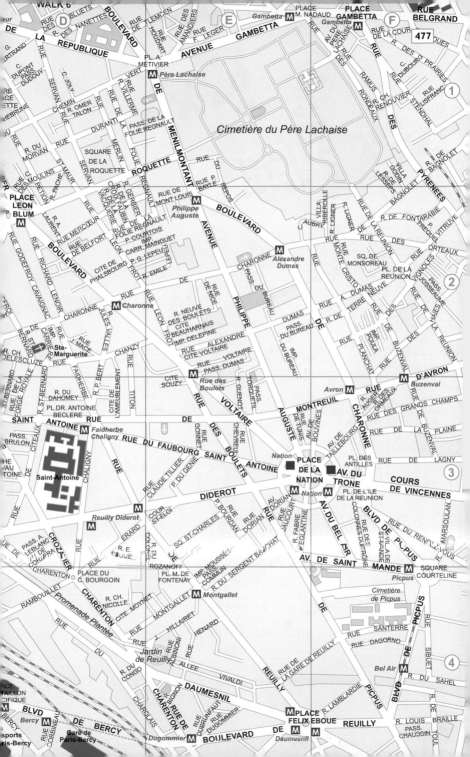

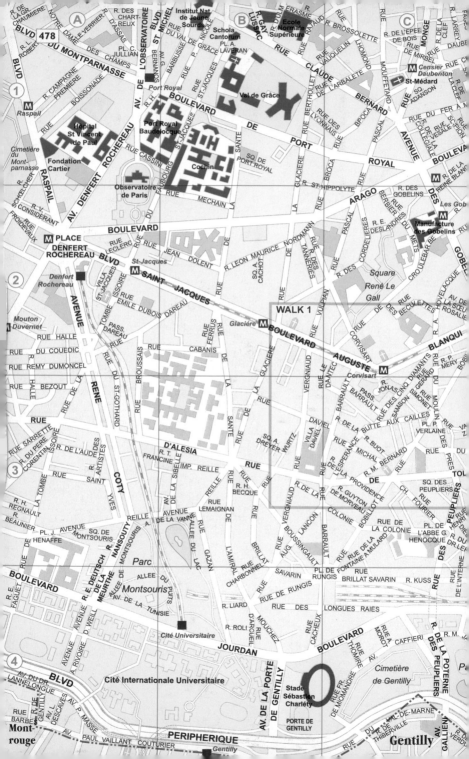